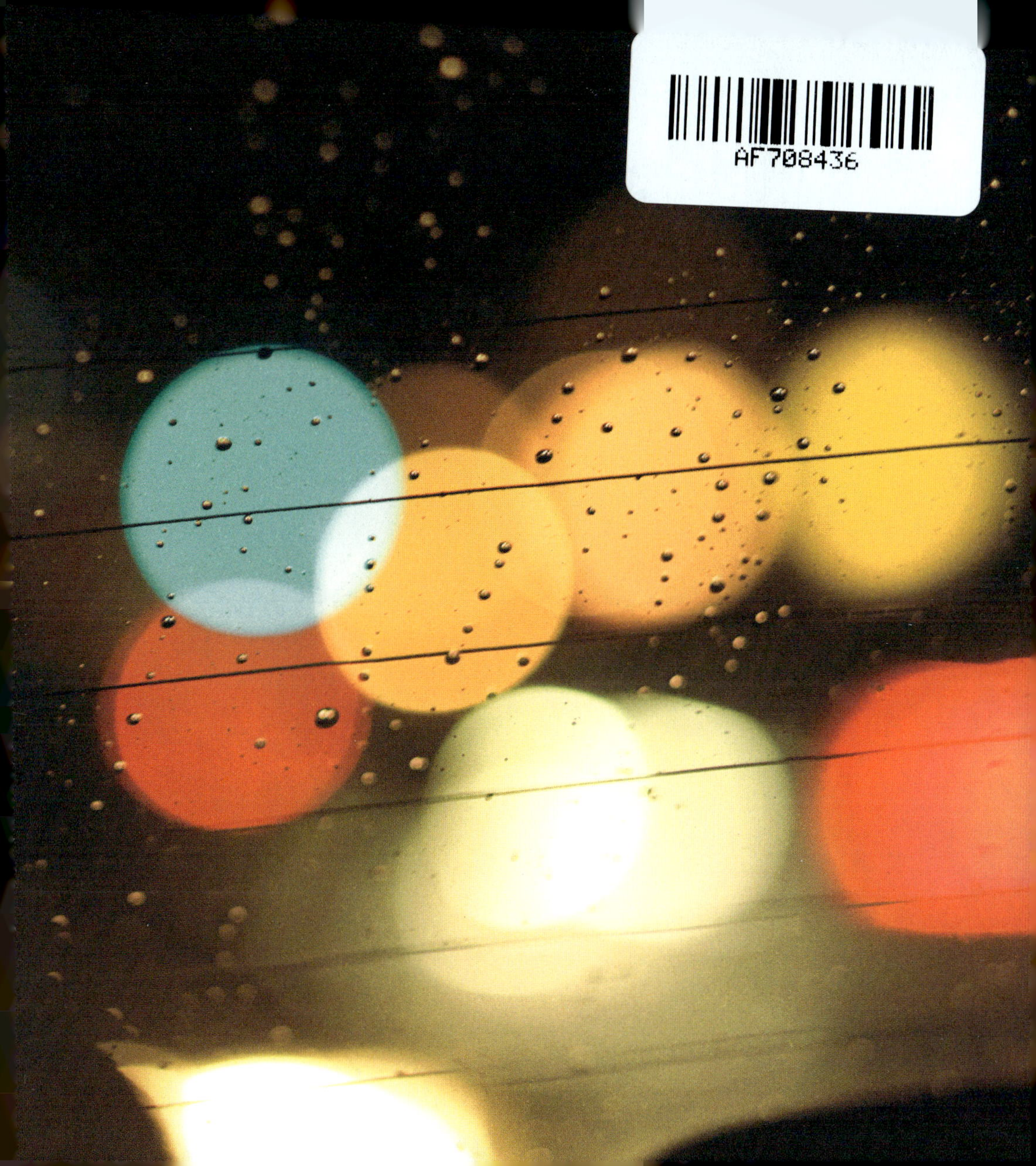

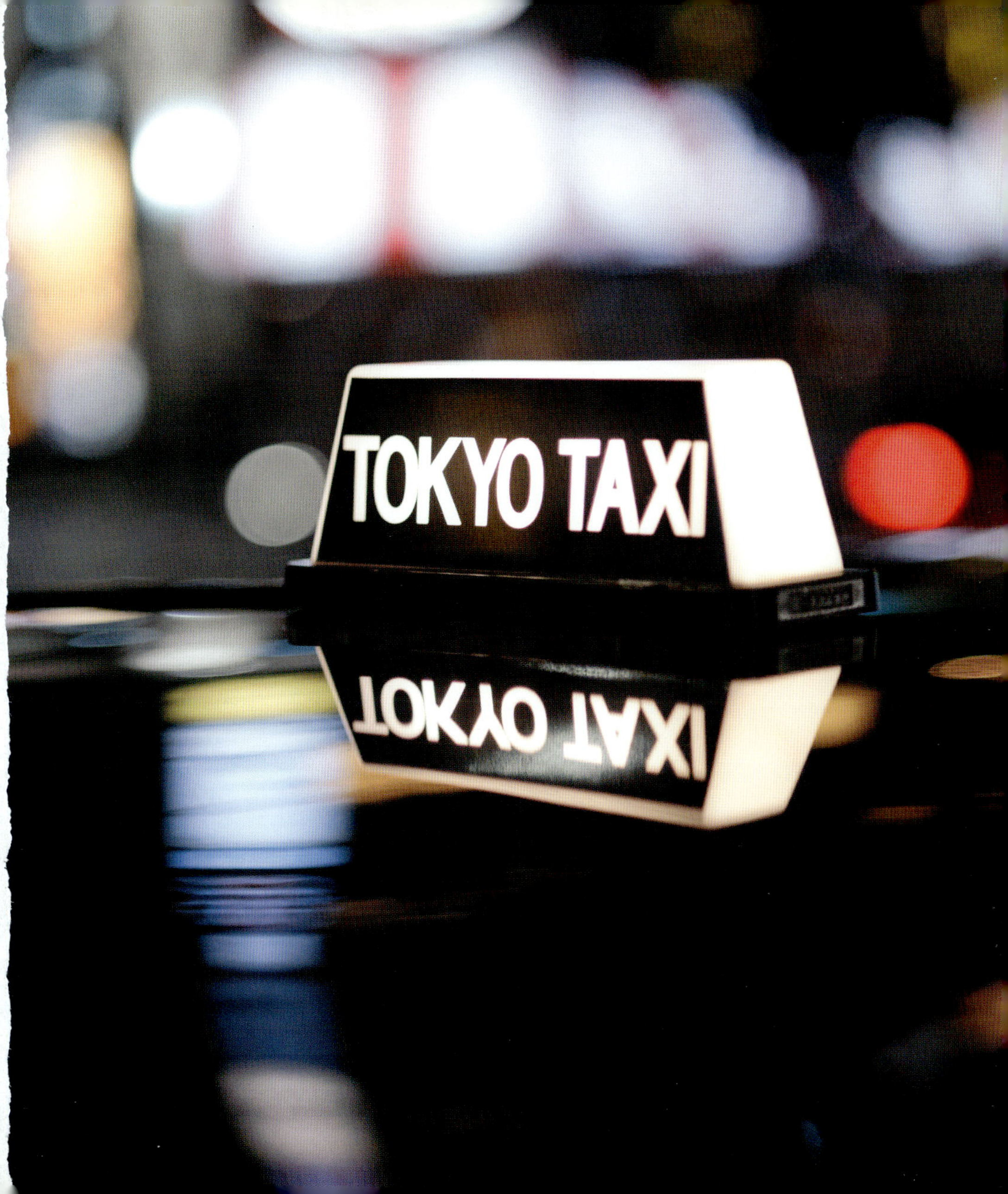
TOKYO TAXI

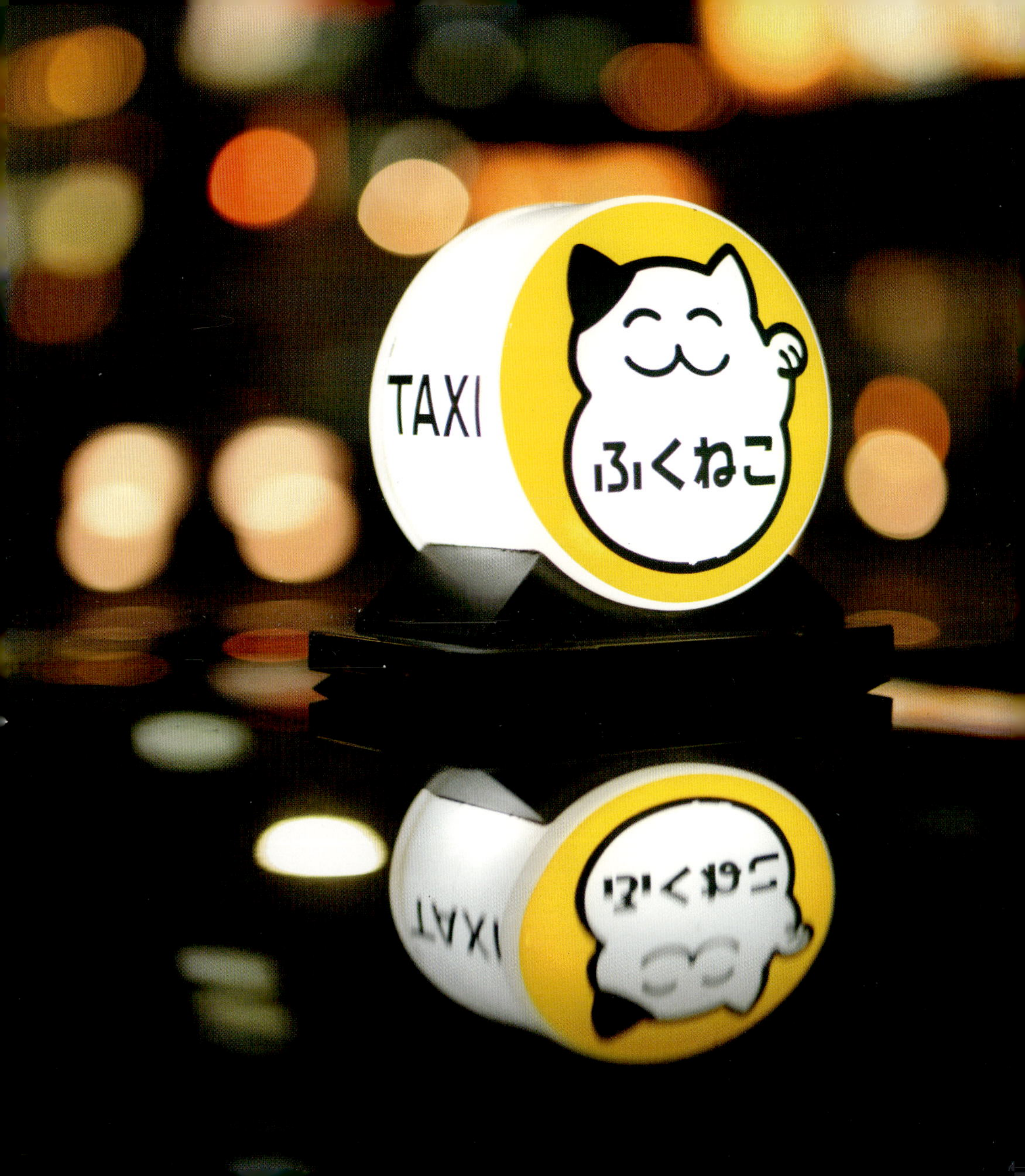
TAXI
ふくねこ

TOKYO TAXI

ALEXANDER JAMES

MERRELL
LONDON • NEW YORK

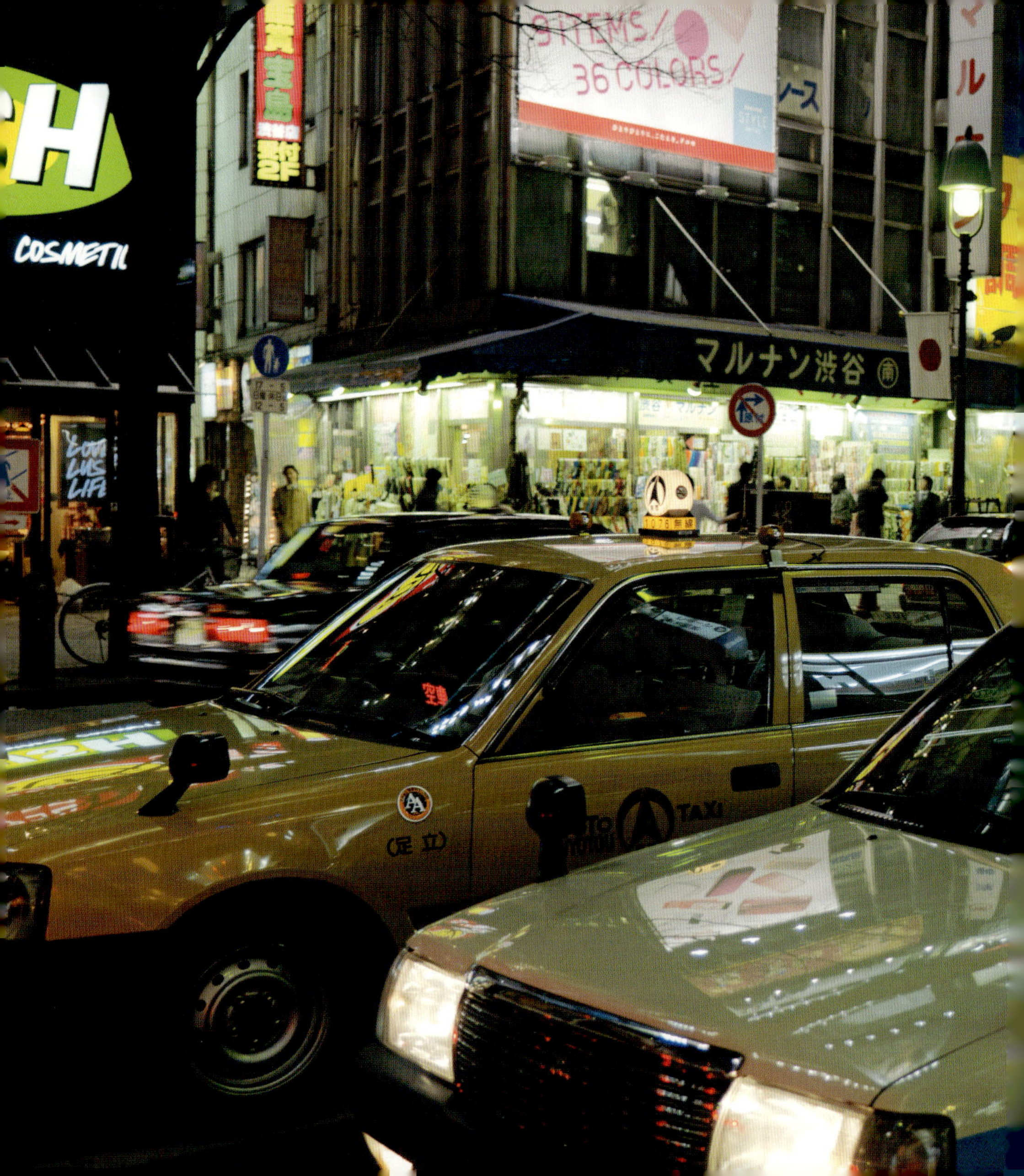

9 ITEMS/
36 COLORS/
宝島
COSMETI
マルナン渋谷
空車
(足立)
TAXI

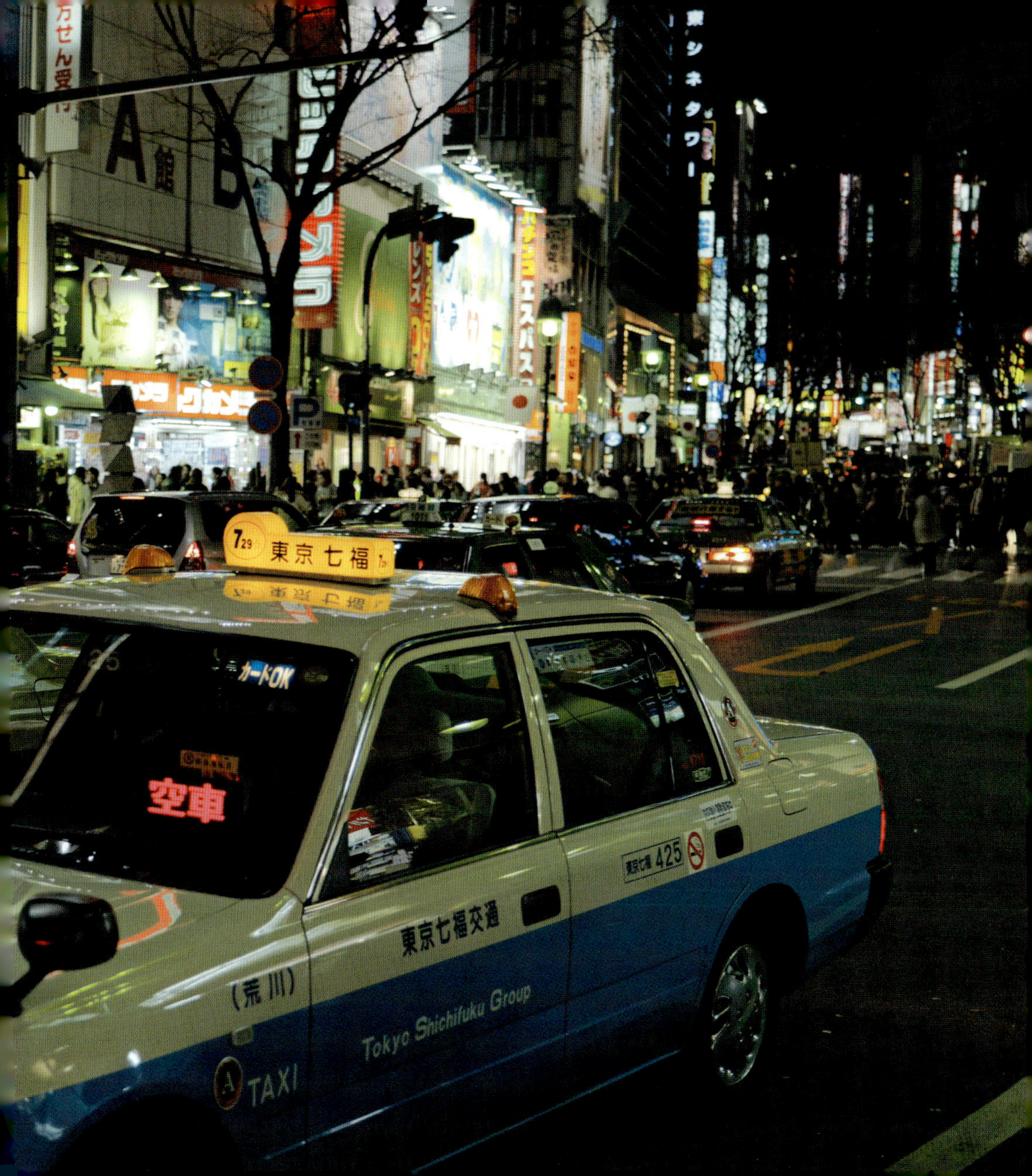

東京七福
カードOK
空車
東京七福 425
東京七福交通
(荒川)
Tokyo Shichifuku Group
TAXI
エスパス

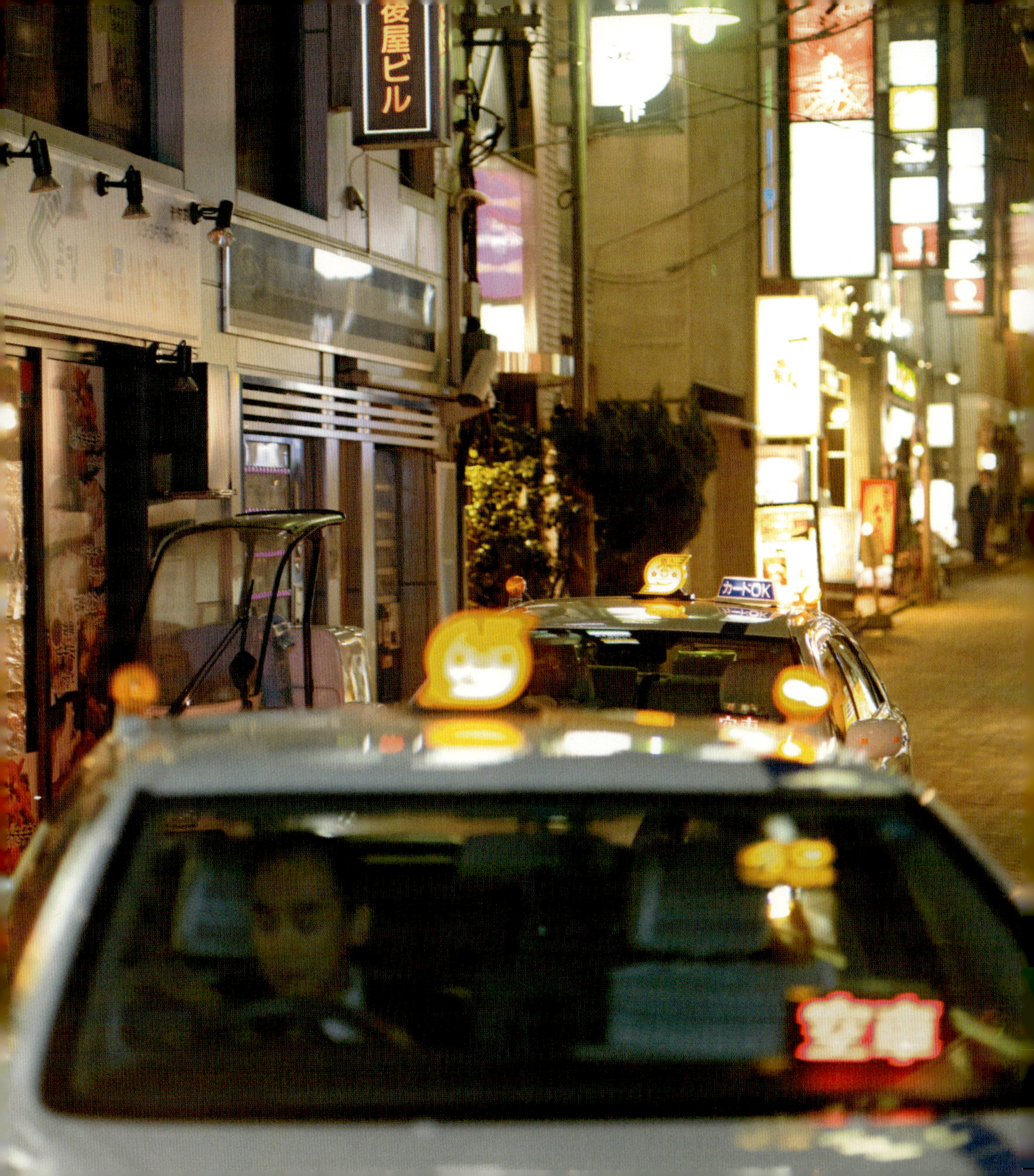
カードOK
空車

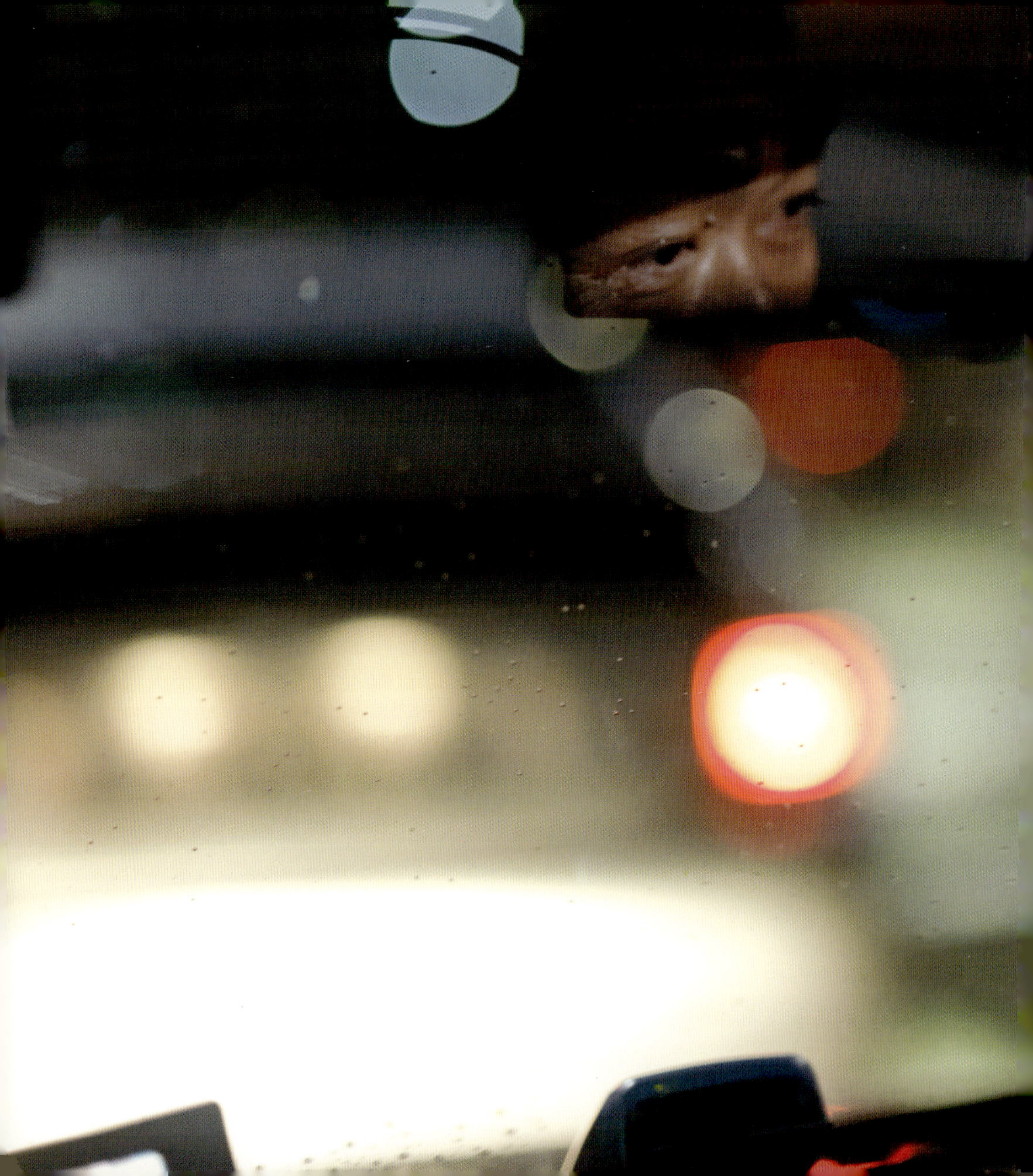

INTRODUCTION

My fascination with Tokyo's taxis began more than ten years ago, when I first saw them at night. Each taxi company sports a unique sign on the roof of its vehicles; after dark, these signs – illuminated when a taxi is vacant – produce a captivating display. In terms of sheer numbers and variety, they are like no other taxi signs anywhere else in the world.

This book is a visual exploration of a selection of these signs, punctuated by anecdotes from some of the drivers with whom I have spoken over the course of many visits to Japan. Creating the near-comprehensive series from which this selection is taken was no easy task: there are 58,000 taxis on Tokyo's roads, registered to 1024 companies. Approximately 90 per cent of the taxis belong to one of the six main firms operating in the city, so tracking down the much rarer

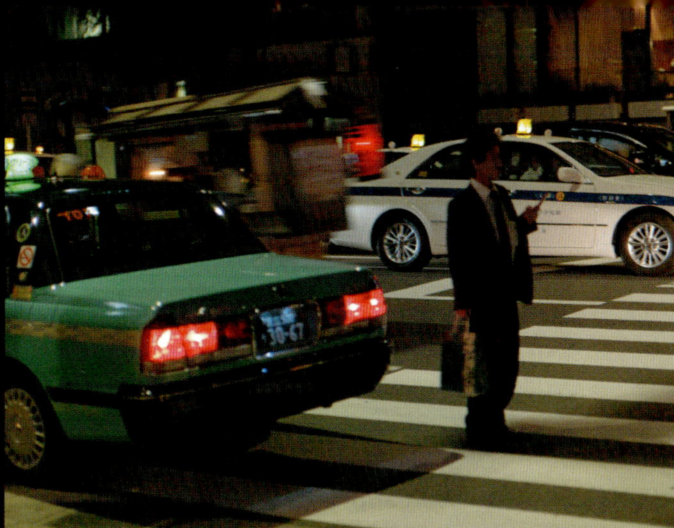

A man waits for a taxi on a crossing in the Ginza district of the city.

companies – some of which have as few as four cars to their name – proved a lengthy process. And then there are the hundreds of *kojin* taxis, run by individuals. My favourite signs include the bubblegum-pink floral motif of the Sakura (or 'cherry blossom') Taxi Co. (page 165) and the striking green star of the Edosou Group Taxi Co. (page 27).

To me, the signs are a remarkable form of advertising; glowing and buzzing with a sense of urgency, they promote the quality of the service offered by the companies they represent. The way in which the landscape of the city interacts with the reflective surfaces of the taxis can also be overlooked. Each vehicle is engaged in a vigorous dialogue of light and energy as it weaves its way through the streets, in dramatic contrast to the stillness of the seated passenger inside.

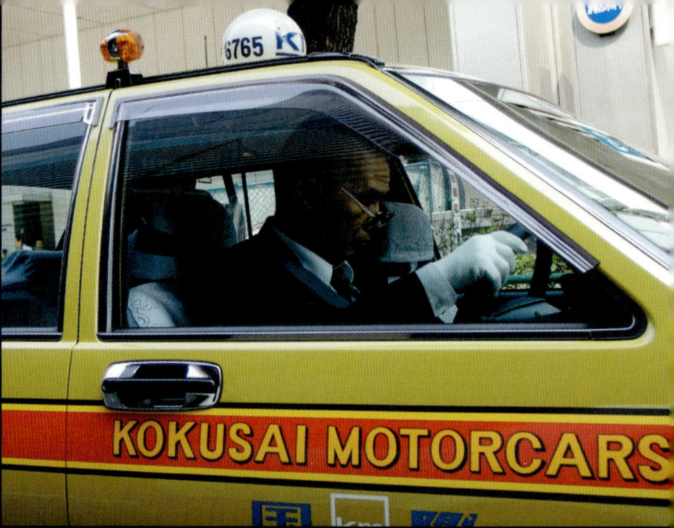

A Kokusai Motorcars driver waits for a fare

I took many of the photographs while riding a bicycle, a genuine pleasure on Tokyo's smooth-as-glass streets. Cycling with one hand while holding a primed medium-format camera in the other, however, was something of a guerrilla affair. I had to be very quick when I spotted a new company sign – literally chasing after the unsuspecting driver as he looked for a fare – so quite a few of the images were taken while I was still in the saddle. When I eventually caught up with my target, usually only after it had joined a taxi rank, I always asked the driver's permission before taking any photographs. The drivers are more than happy to chat, which has helped me understand what their working lives are really like. One thing that becomes immediately apparent is just how hard it is to get started in the job; even with the

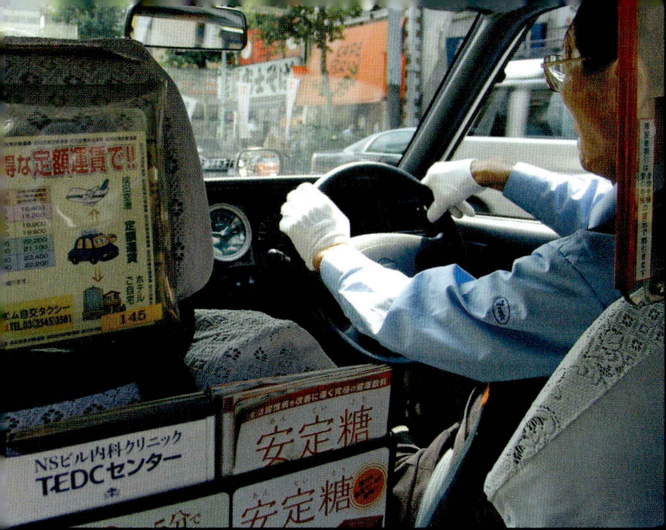

he white gloves worn by many drivers reflect the great pride they take in their work.

help of satellite navigation, there is an enormous number of often complex streets to learn and navigate successfully.

When talking to the drivers, the vast majority of whom are male, you soon begin to hear stories about the people they have met and the funny things that have happened to them. Such stories are clearly an important source of light relief for the drivers; the hours are long and hard, and many of them talk of the time they have to spend away from their families. If it were not for the social aspect of the job, I am sure many of them would change career. They all seem genuinely to enjoy talking to their customers.

The taxis themselves are immaculate. Even twenty-year-old models are spotlessly clean, both inside and out, with no scratches or dents in the bodywork. Great pride is taken

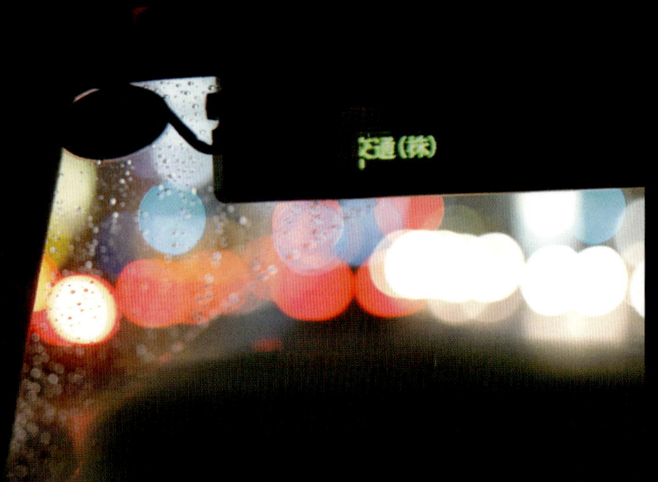

A digital information screen inside a taxi operated by Teito Taxi Co.

Mr Harada of Teito Taxi Co. in the smart attire commonly worn by drivers from the more reputable taxi firms.

over the service offered: drivers often wear white gloves, while the seats are covered in white cloth. With the aid of a hydraulic ram, the driver opens the passenger door for you as he skilfully pulls up beside the pavement, allowing you to glide effortlessly into your seat. I always keep an eye out for one of my favourite models of Japanese taxi, an early generation Toyota Crown (see, for example, page 16). Although it may seem dated by today's design standards, it is as integral to the city's streets as the black cab is to London's.

The majority of the research and planning for each shoot was undertaken late at night in the sushi and noodle bars buried deep in the backstreets of the Akasaka neighbourhood. The tables of these venues – their names

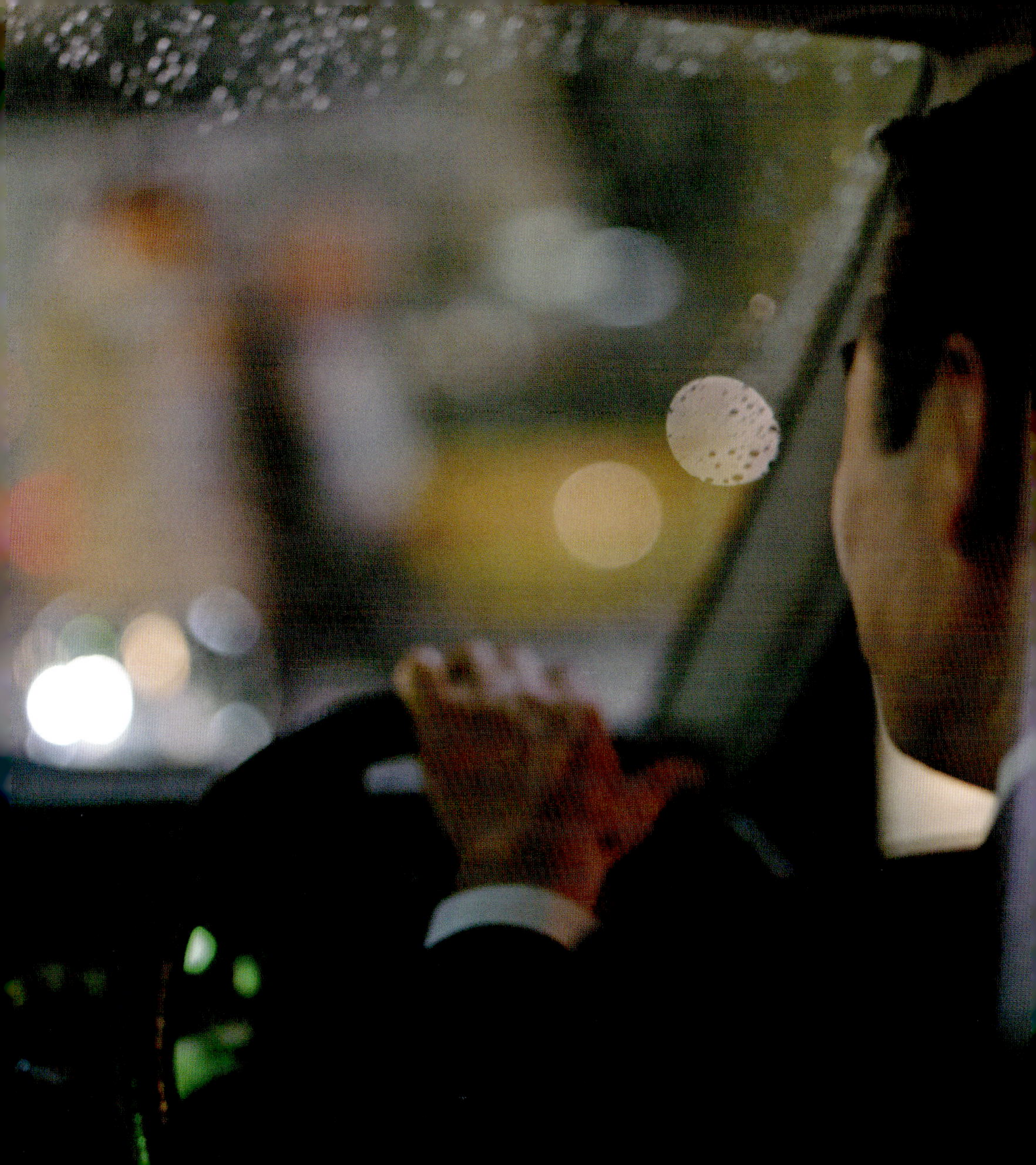

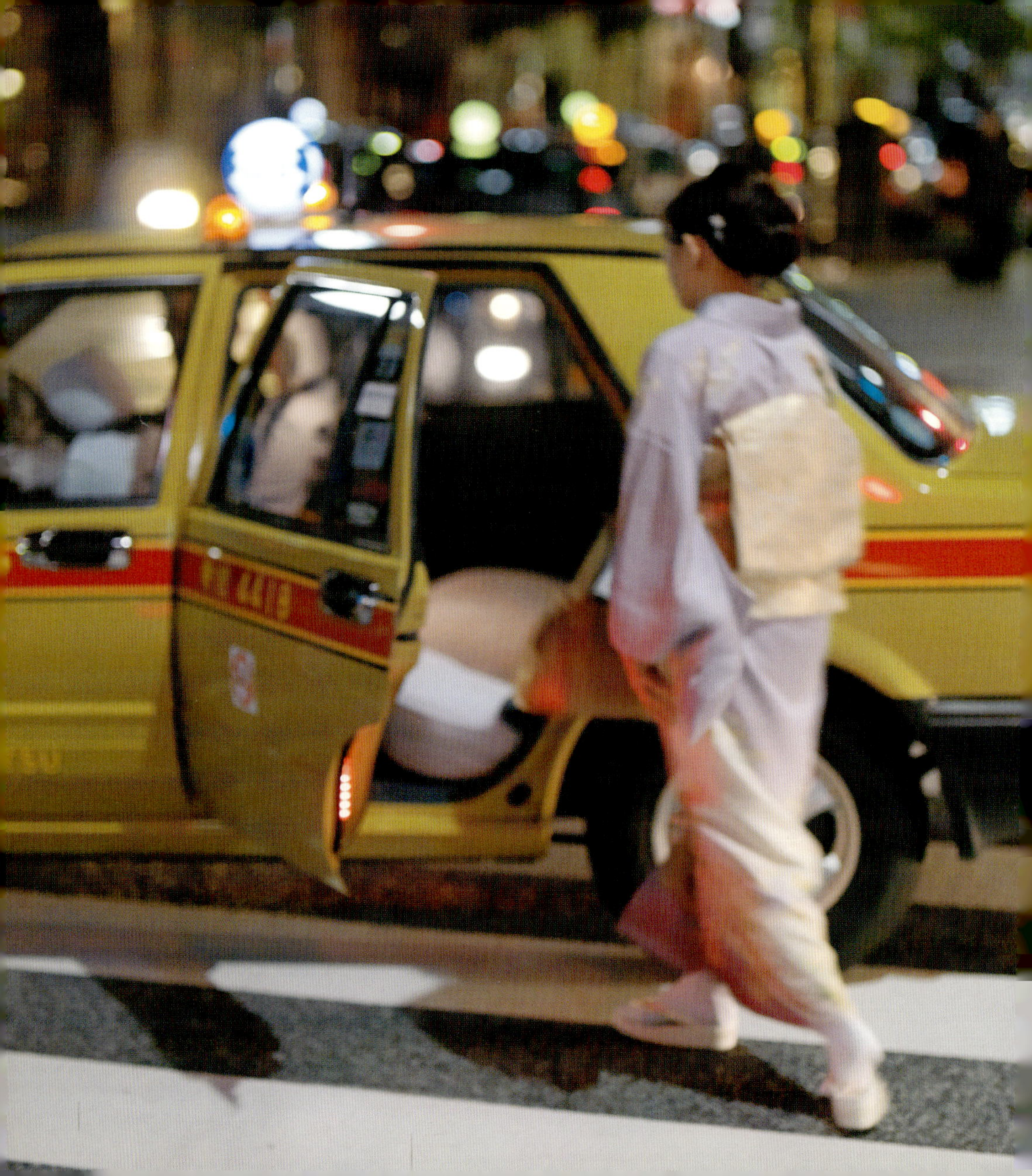

A traditionally dressed woman hails a taxi in the Akasaka entertainment district.

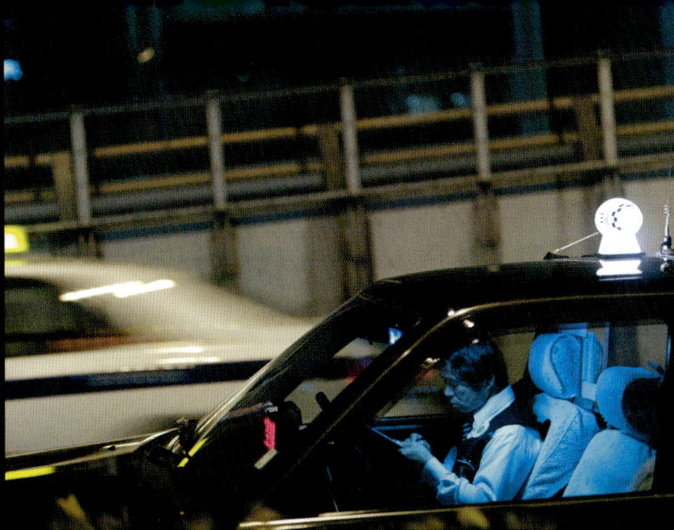

Illuminated by the glow of his reading light, a driver waits on a taxi rank in Akasaka.

and menus written only in kanji – were full of men from every age group, all wearing dark suits, all smoking and drinking heavily, and all laughing and joking with one another. I could not have asked for a more authentic place in which to work. In fact, Akasaka proved an ideal base of operations, since it is well known for being an area in which the locals like to socialize after work, providing a steady stream of taxi fares into the early hours of the morning.

Tokyo is a place that has to be experienced to be believed. Only then can you begin to appreciate how utterly different it is from every other city in the world. The infrastructure, for example, blends seamlessly with the daily life of a true metropolis. Motorways pass overhead, right through the busiest of districts, while thousands of people

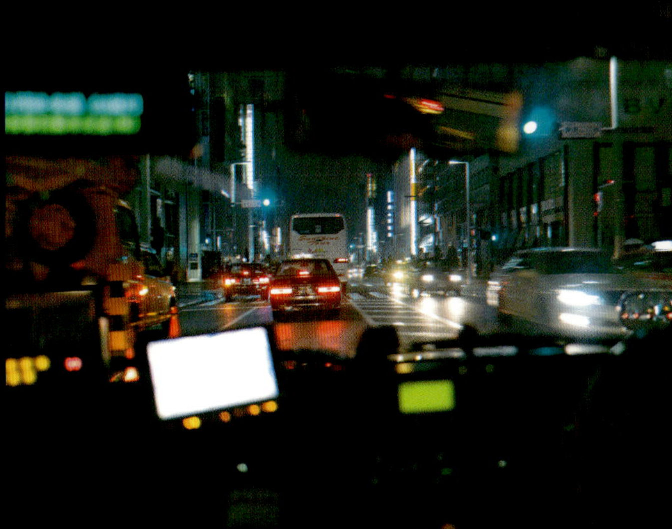

The streets of Tokyo's Shimbashi district seen from a taxi driver's point of view.

go about their business on the streets below; only the *gaikokujin* (foreigners) tend to take any notice. Through the soles of your feet, meanwhile, you can feel the subway trains thundering through underground tunnels: the place pulses with such energy that your heart is liable to skip a beat. I take very few daytime shots whenever I visit Tokyo; for me, its transformation at night is simply magical, and I never tire of my self-imposed night shift. With a pocket full of unexposed film, the possibilities seem endless.

If you have never been to Tokyo, then I can heartily recommend it, on every level; in fact, it should be on everyone's must-do list. During my many trips to the city I have had nothing but the best of experiences, both professionally and personally. Riding around such a city

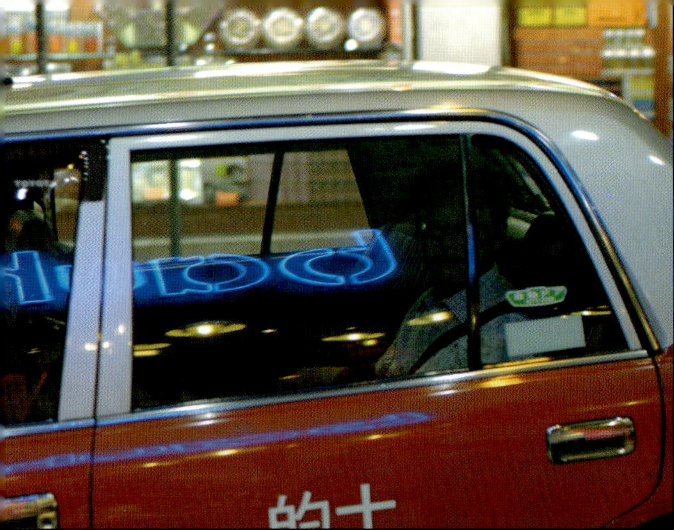

he windows of a passing taxi reflect a neon shop sign.

as New York or London at night with a high-end camera n your hand could result in a very different story. But this s Tokyo, where crime rates are extremely low, especially n relation to foreigners. Etiquette plays an important role n Japanese society, which makes every interaction a genuine pleasure. The food is delicious and extremely varied, even for the budget-restricted epicurean, while the people themselves are warm, helpful and fun to be around. Once you add the dramatic location into the mix, you have everything that a great travel experience should be. Just be sure to take a ride around the city at night in one of its conic taxis. And don't forget your camera.

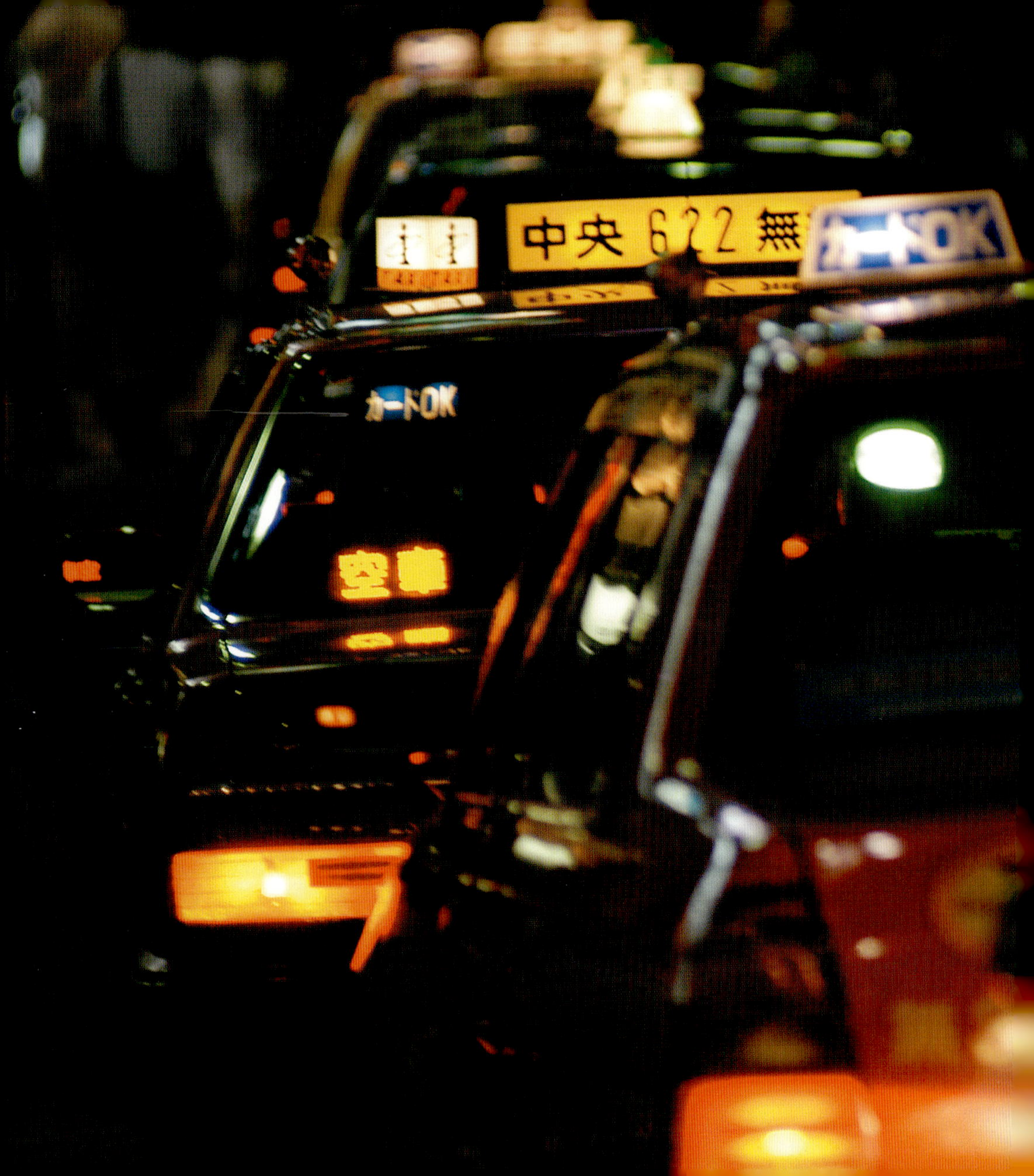
中央 622 無
カードOK
空車

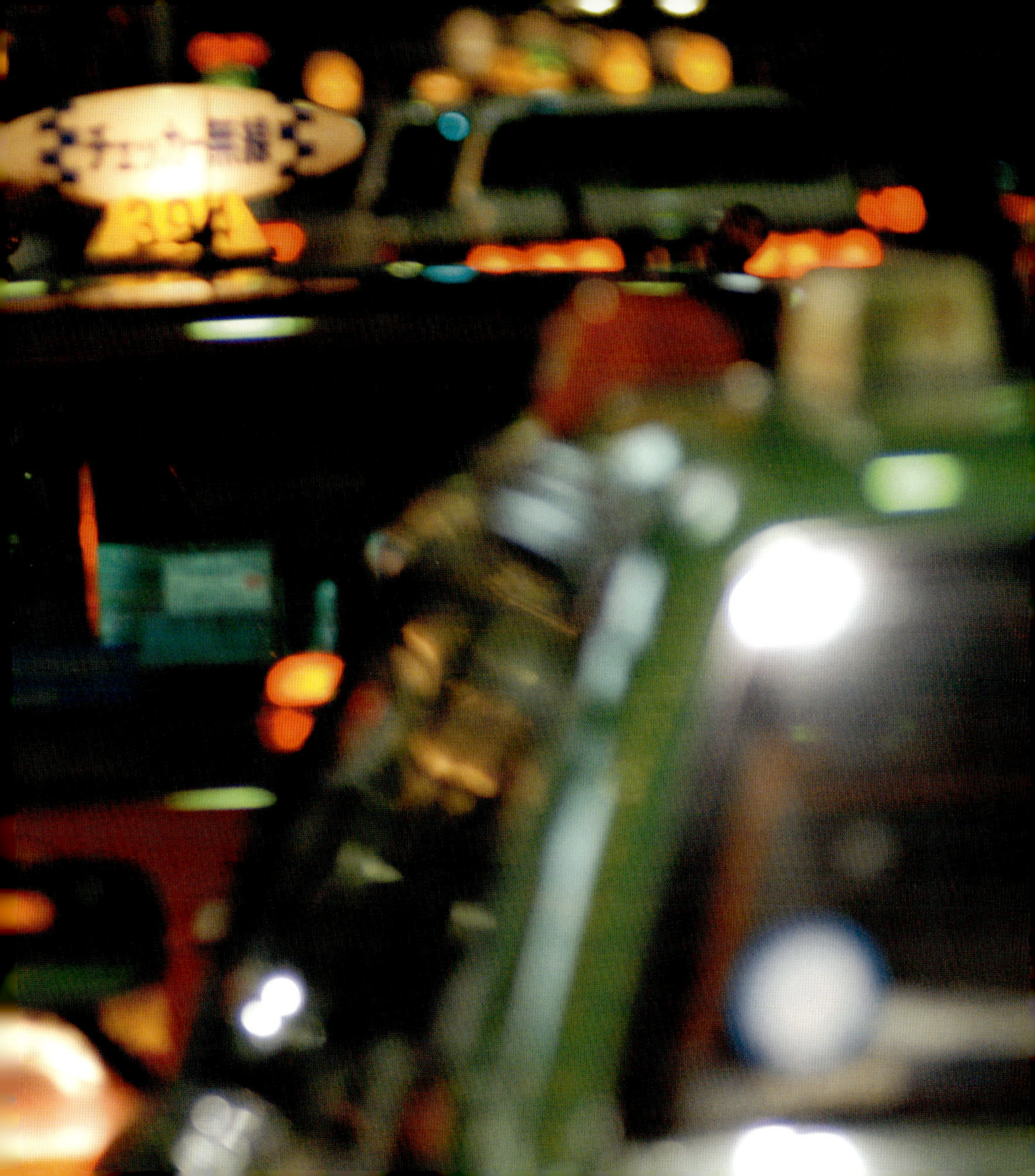

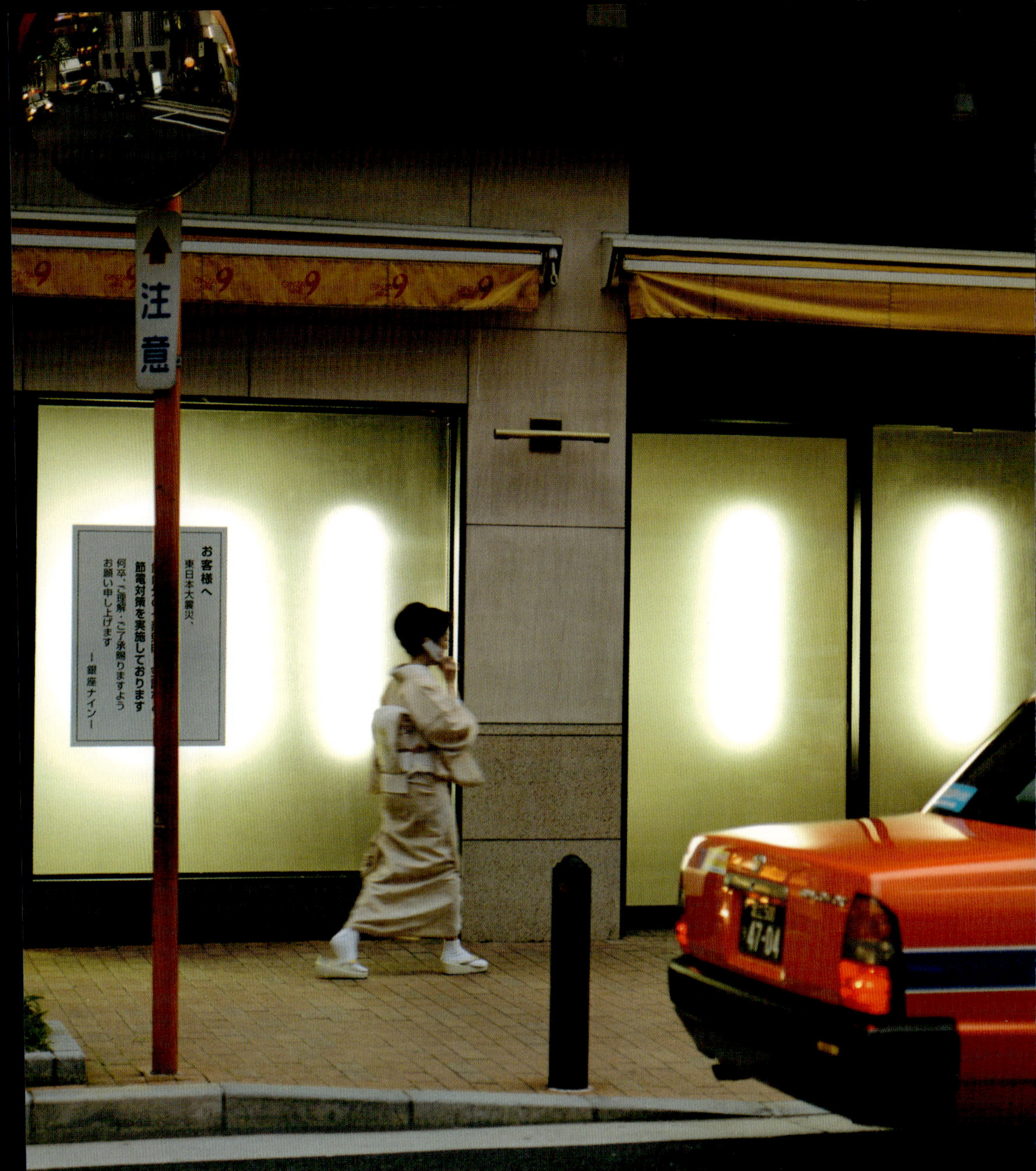
注意
お客様へ
東日本大震災、
節電対策を実施しております
何卒、ご理解・ご了承賜りますよう
お願い申し上げます
ー銀座ナインー

TOKYO TAXI

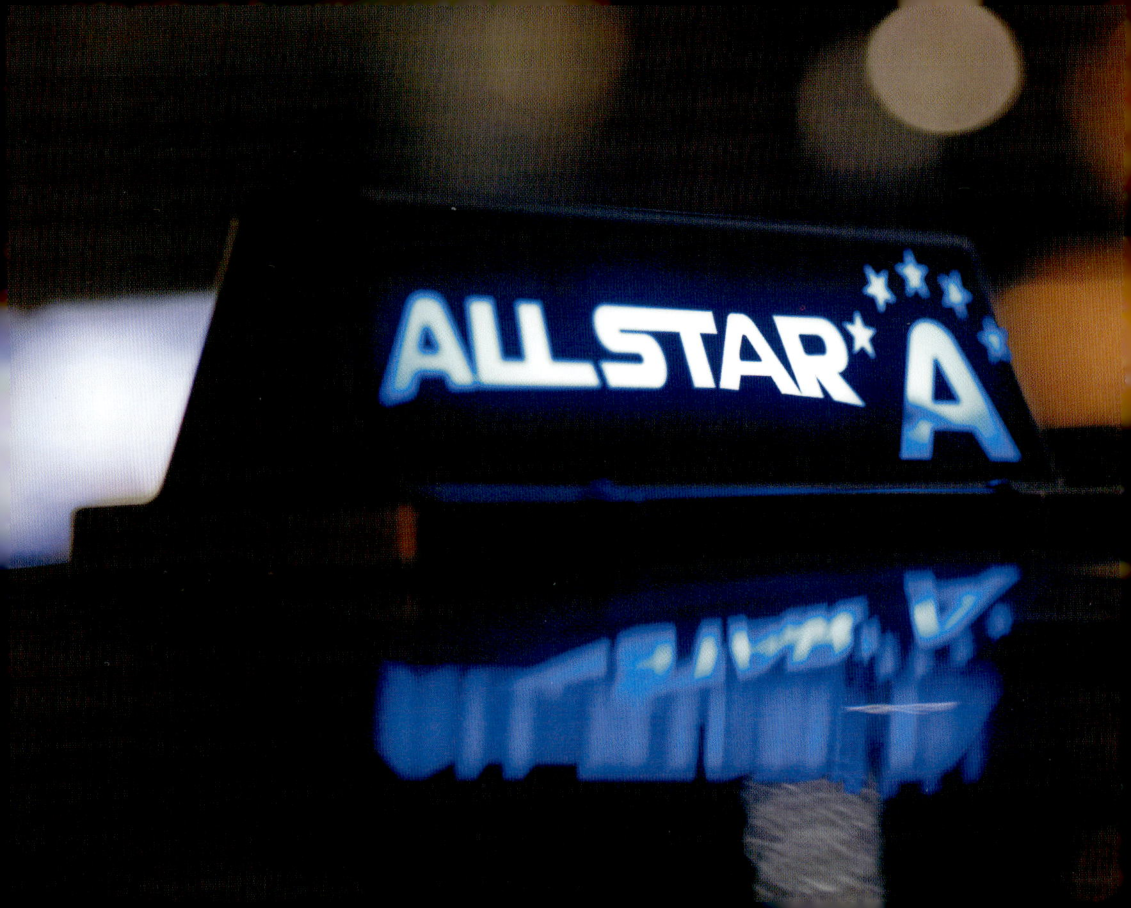
ALLSTAR A

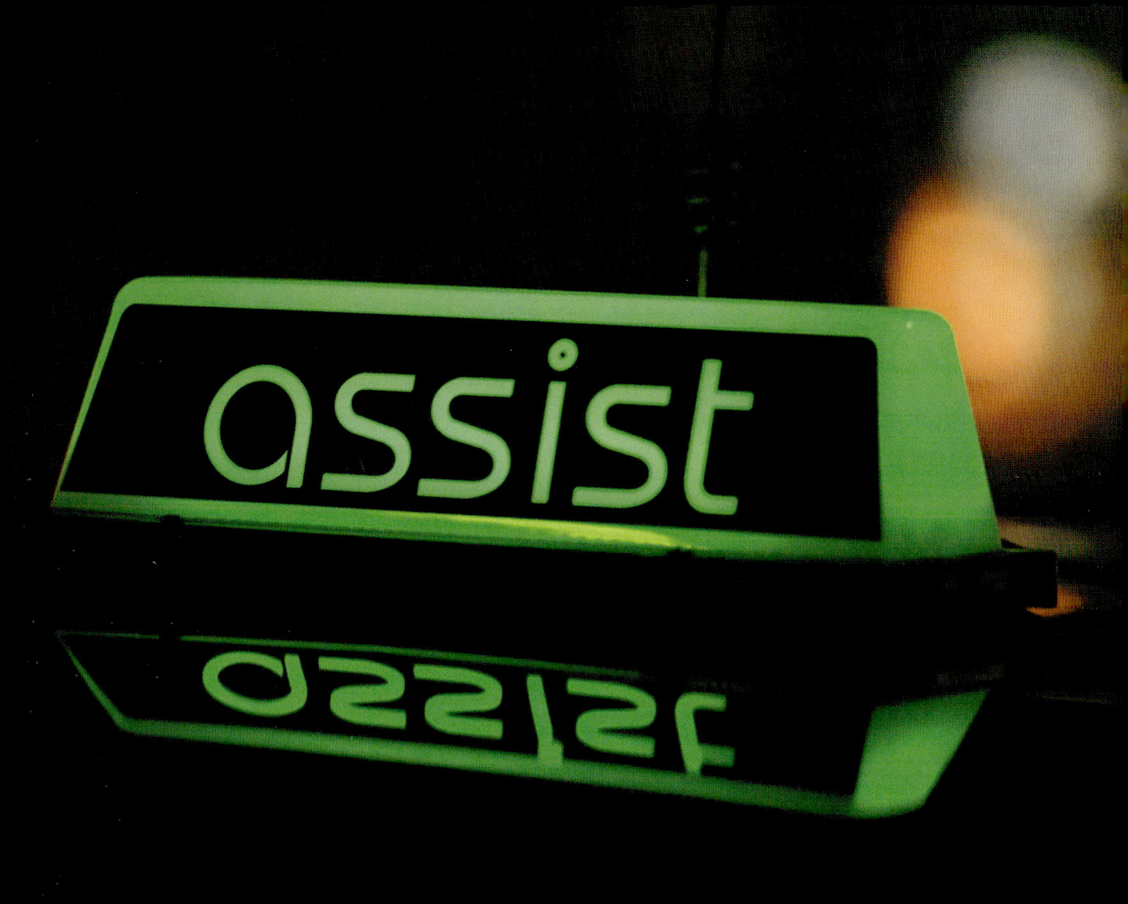

ASSIST TAXI CO.

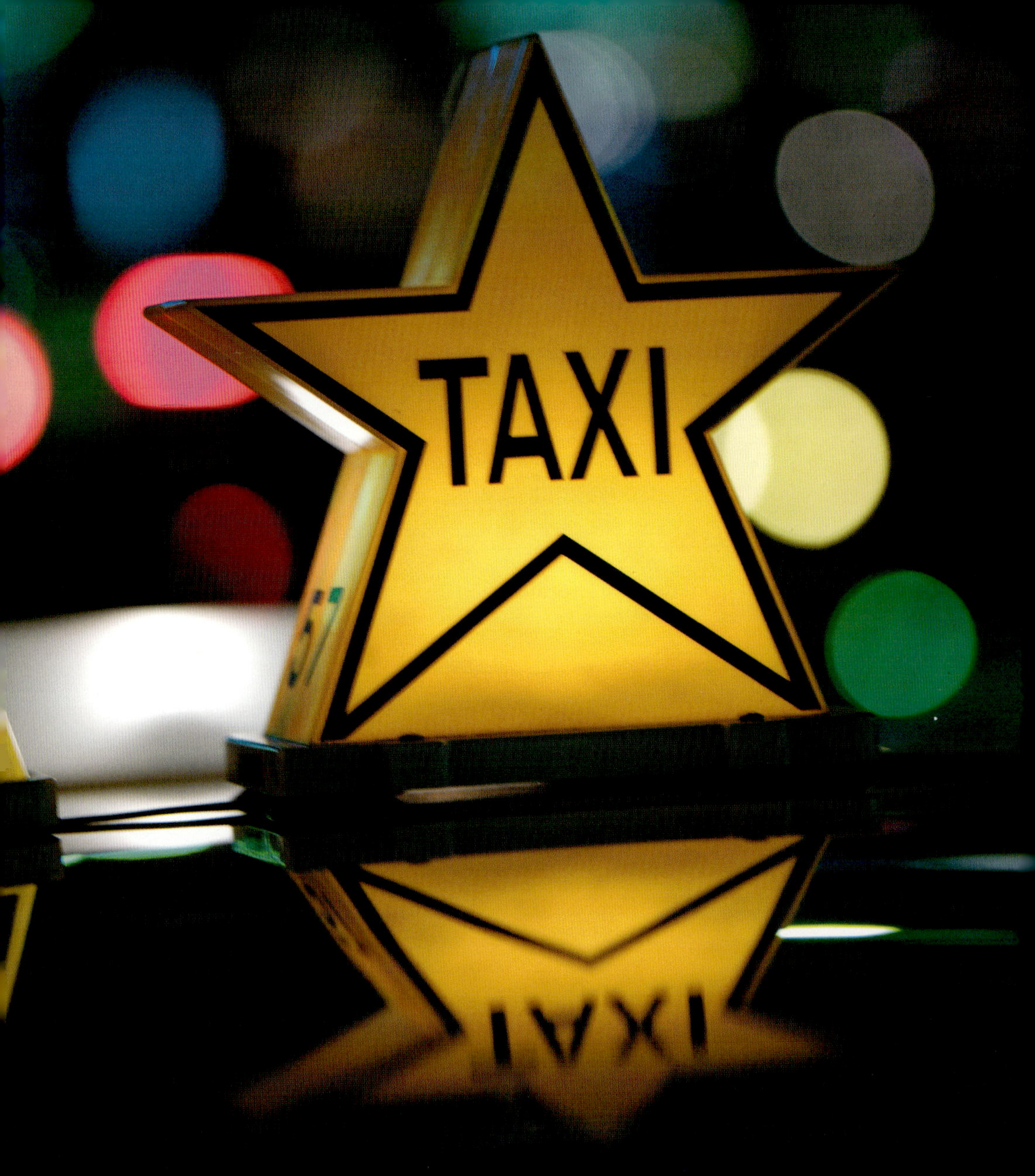
TAXI

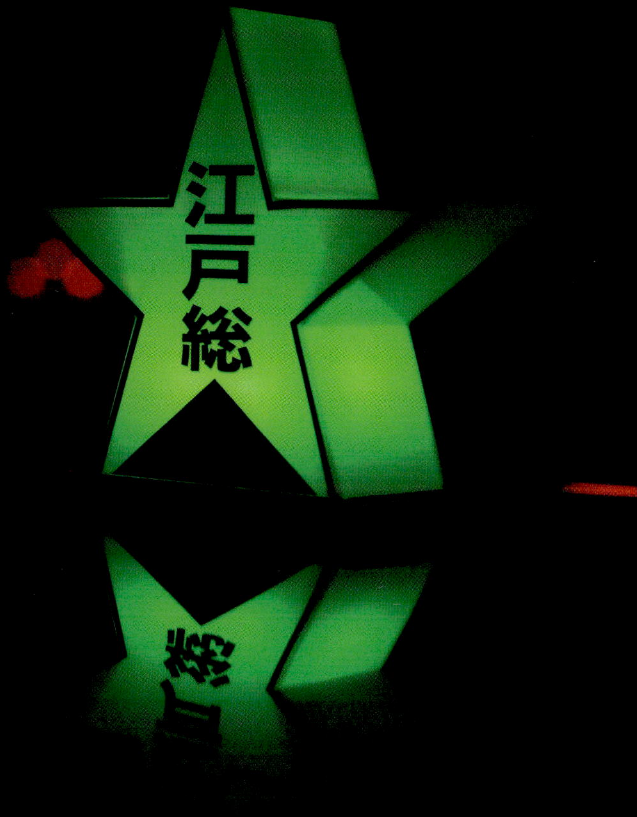

EDOSOU GROUP TAXI CO.

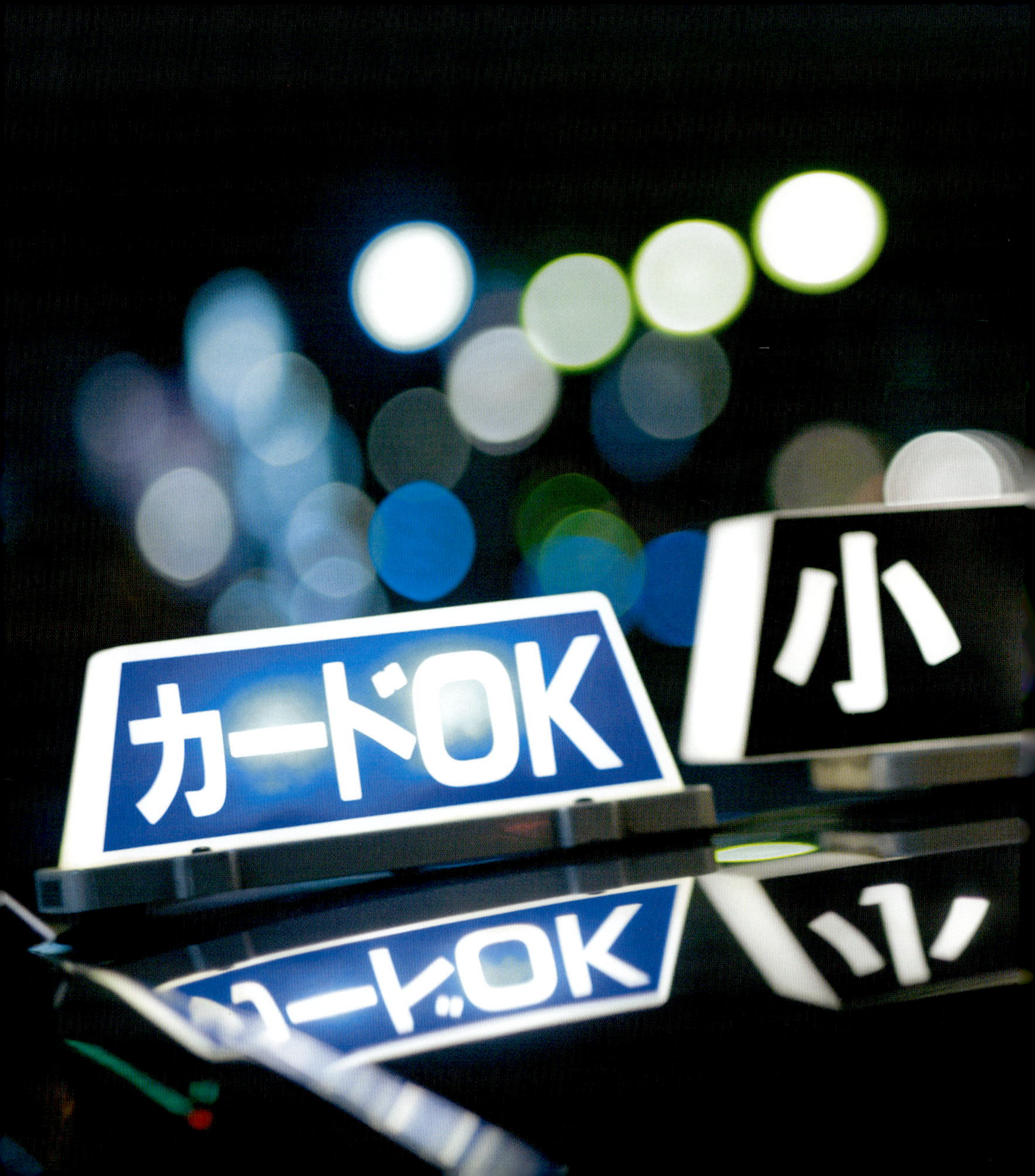
カードOK
小

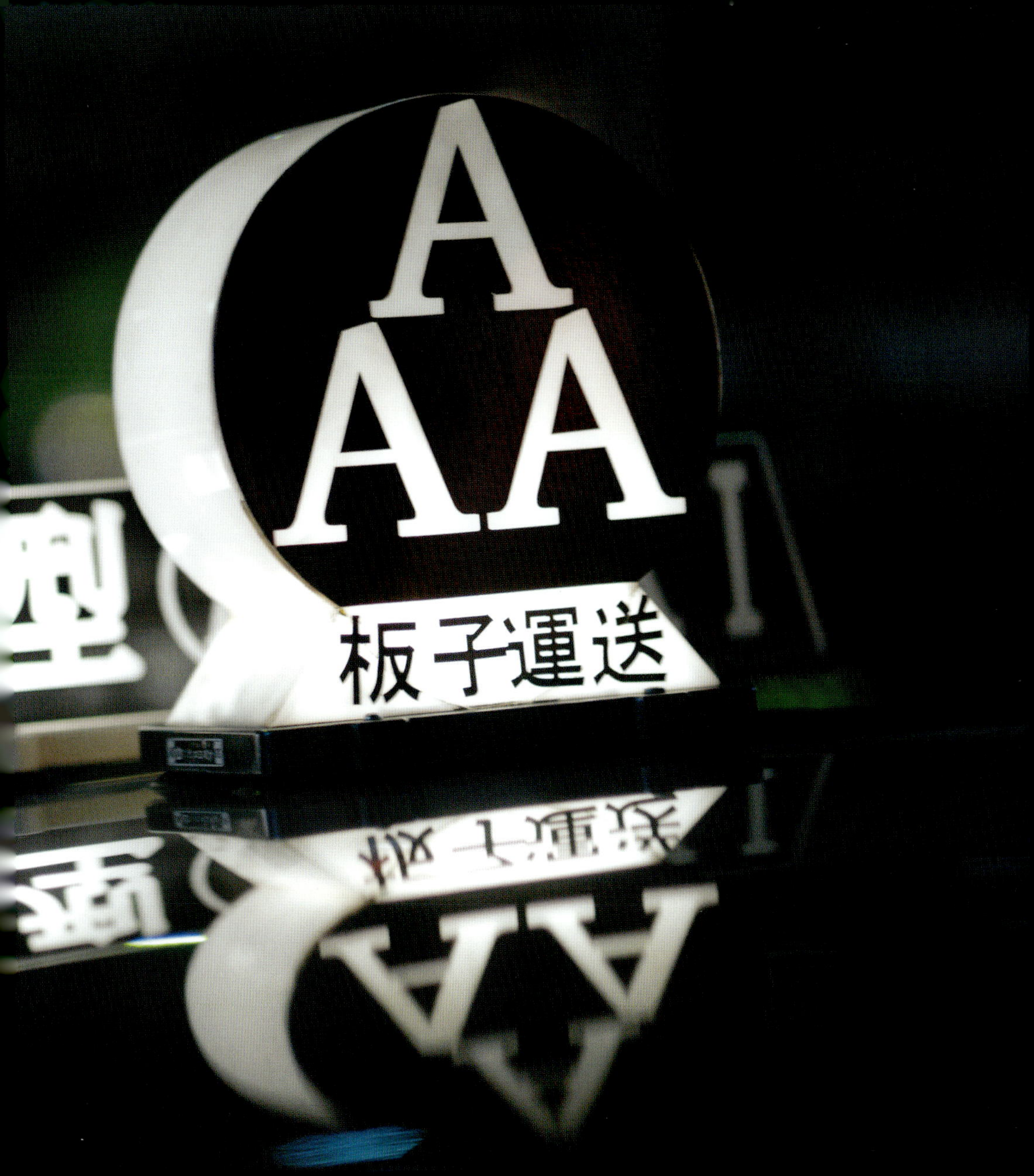
AAA
板子運送

UNNAMED DRIVER

I remember one passenger who, when he was bowing after a few too many drinks, would not turn his back on his friends and work colleagues. He tried to get into the taxi backwards and missed, ending up on his backside in the street. He still tried to maintain decorum when getting up – poor guy.

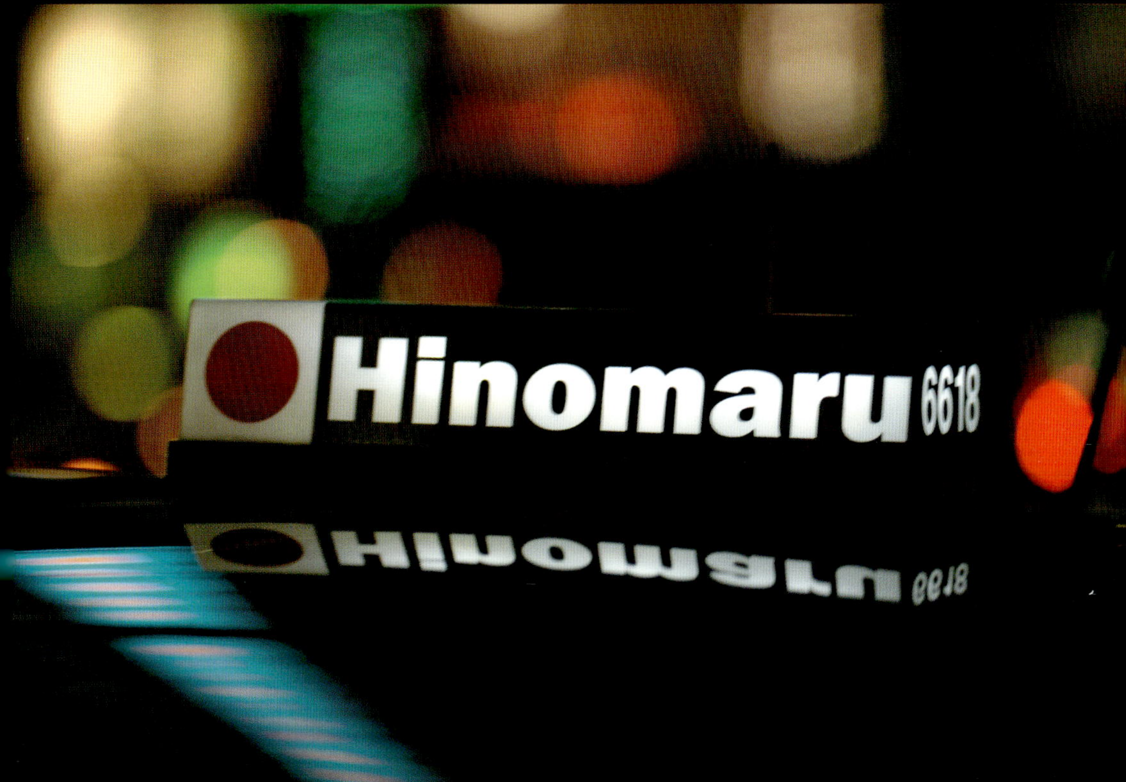

HINOMARU TAXI 6618

KOJIN TAXI

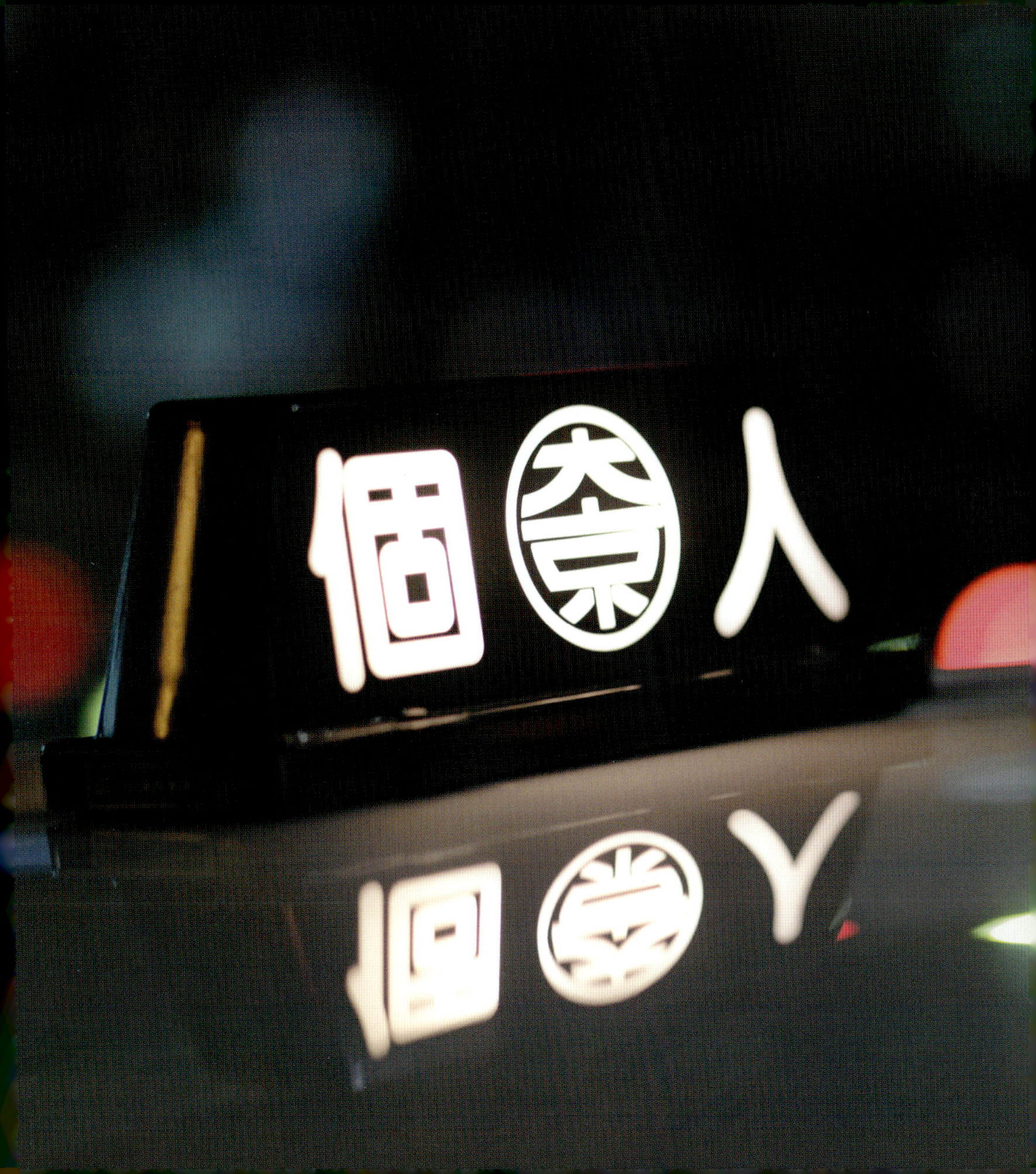
個
奈
人

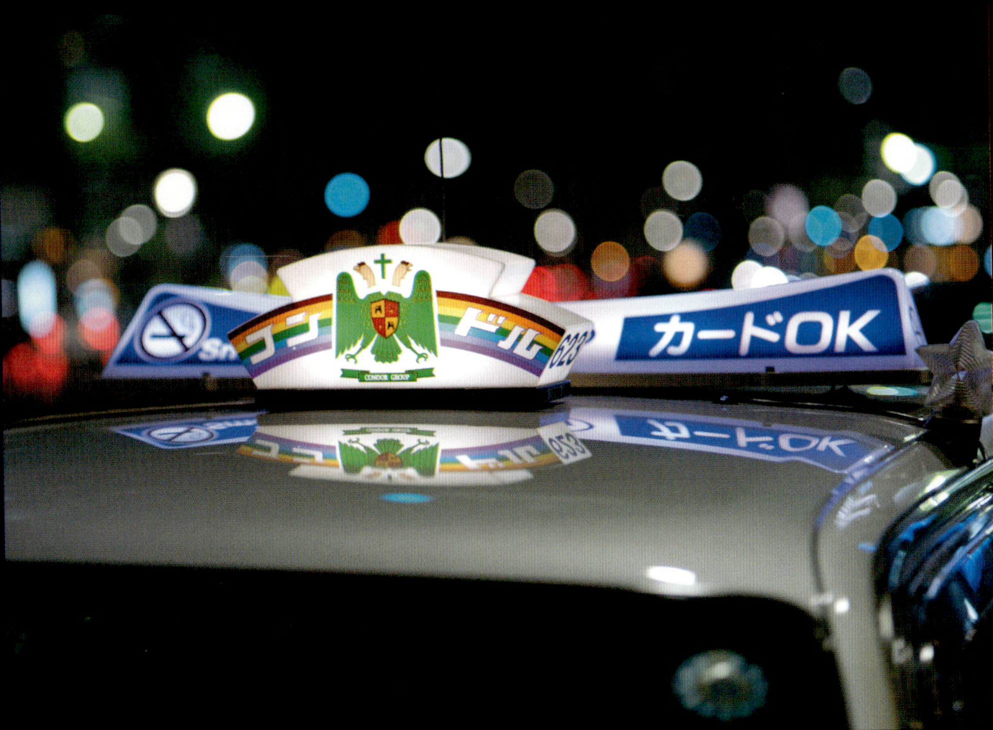

CONDOR TAXI CO.

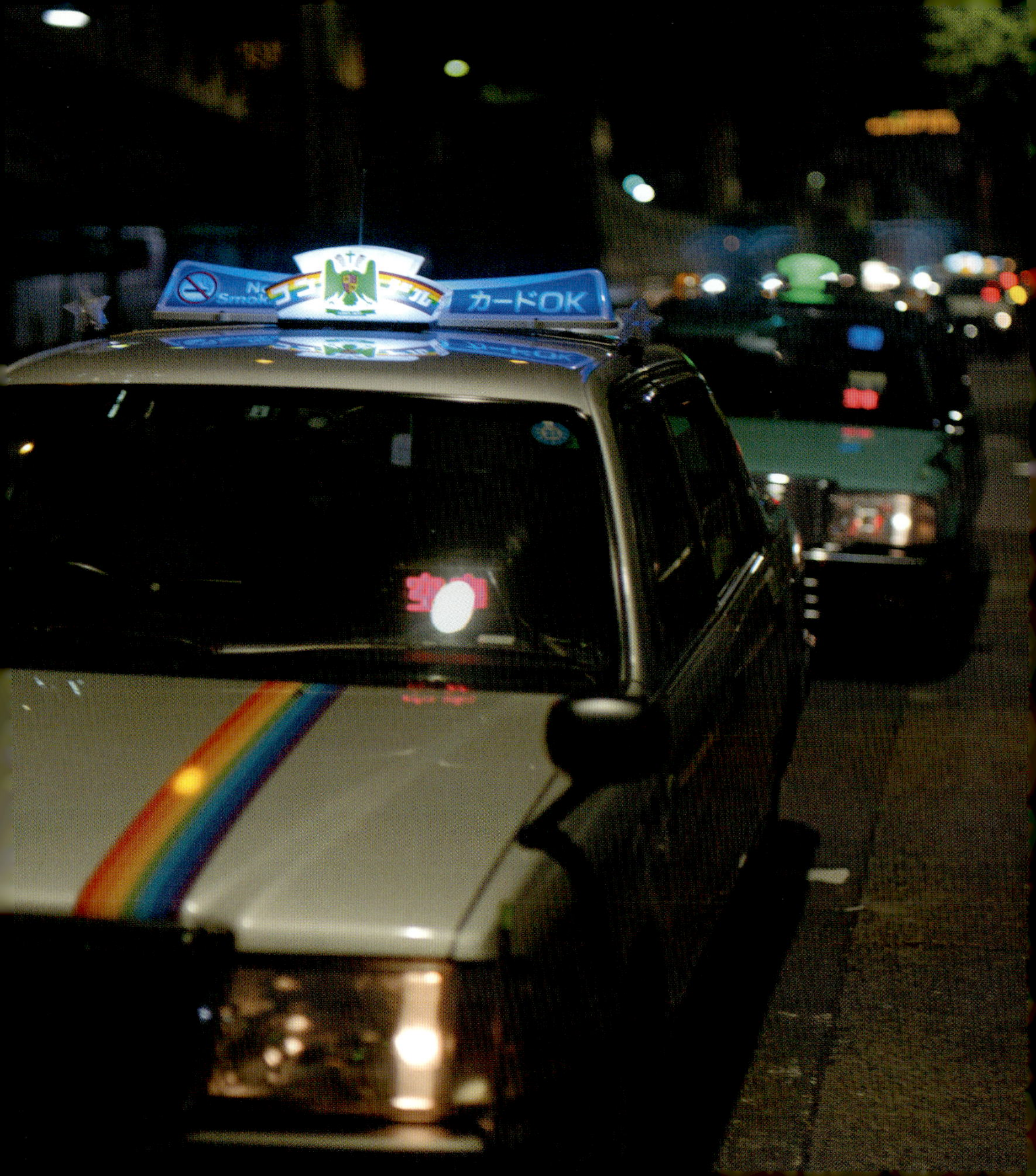
カードOK

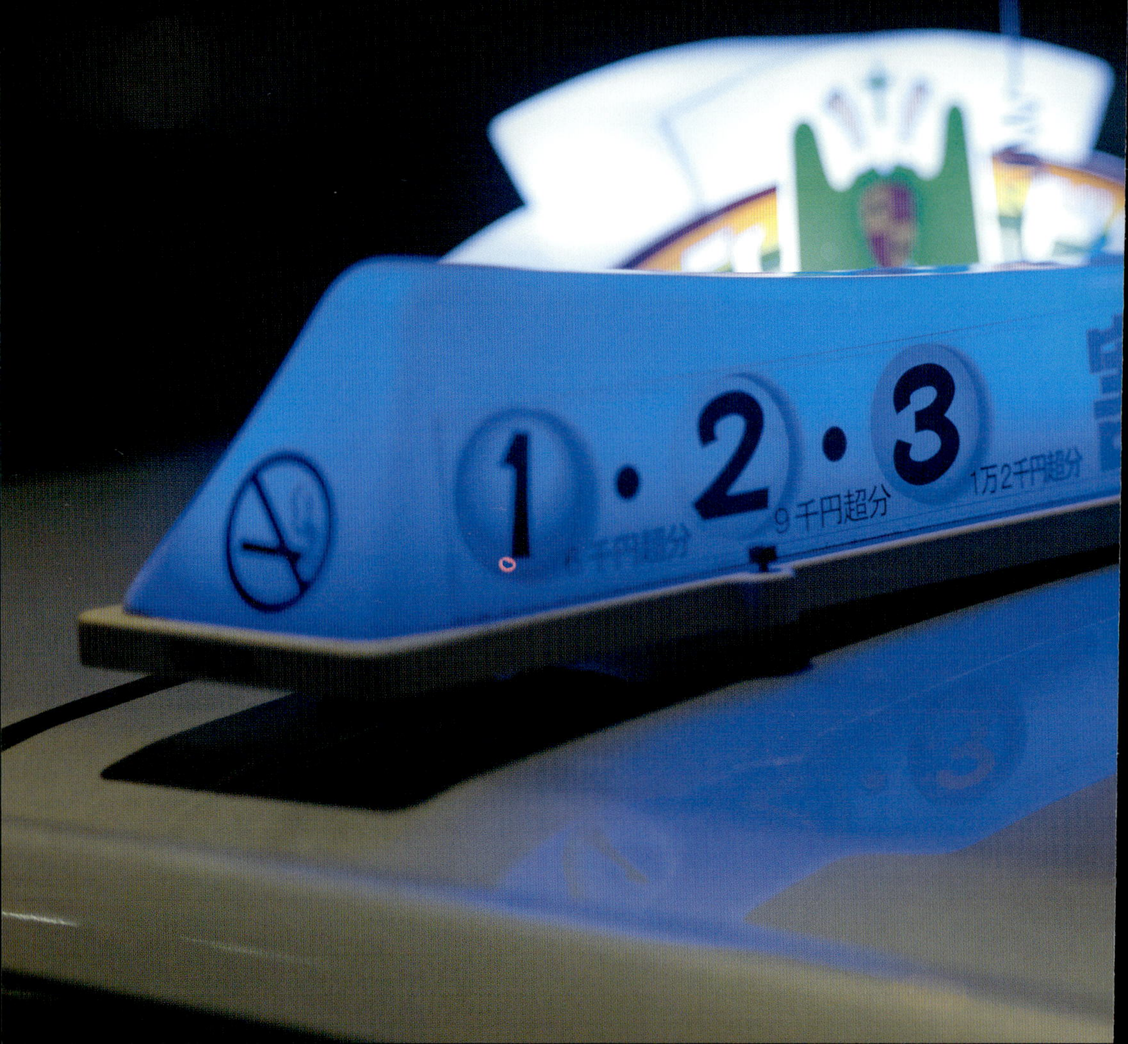
1・2・3
9千円超分
1万2千円超分

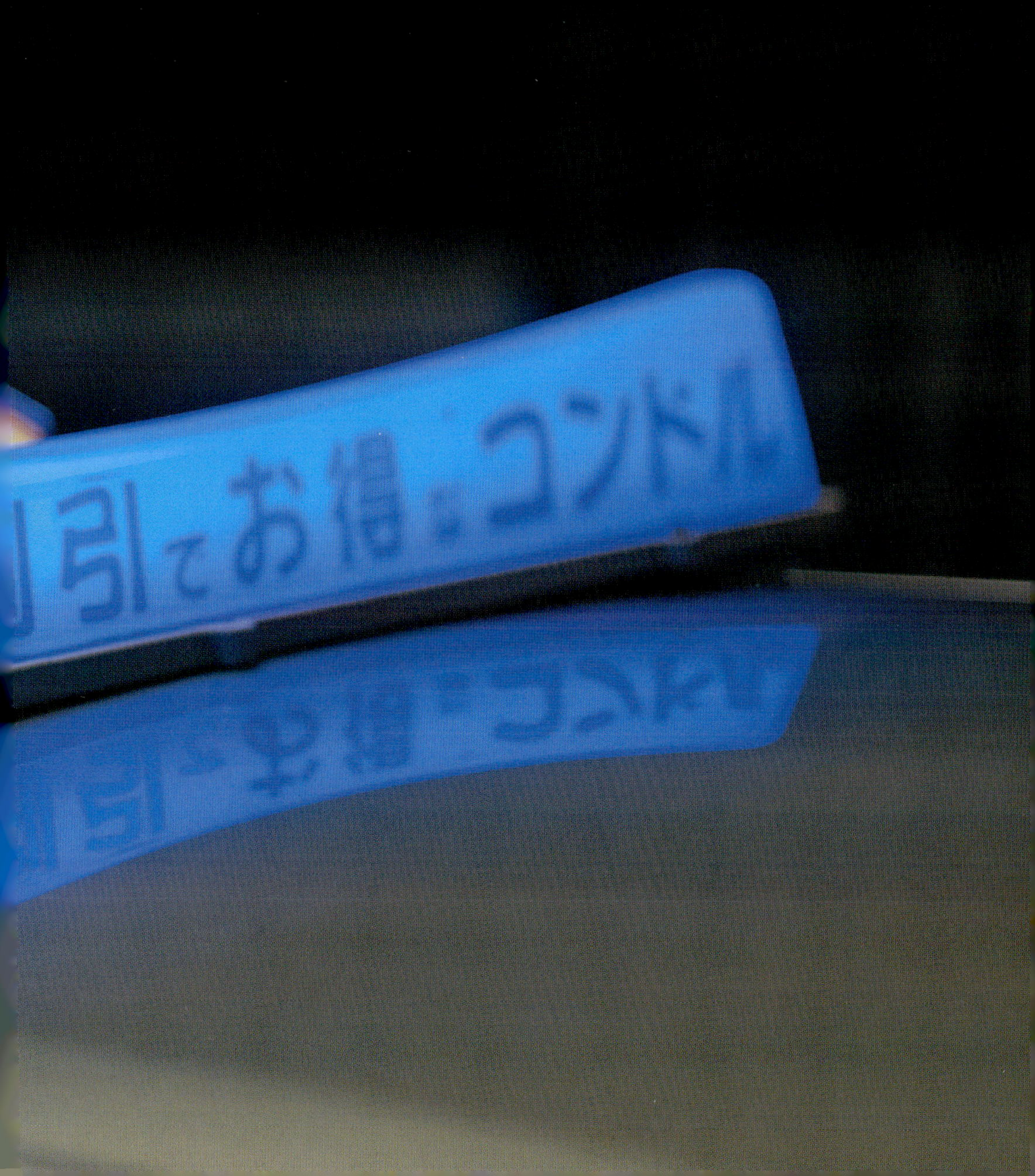
引でお得。コンド

‘RAISED FINGER’

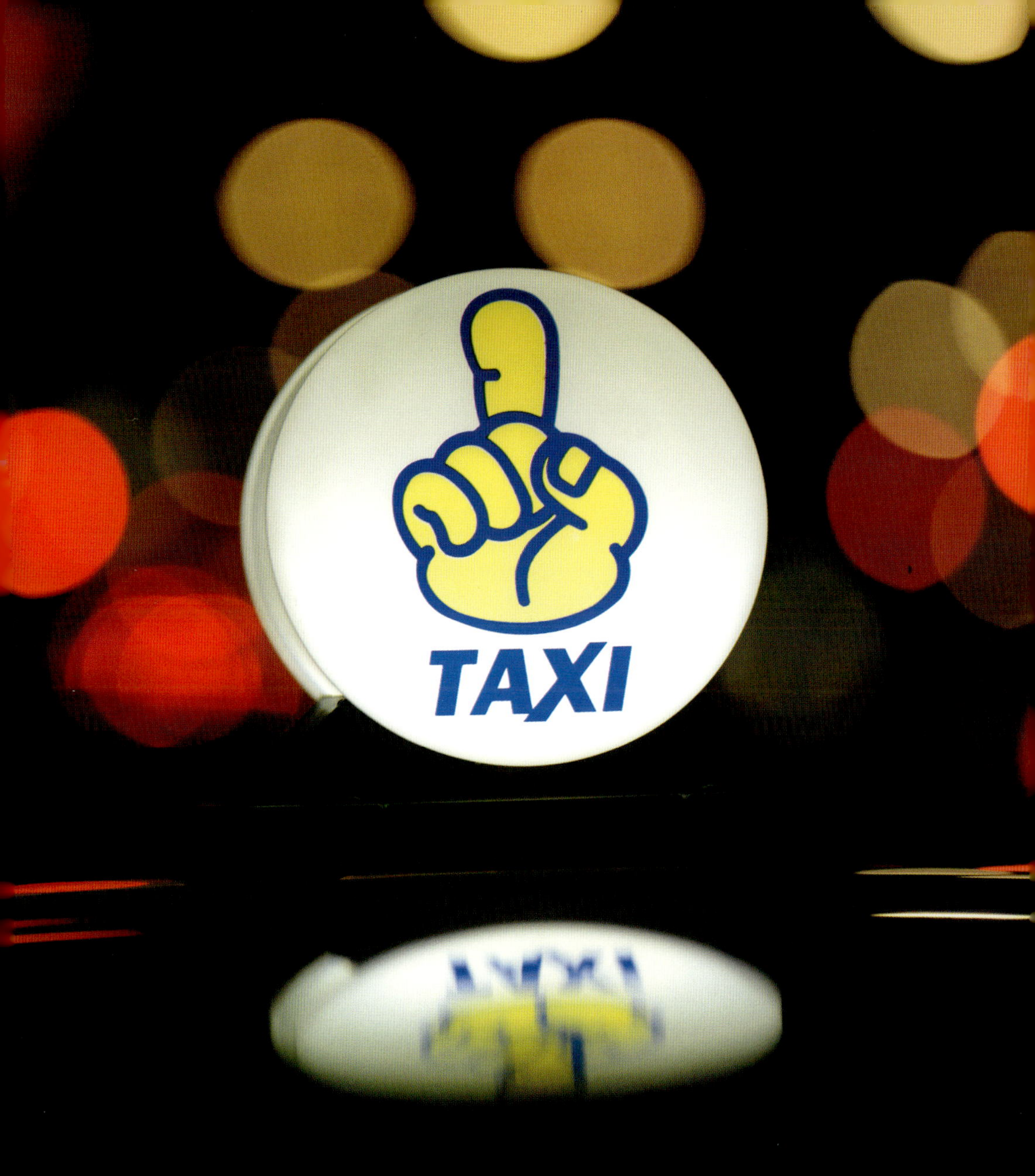
TAXI

MR SUZUKI

I've worked for Teito for more than
six years now, and I love having the opportunity
to work hard and be rewarded for it.
You get out what you put in.

Pages 42–43: TOKYO TAXI

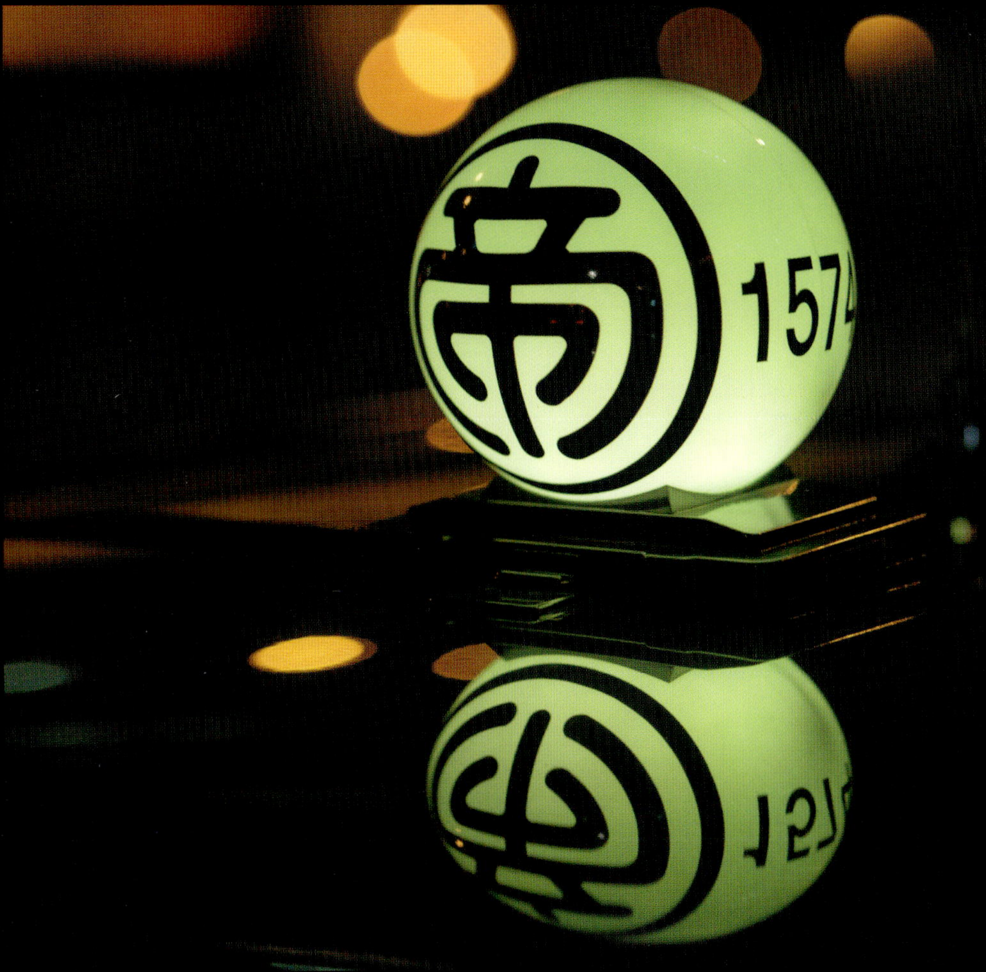

TEITO TAXI CO. 1574

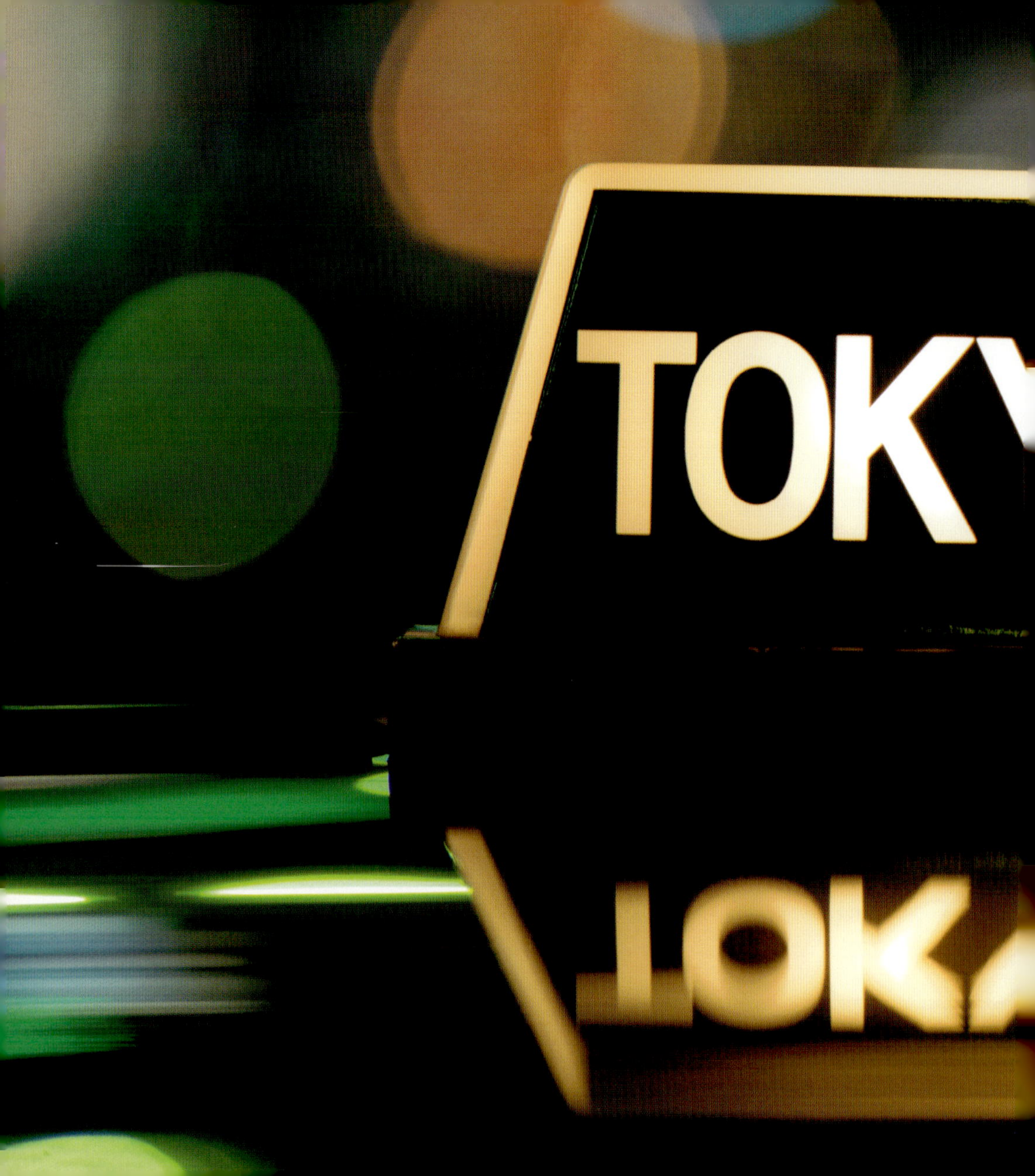
TOKY

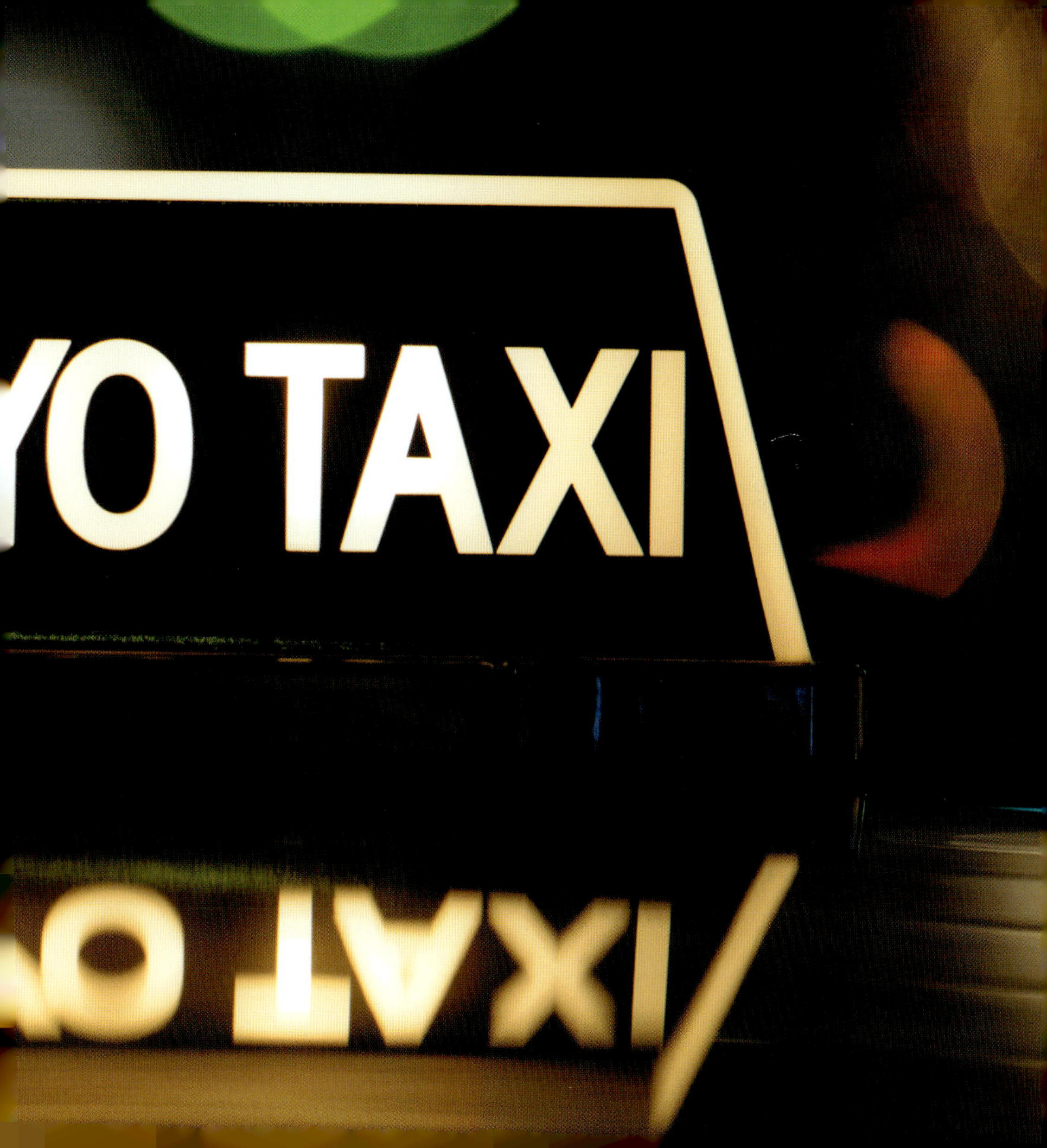
YO TAXI

TONAN KOUTSUU 124

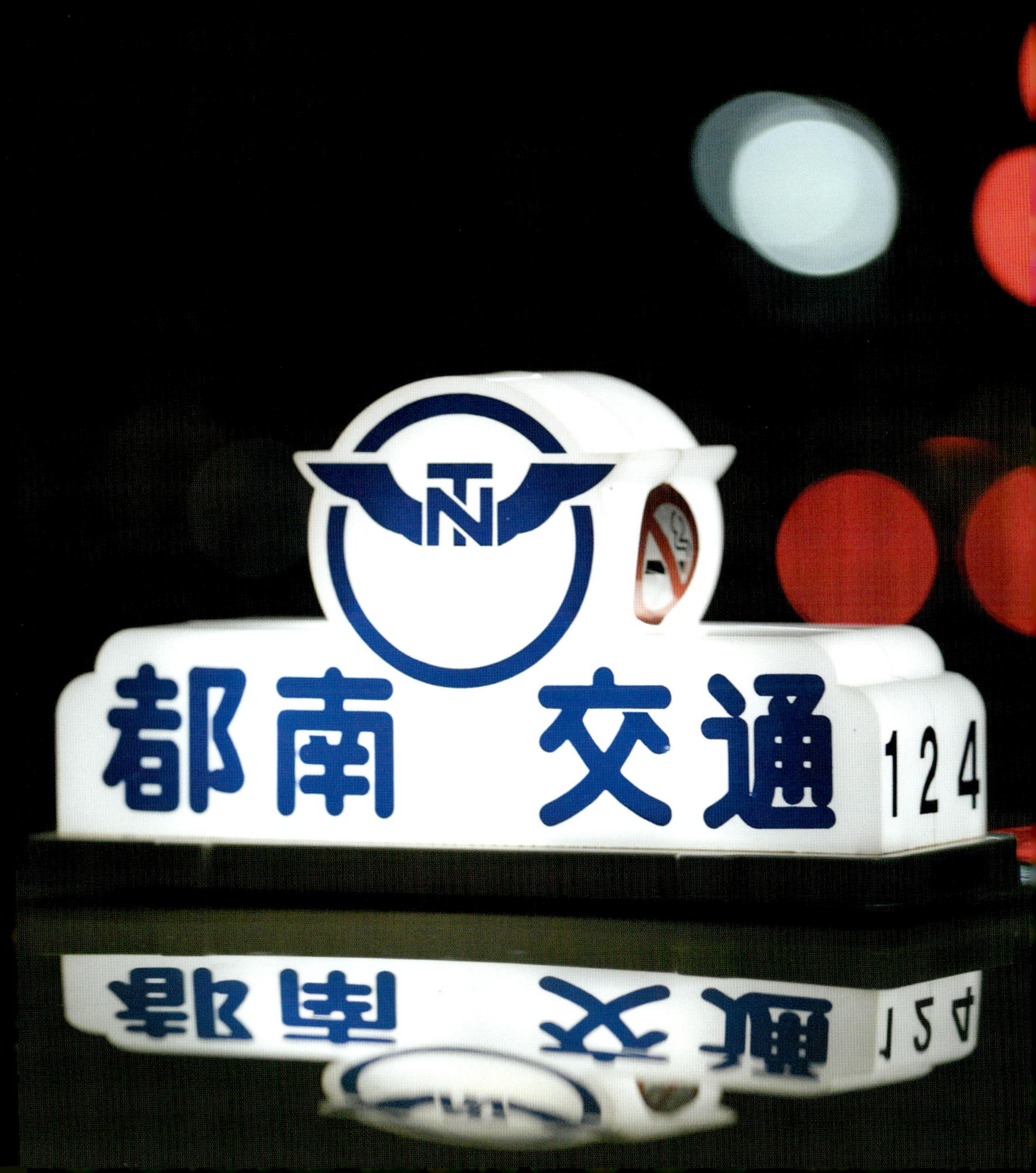
都南　交通
124

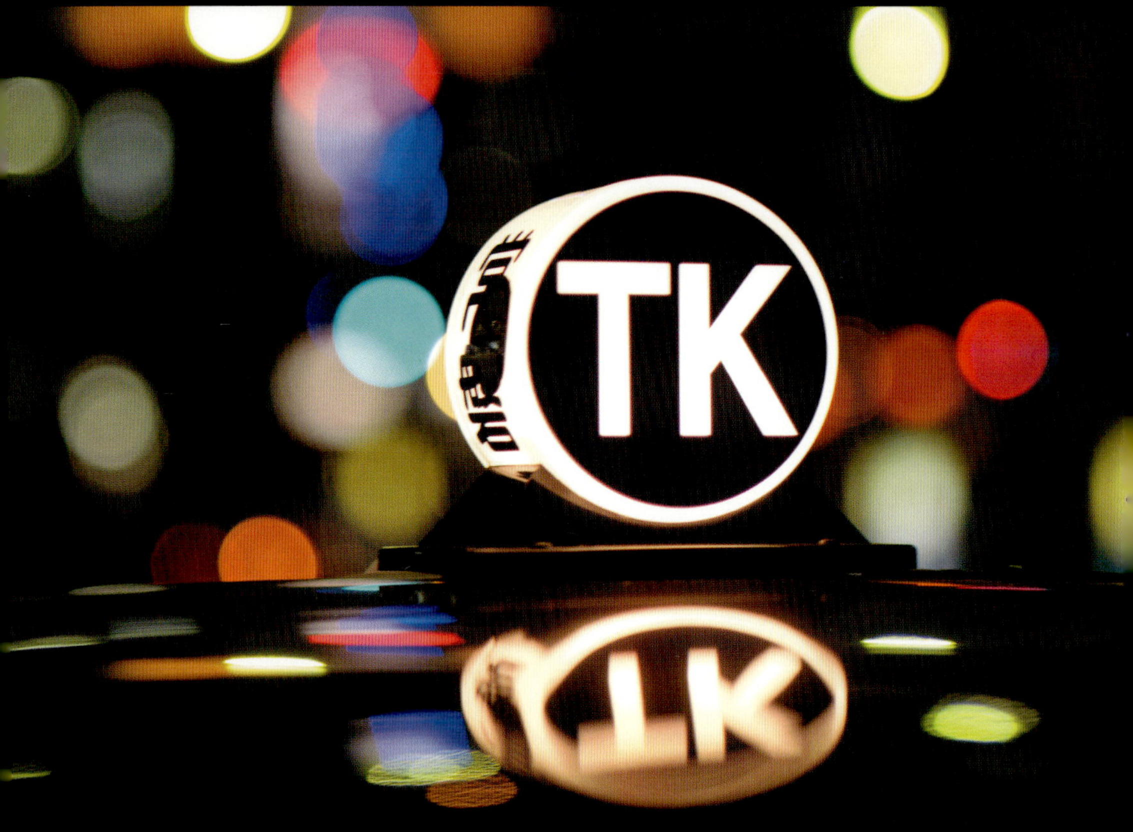

‘TK’ TAXI

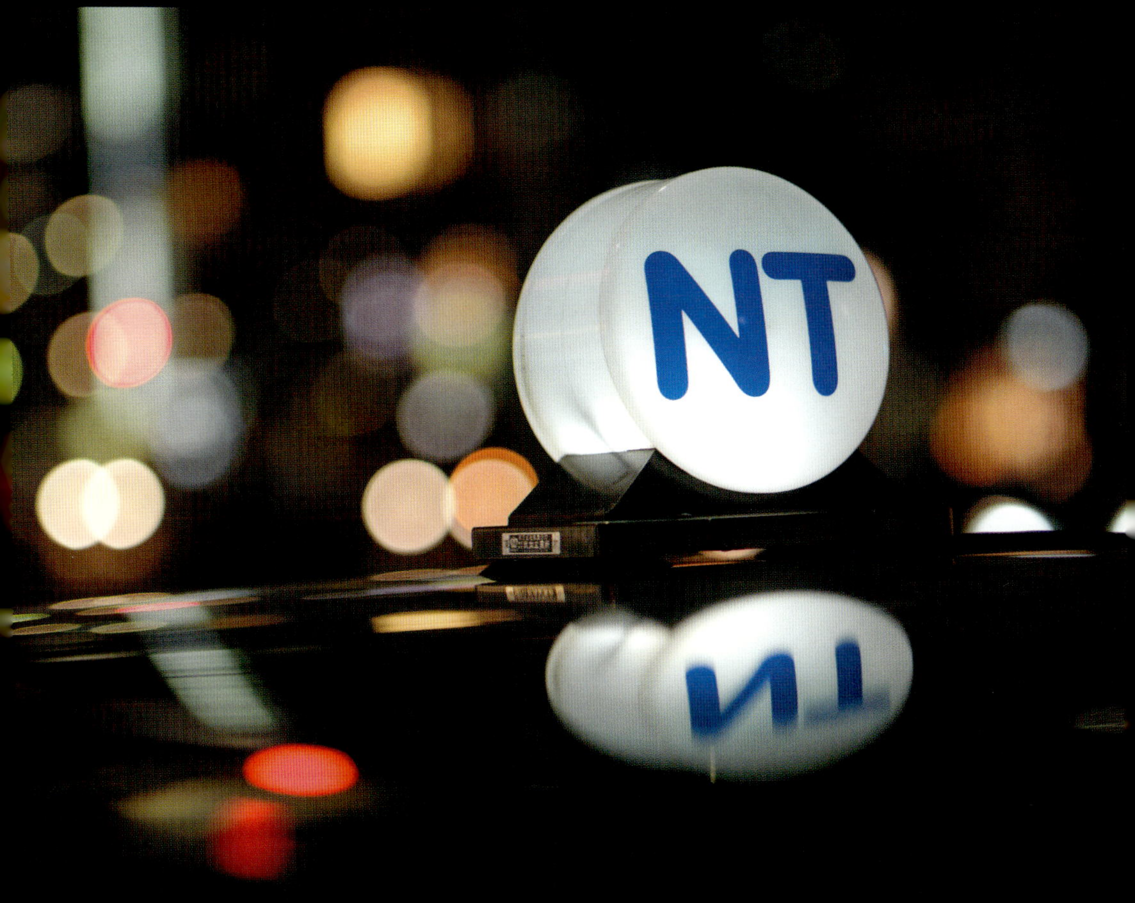

'NT' TAXI

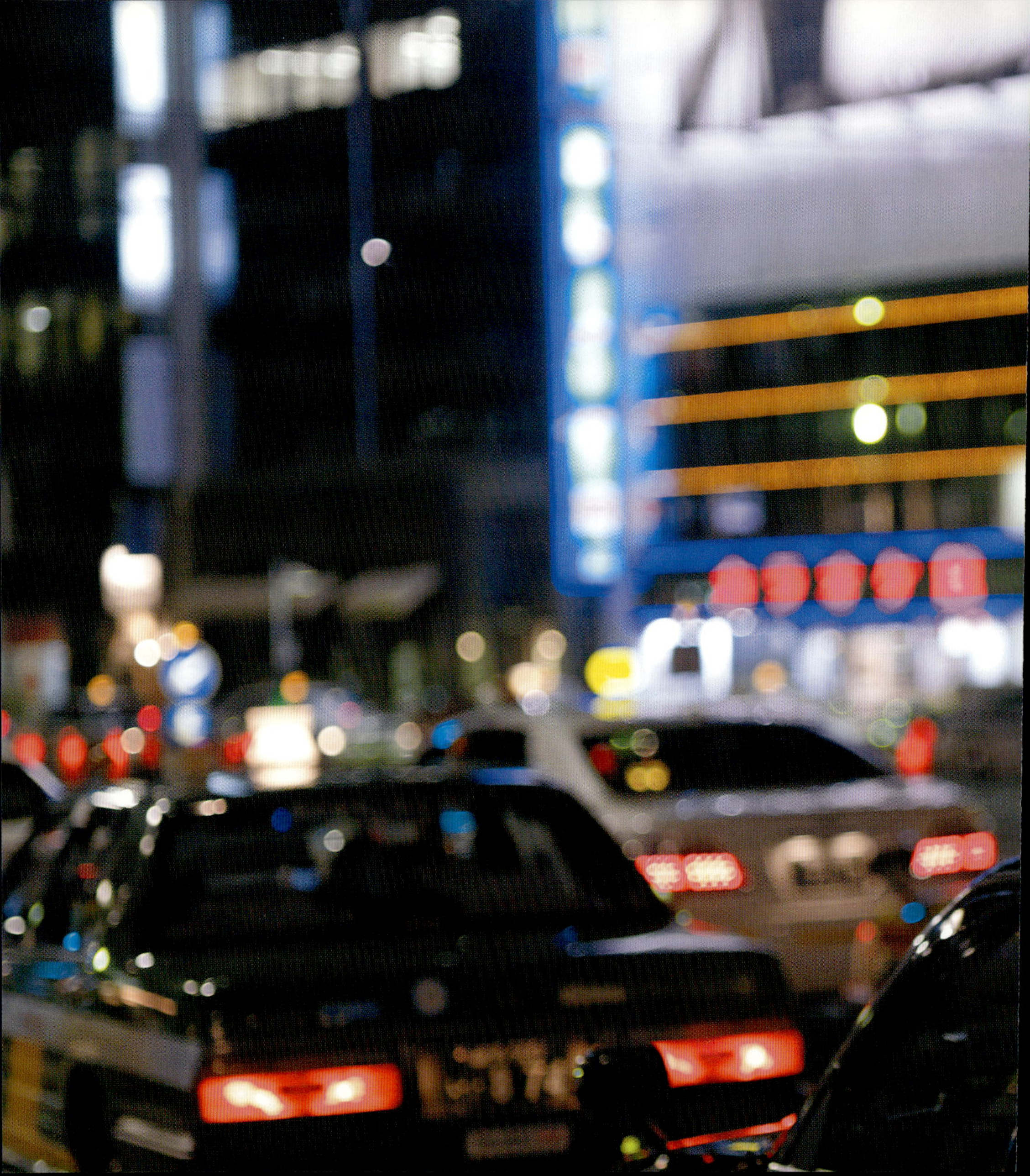

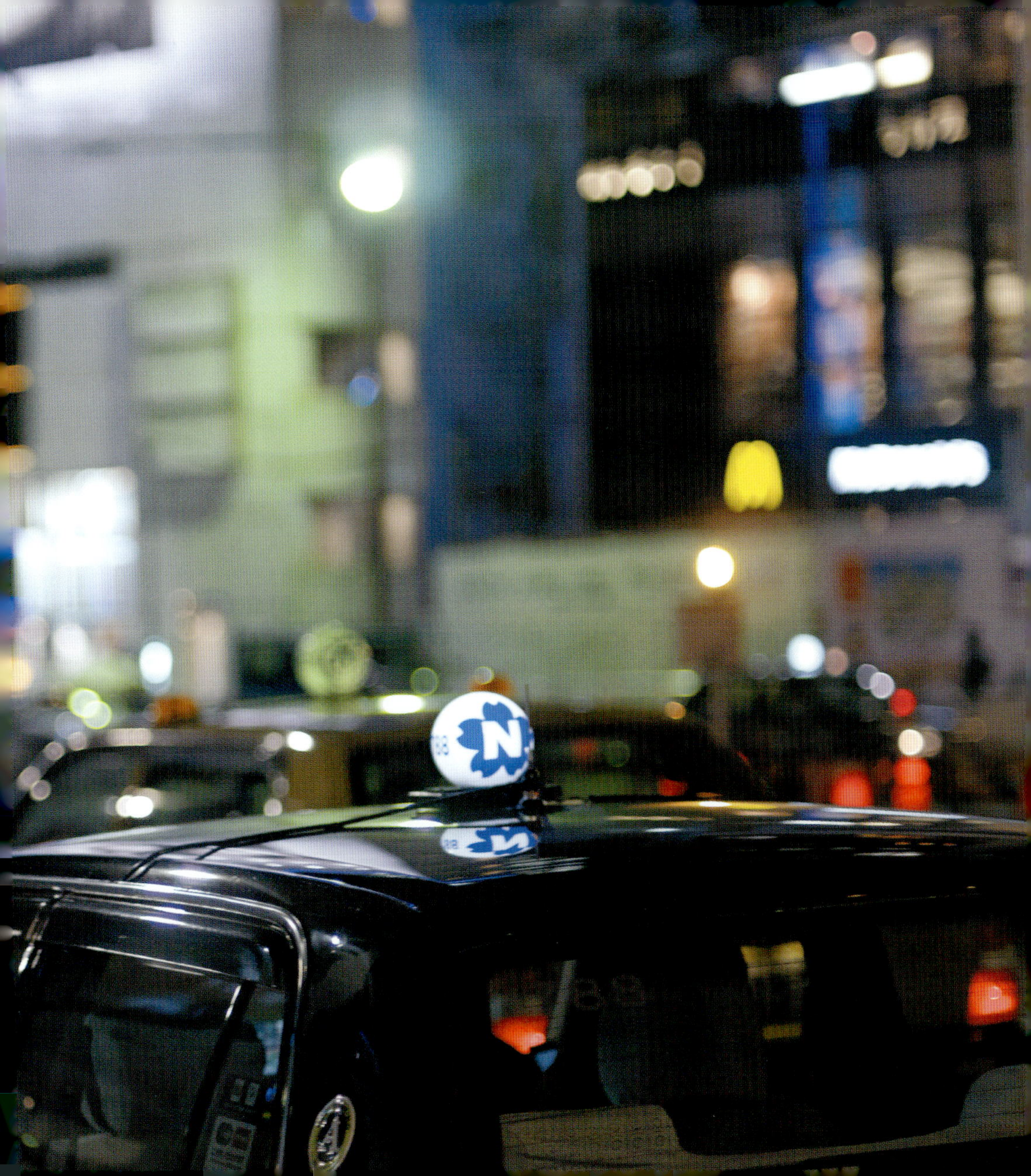

NIHON KOTSU GROUP 3707

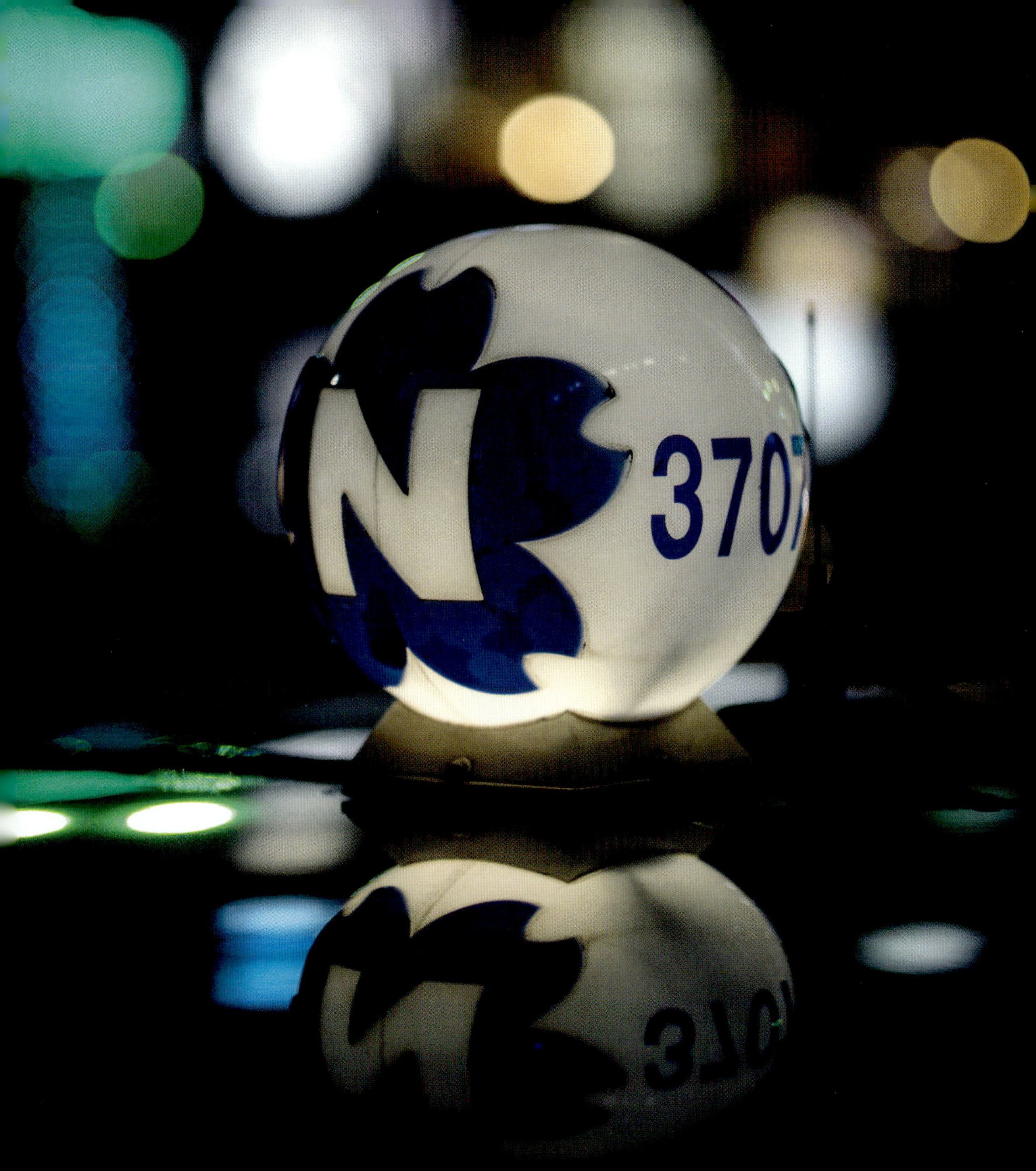
370

MR KAWANANO

Sometimes a *gyaru* [a woman with big hair and/or lots of make-up] will catch a cab with a businessman and tell him that their ride home will cost 20,000 yen. After lots of flirting she'll drop the man off, and will then ask the driver to drop her back round the corner where she works or lives, pocketing all the money. It's surprising how often this happens. Guys are so easy to fool.

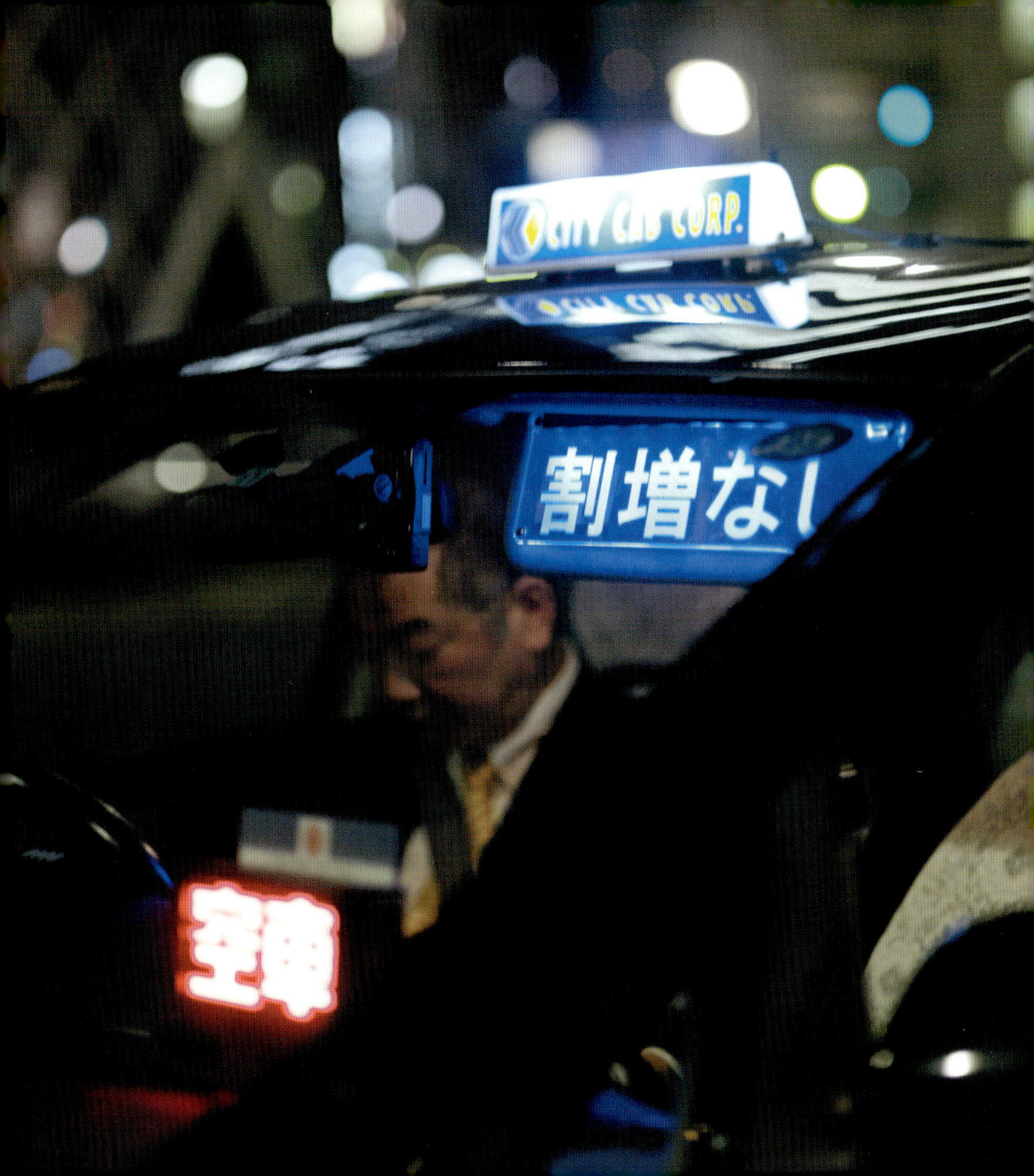
CITY CAB CORP.
割増なし
空車

CHUO MUSEN 1402

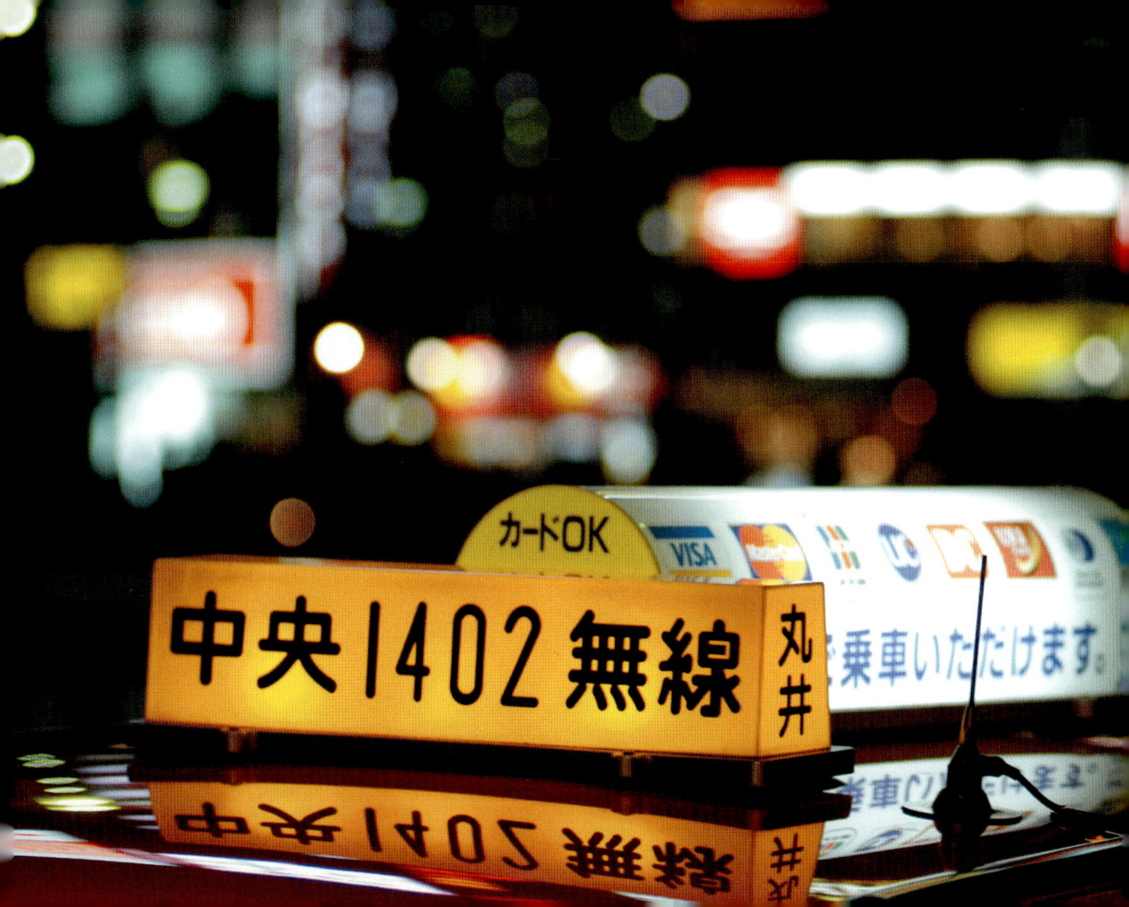
カードOK
VISA
中央1402無線
丸井
乗車いただけます。

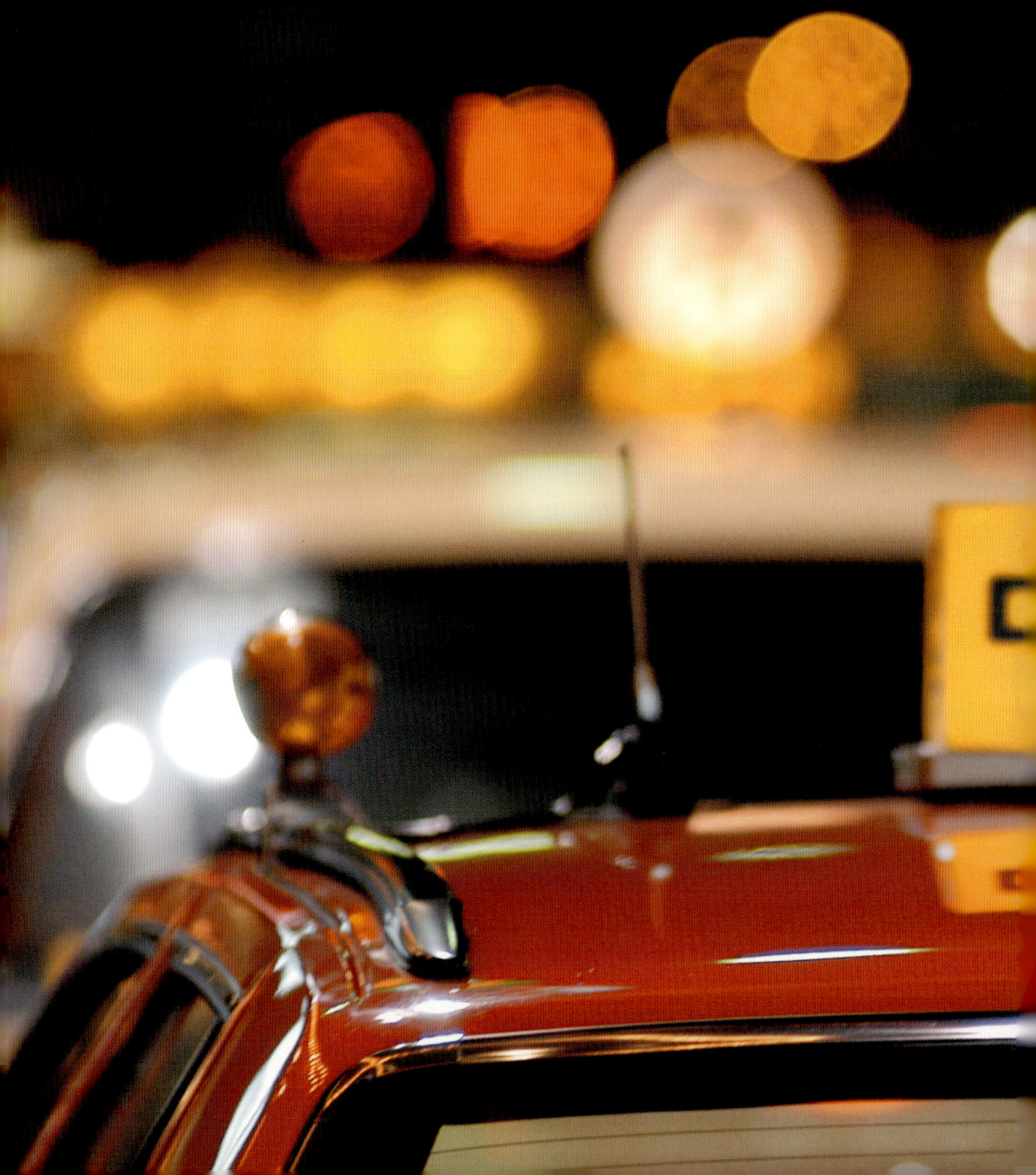

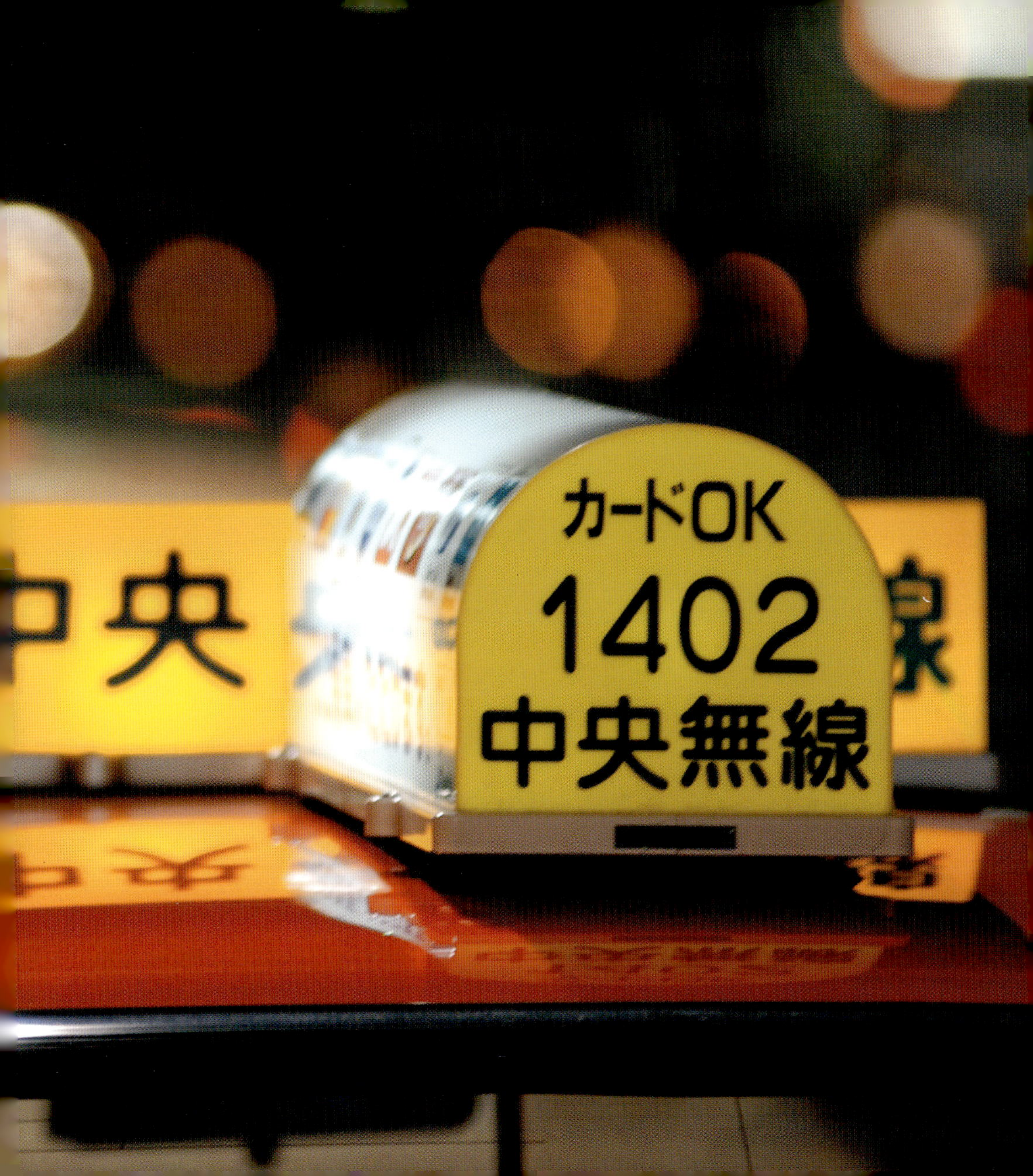
カードOK
1402
中央無線

KAKINOKI TAXI

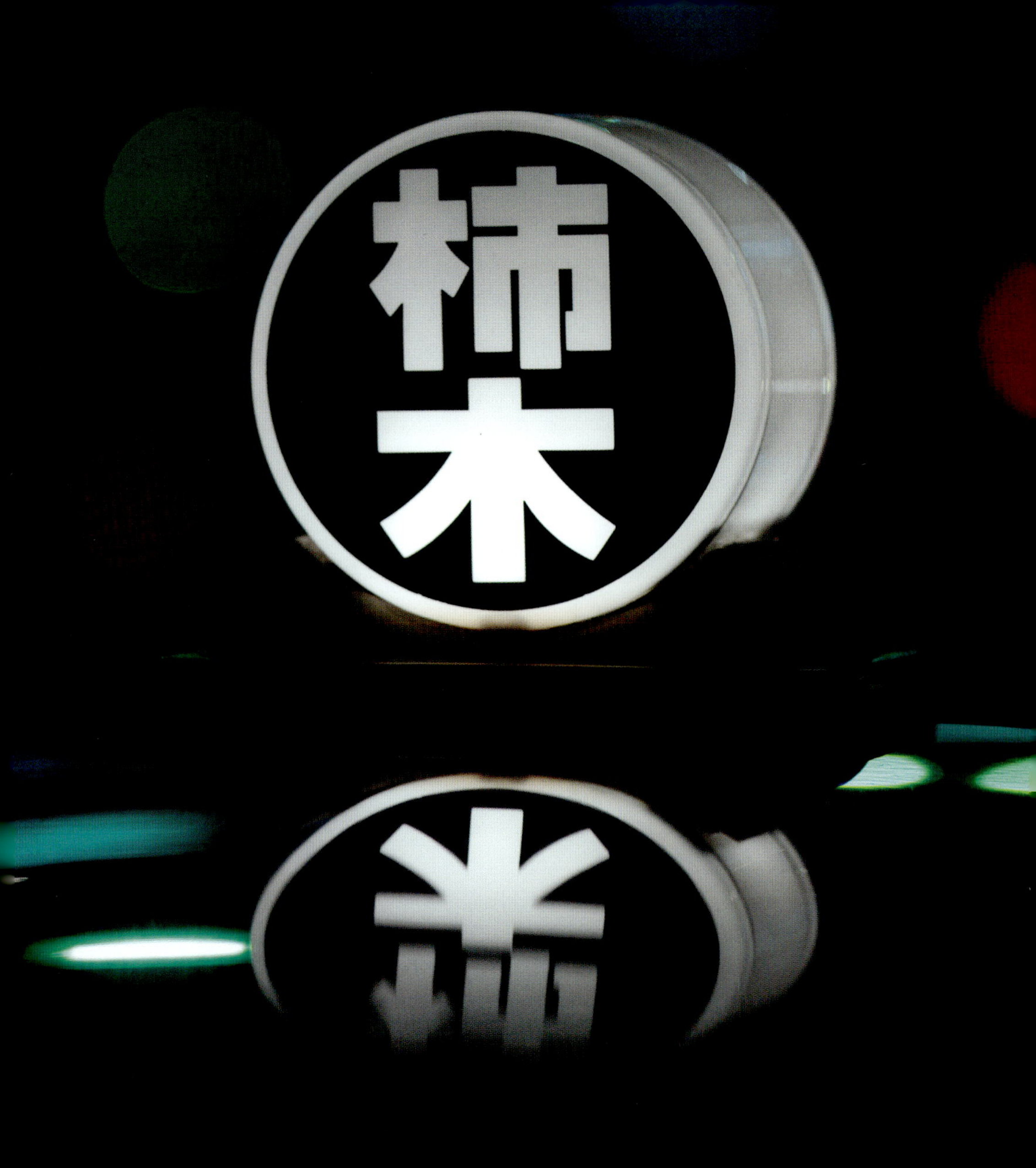
柿
木

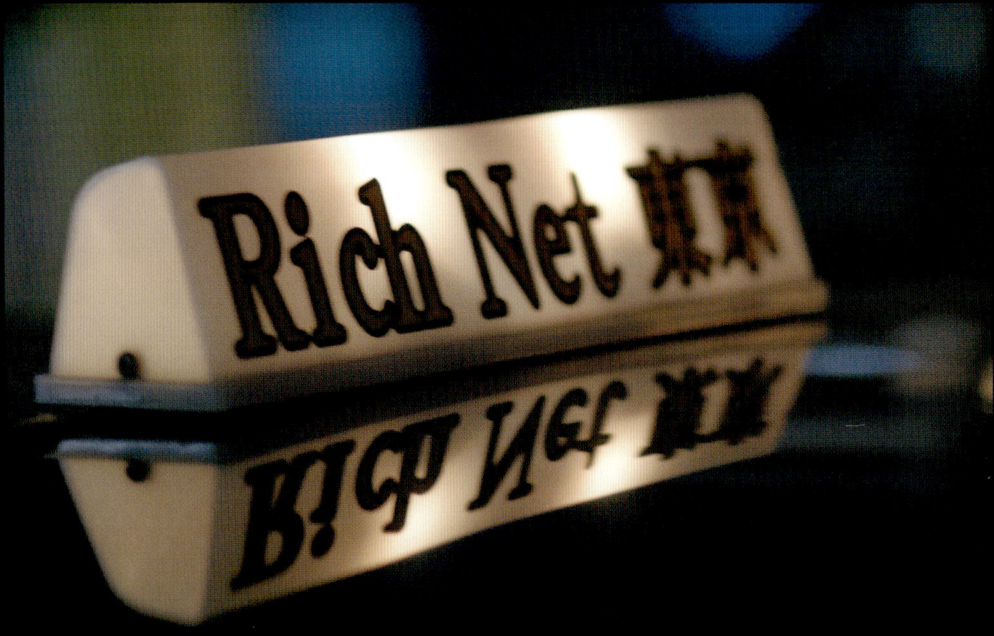
Rich Net 東京

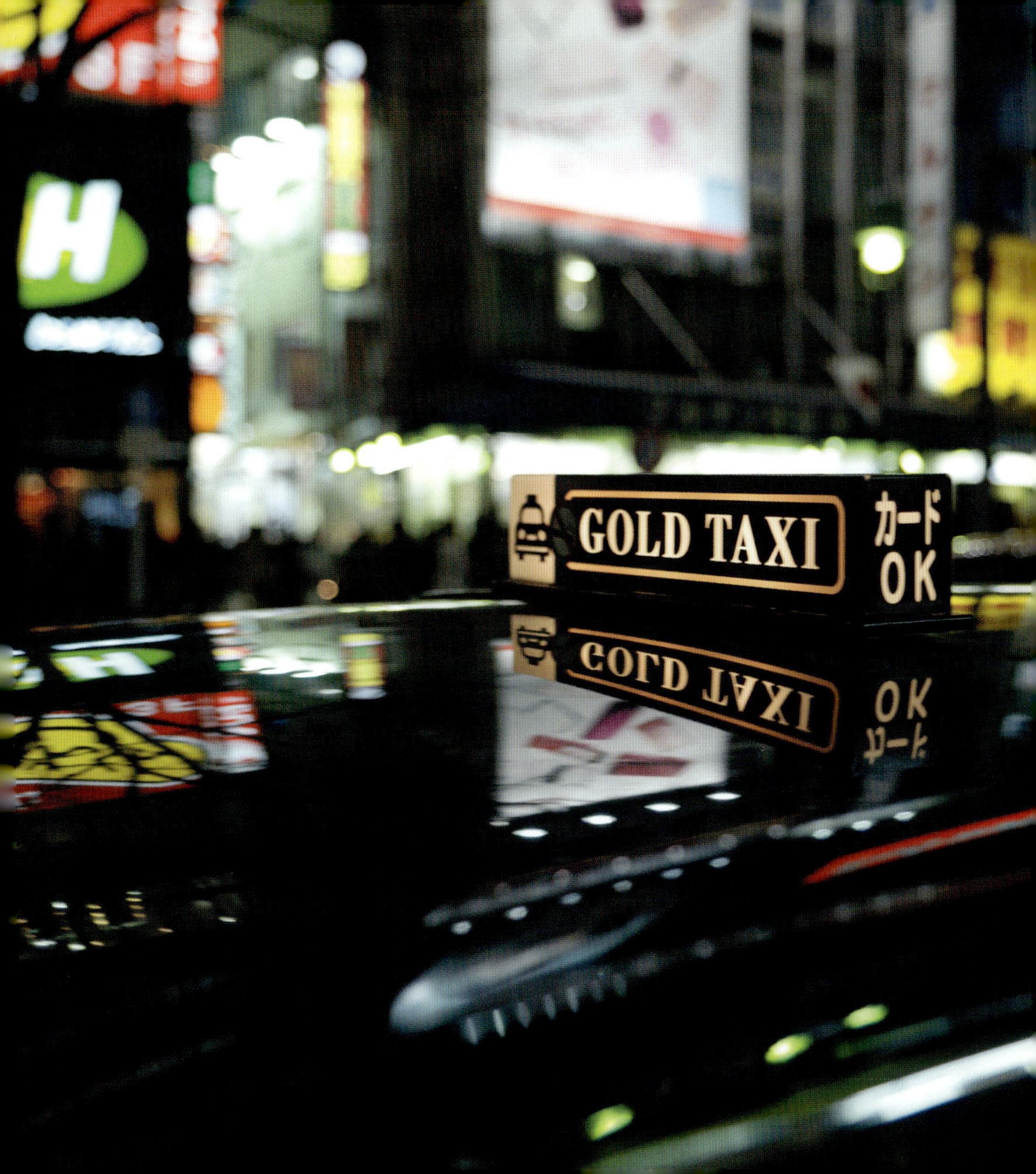
GOLD TAXI
カード
OK

UNNAMED DRIVER

The events of March 2011
[the earthquake off the coast of Japan
and the subsequent tsunami] have changed
the customers in the city. There are fewer of them,
and some shops are closed because of power shortages.
Fewer businessmen are going out drinking at night,
although the youth are picking up the slack.
Only about one in seven fares is a
gaikokujin [foreigner].

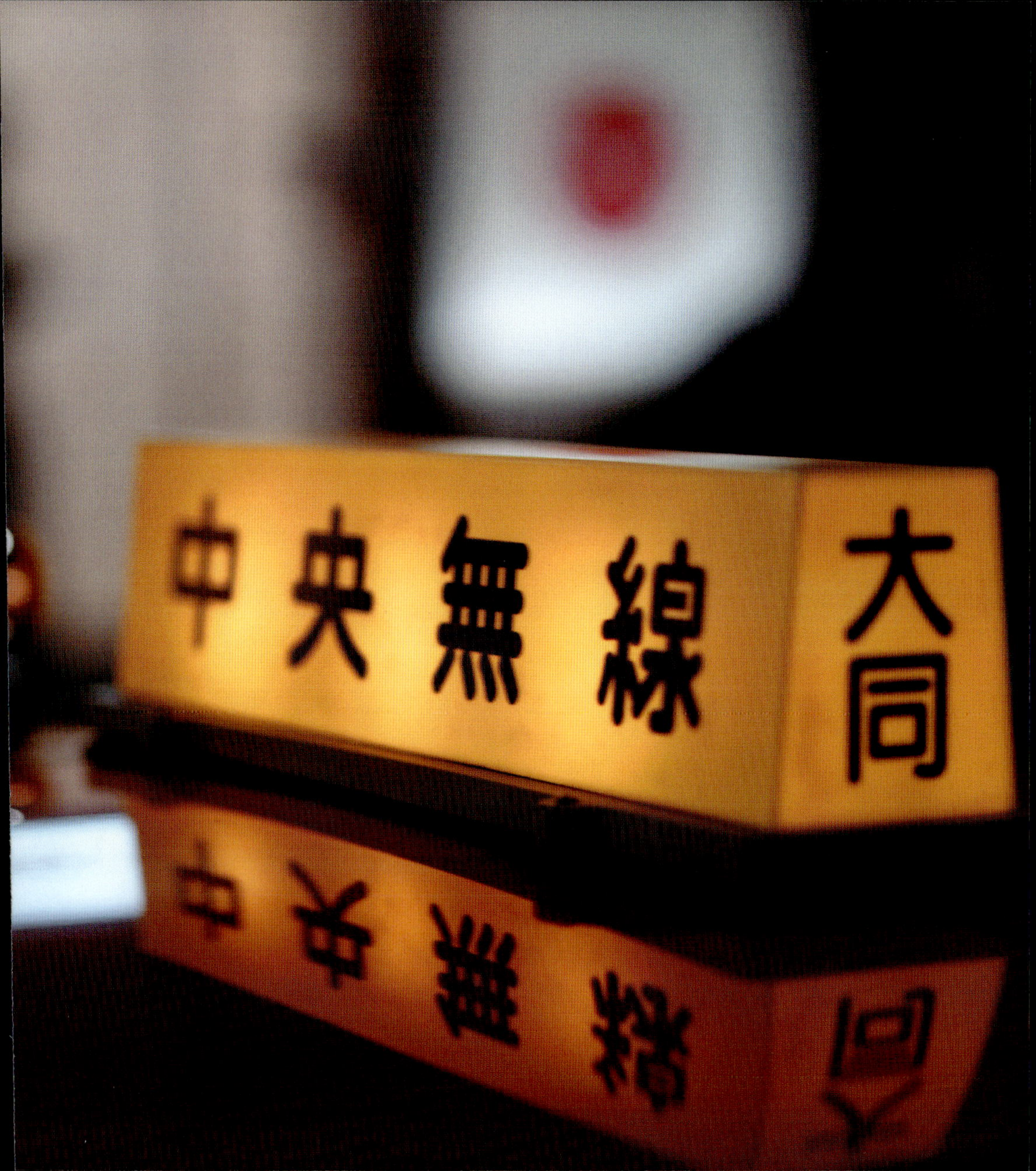
中央無線
大同

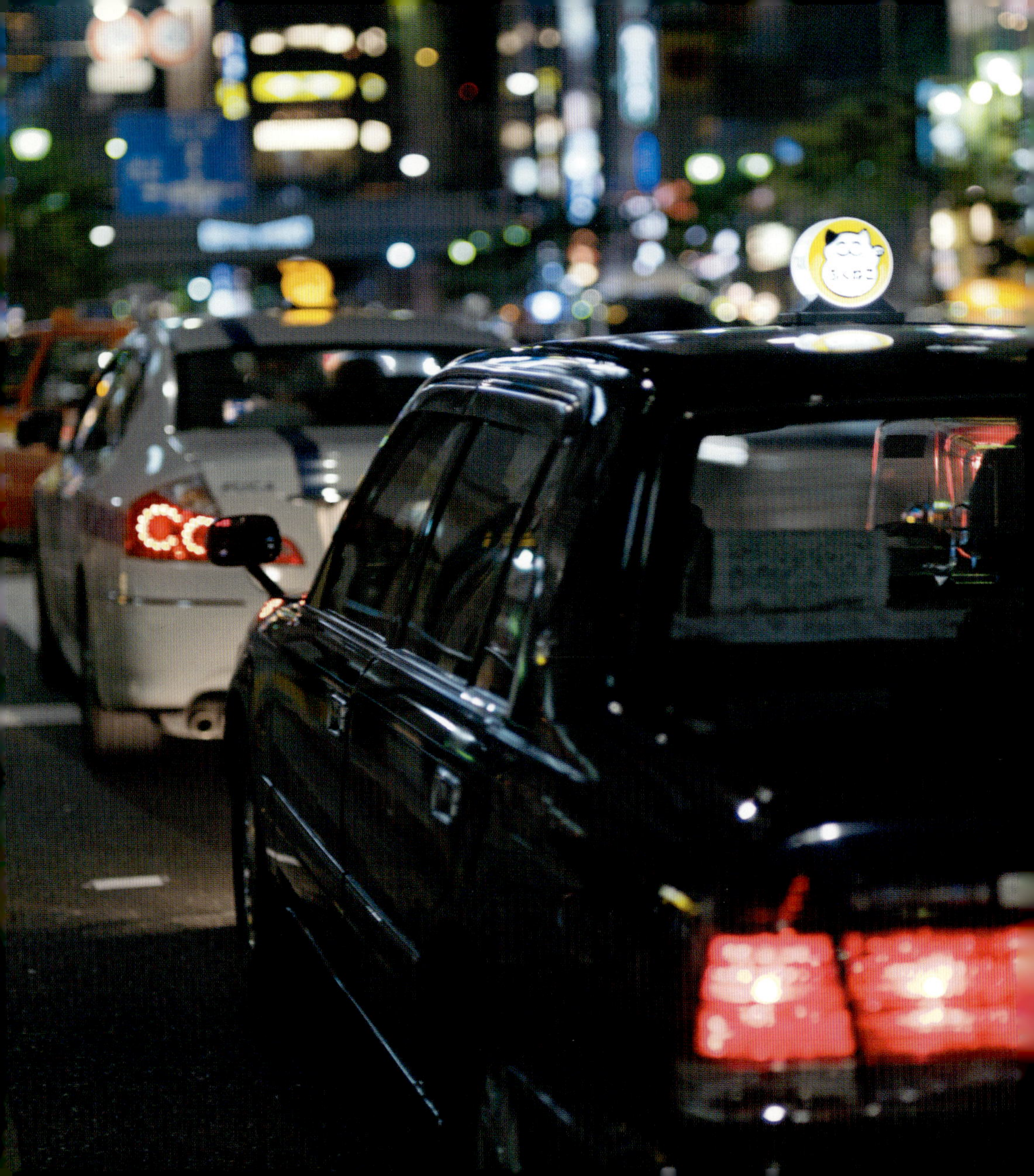

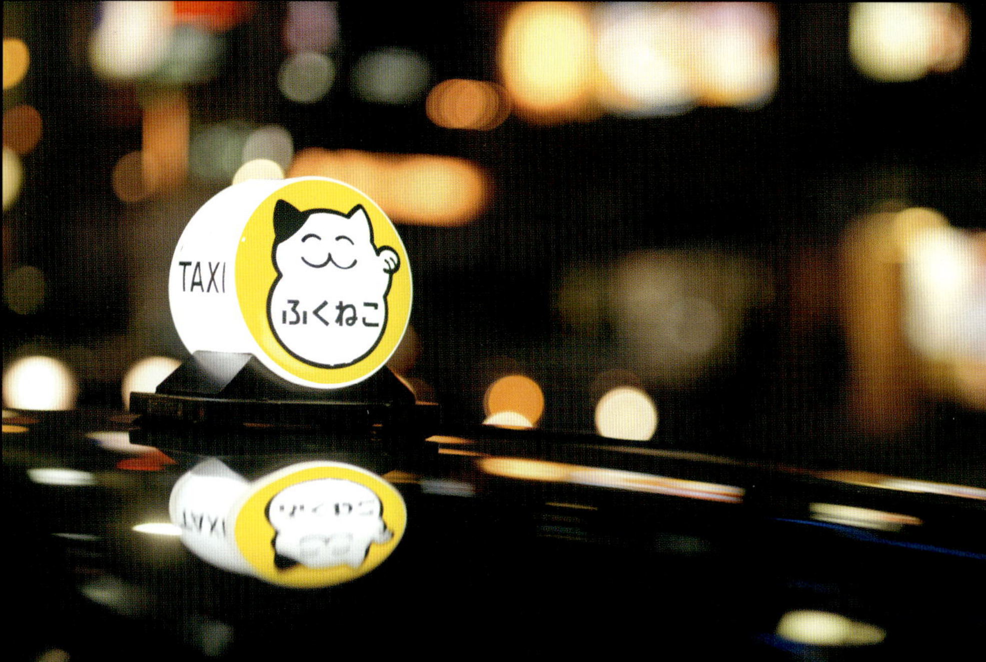

YAMASUIRO KOTSU TAXI CO.

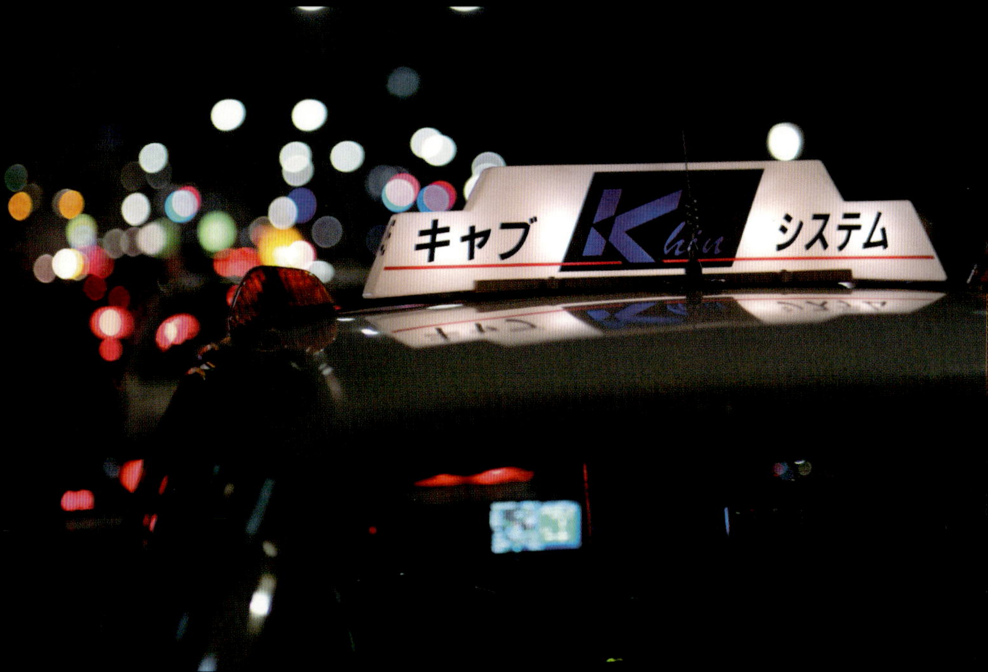

CAB KEIHIN

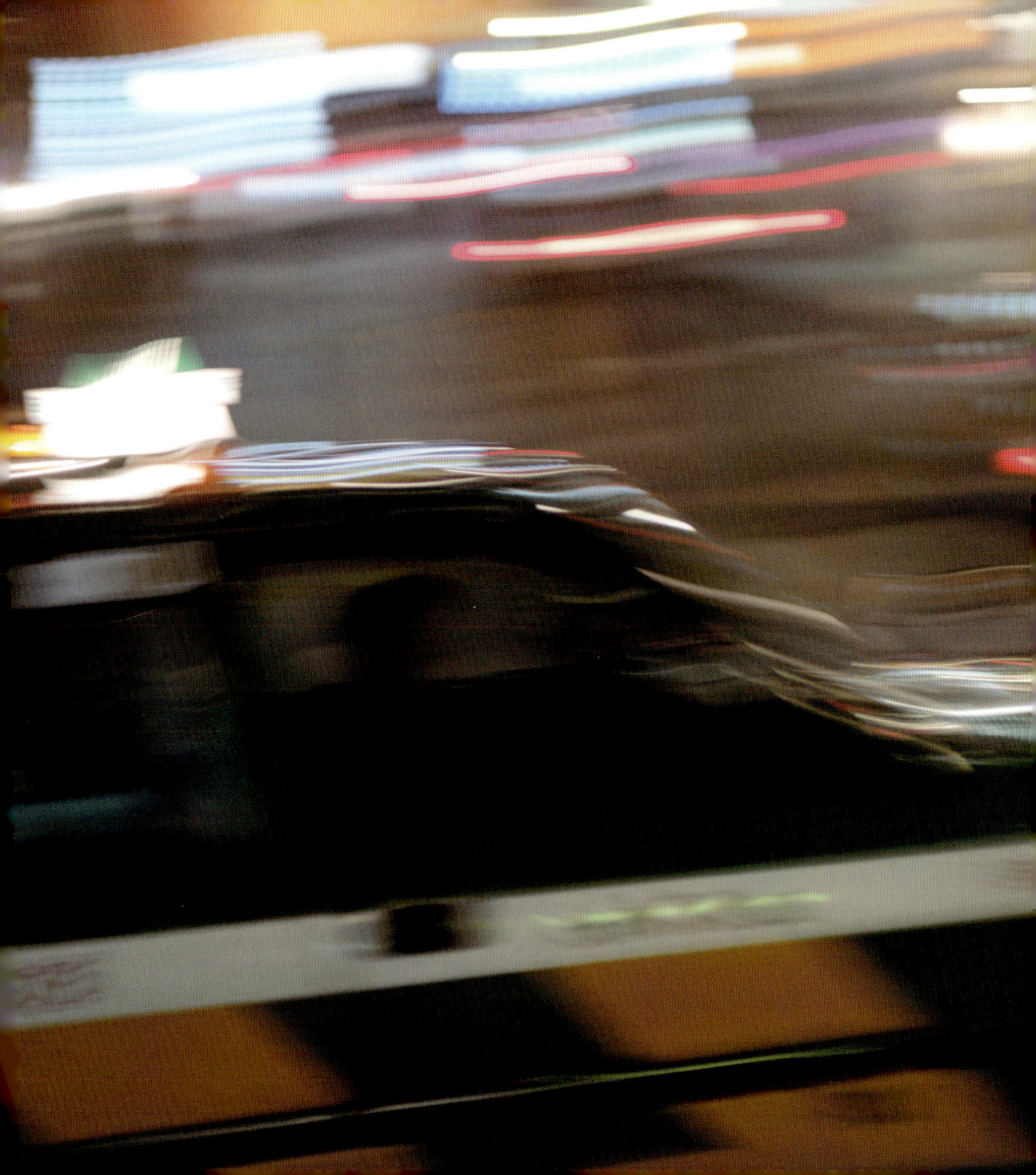

HELIX TAXI CO.

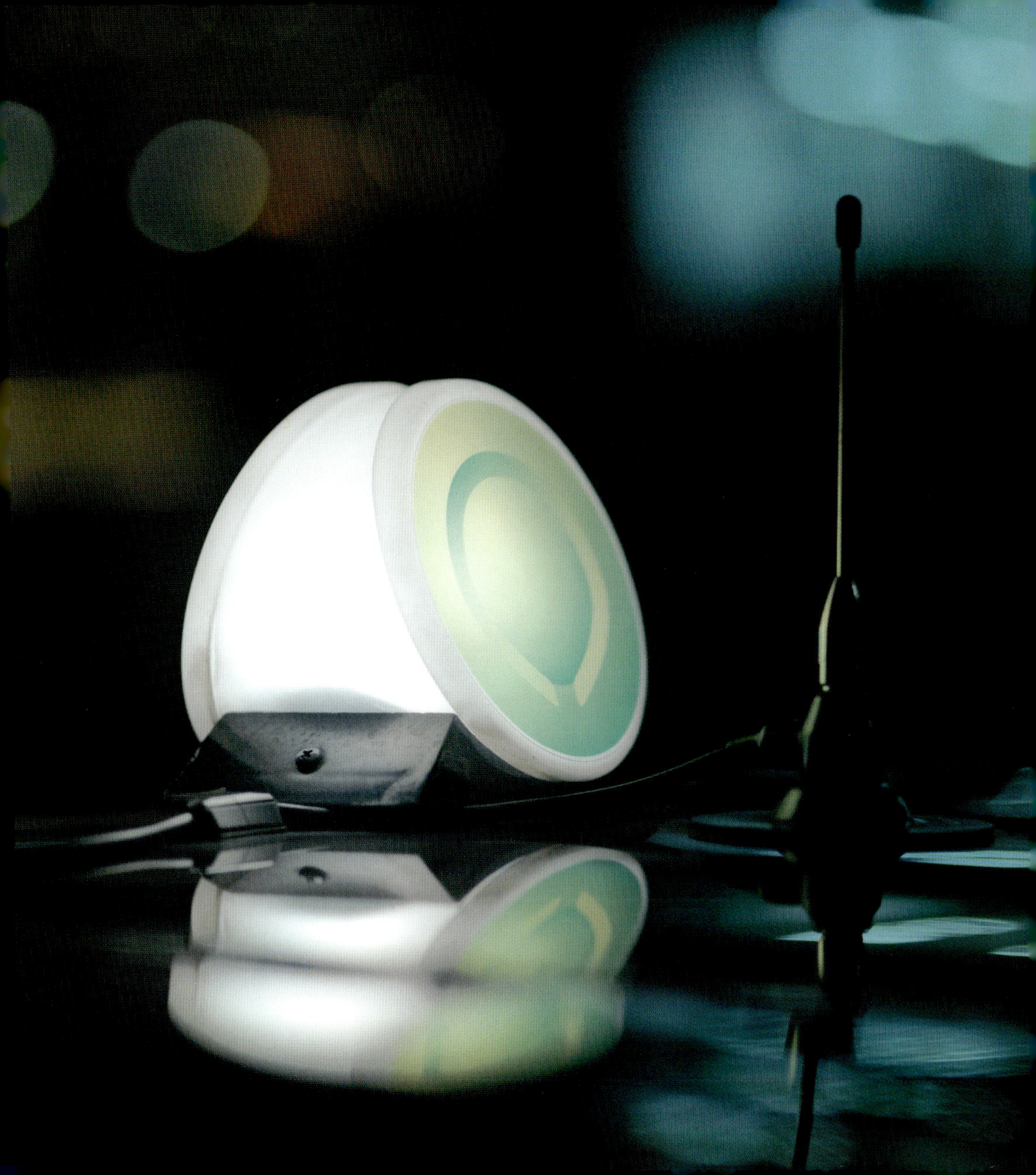

YUME TAXI CO.

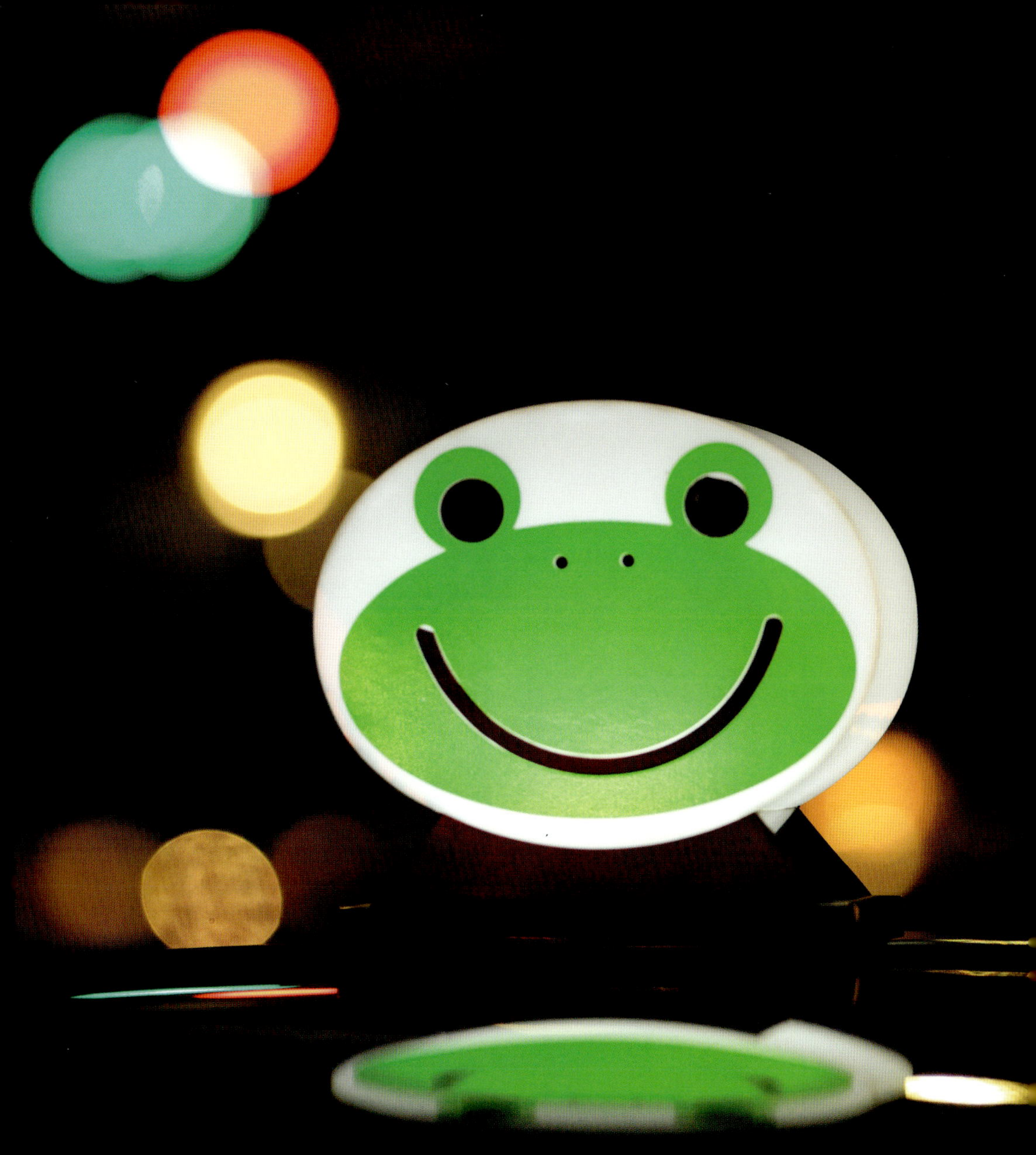

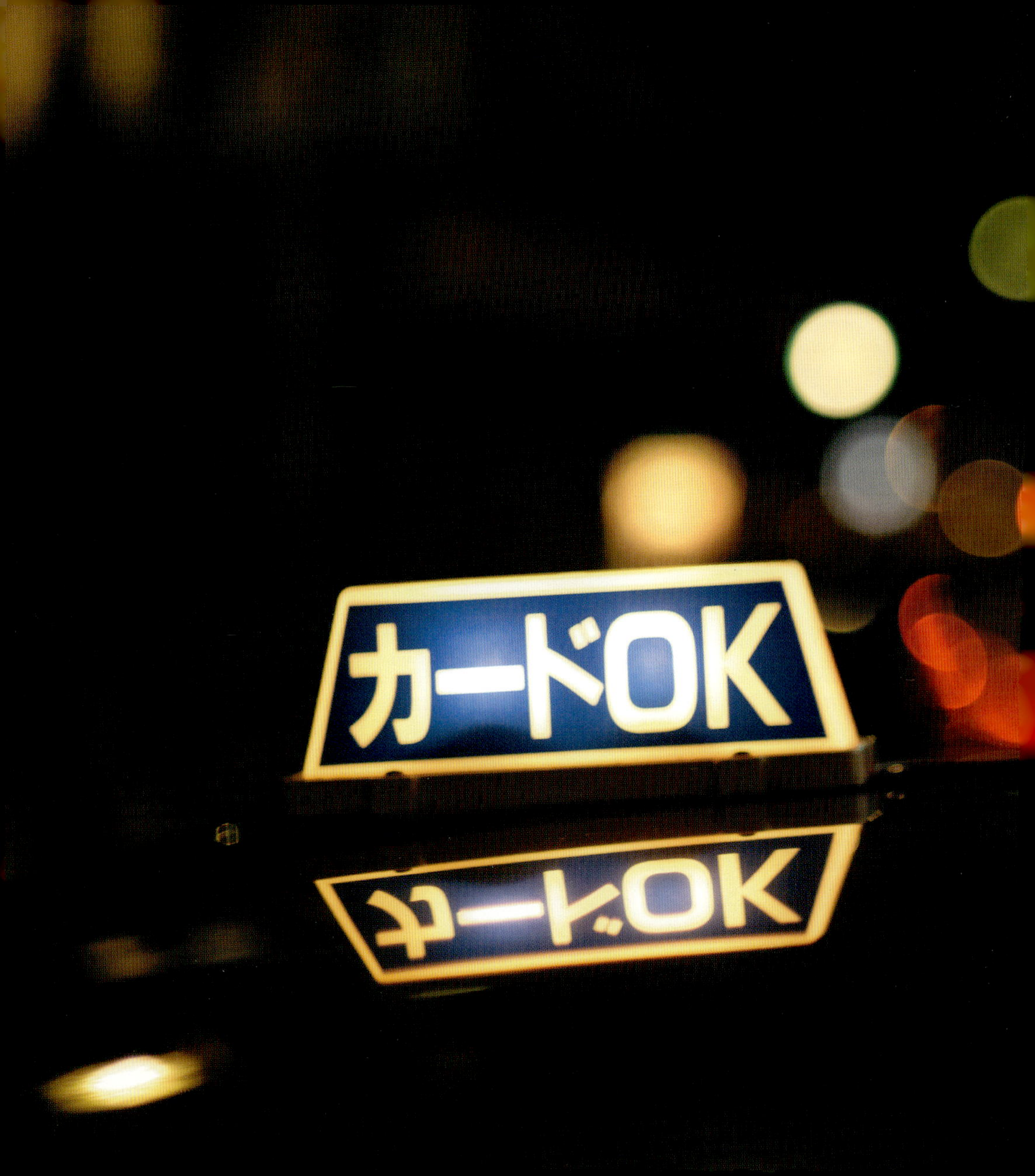
カードOK

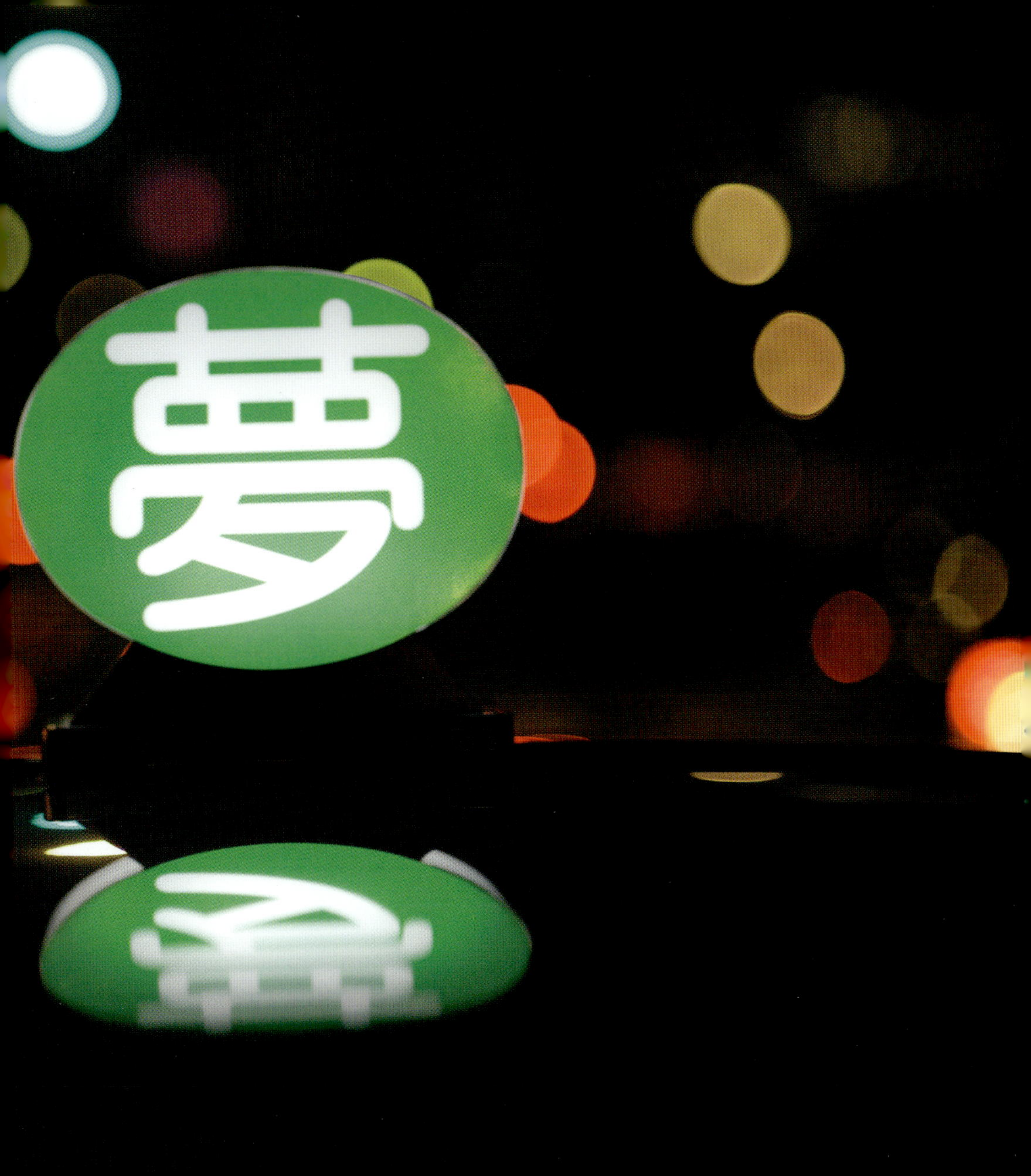
夢

Pages 72–73. YUME TAXI CO. (REAR VIEW)

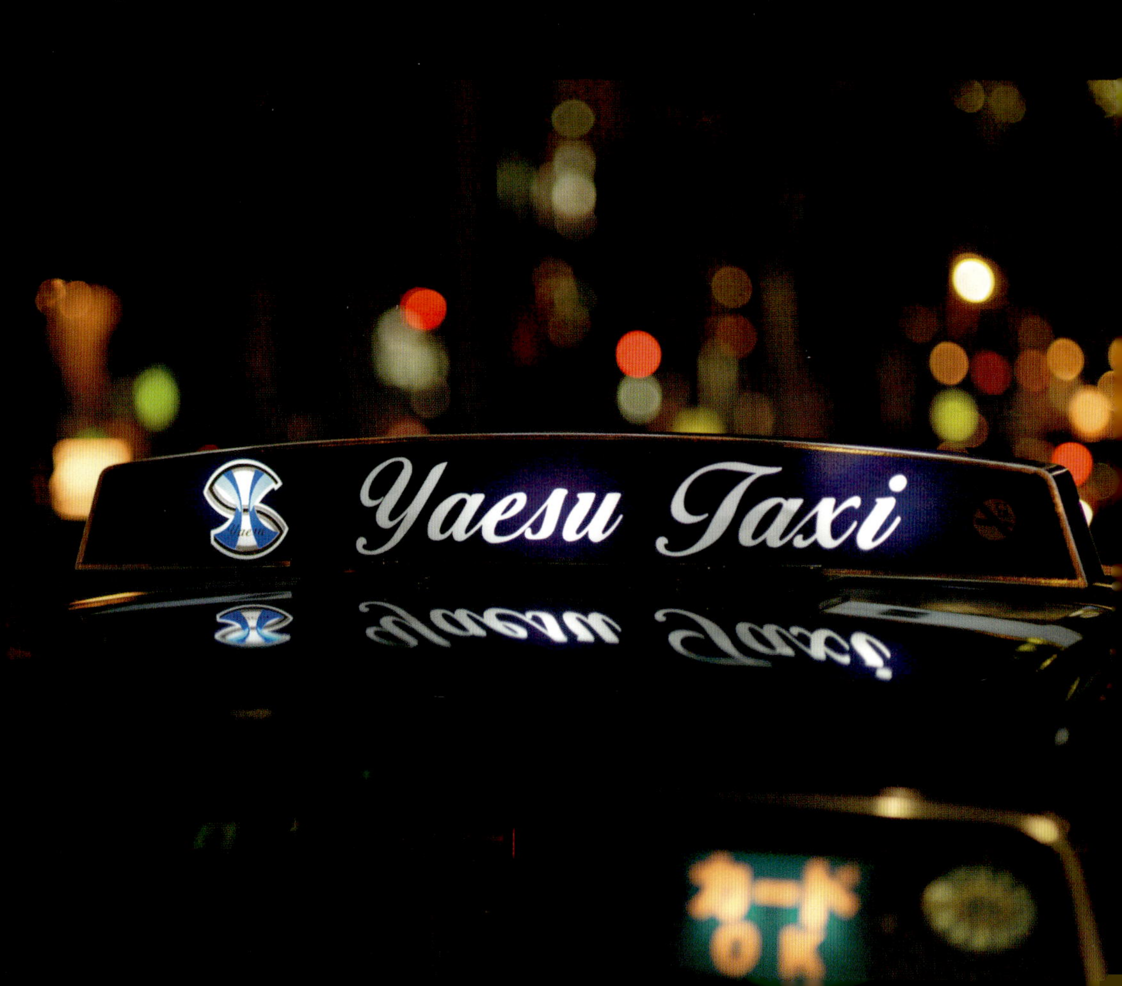

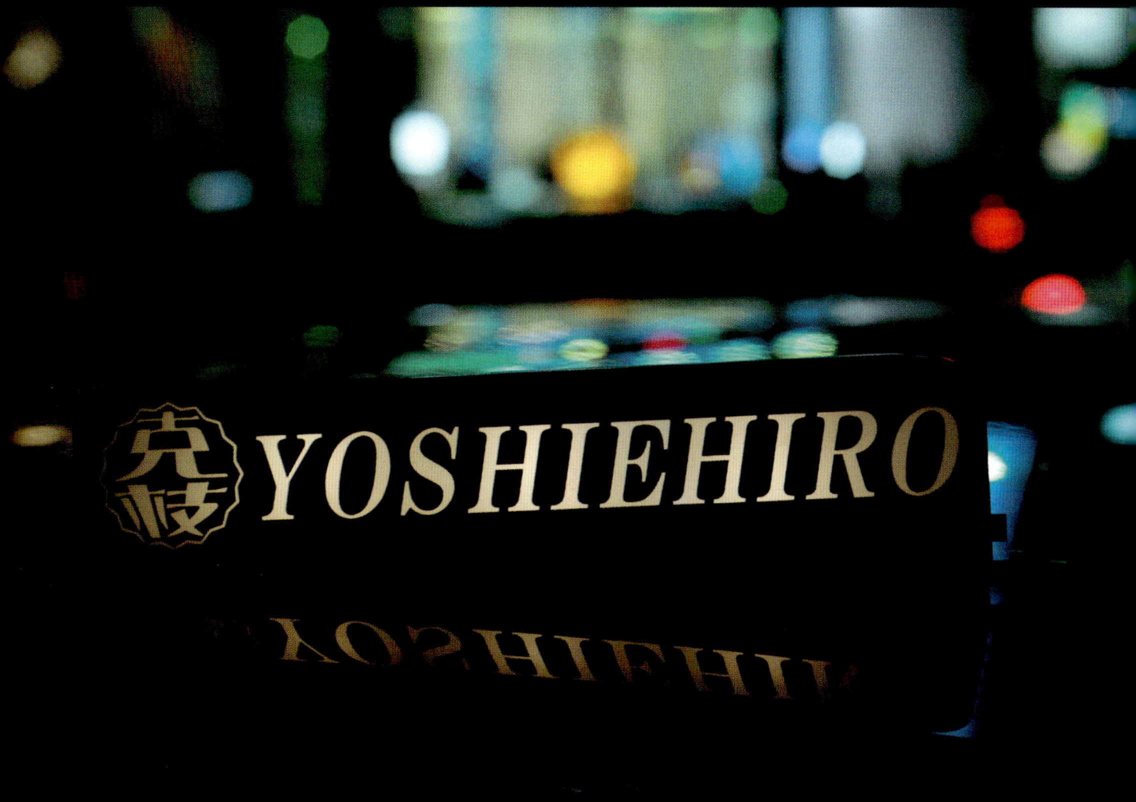

YOSHIEHIRO TAXI CO.

UNNAMED DRIVER

The best part of my job is being in different locations around the city and seeing the sun come up. Tokyo is such a beautiful place at dawn.

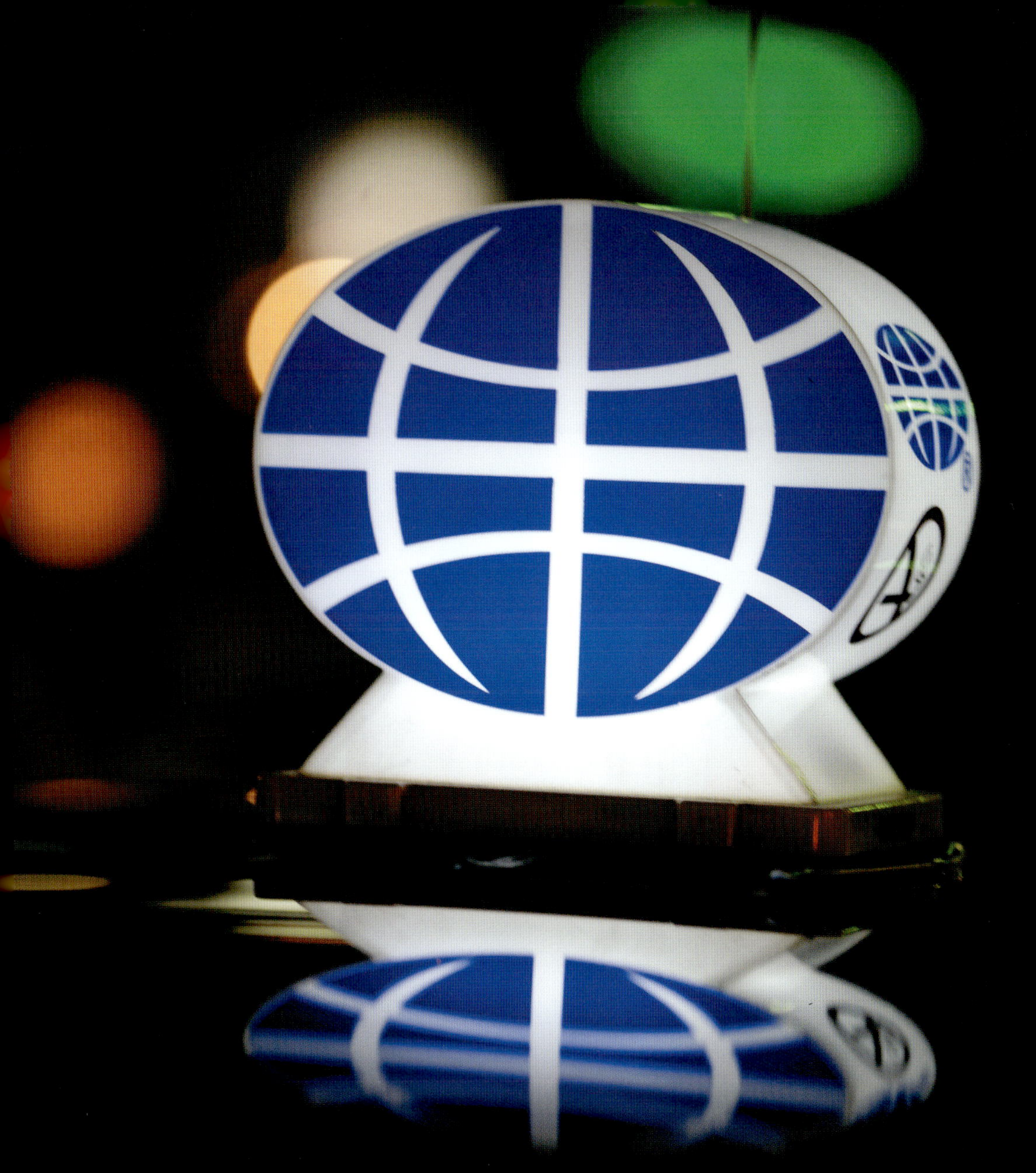

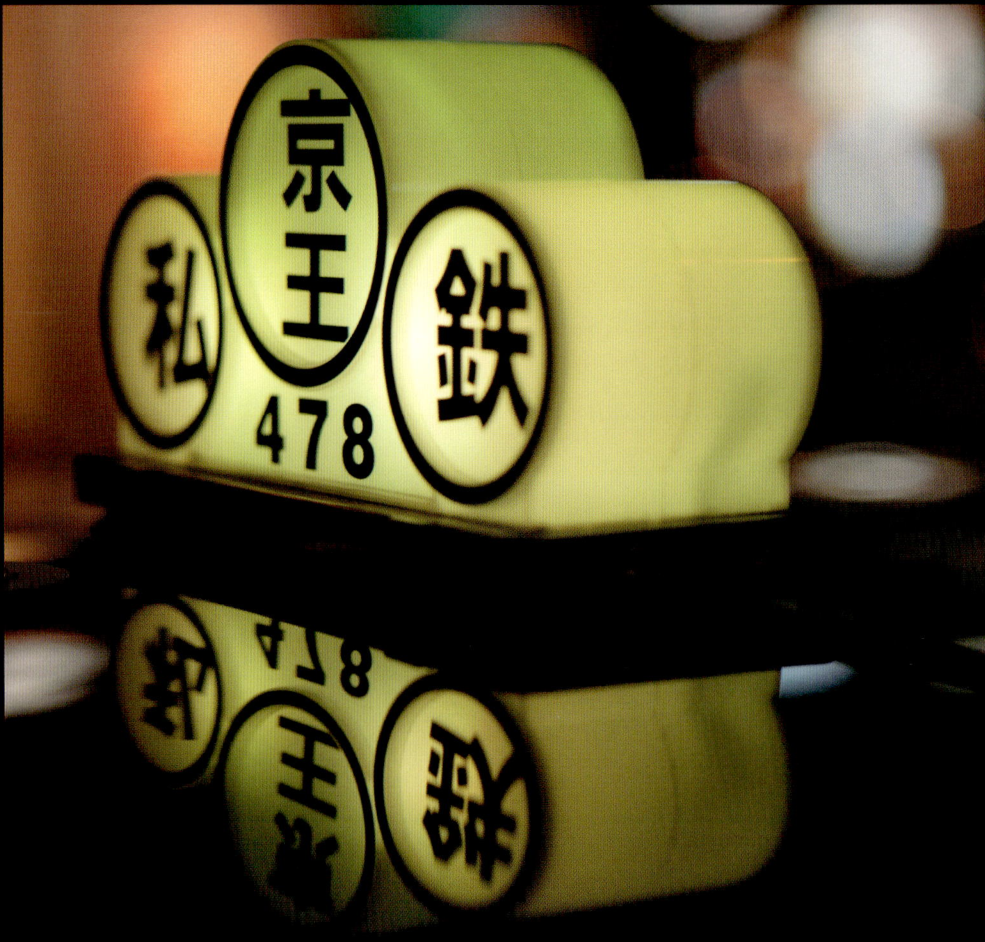

KEIKYU GROUP 478

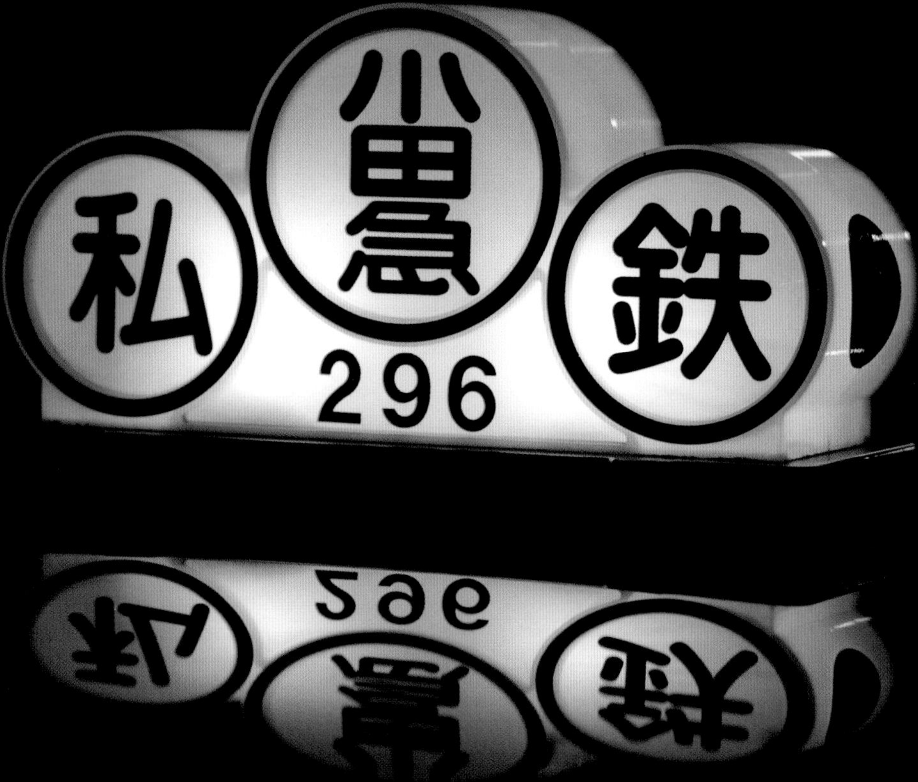

ODAKYU SHITETSU TAXI CO. 296

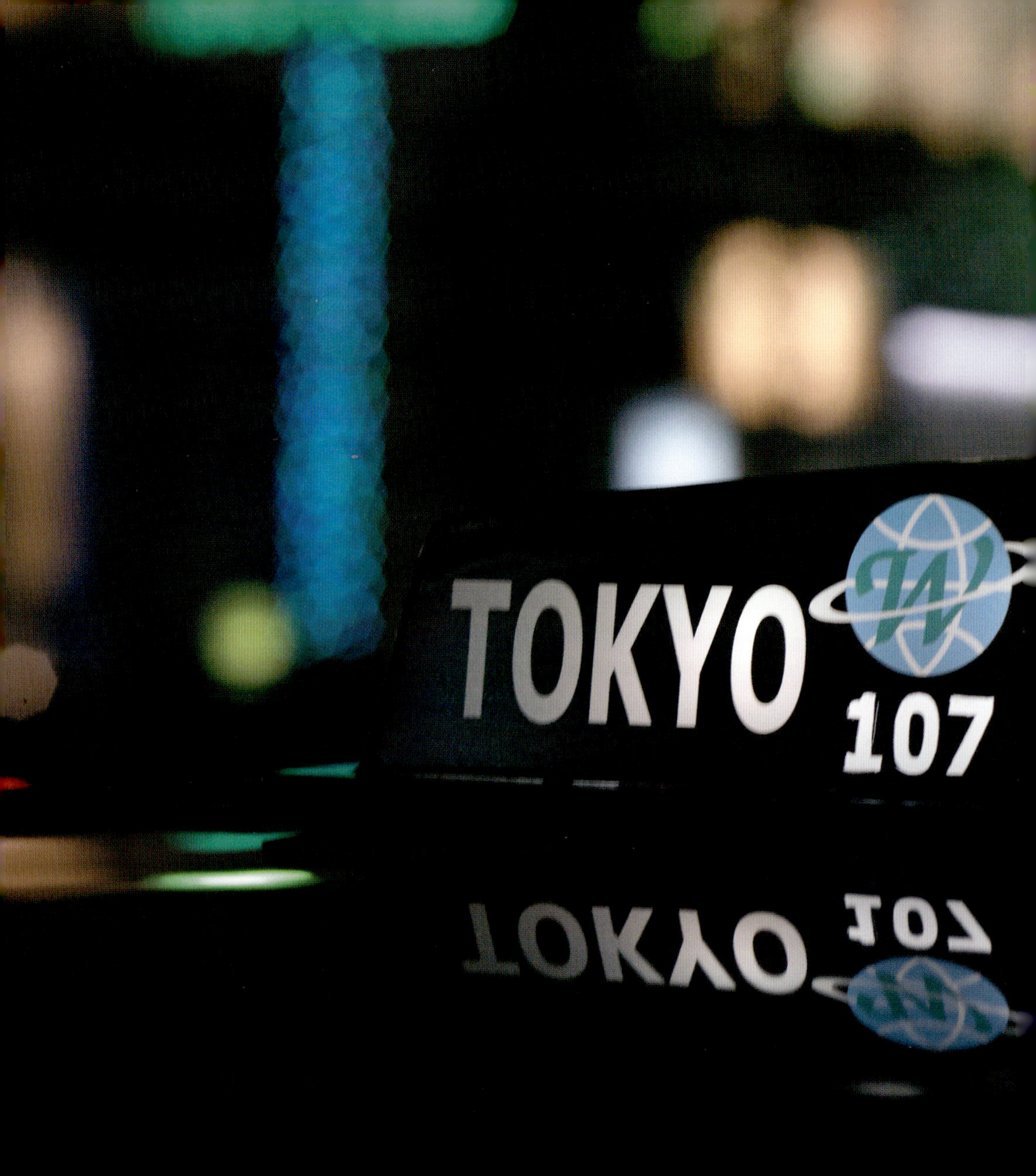
TOKYO
107

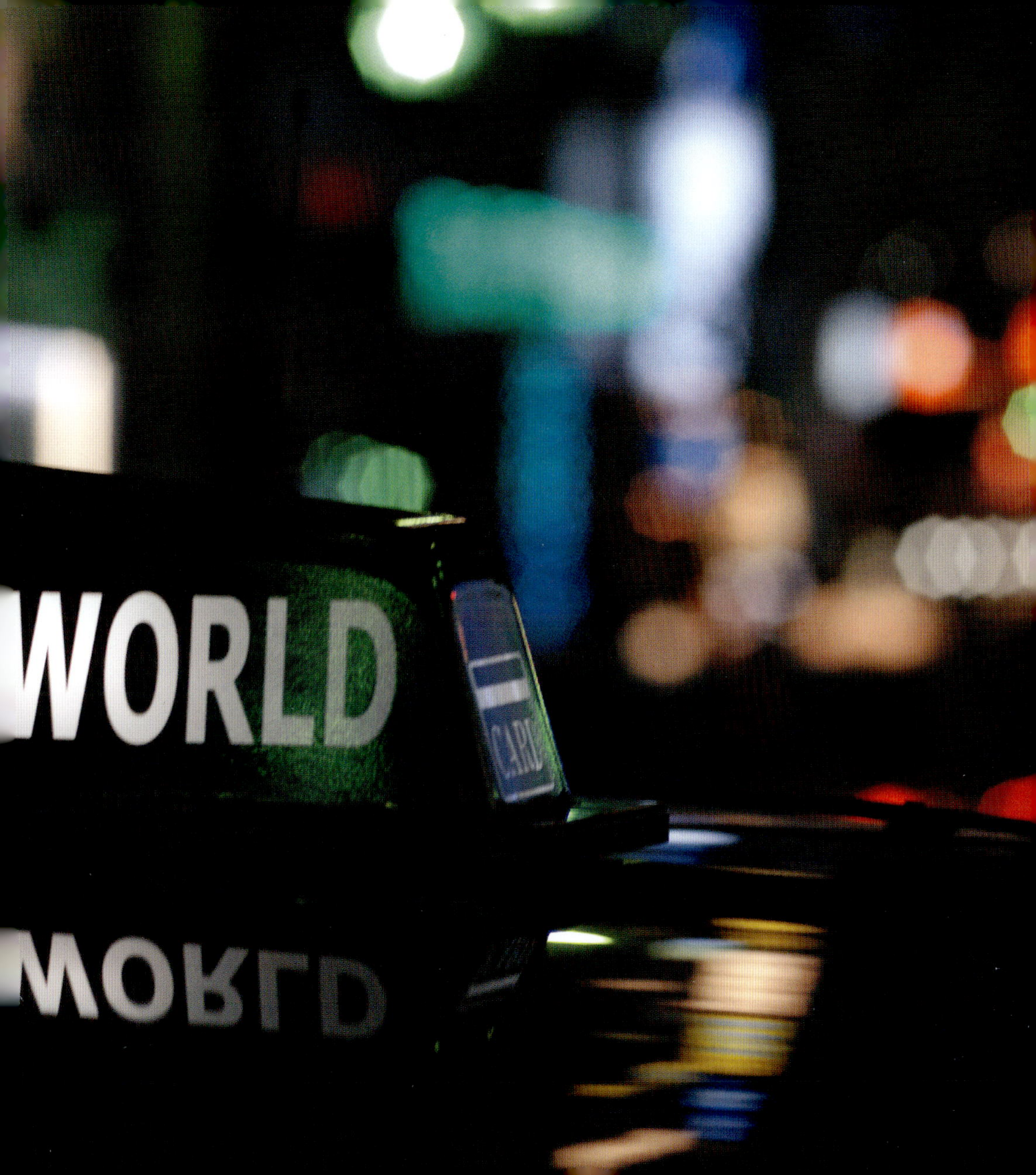
WORLD
CARD

Pages 80–81: TOKYO WORLD TAXI 107

EBISU TAXI

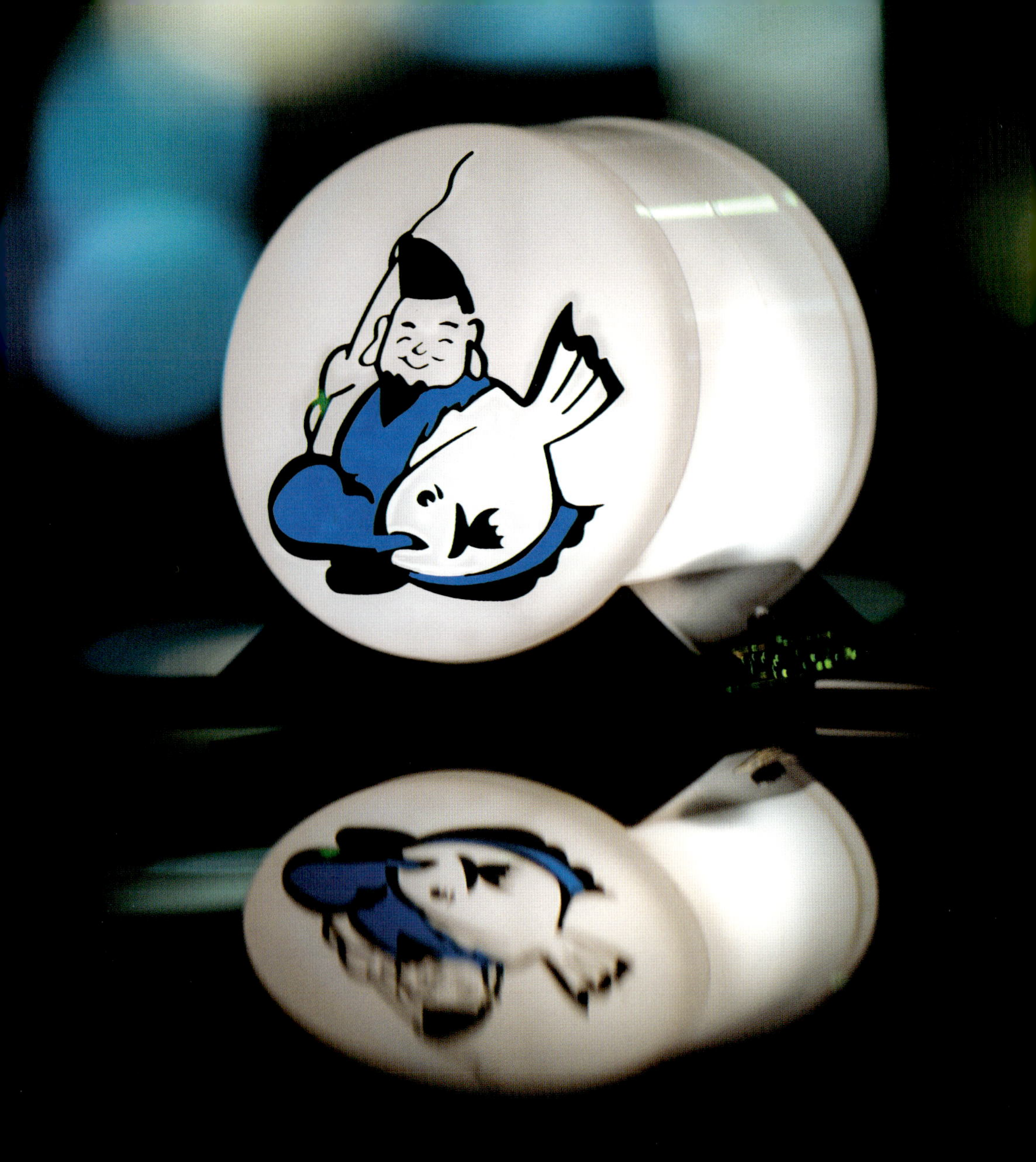

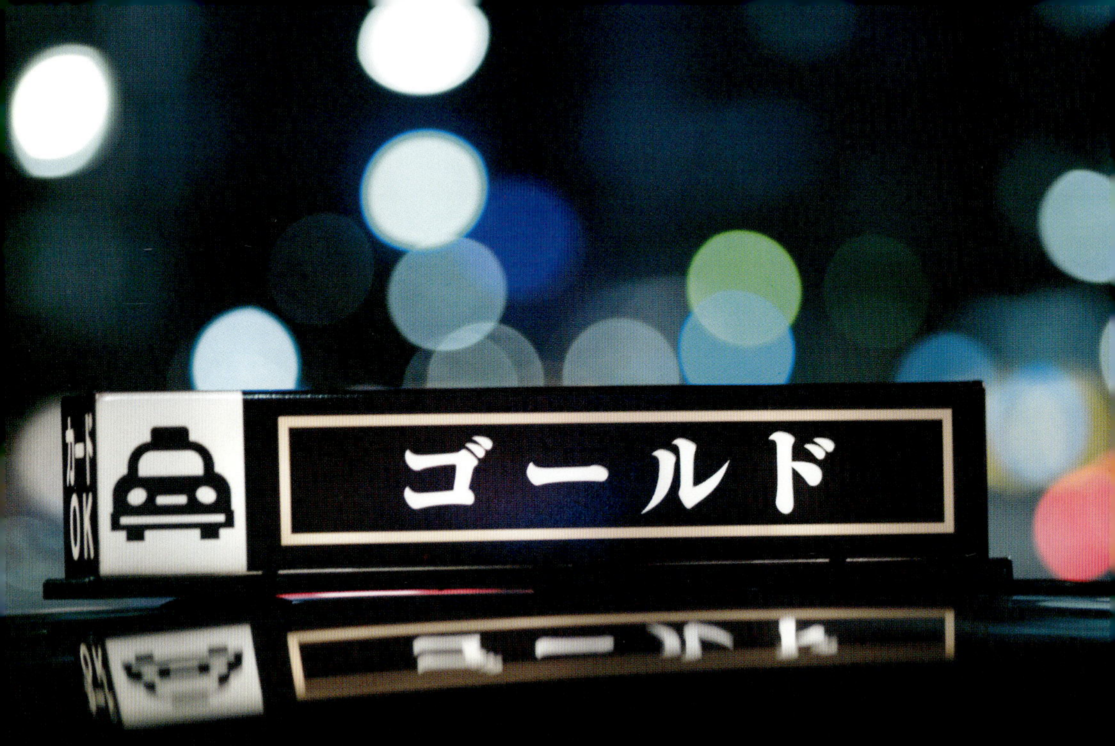

GOLD TAXI CO.

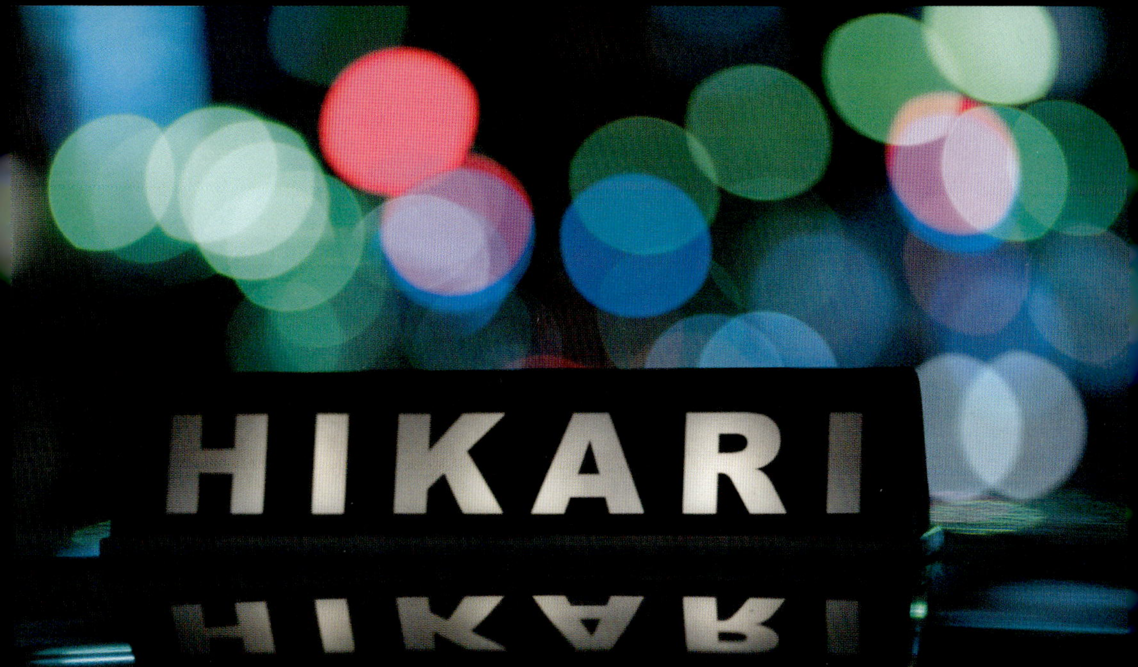

HIKARI TAXI CO.

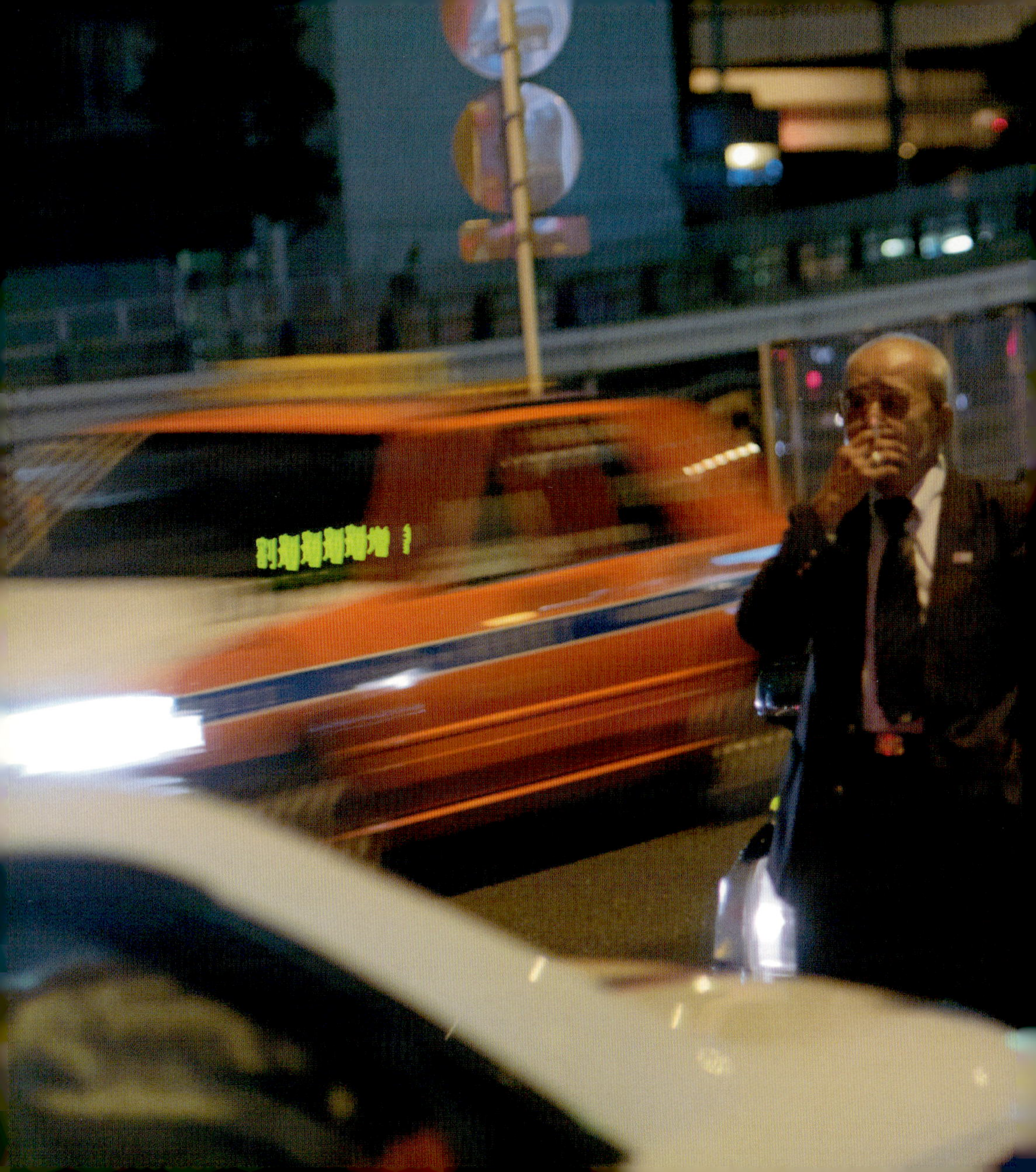

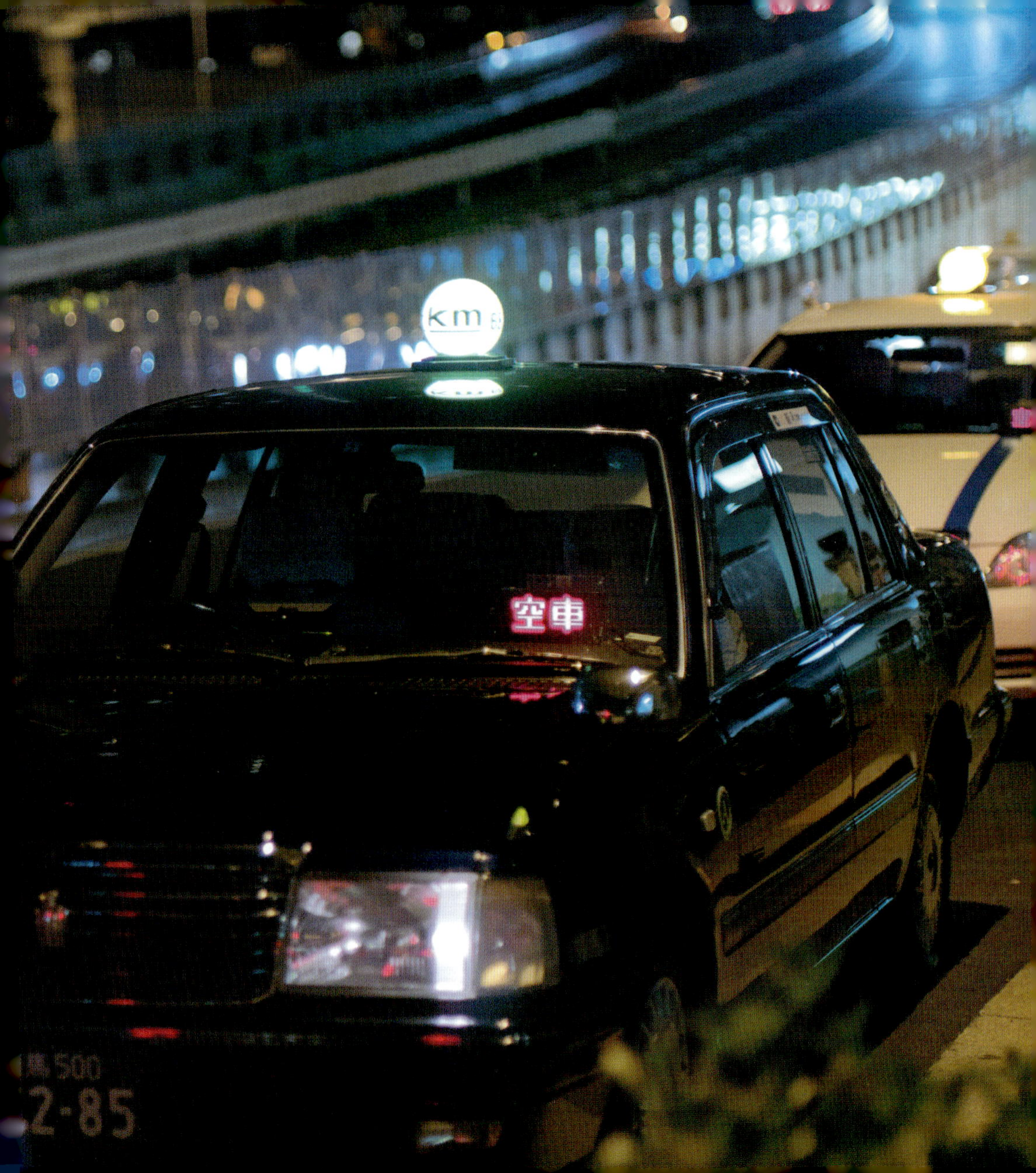
km
空車
500
2-85

MAINICHI TAXI CO.

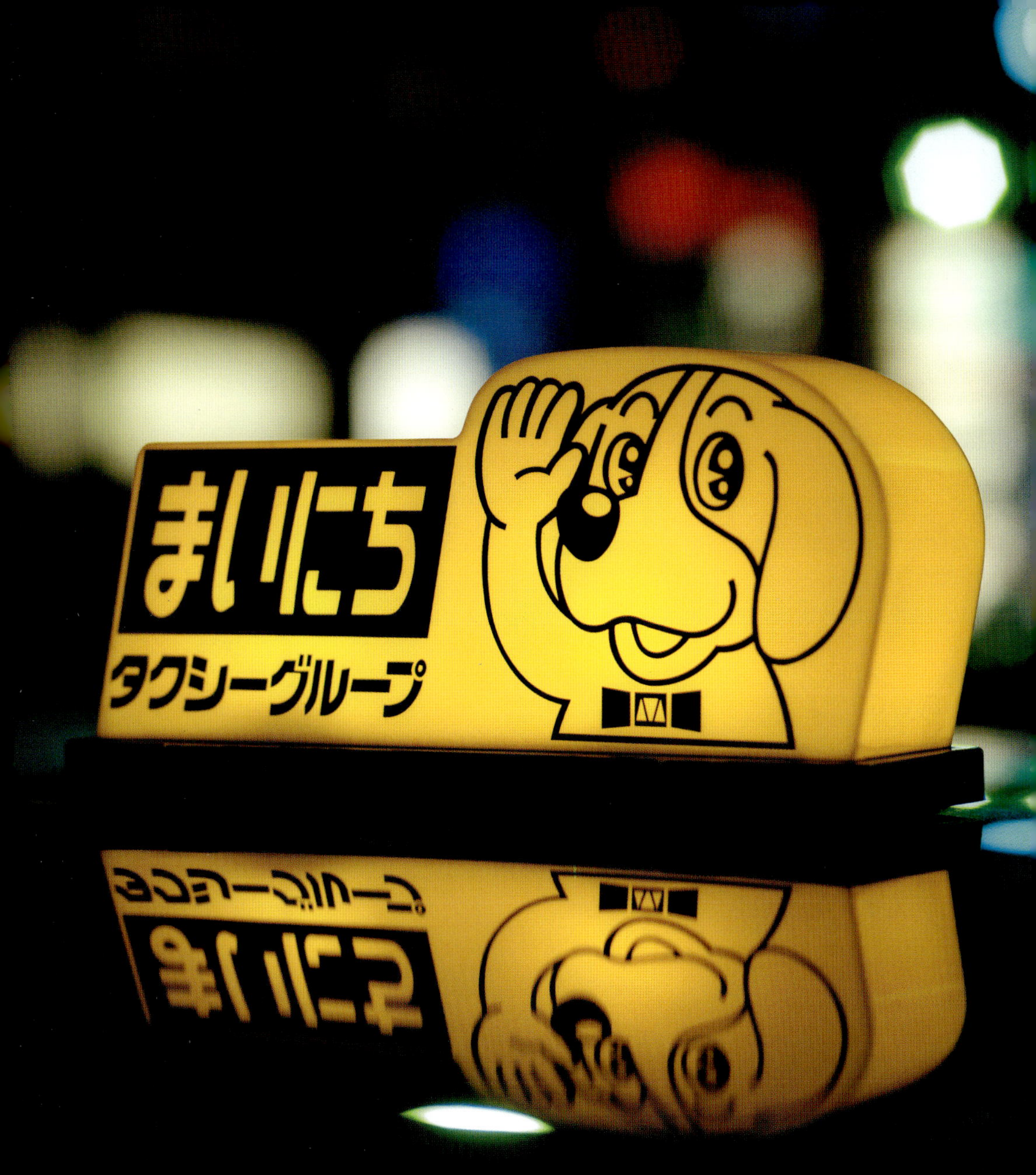
まいにち
タクシーグループ

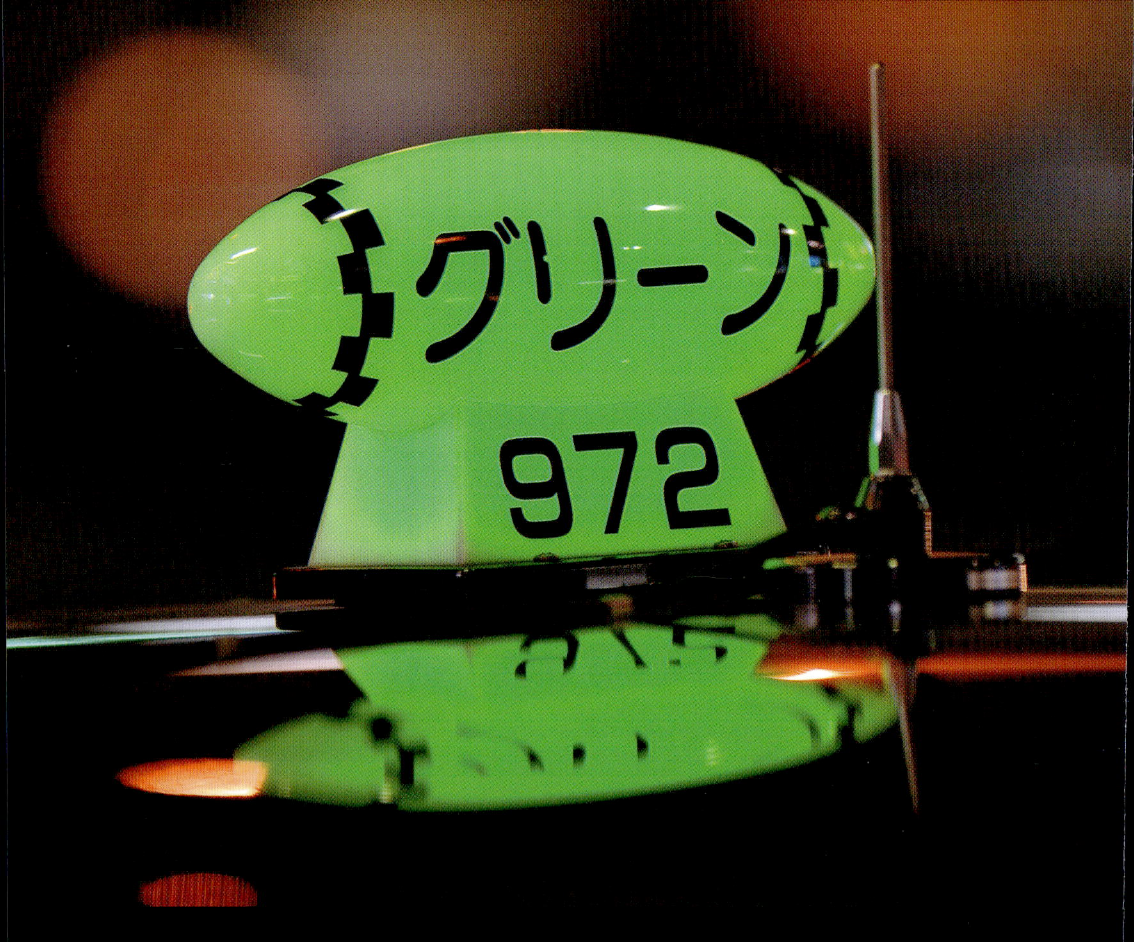

GREEN CHECKER TAXI CO. 972

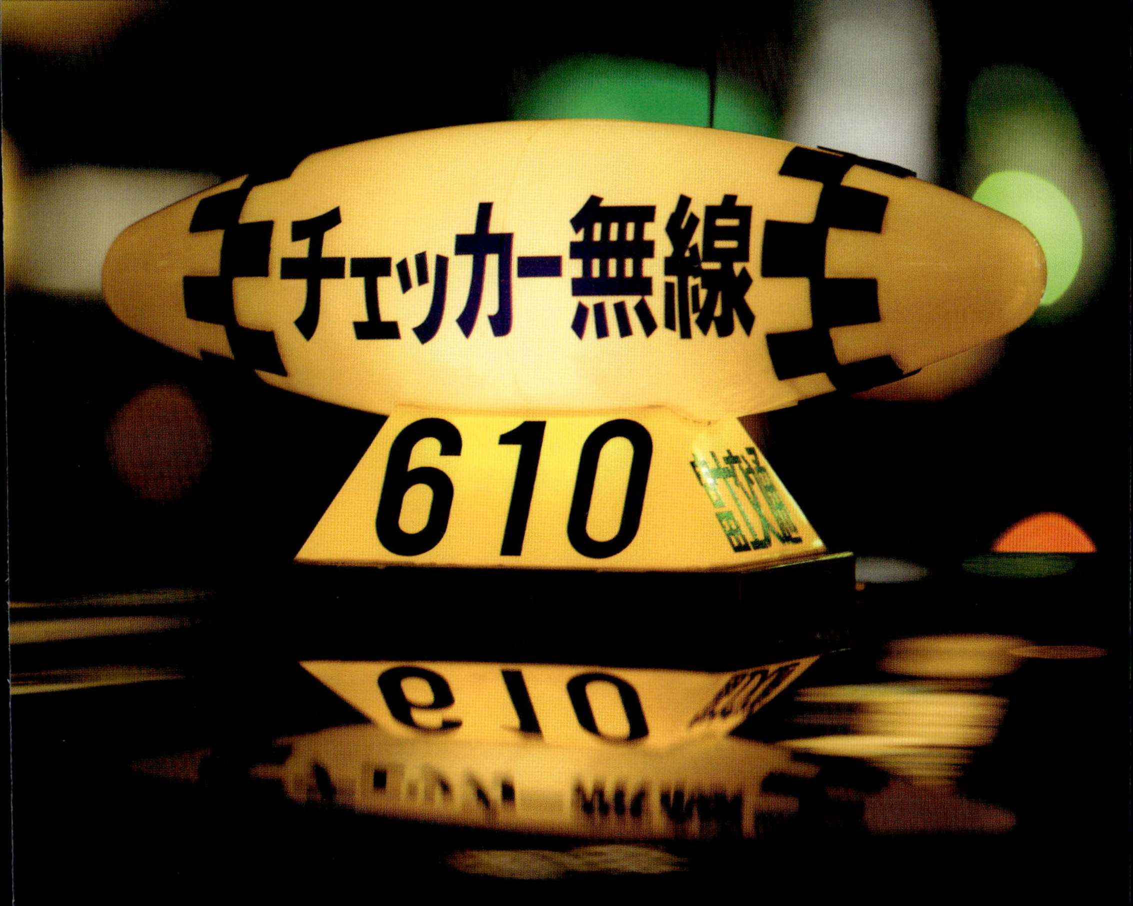

CHECKER TAIYO TAXI CO. 610

UNNAMED DRIVER

Once I had a wonderfully happy young man in my taxi.
He asked to stop at a florist's, and bought their entire stock
of cut flowers. I then took him to his girlfriend's house.
Something must have happened when he got there, because
he came out ten minutes later, paid the fare, told me
to give the flowers to my wife, and walked off.
I'm not married.

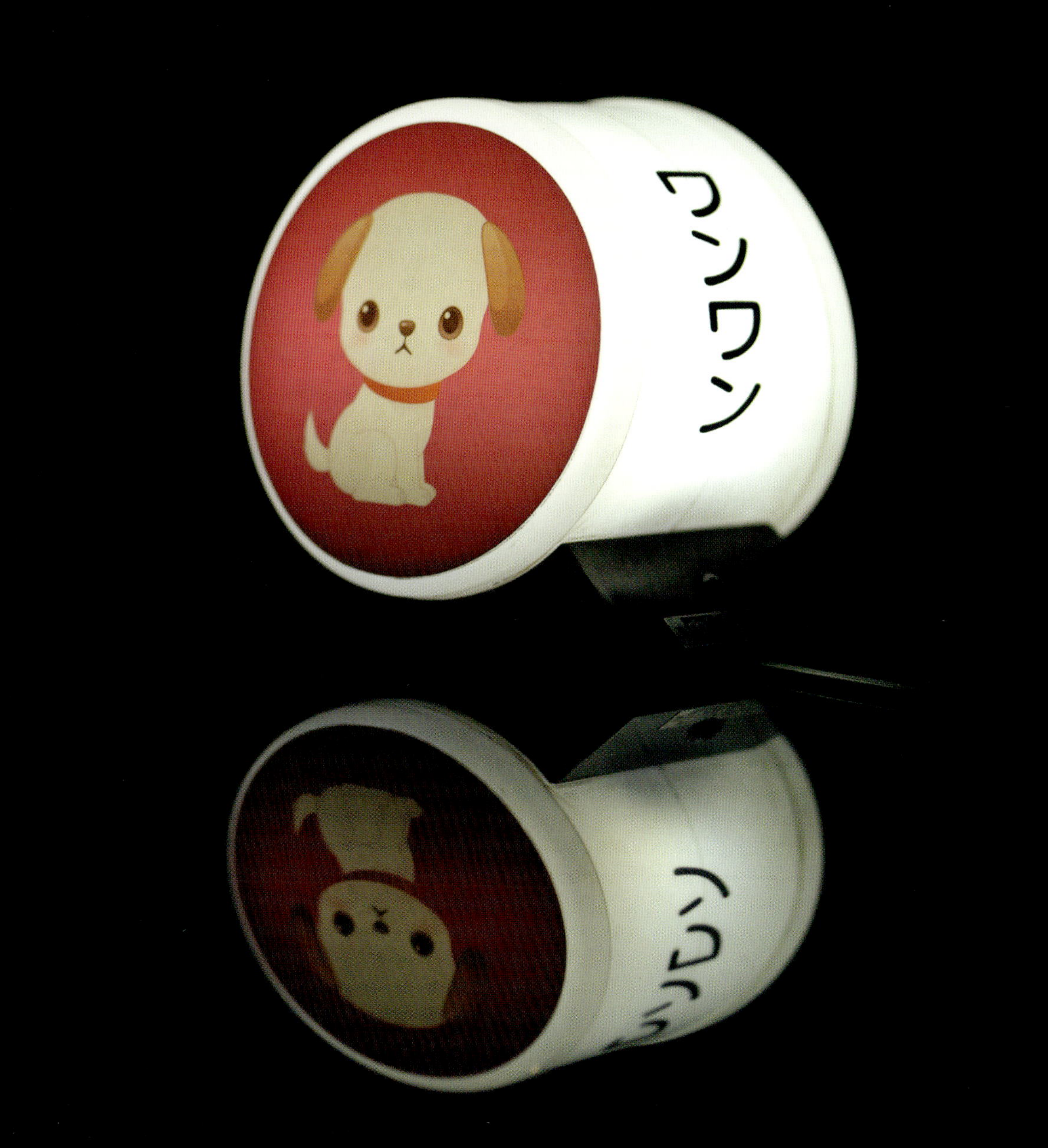
ワンワン

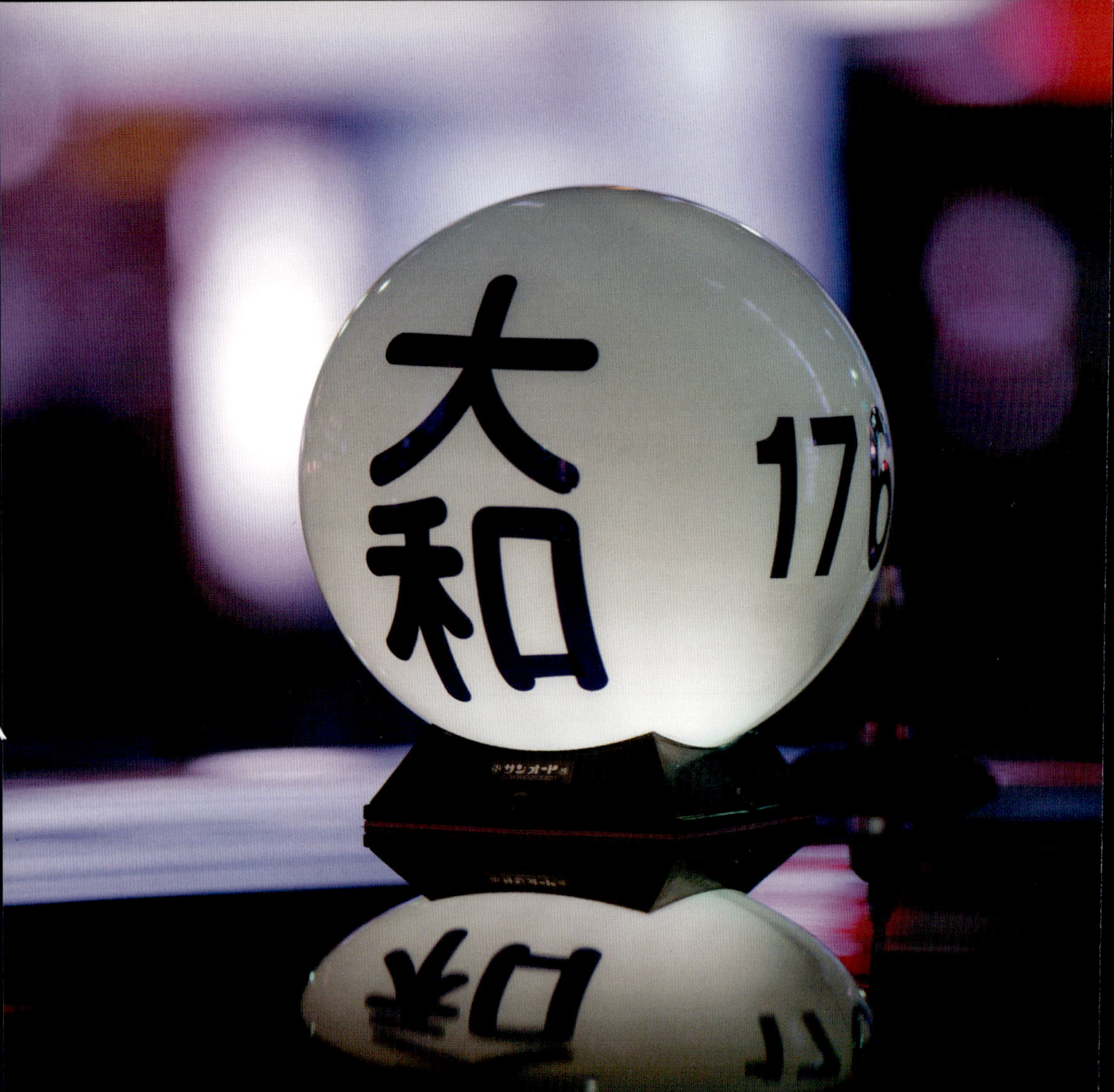
大和
17

DAIWA TAXI CO. 176

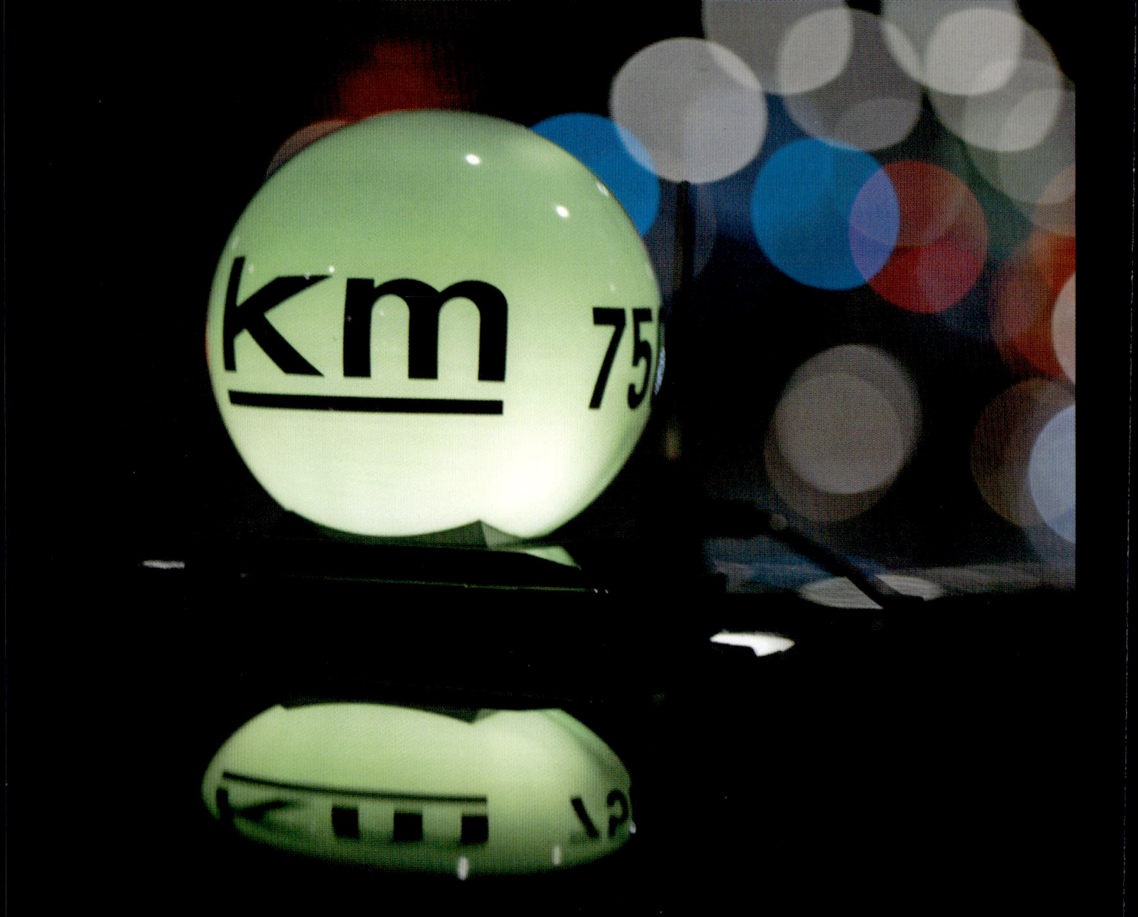

KOKUSAI MOTORCARS 750

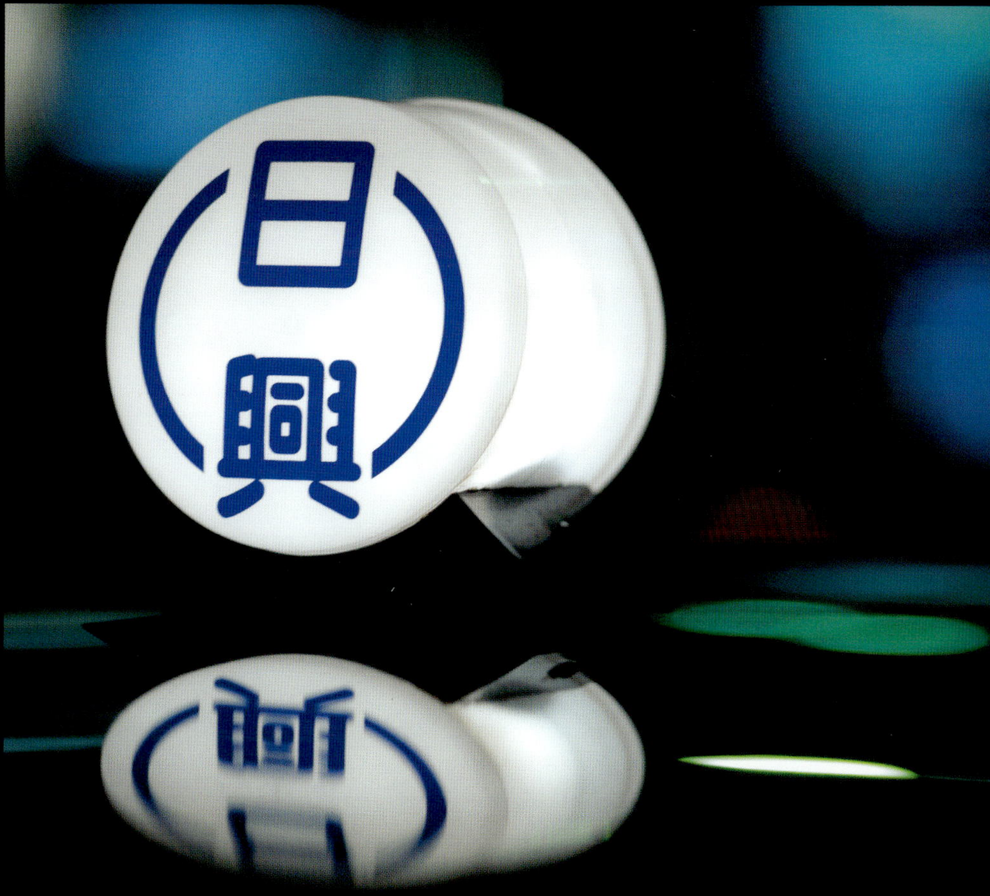

NIKKOU TAXI

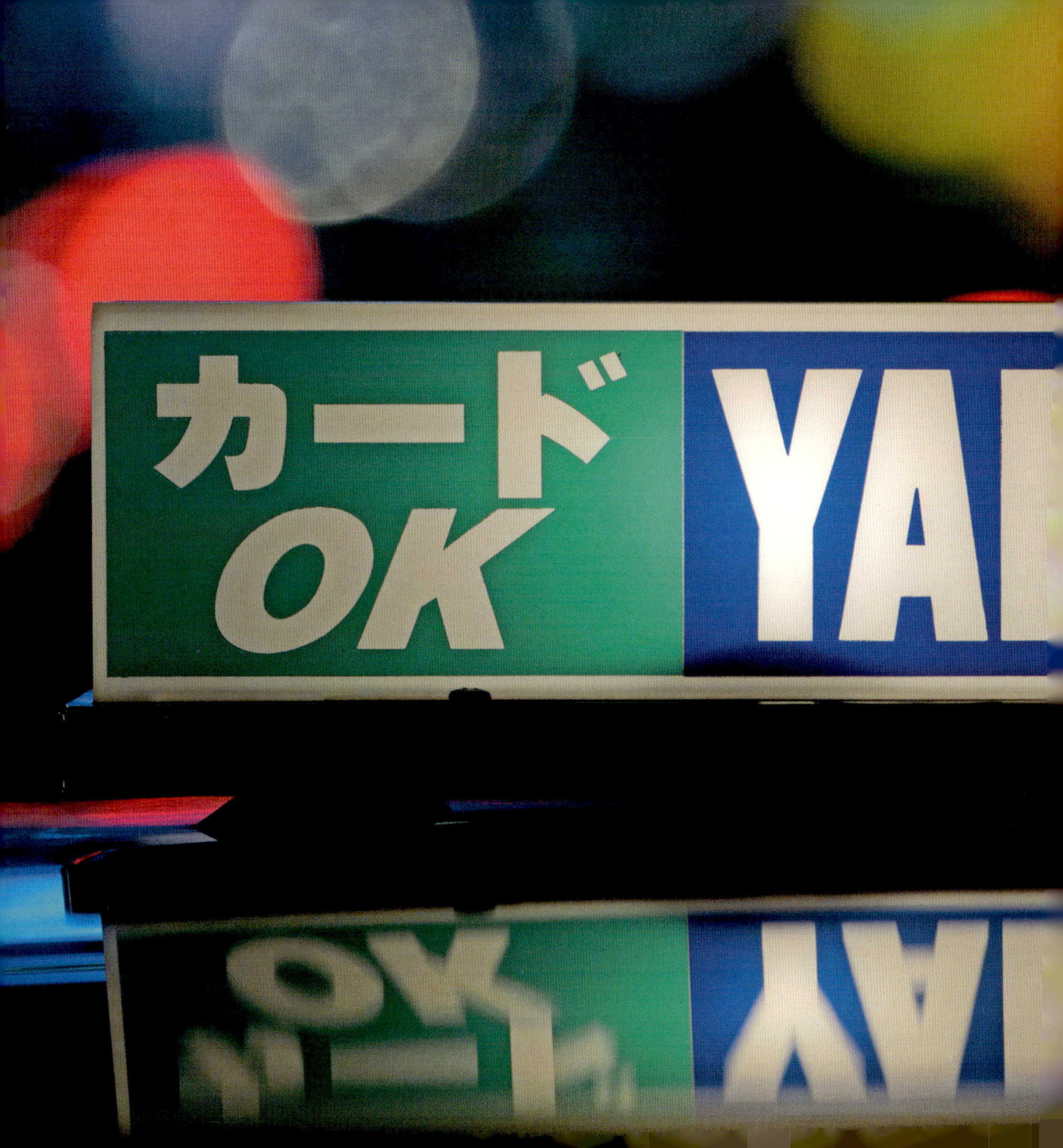
カード
OK

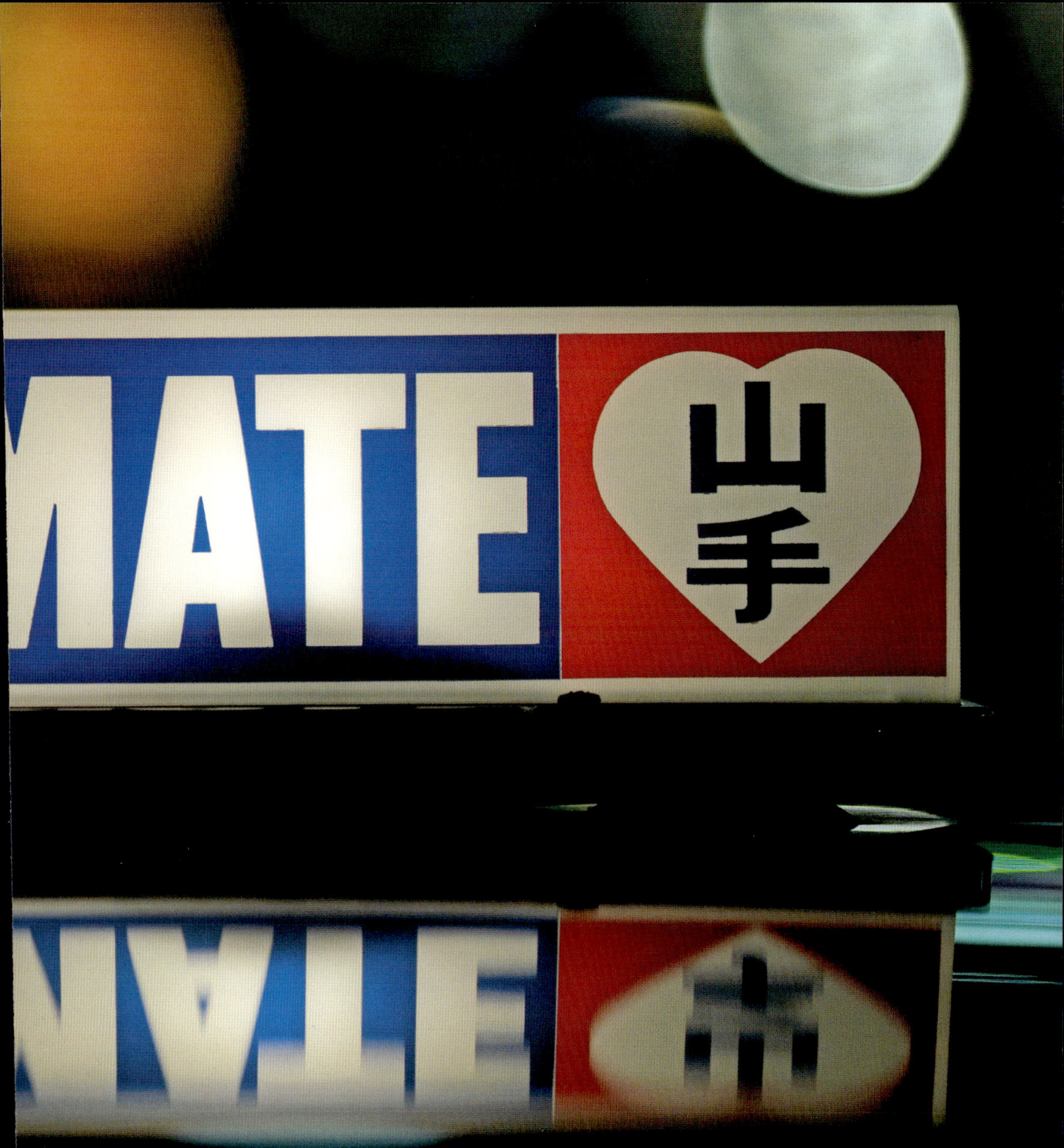
MATE
山手

Pages 98–99: YAMATE TAXI CO.

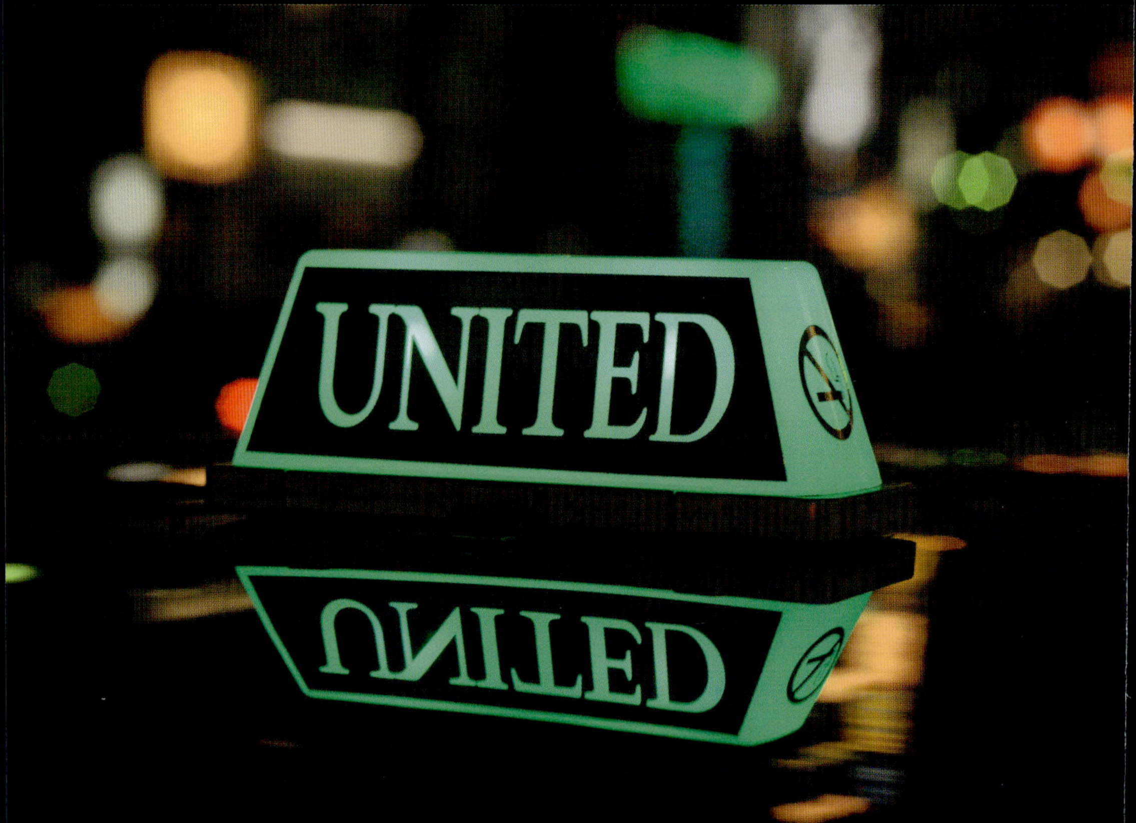

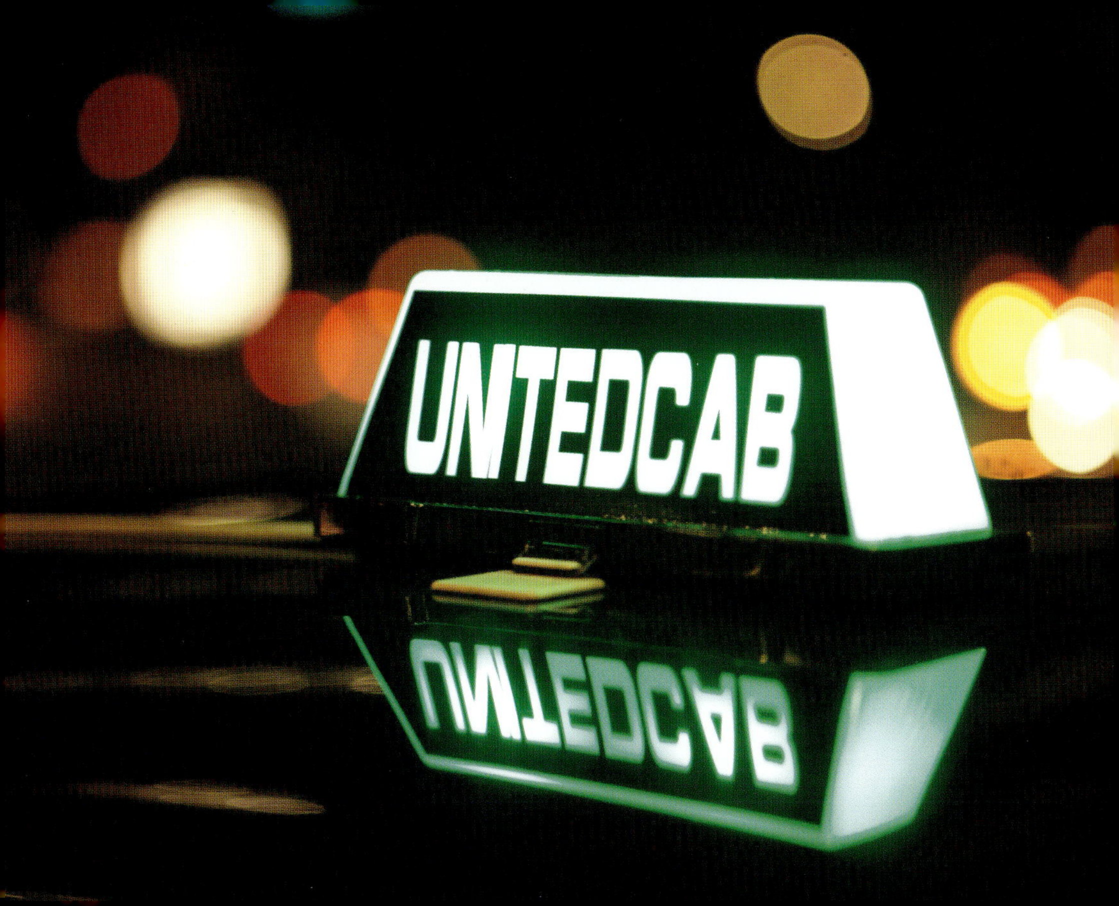
UNITEDCAB

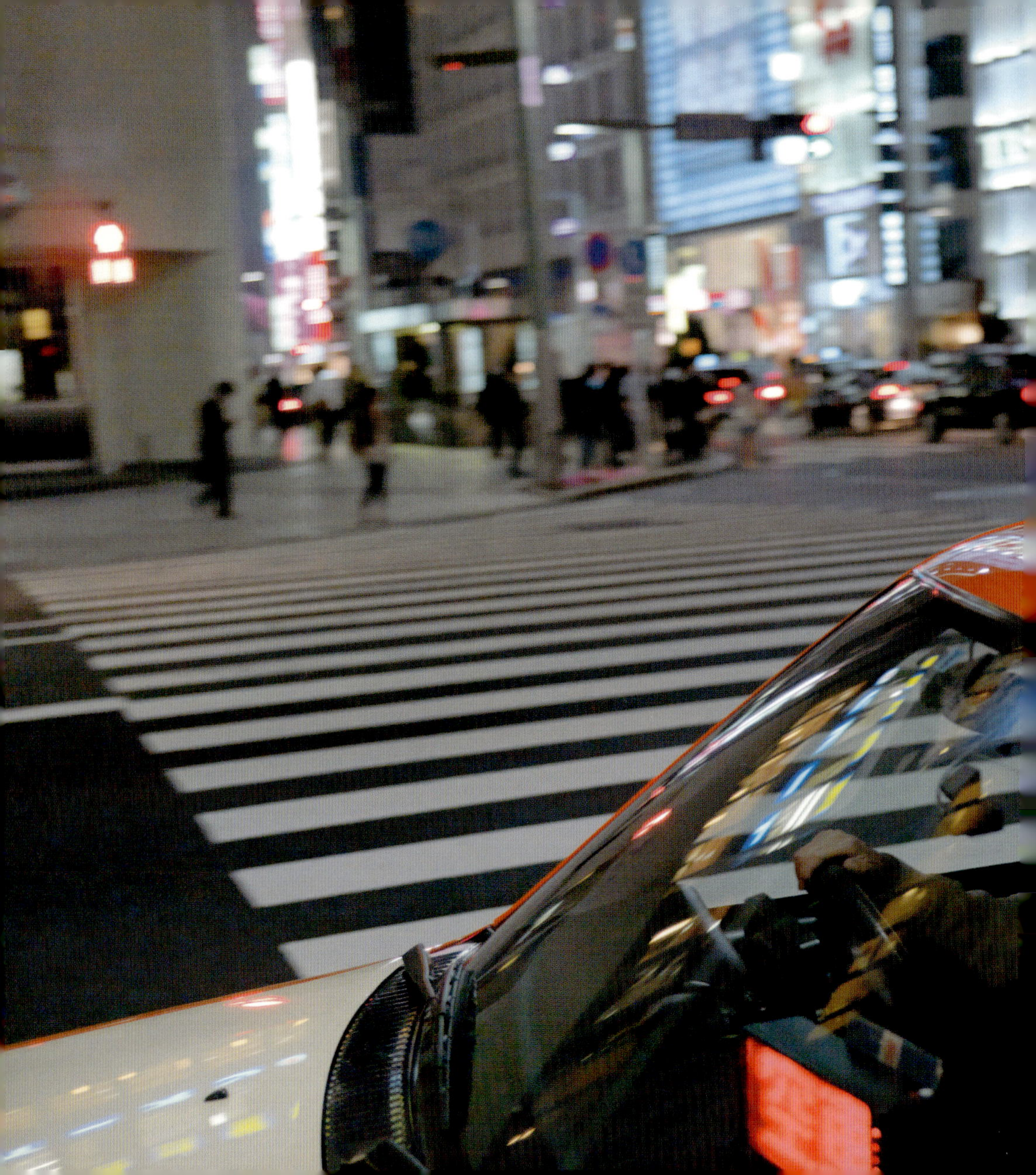

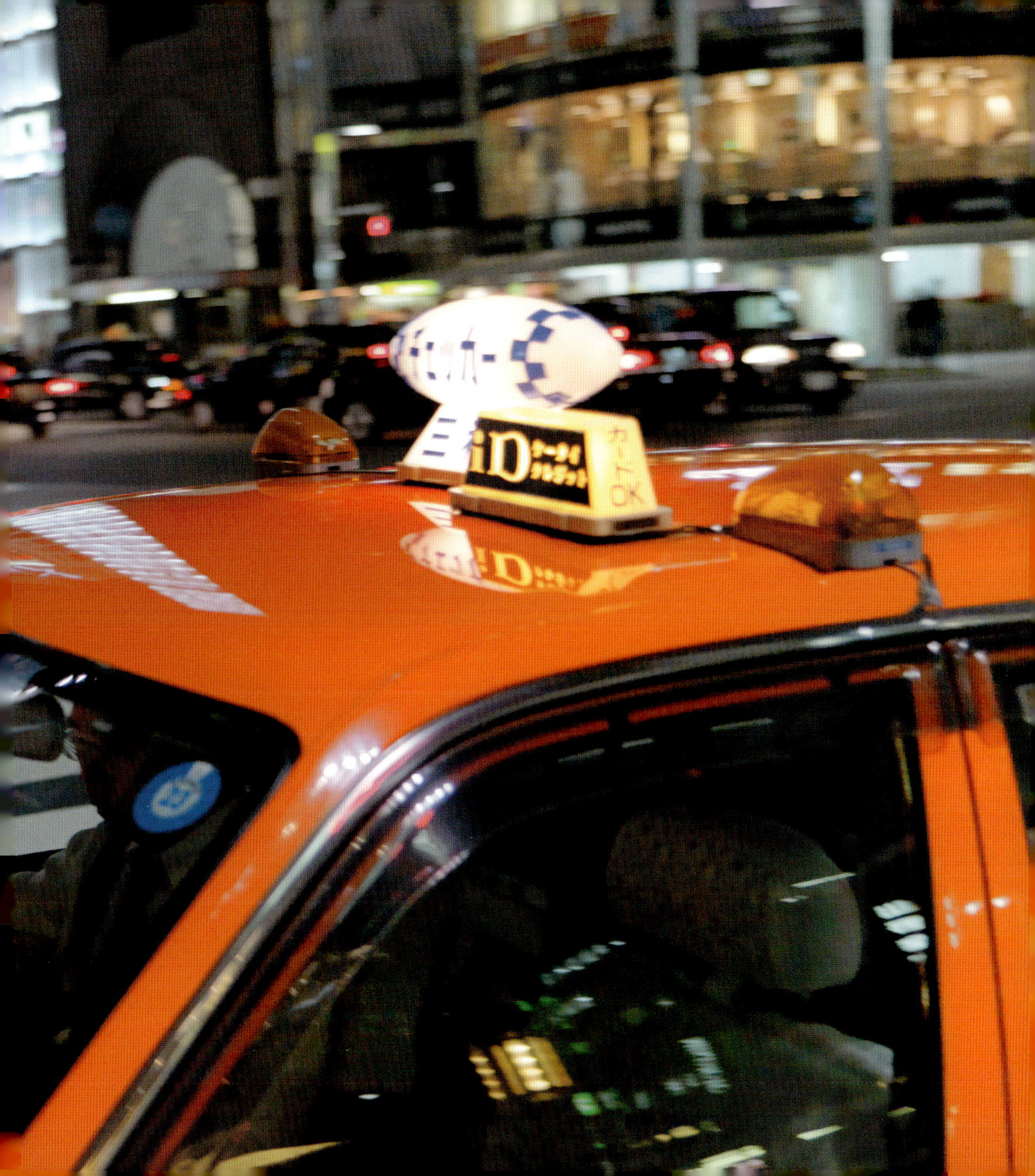
iD
カードOK

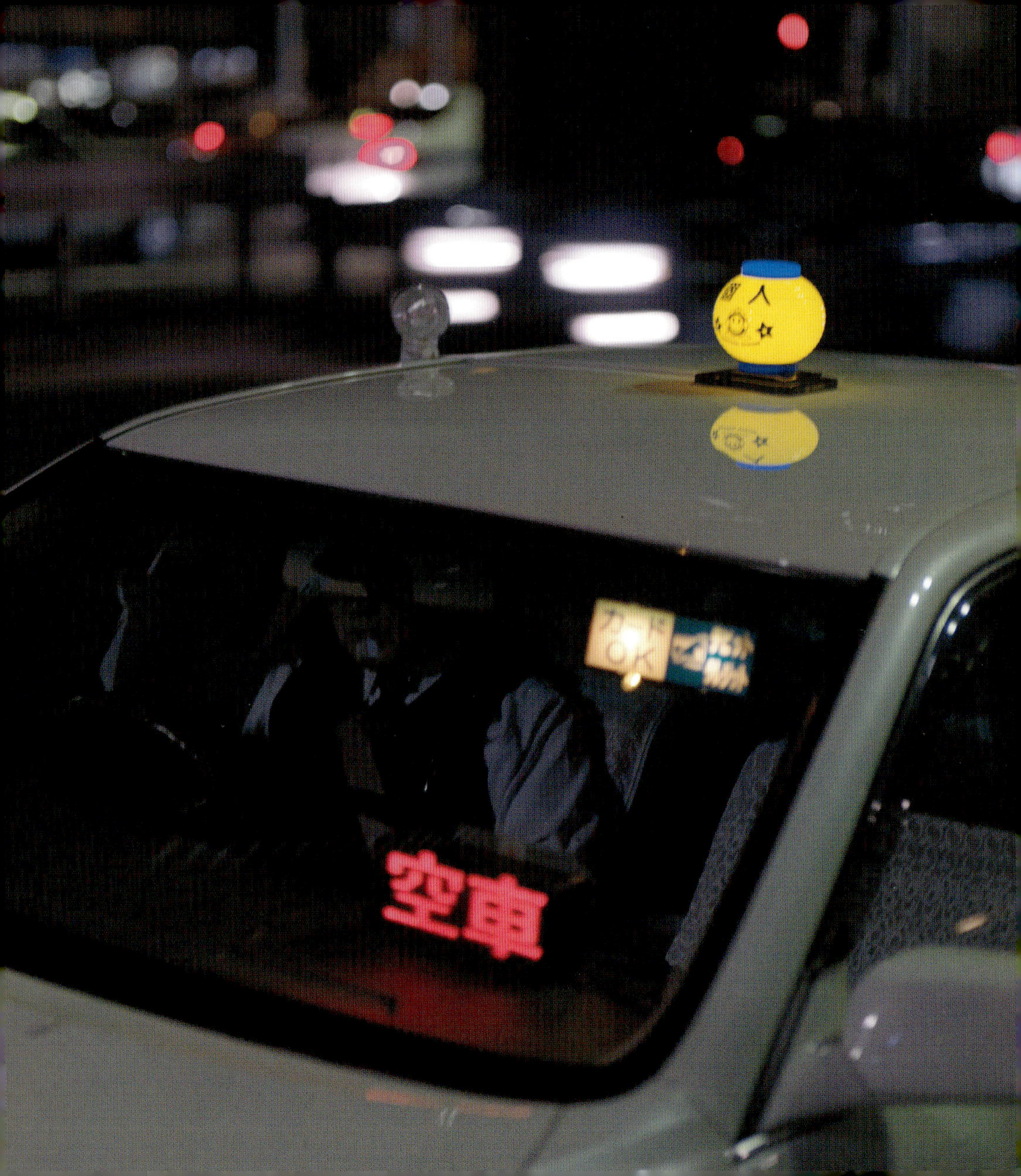
空車

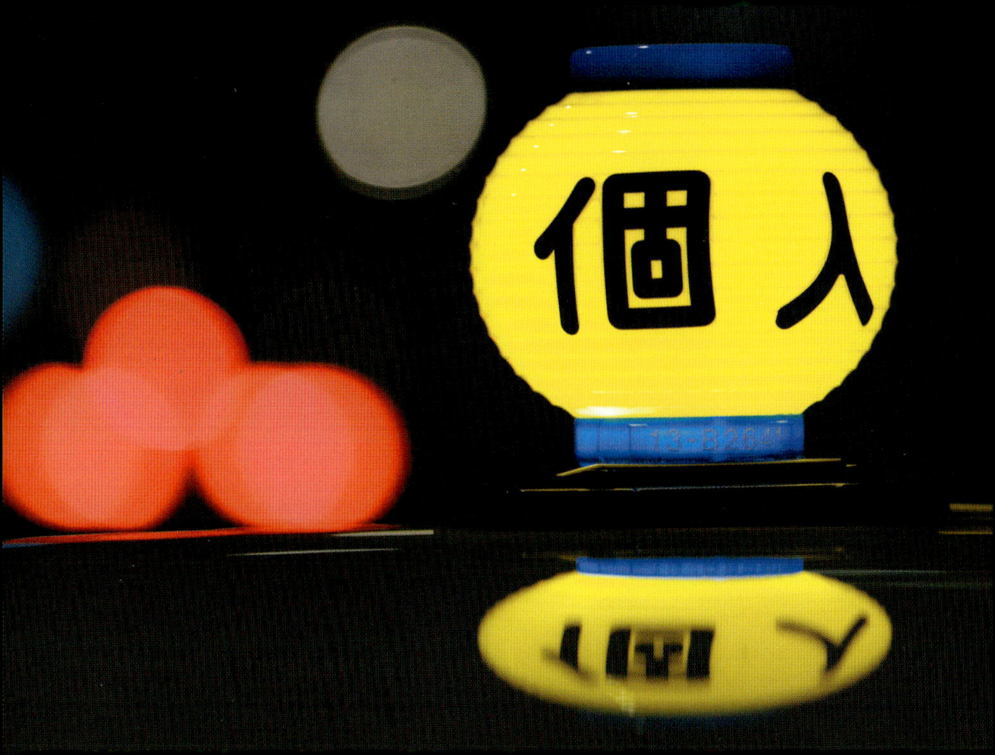
個人

YOTSUBA TAXI CO.

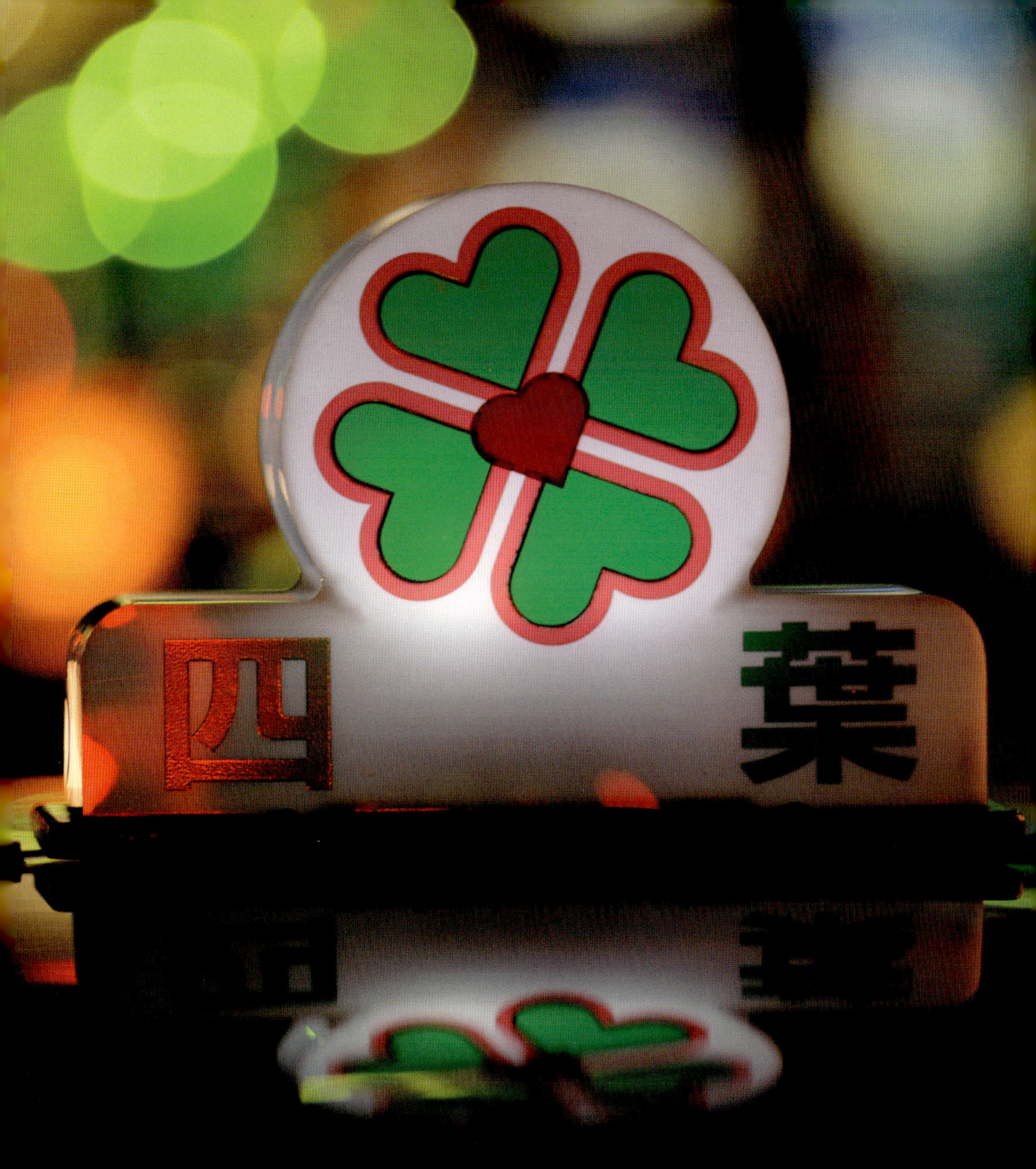
四
葉

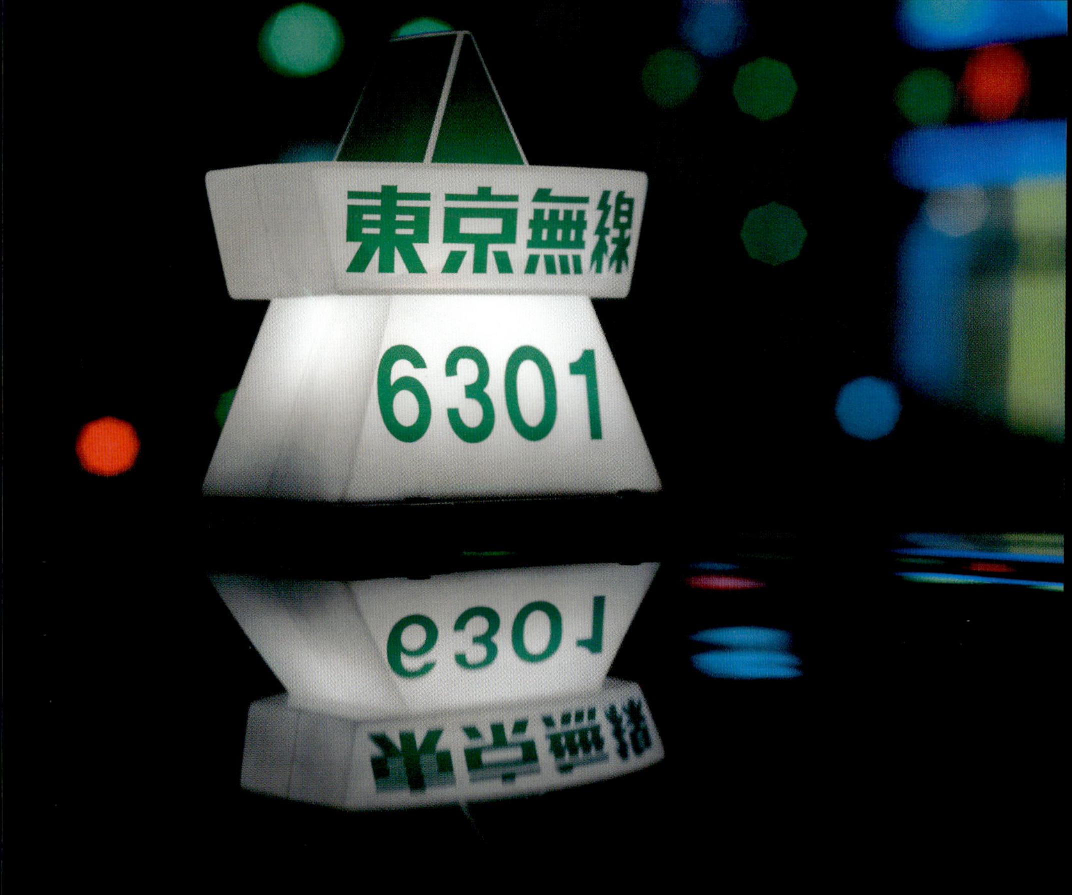

TOKYO MUSEN 6301 AND 849

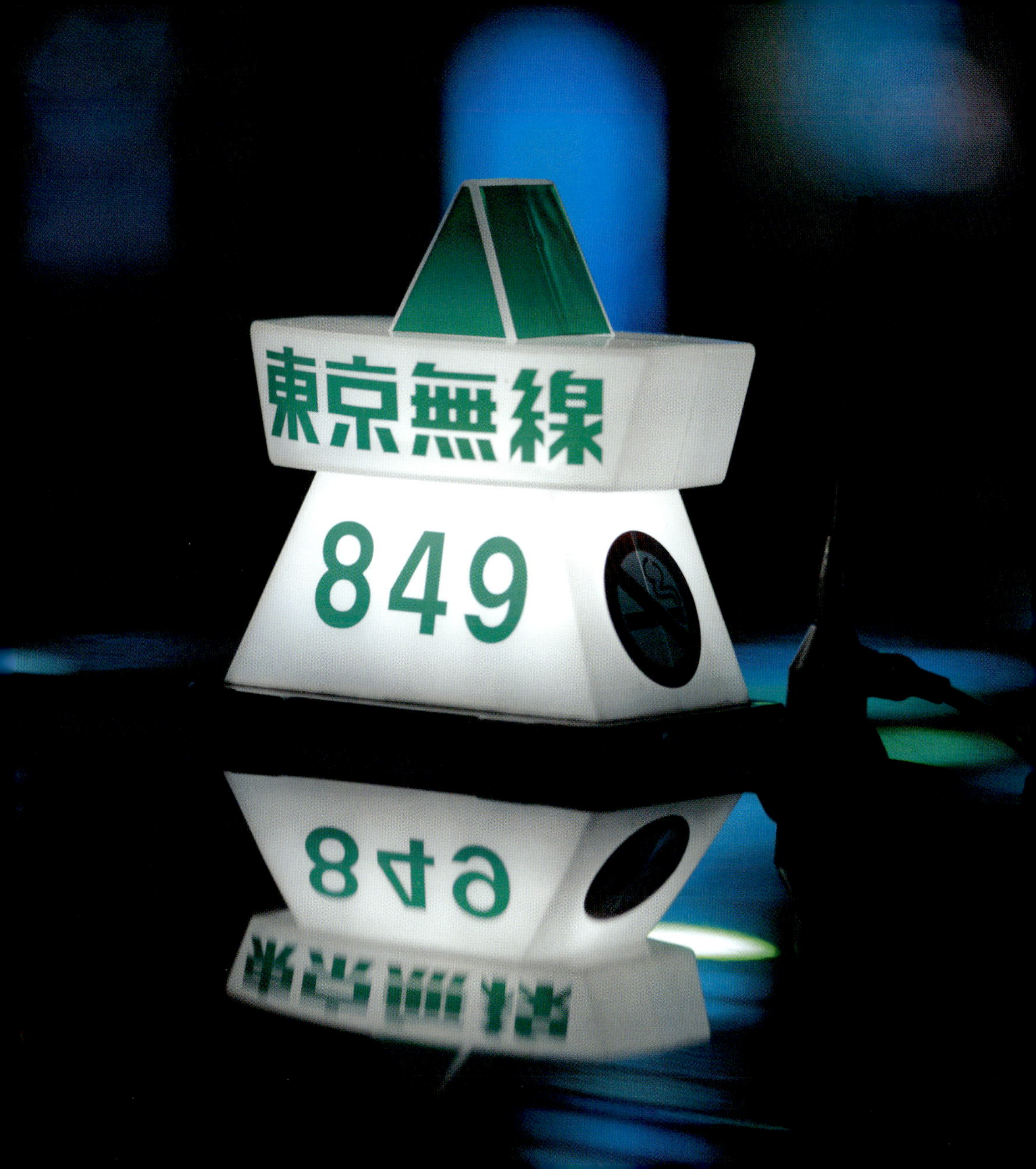
東京無線
849

'DIGITAL INFORMATION SERVICE INSIDE'

MR HARADA

Driver for Teito Taxi Co.

with more than thirteen years' experience

The hardest part of the job is trying to communicate with difficult or drunk customers. No matter how they behave, you must always treat them with respect; their needs come first. The worst thing about my first year was trying to find my way around the backstreets. Even for locals these streets can be overwhelming

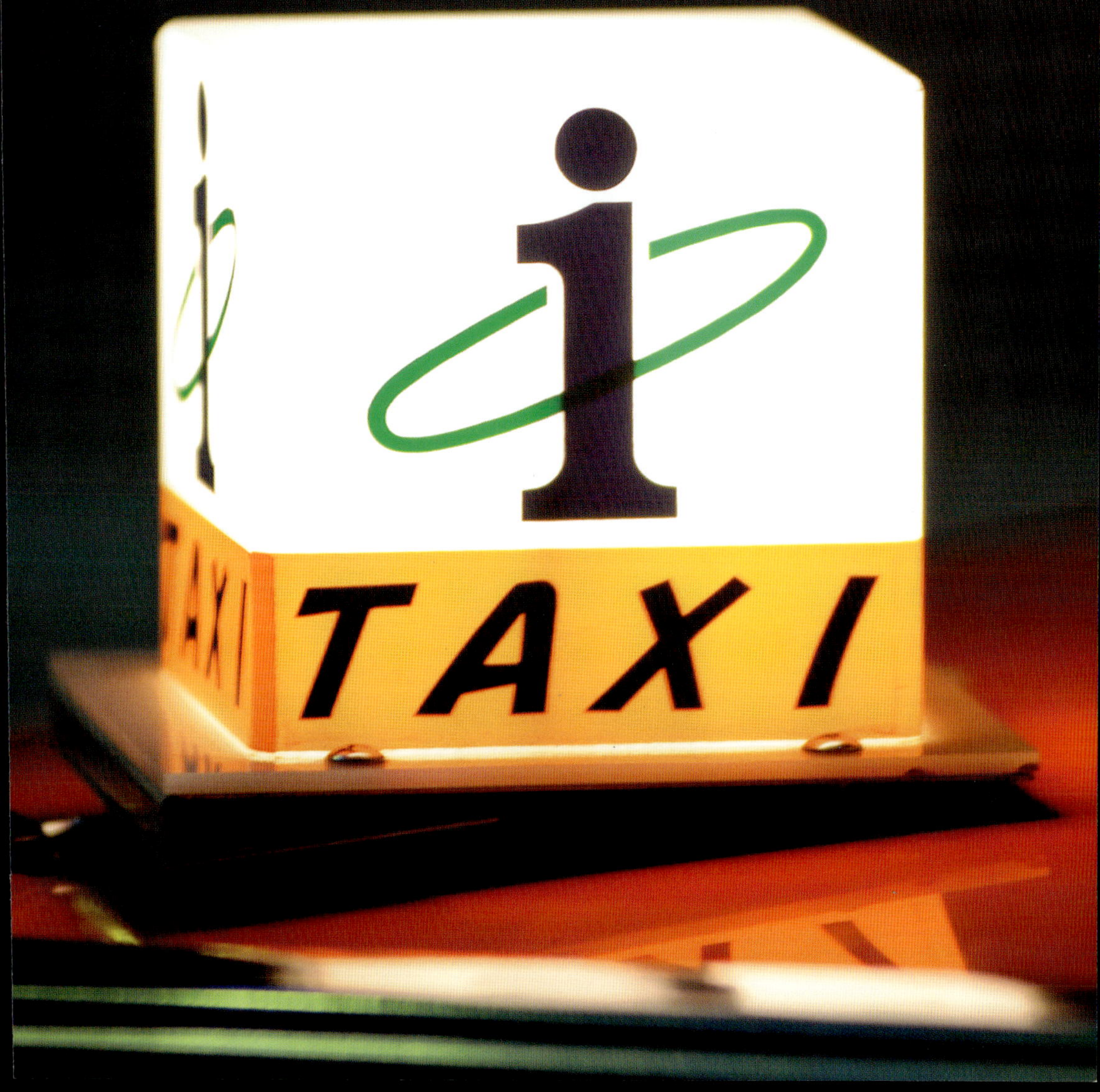
TAXI

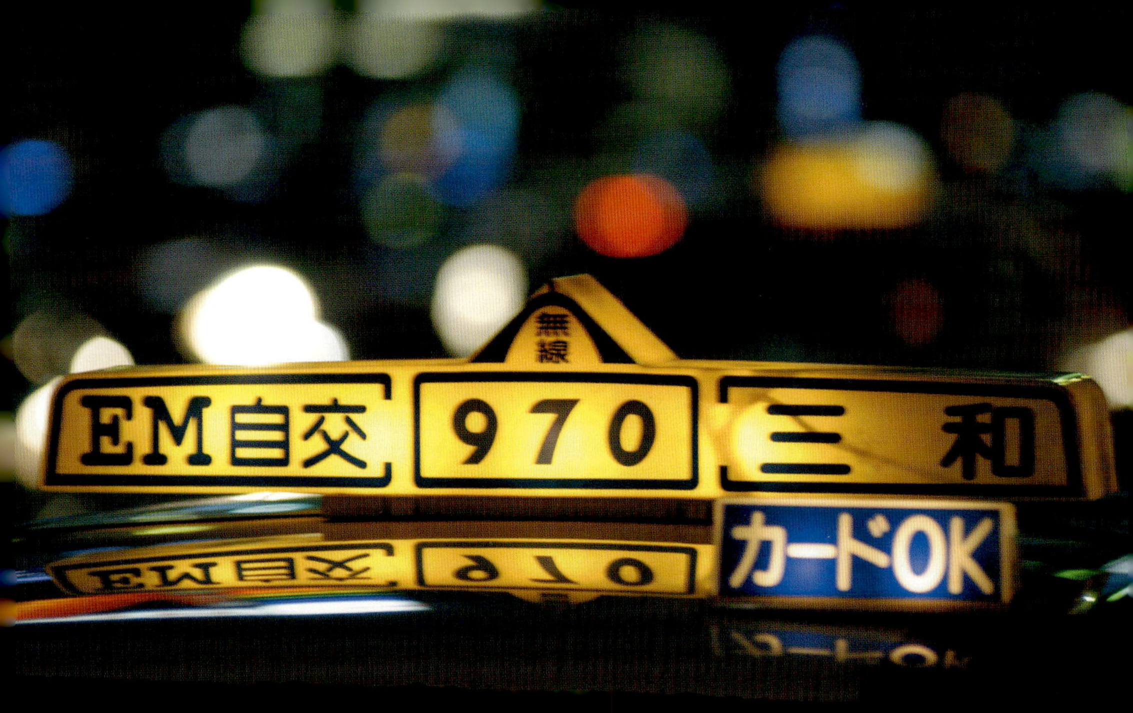
無線
EM自交
970
三和
カードOK

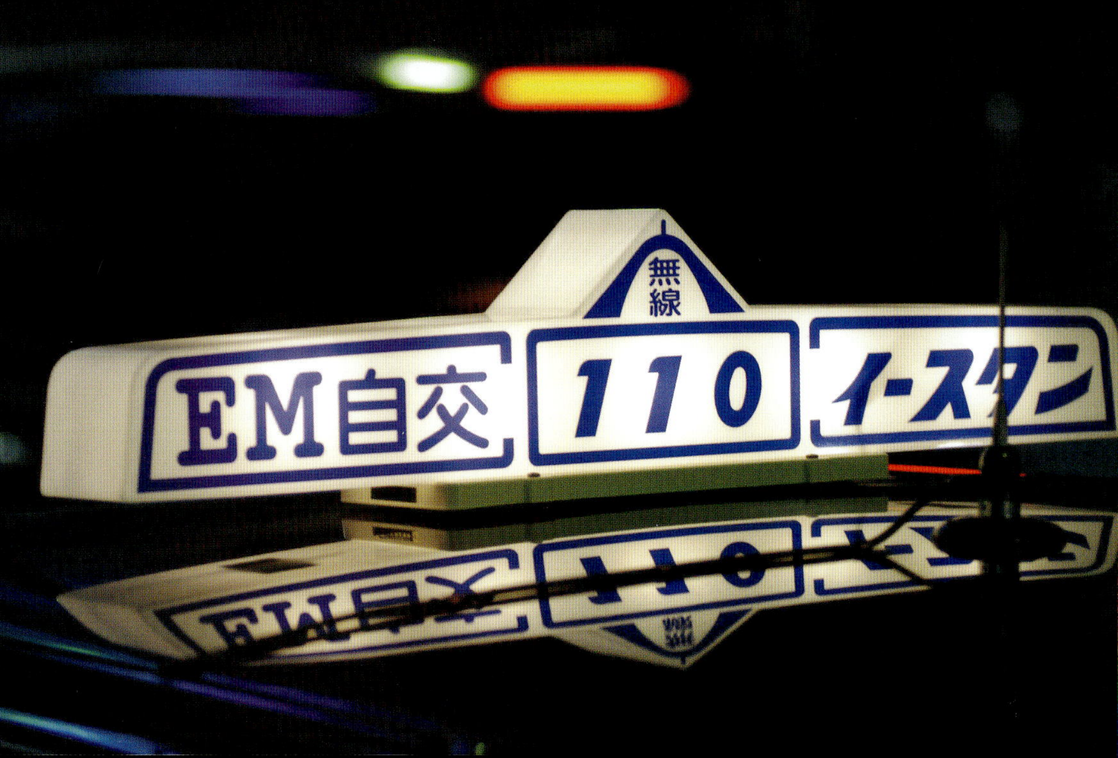

EM JIKOU EASTERN 110

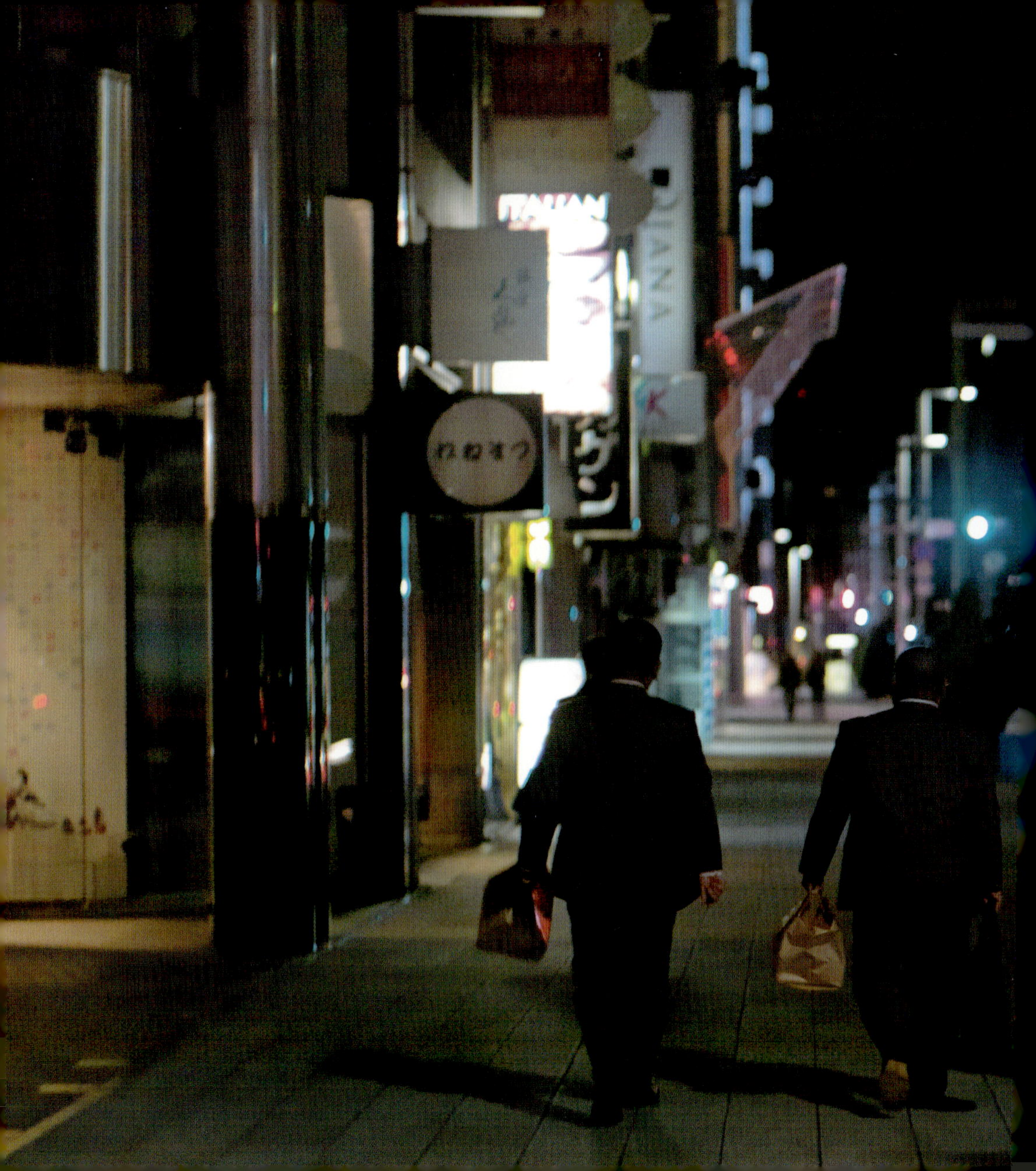
ITALIAN
DIANA

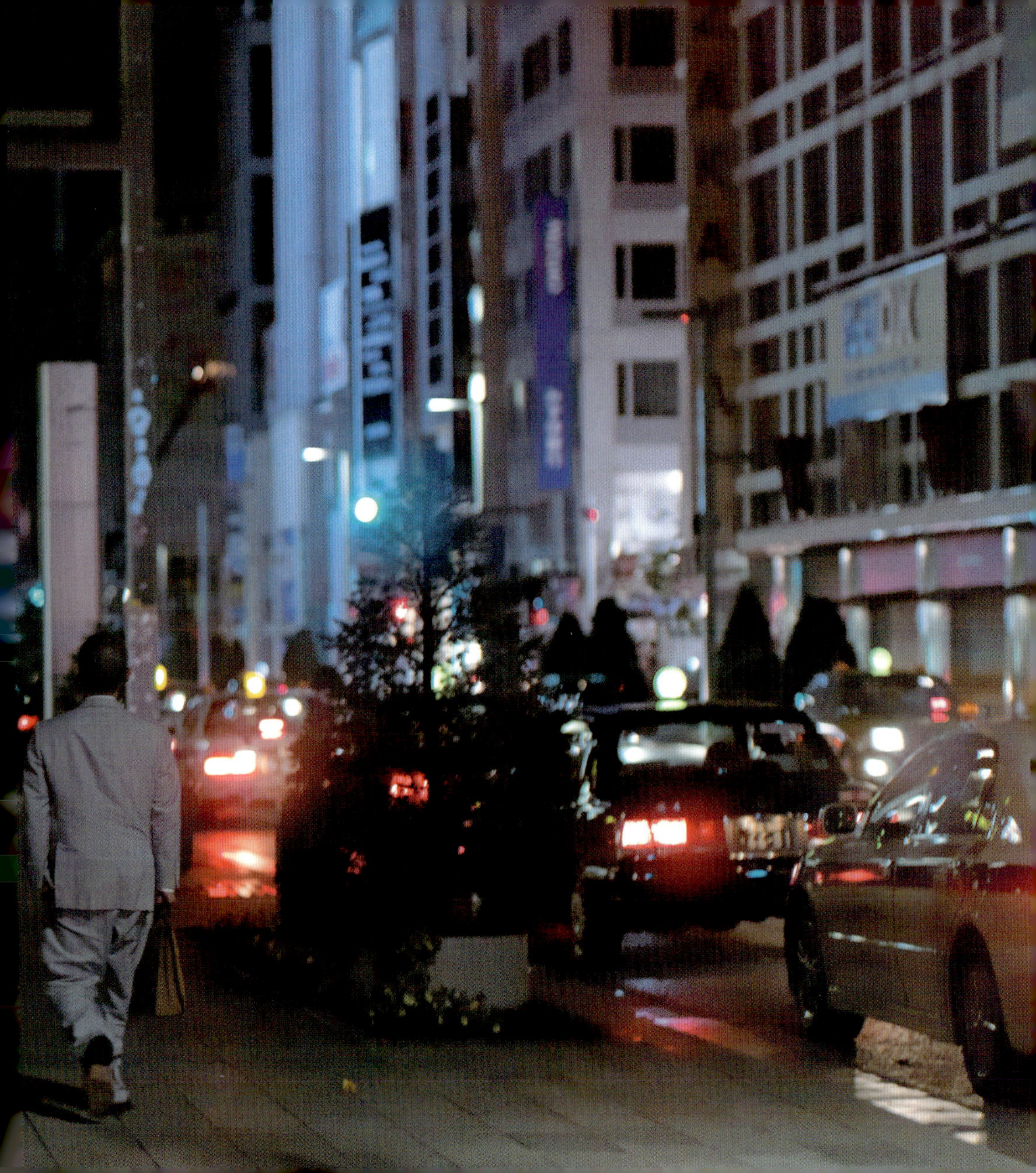

MONKEYS TAXI CO.

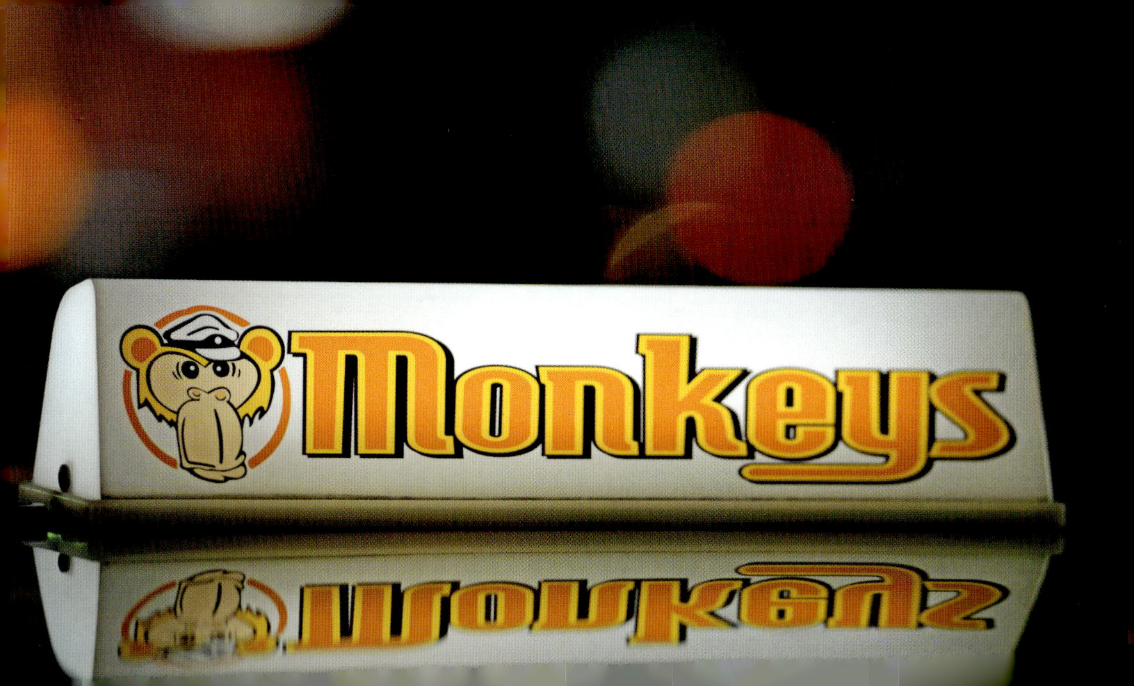
Monkeys

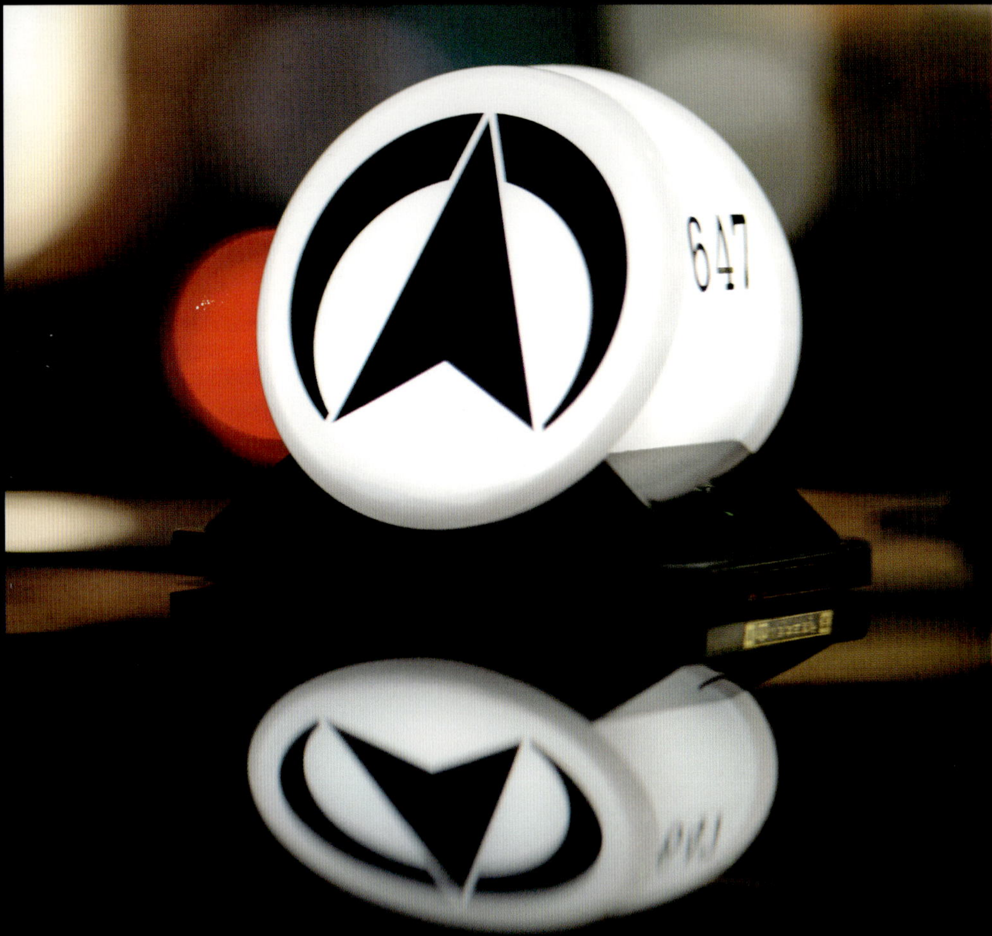

TOUTO TAXI CO. 647

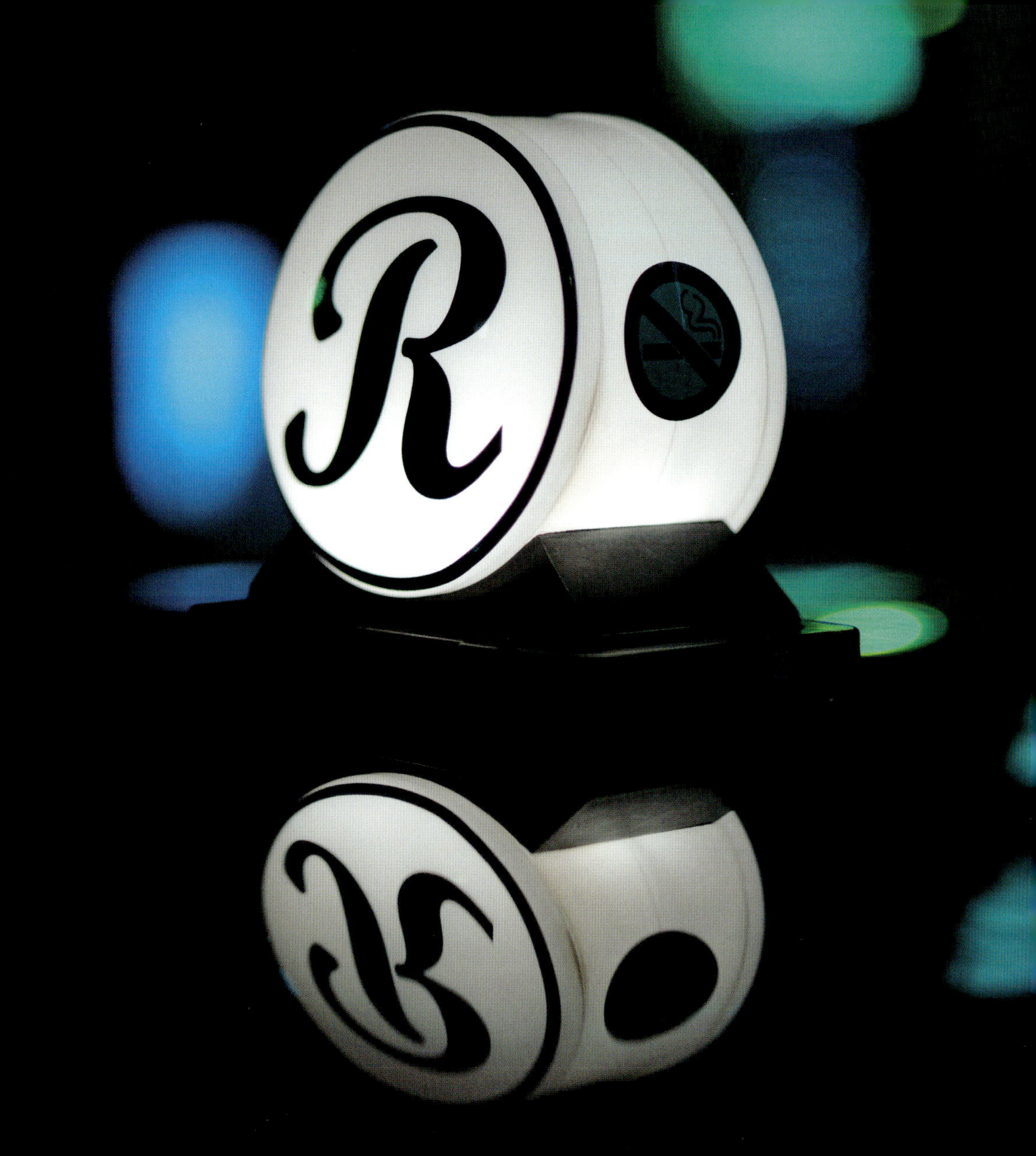

MR INNAMI

I like it when customers are talkative. It would be considered very rude of a driver to start a conversation, but when the customer is chatty it makes for a very interesting journey. I still have to maintain a polite decorum at all times.

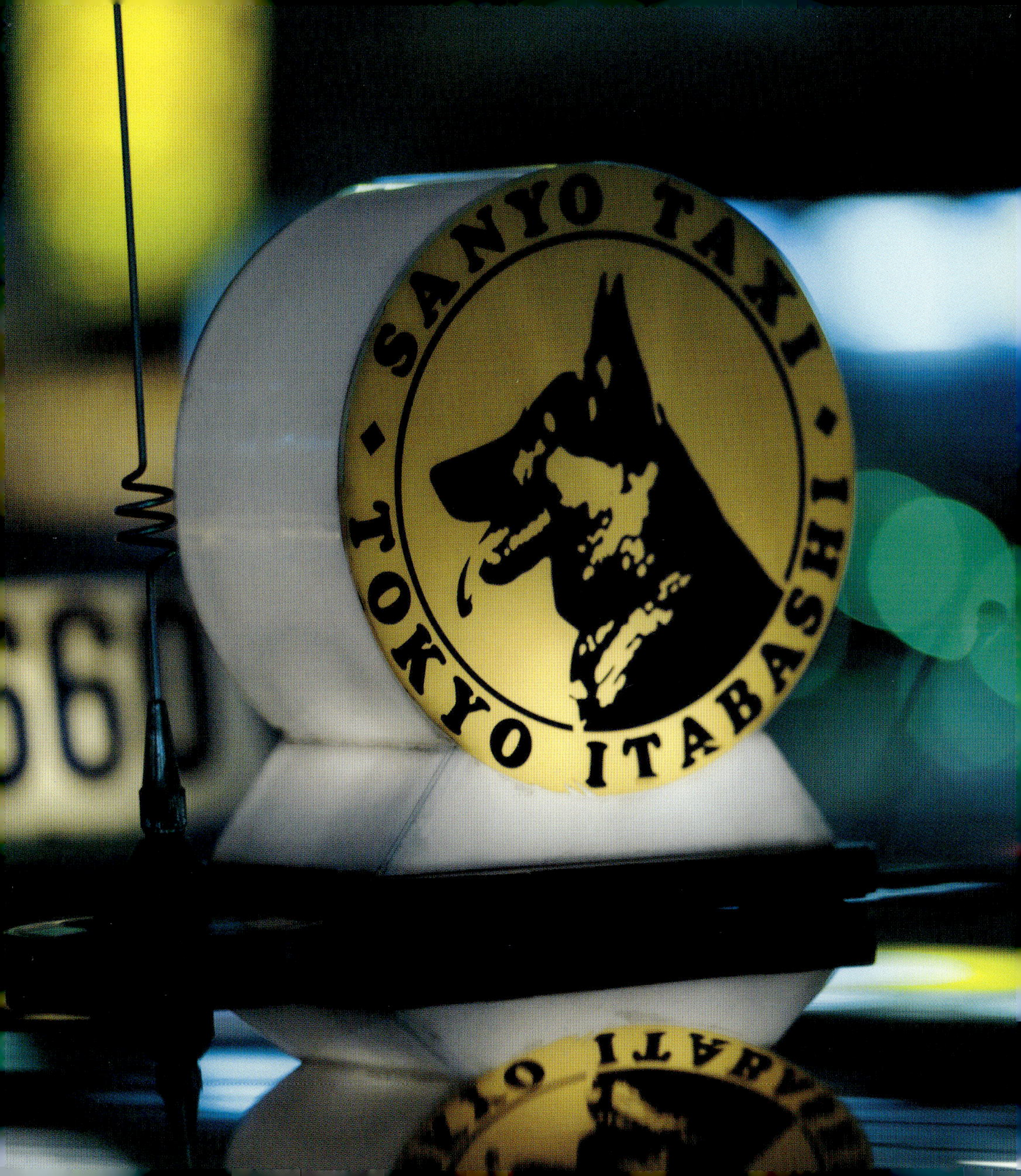
SANYO TAXI
TOKYO ITABASHI

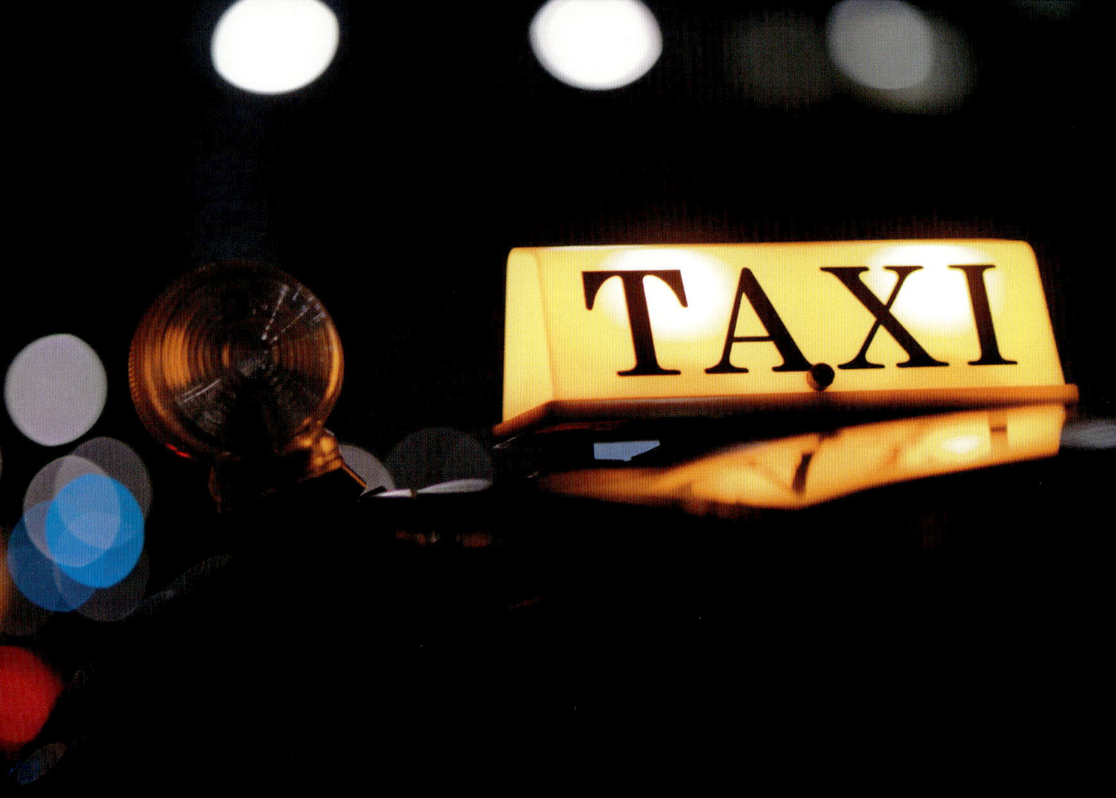

COMPANY UNKNOWN

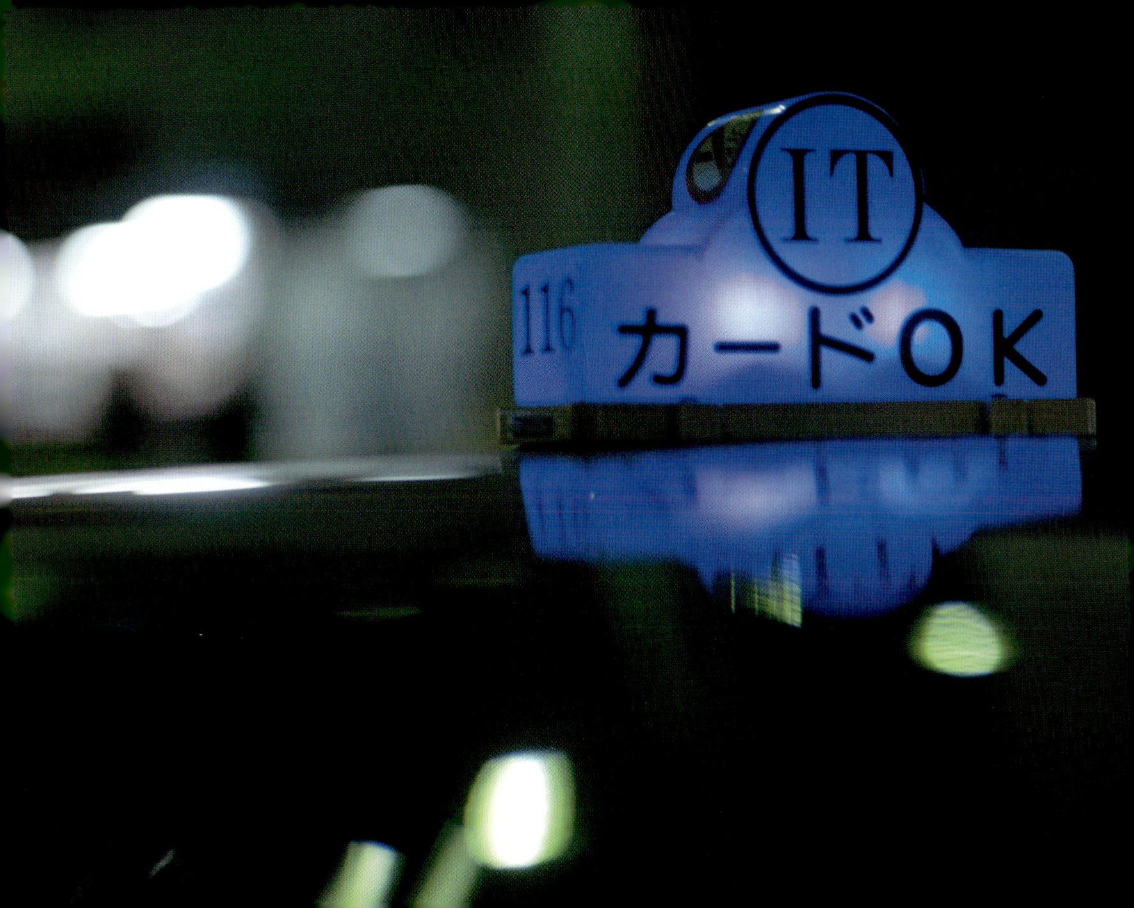
IT
116
カードOK

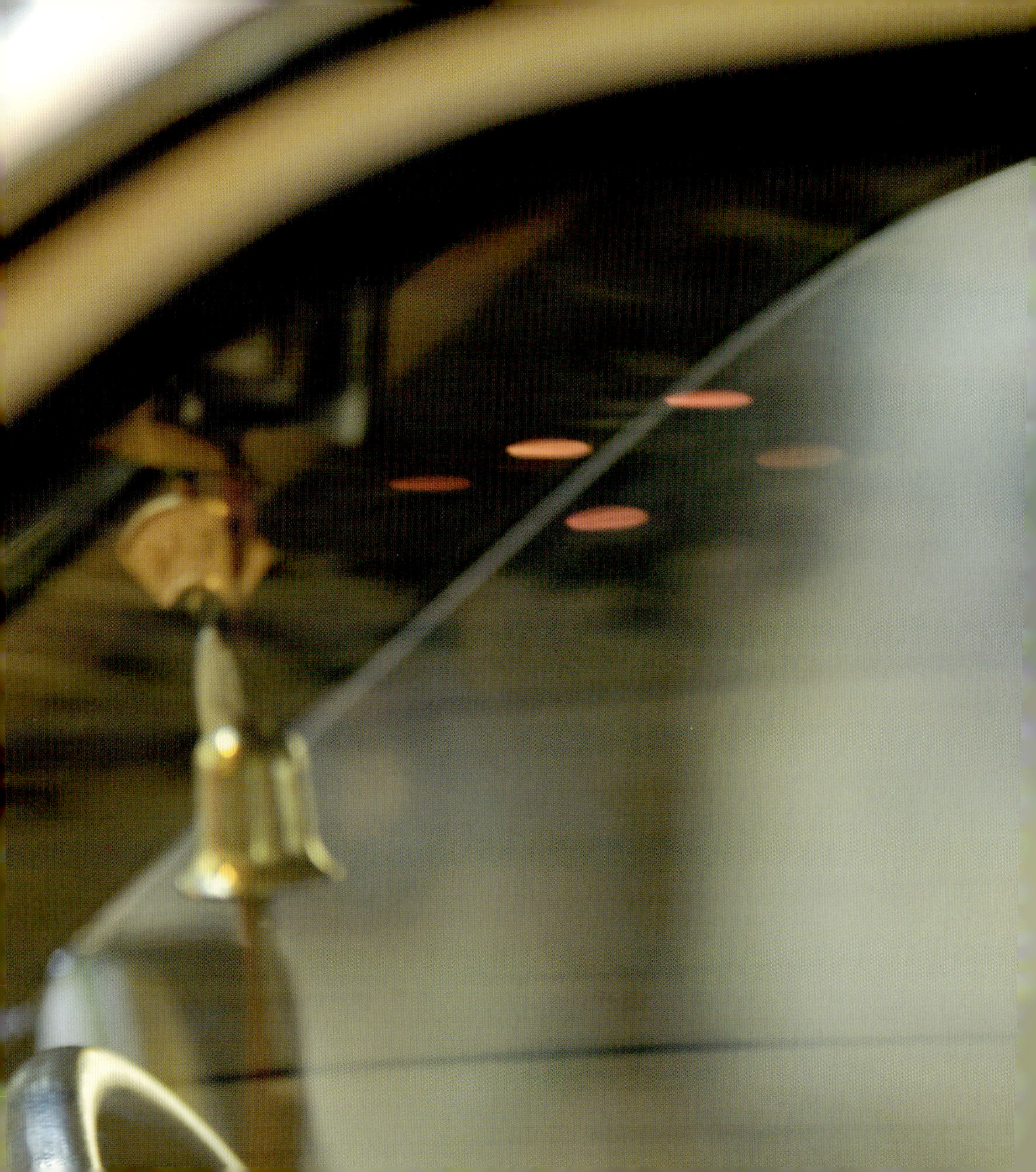

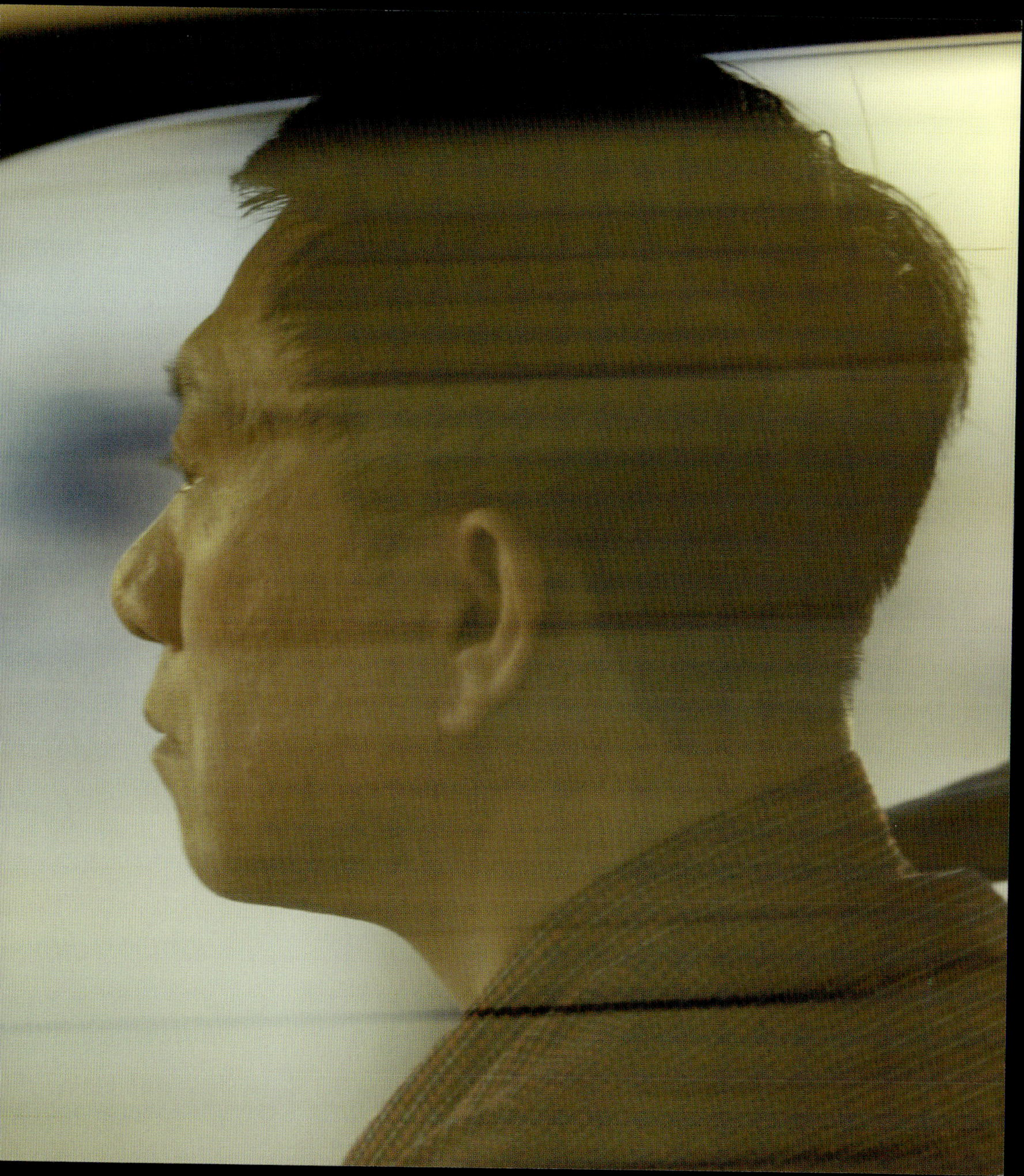

AYA TAXI CO.

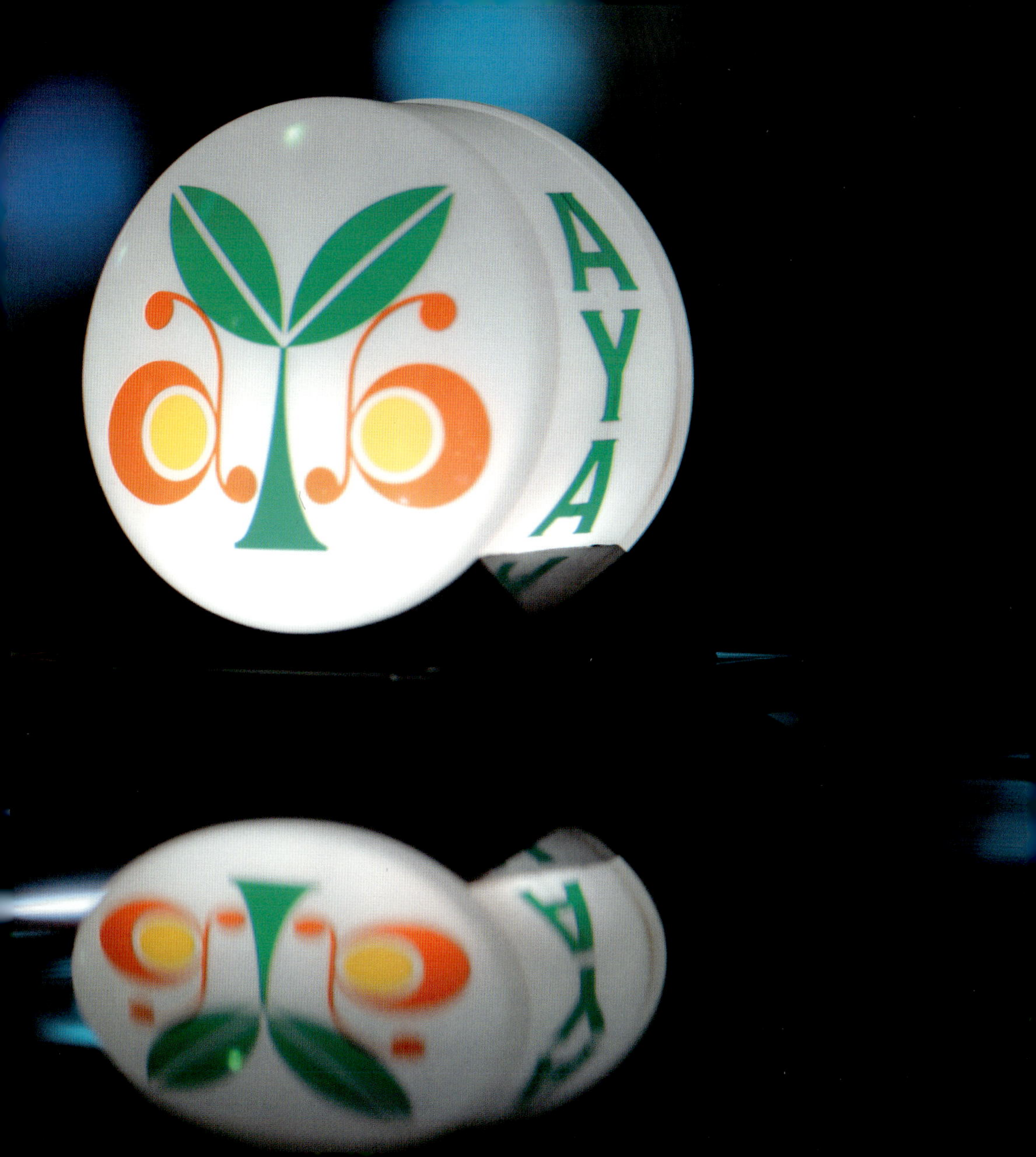
AYA

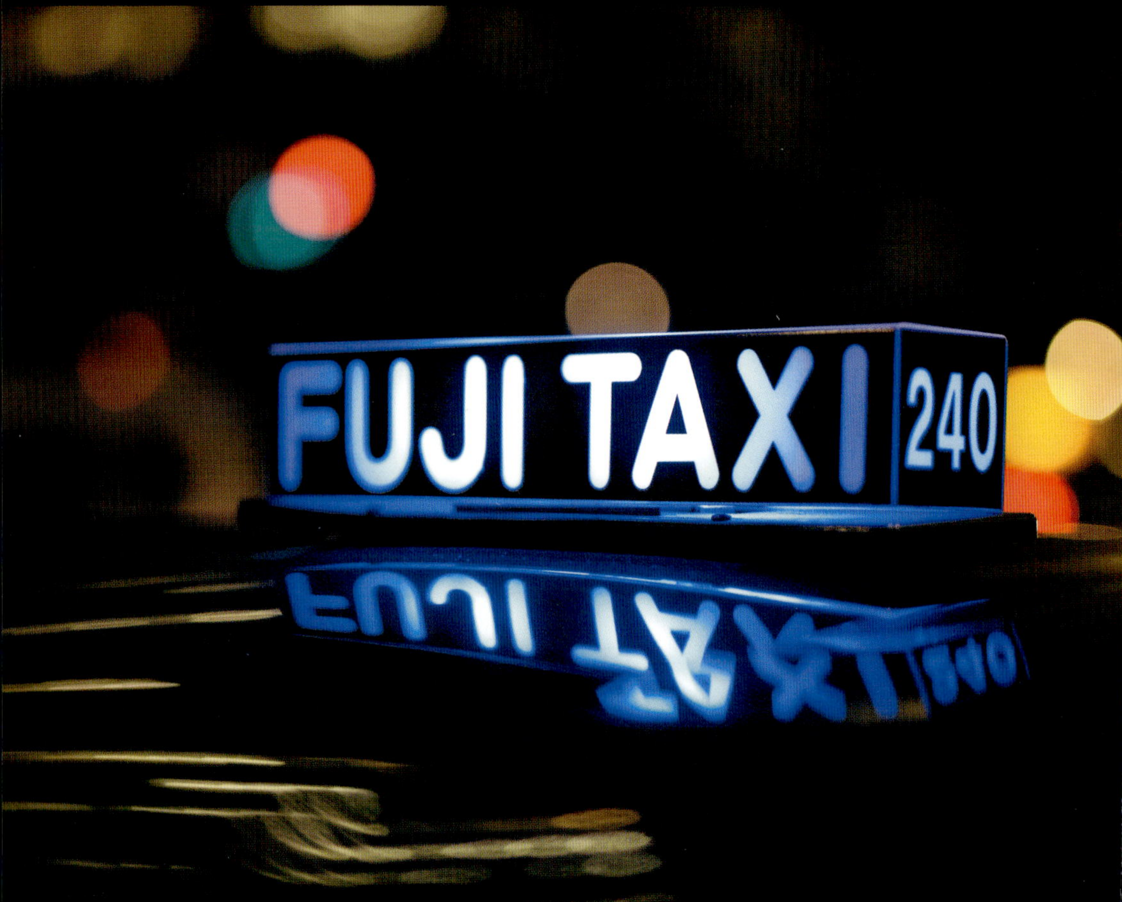
FUJI TAXI
240

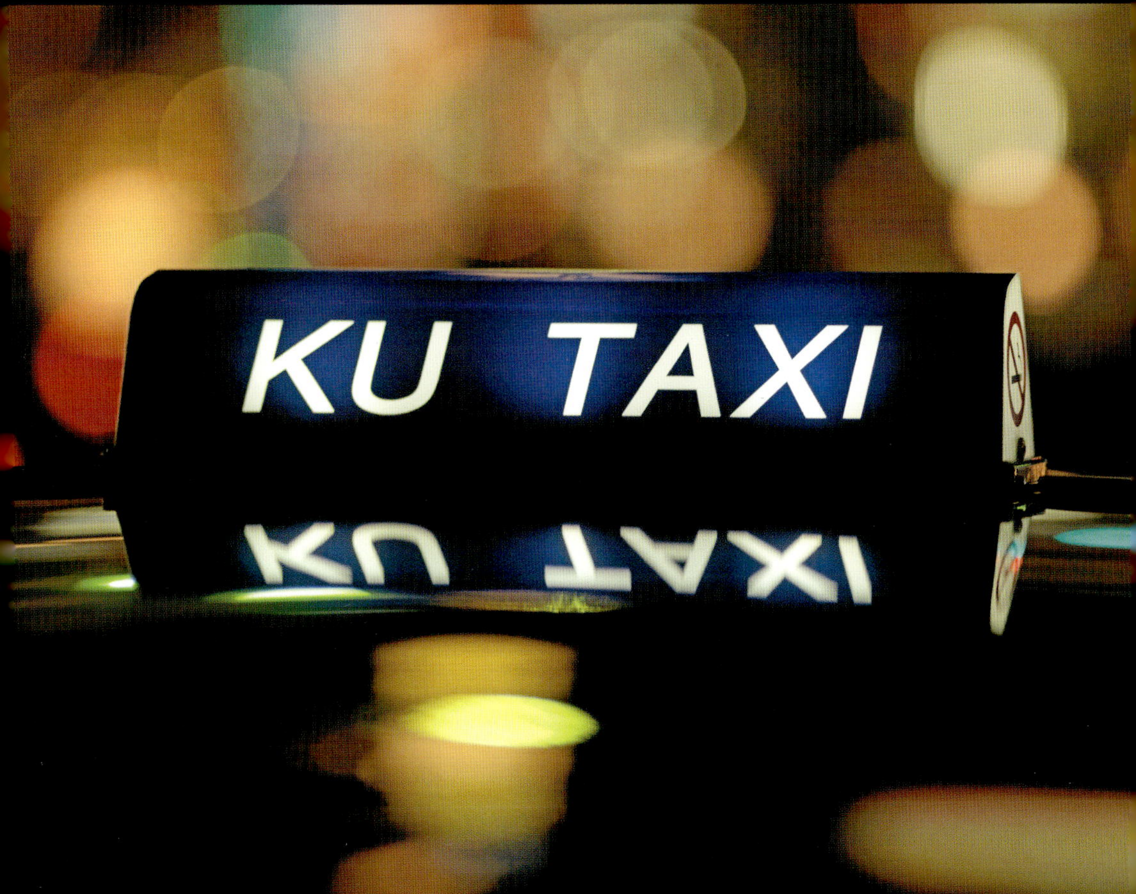

KU TAXI

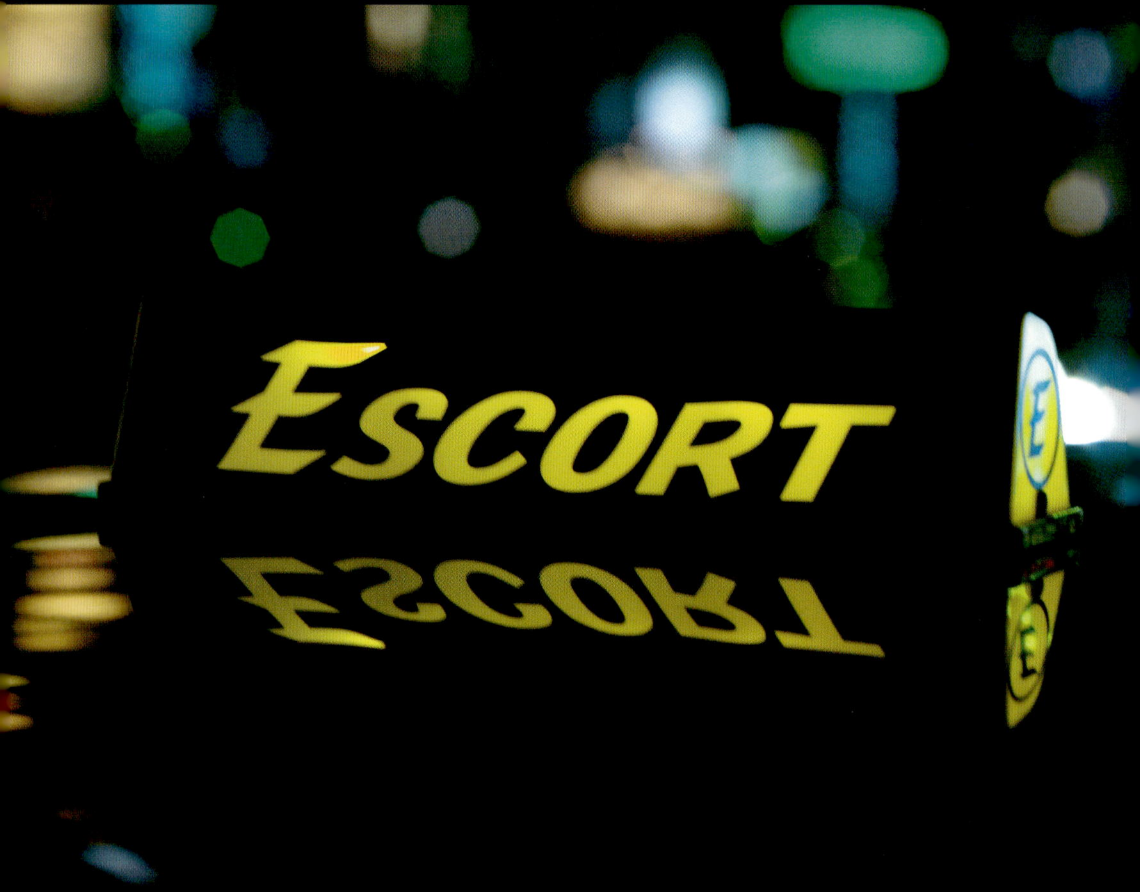

ESCORT TAXI

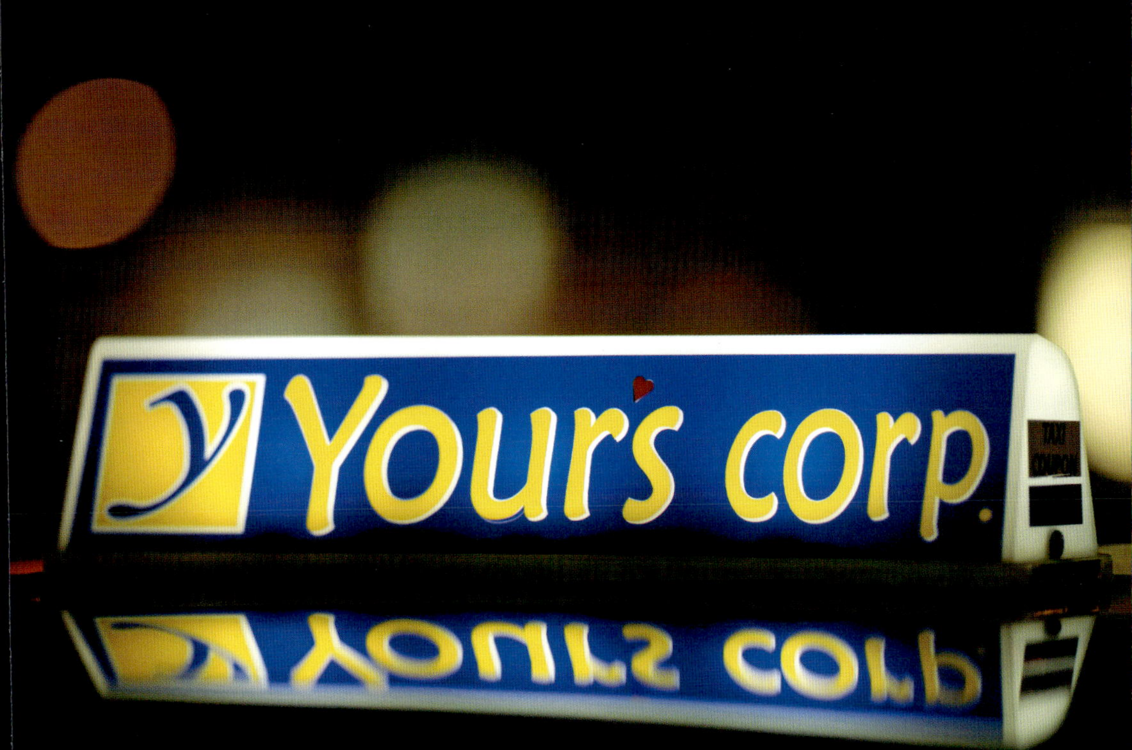
Your's corp.

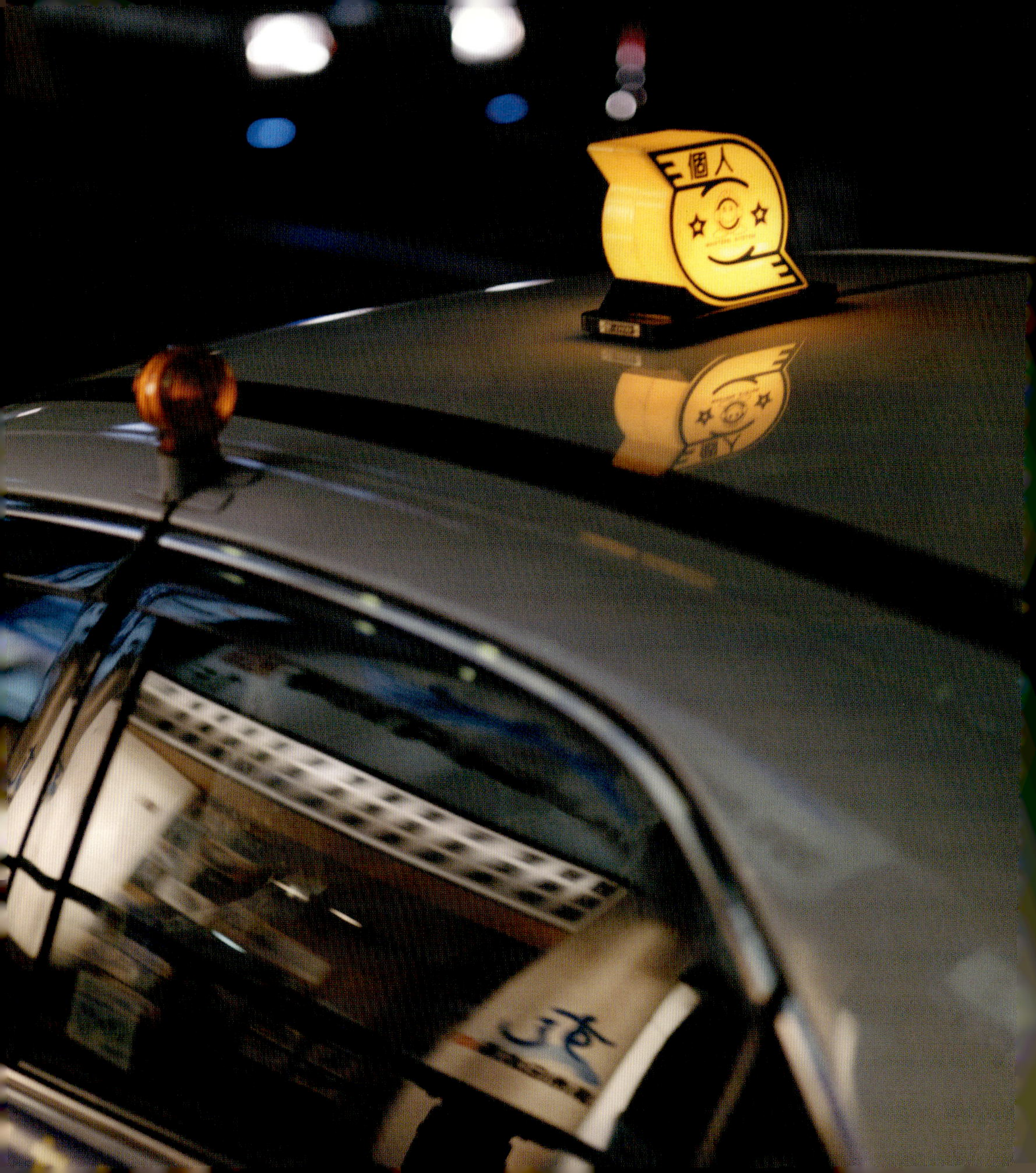
個人

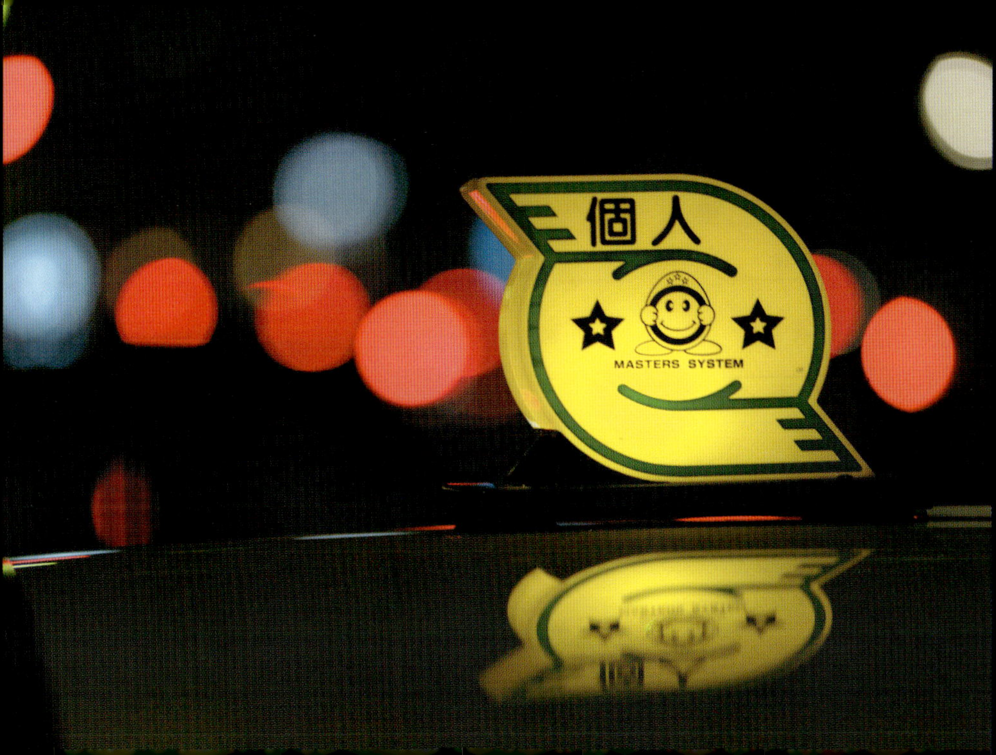
個人
MASTERS SYSTEM

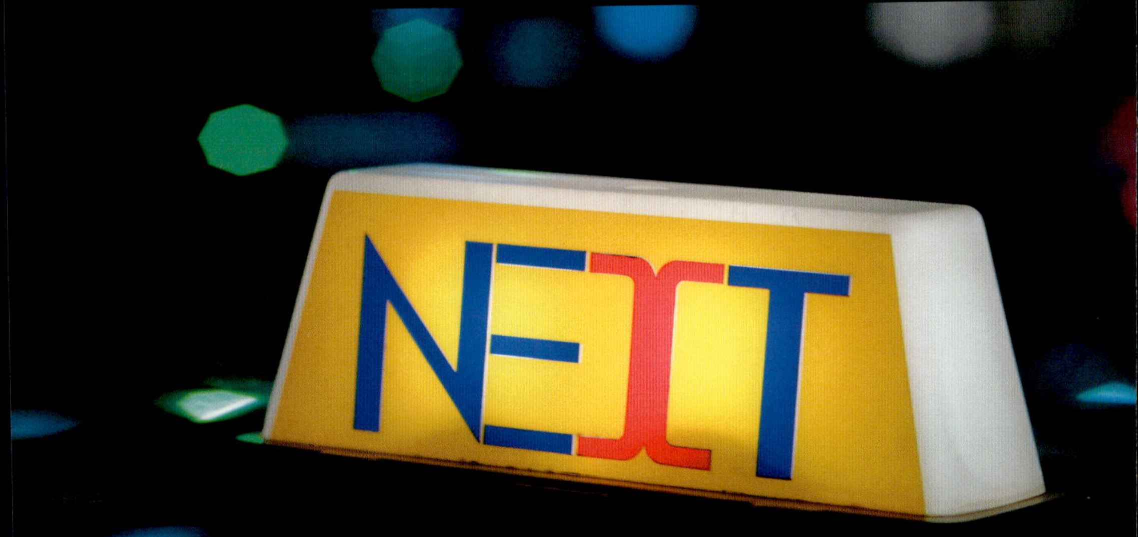
NEXT

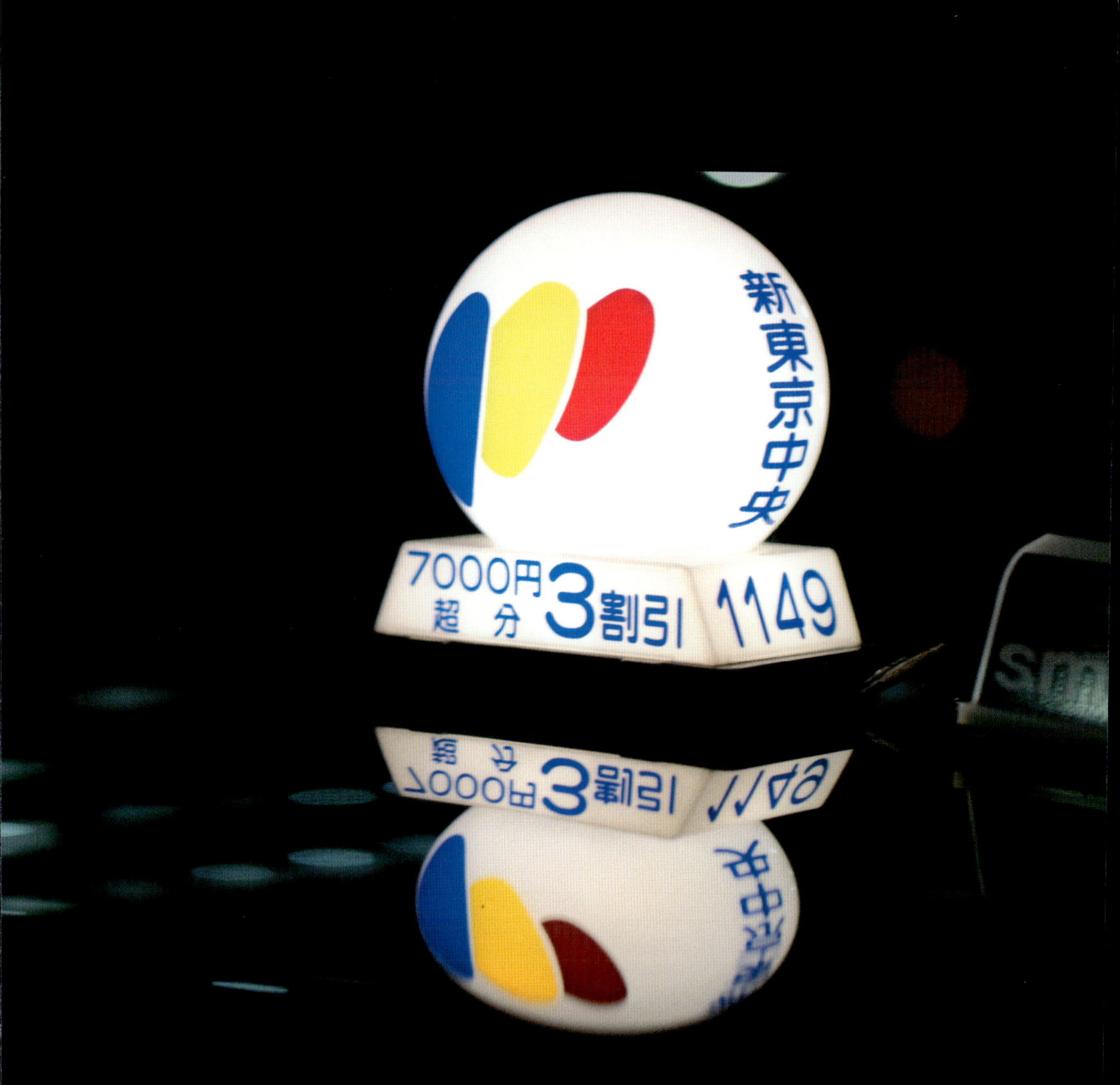

SIN TOKYO CHUO 1149

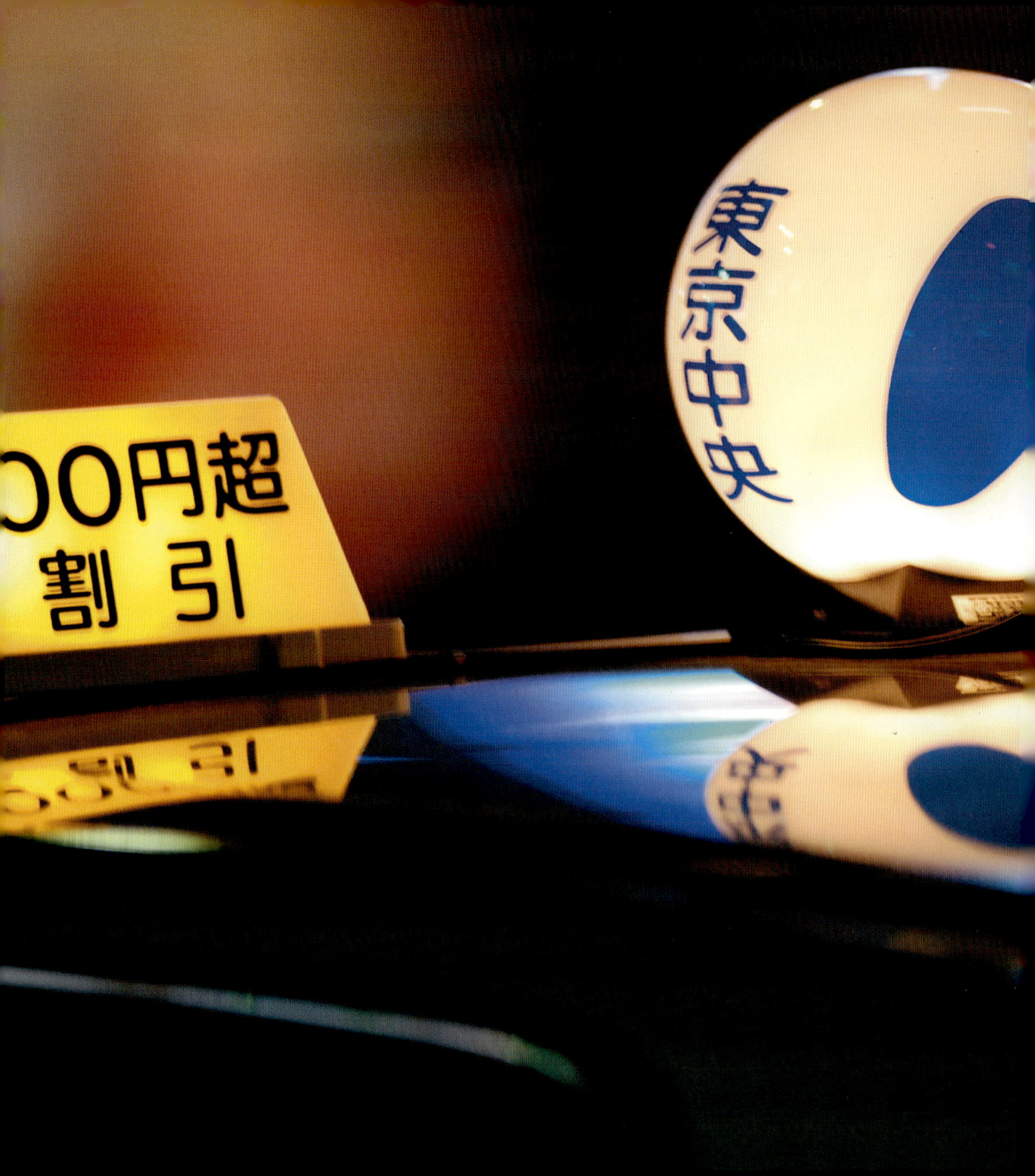
00円超
割引
東京中央

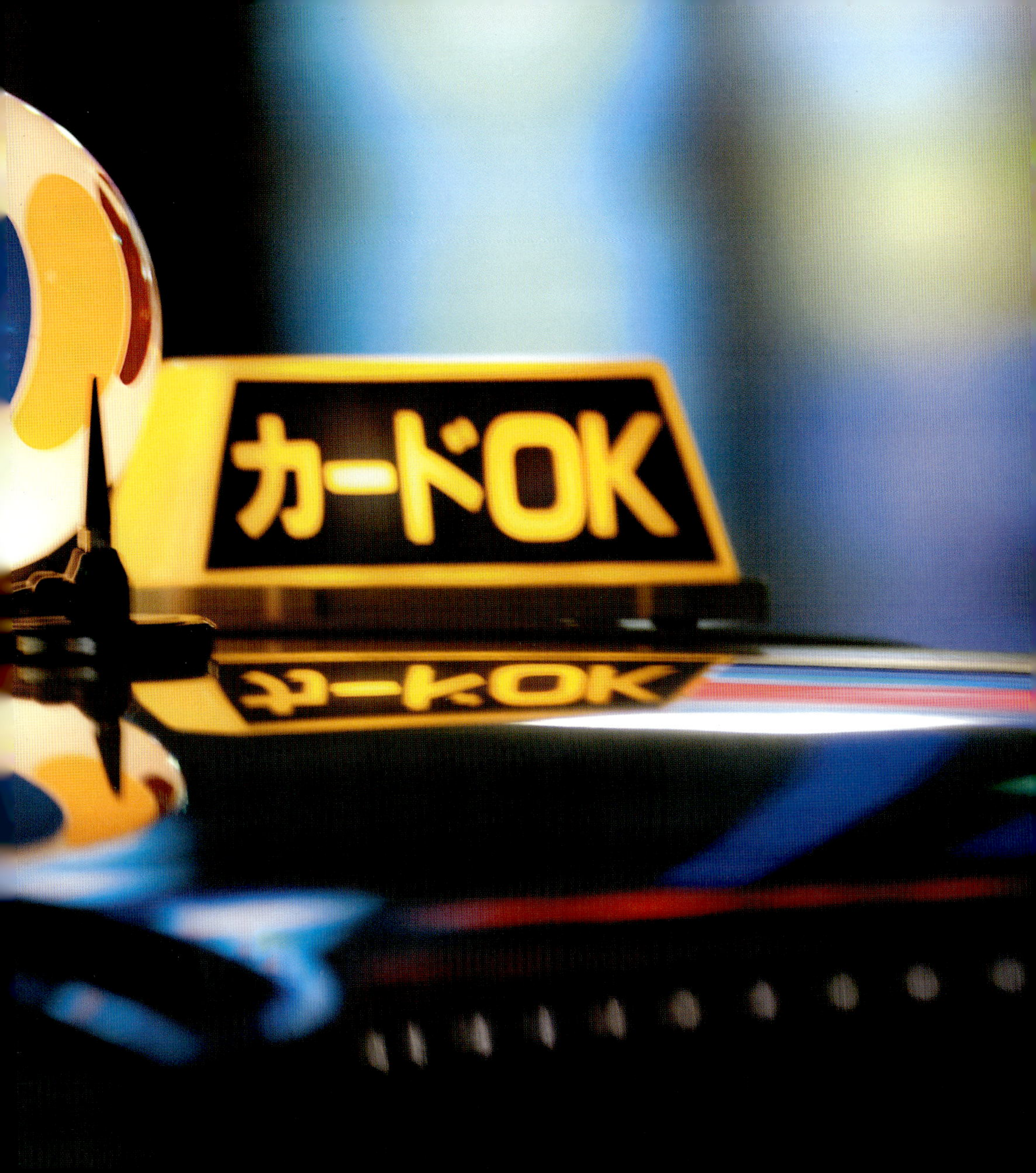
カードOK

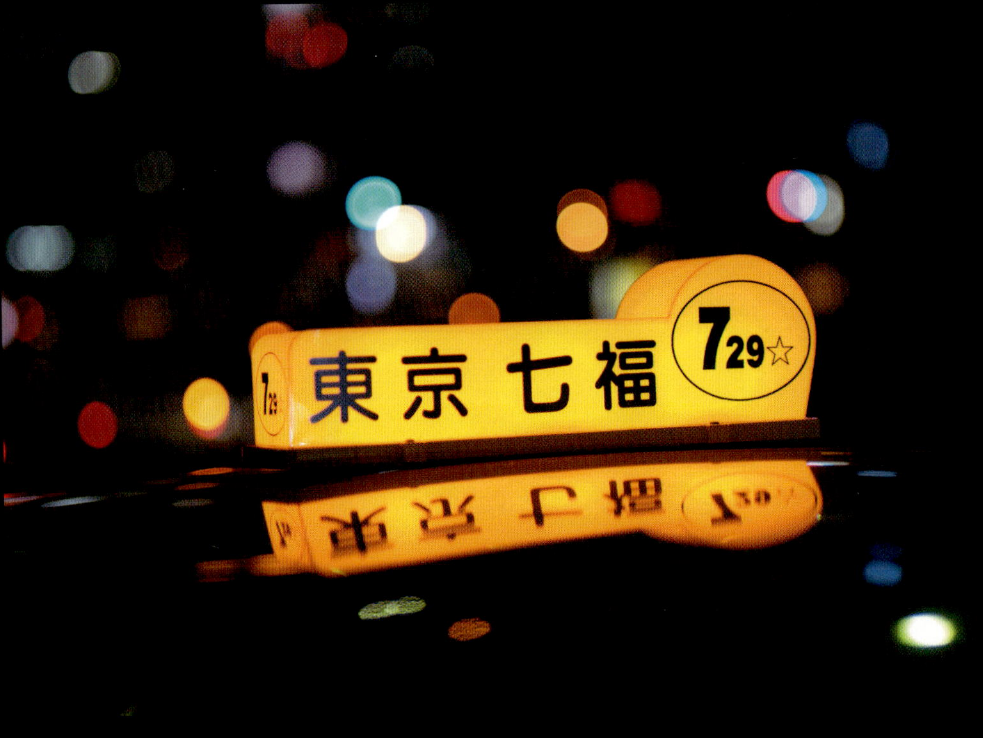

TOKYO SHICHIFUKU 729

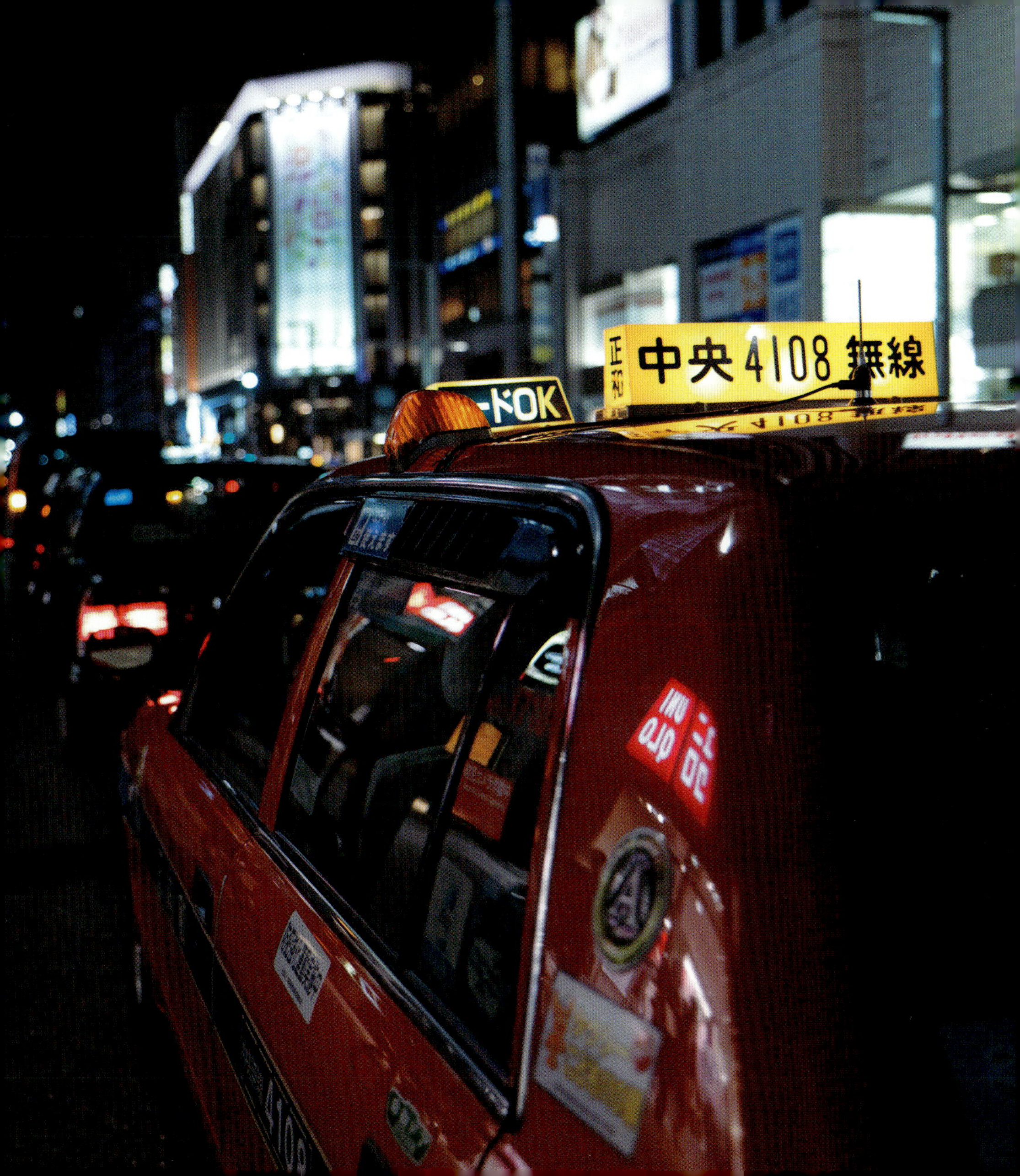
正和
中央4108 無線

HEIWA TAXI CO.

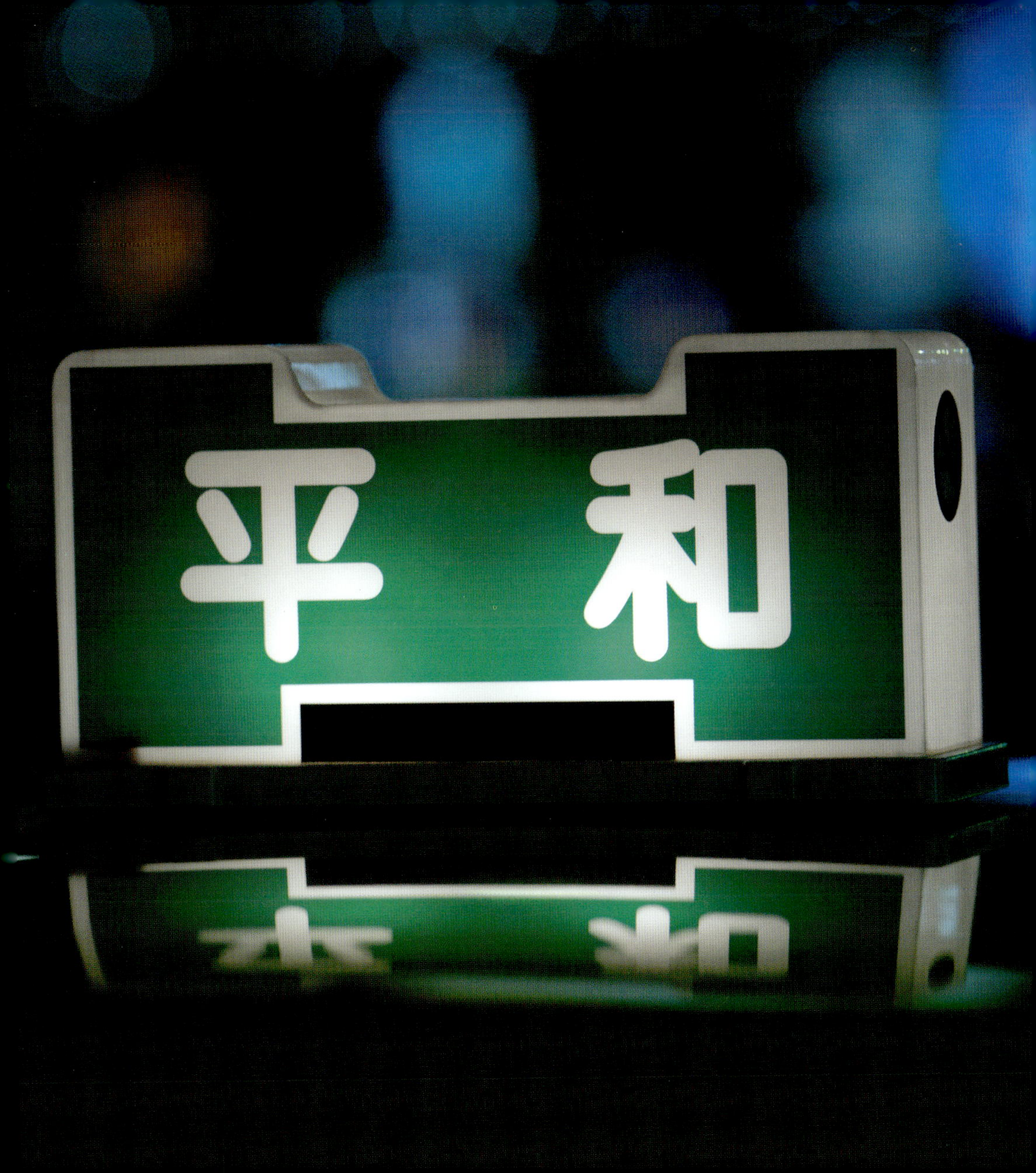
平和

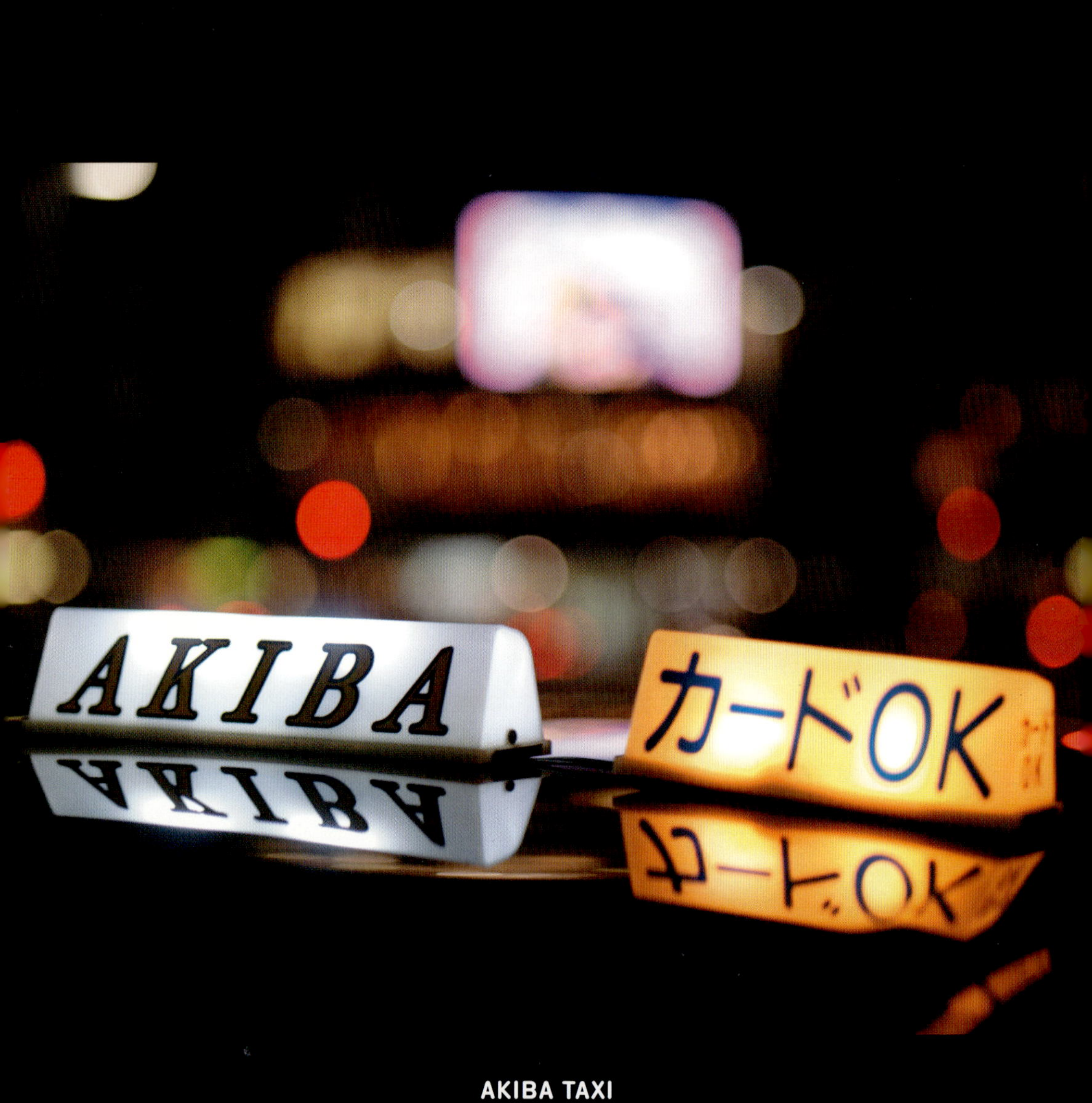

AKIBA TAXI

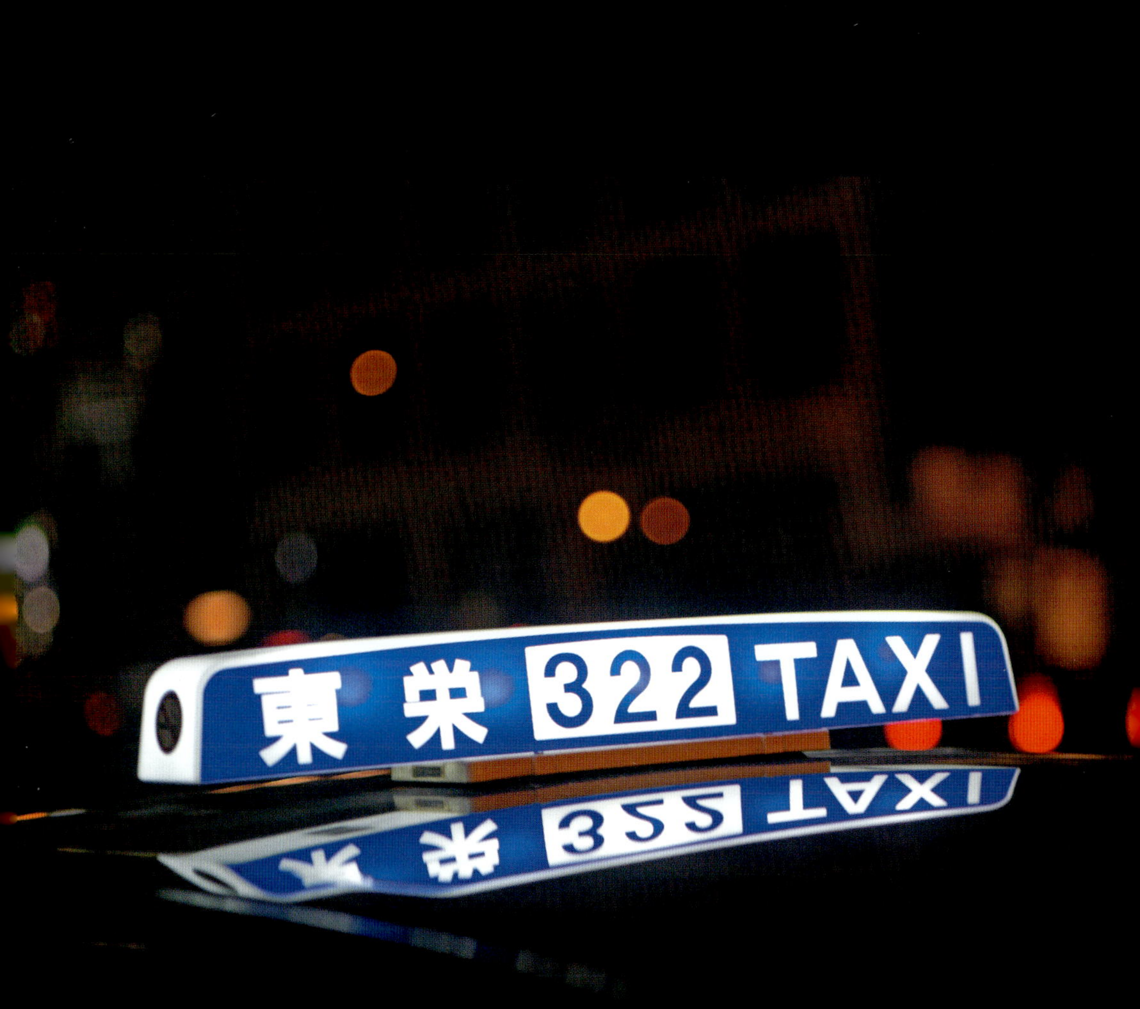

TOUEI TAXI CO. 322

MR FUJIWA

The thing I hate most is when a customer falls asleep in the back of the taxi. You must never touch a customer, so you just have to talk to them to wake them up, which can be really hard.

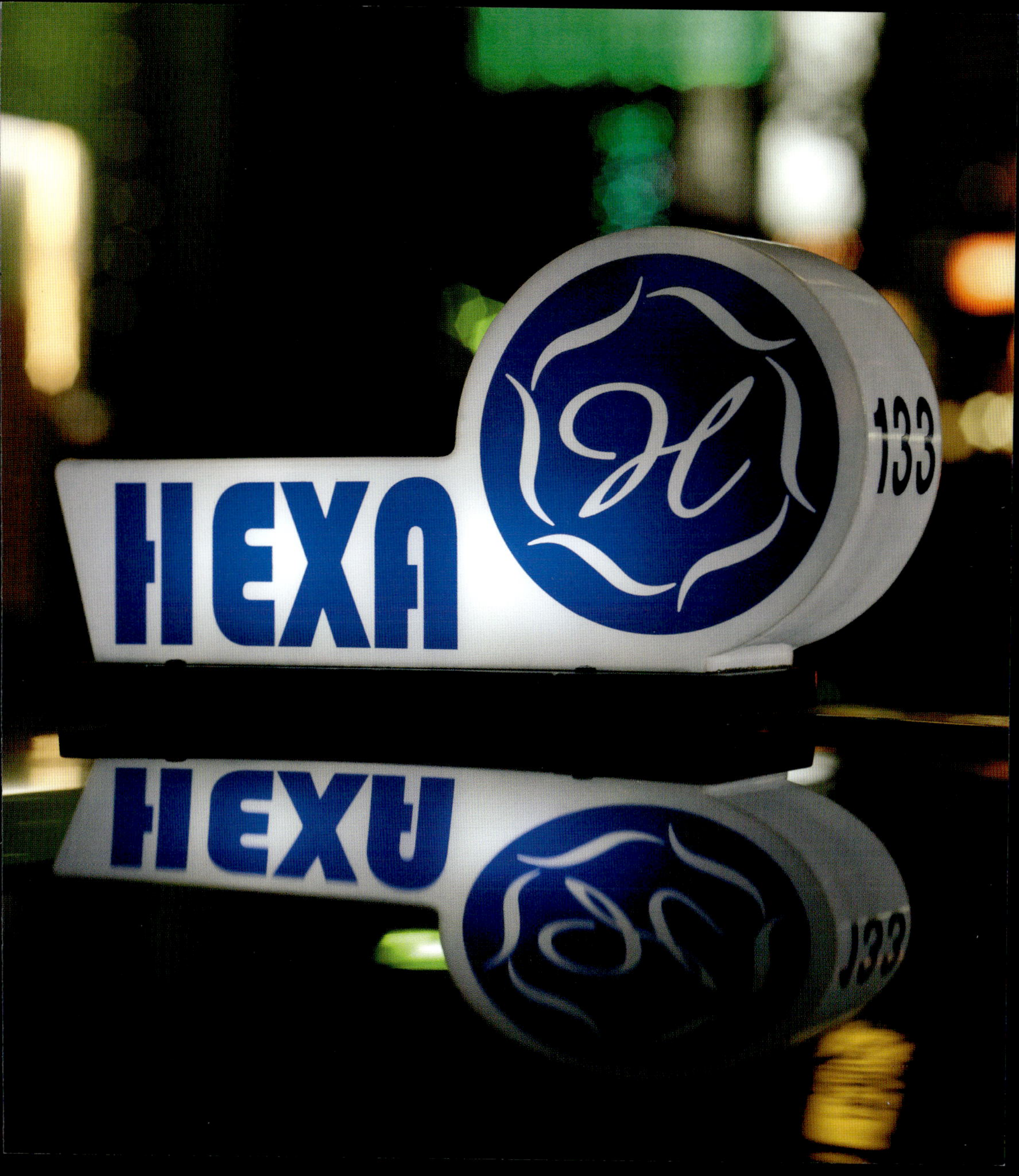
HEXA
133

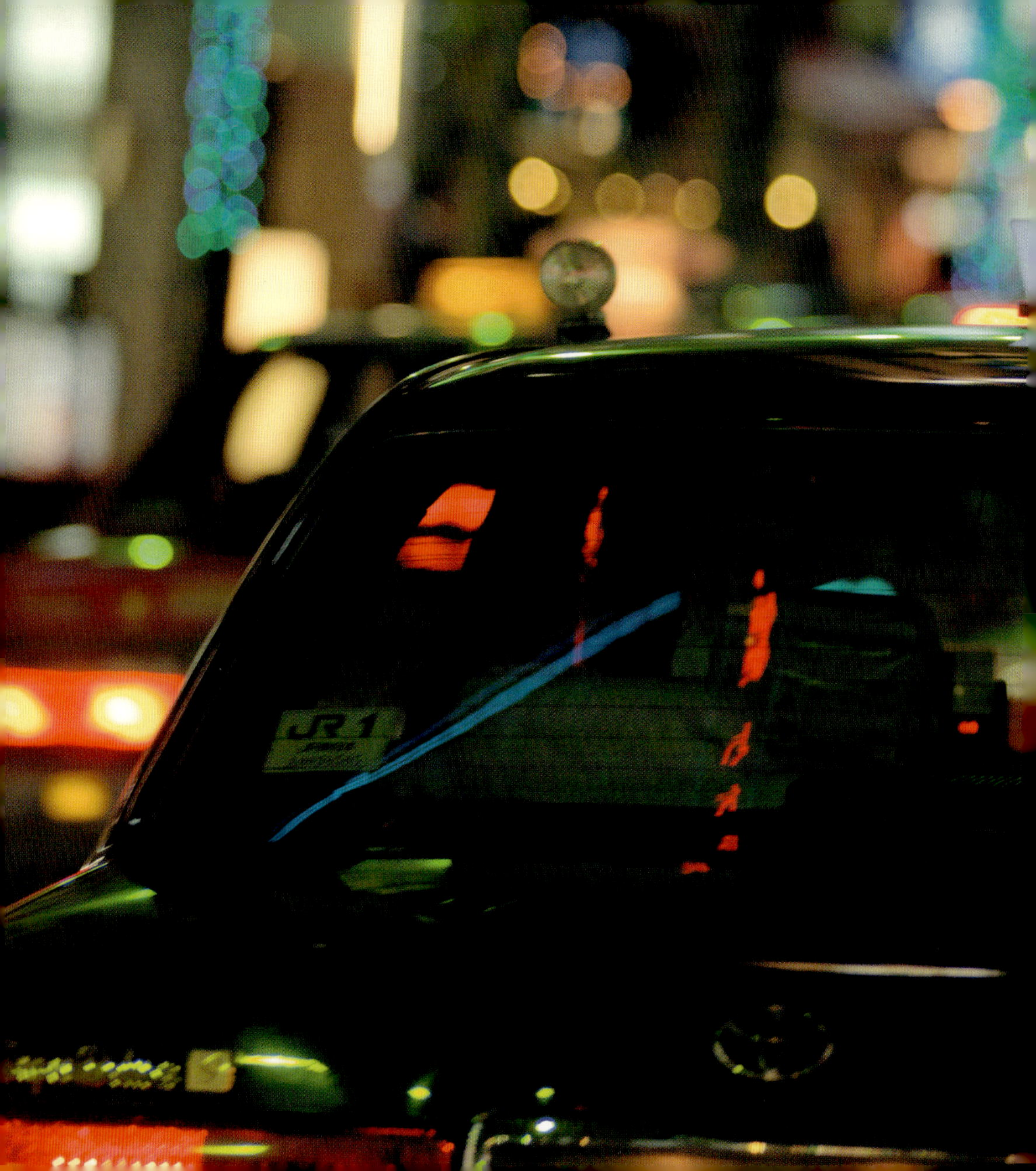
JR 1

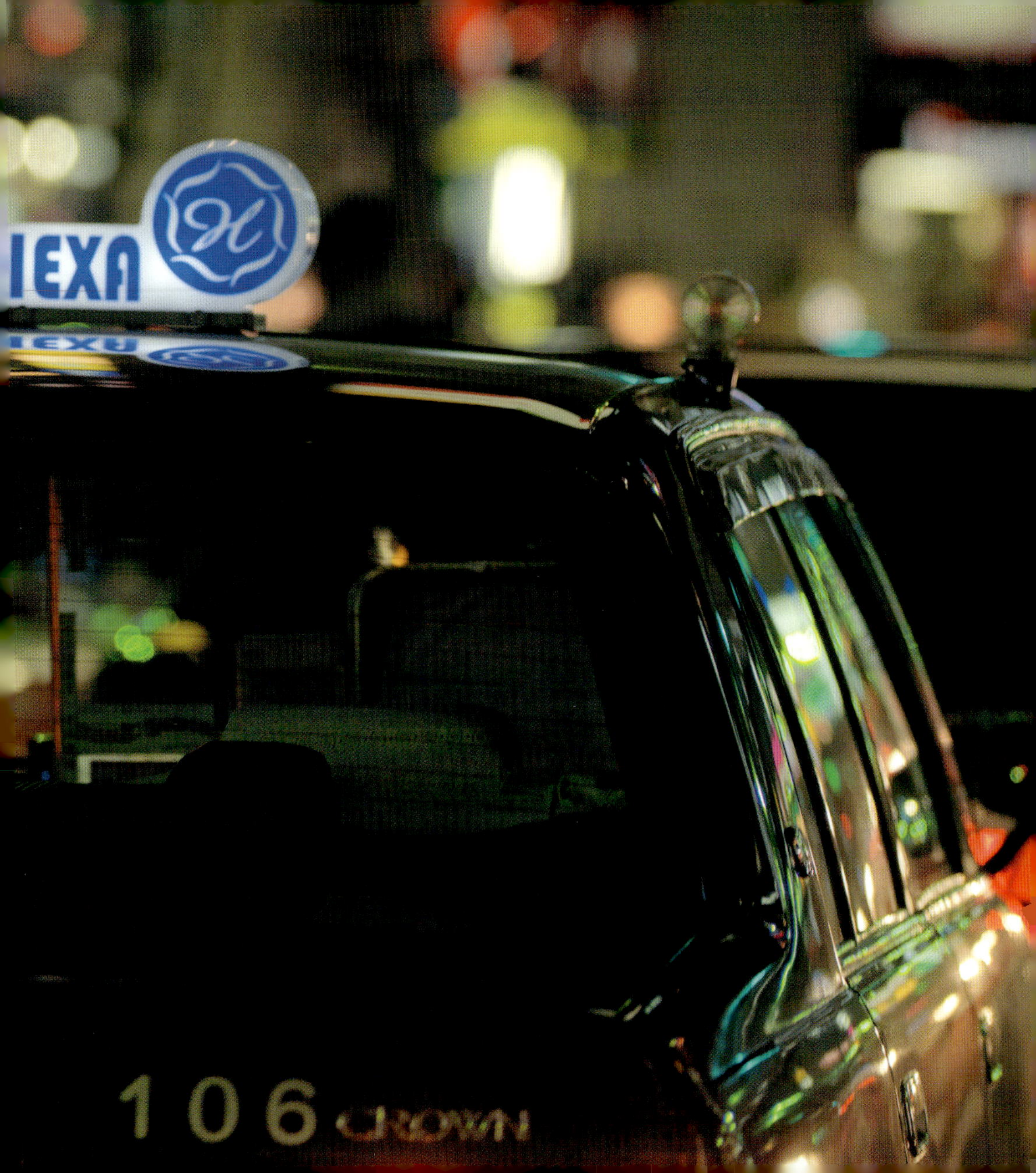
IEXA
106 CROWN

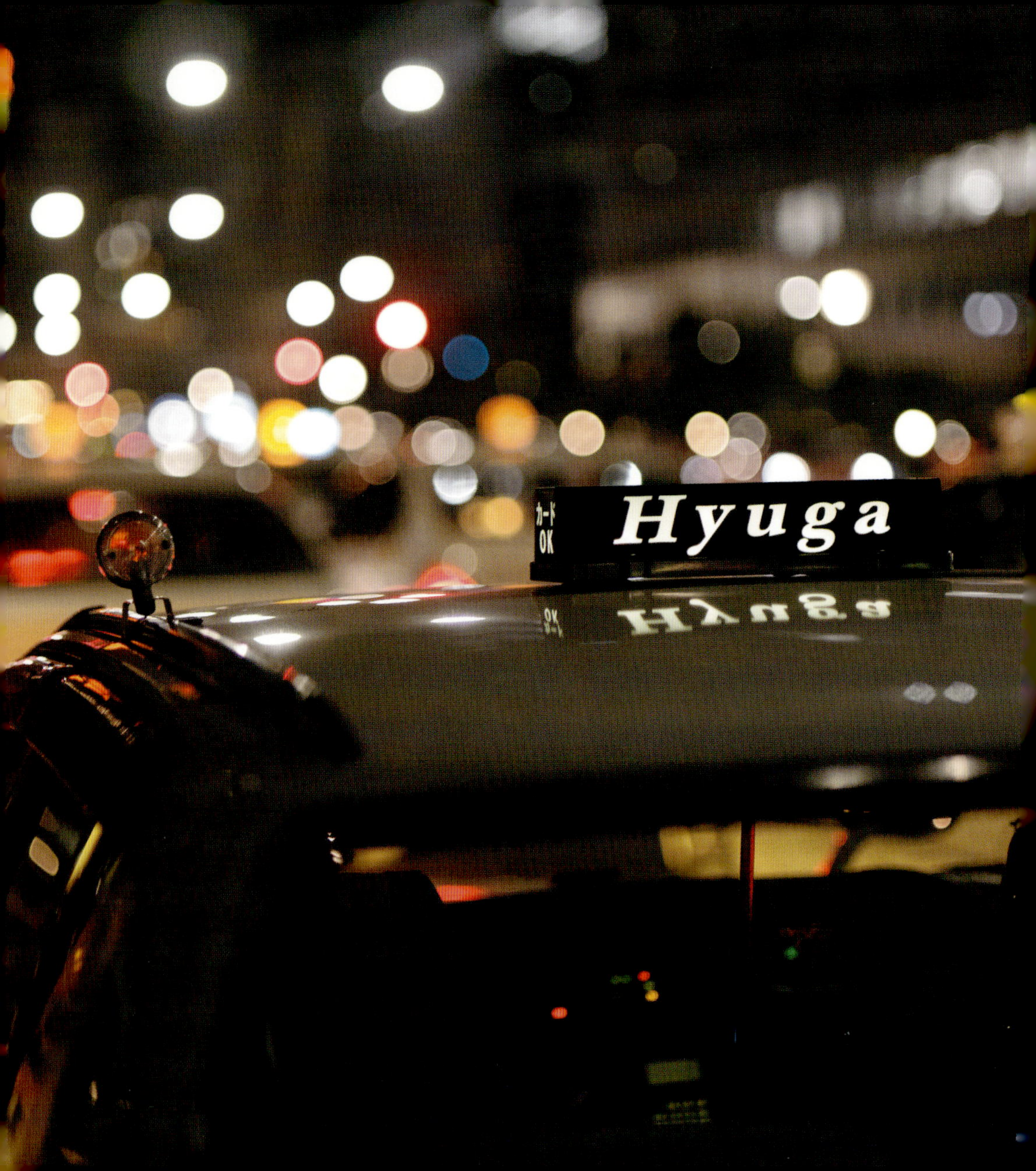
カード
OK
Hyuga

HYUGA TAXI

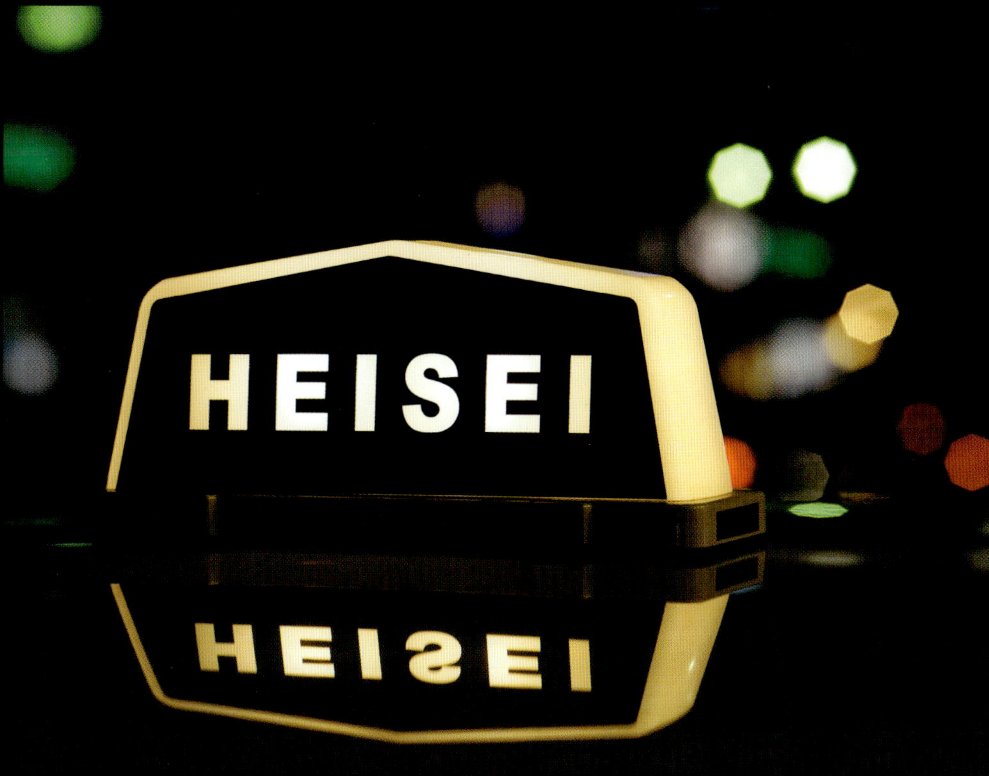

HEISEI TAXI

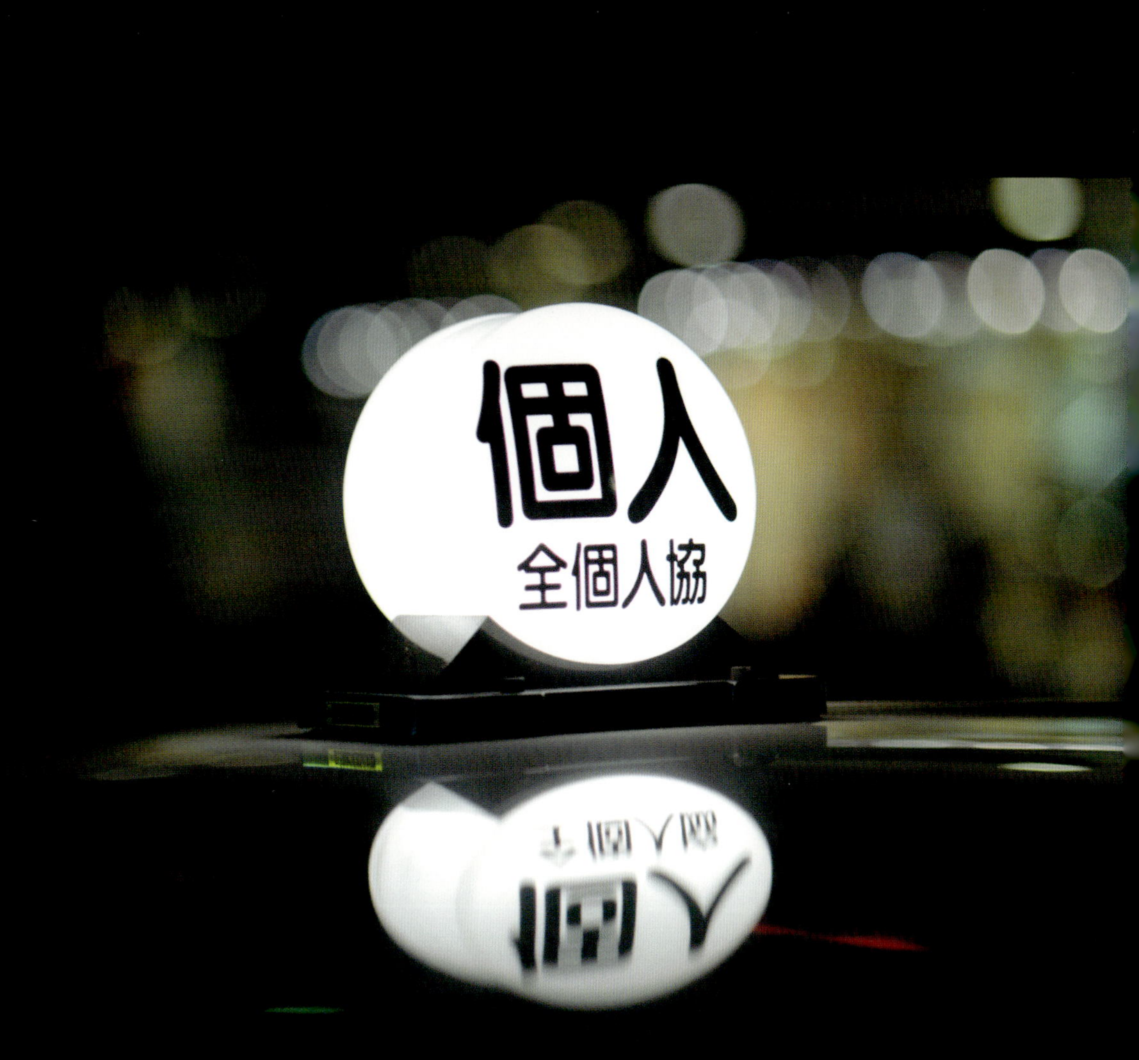

KOJIN TAXI

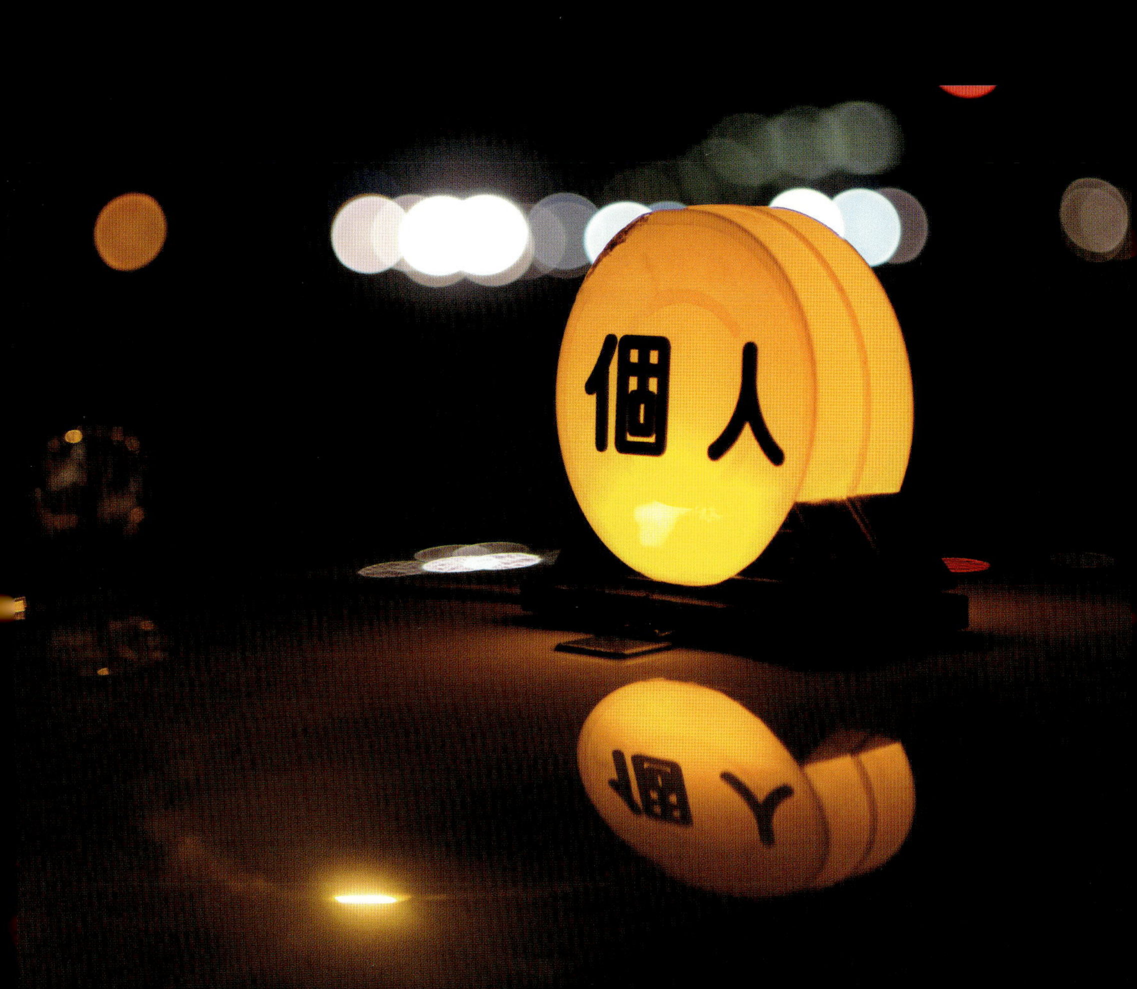

KOJIN TAXI

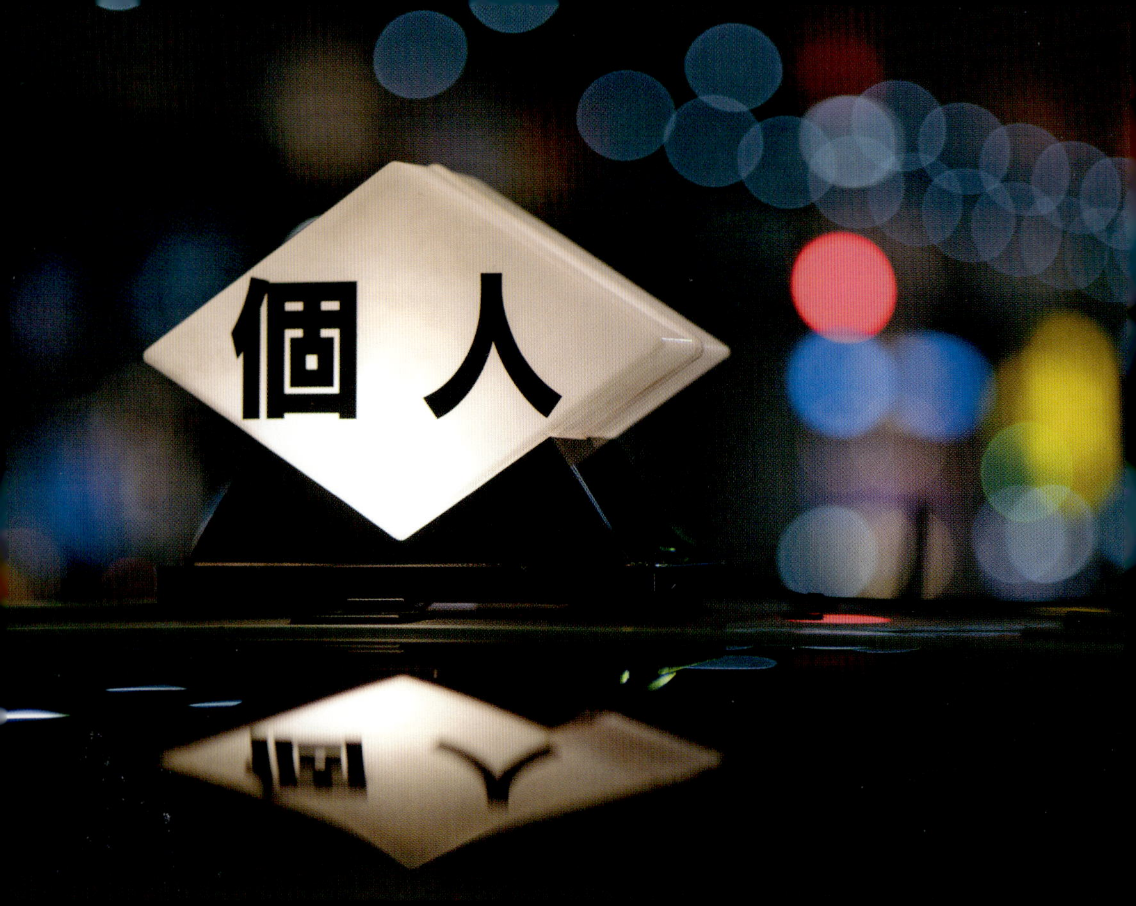
個人

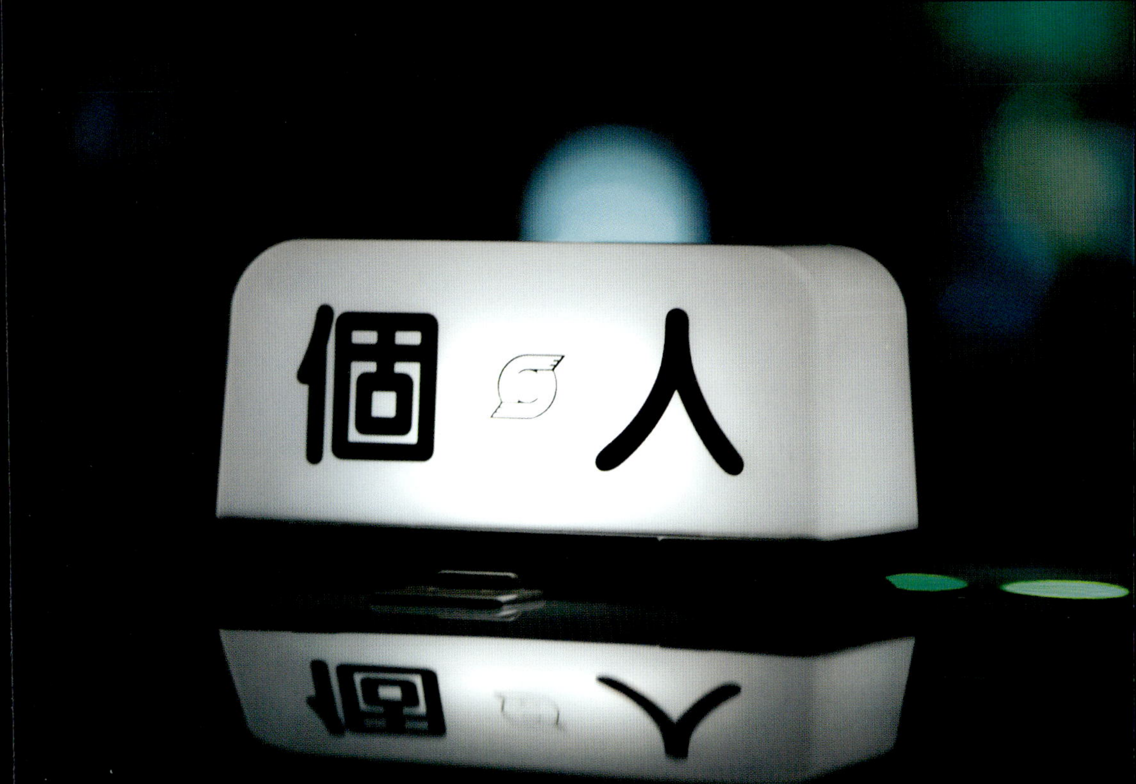
個人

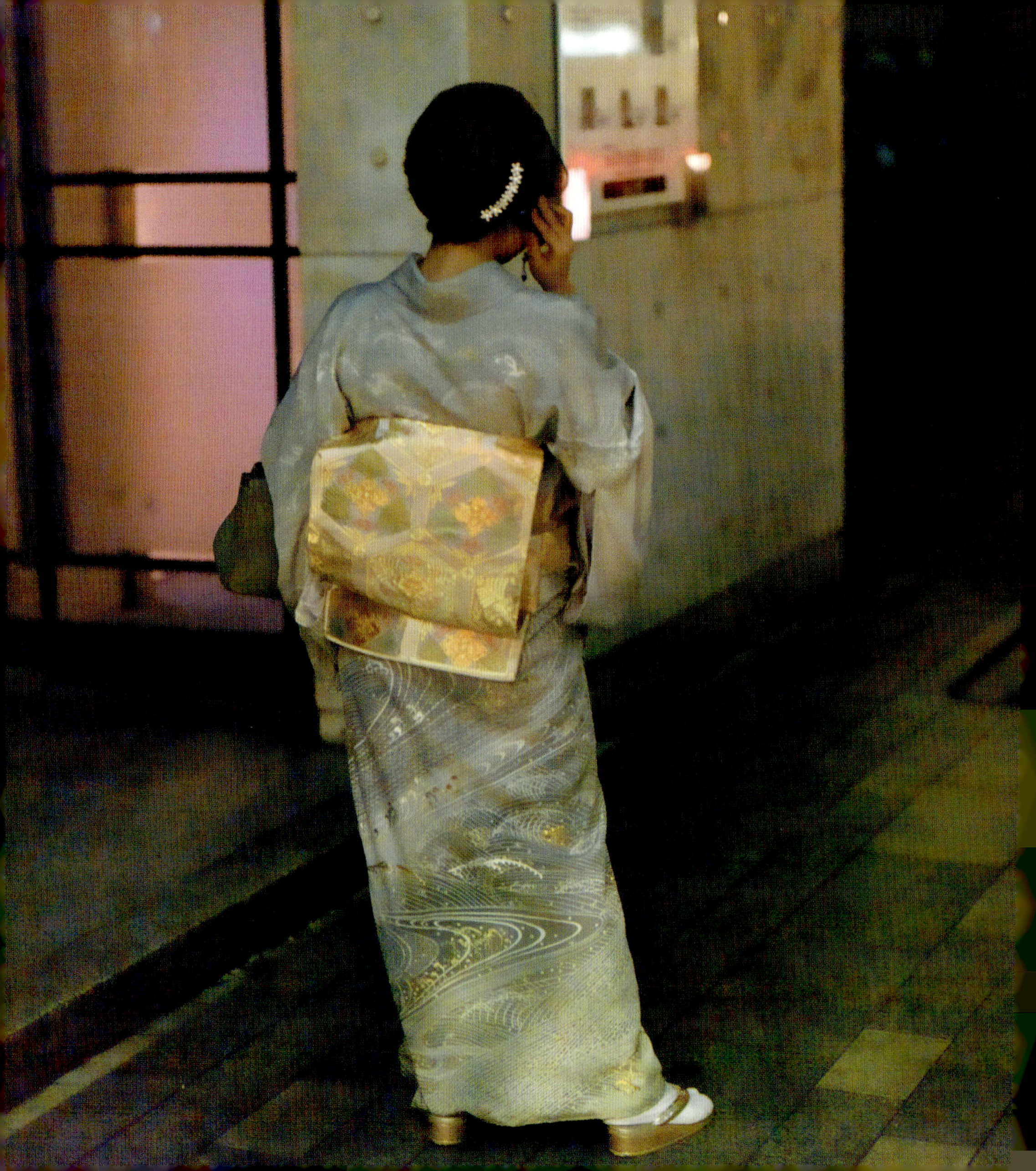

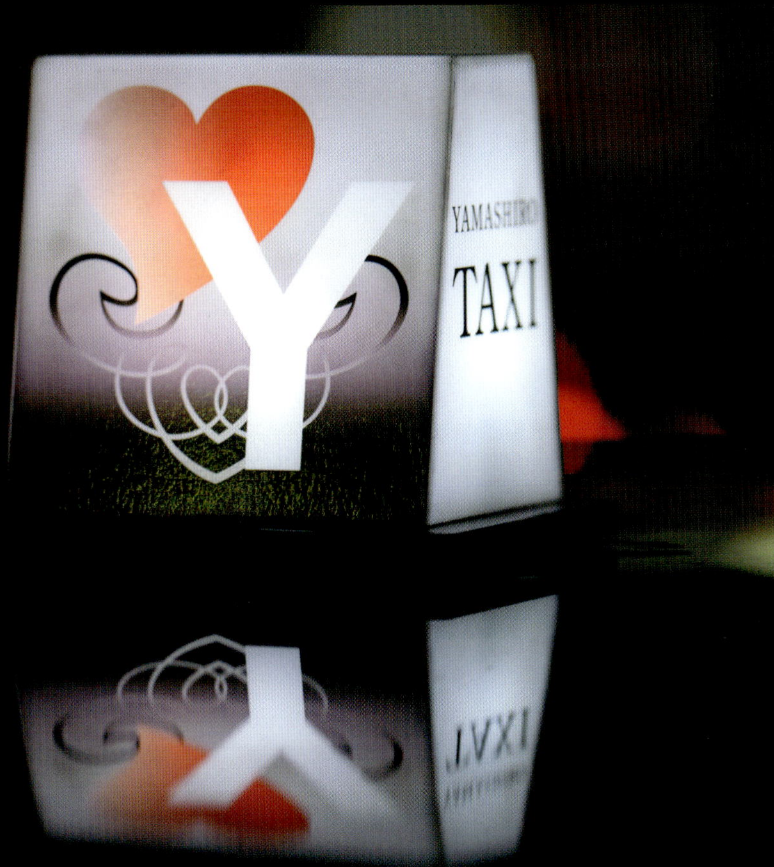

YAMASHIRO TAXI CO.

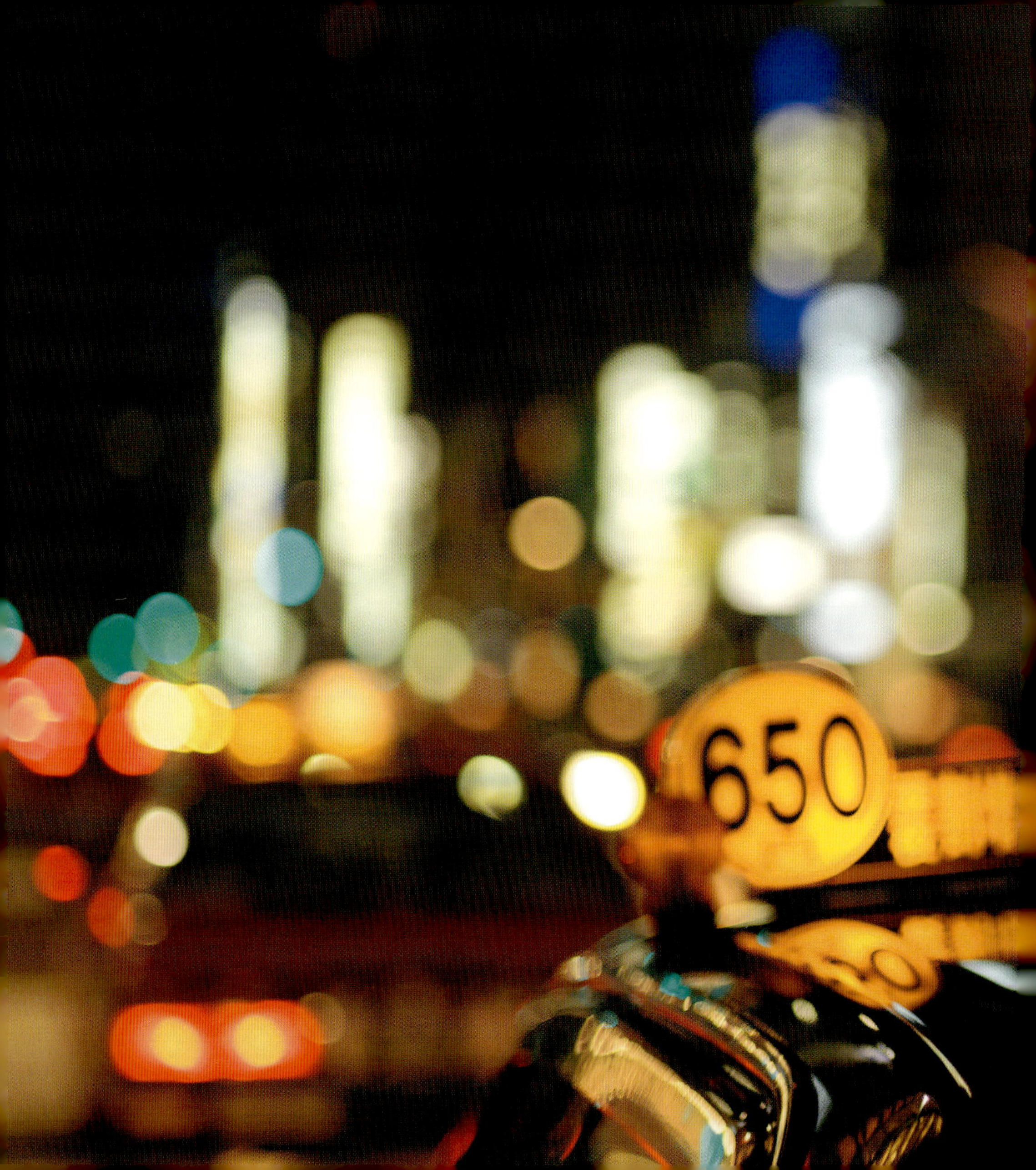
650

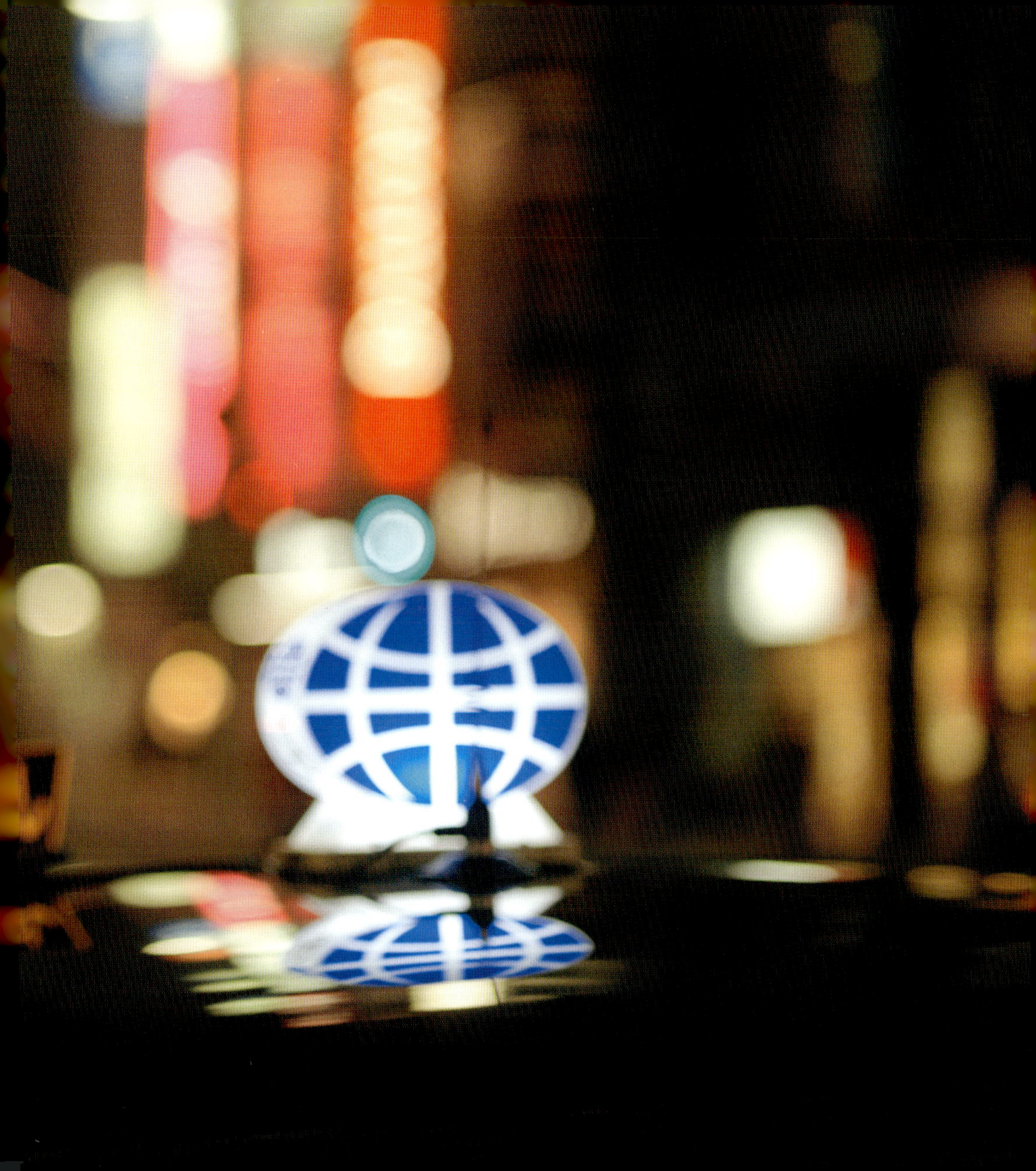

FUKUROU TAXI CO.

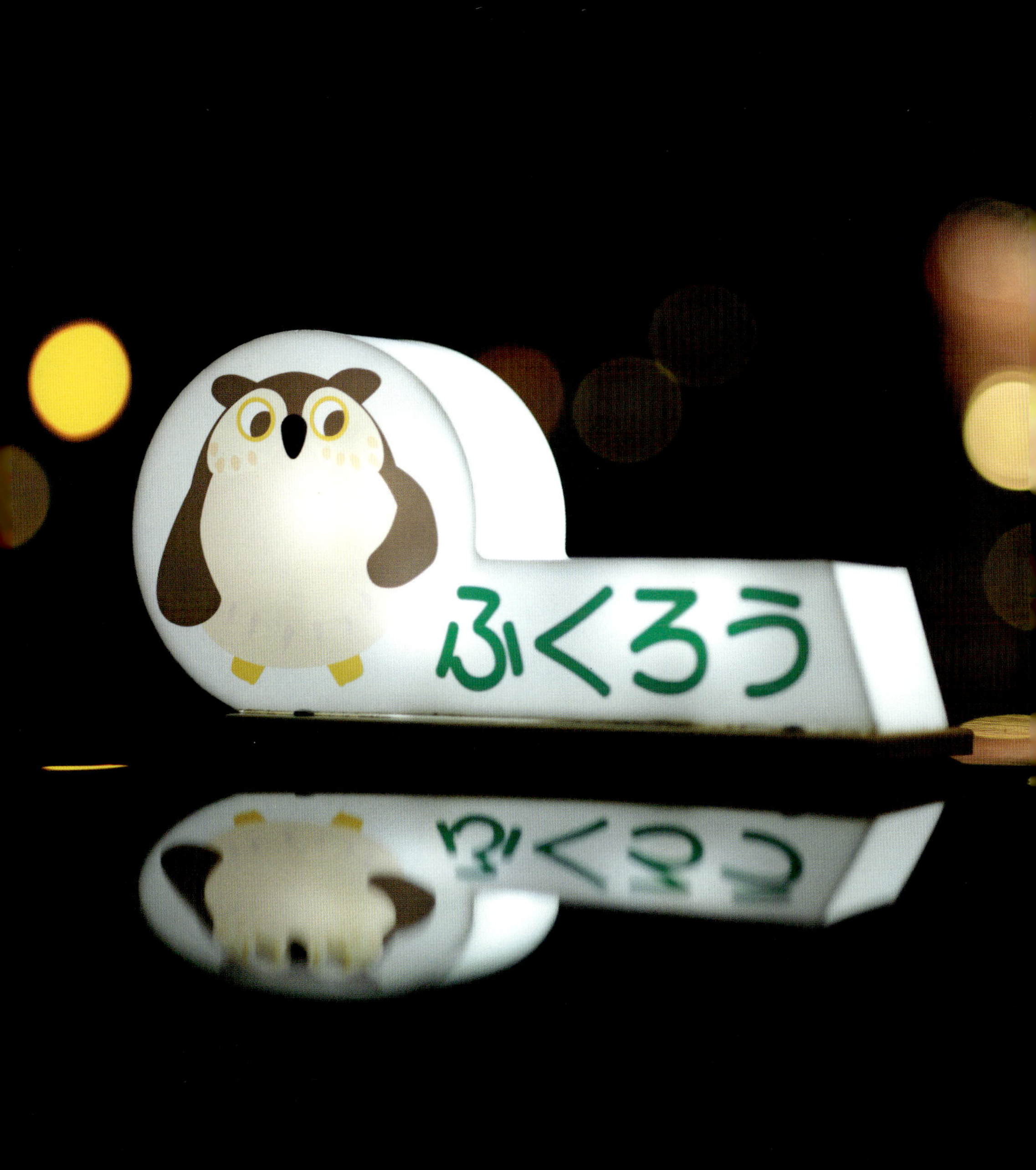
ふくろう

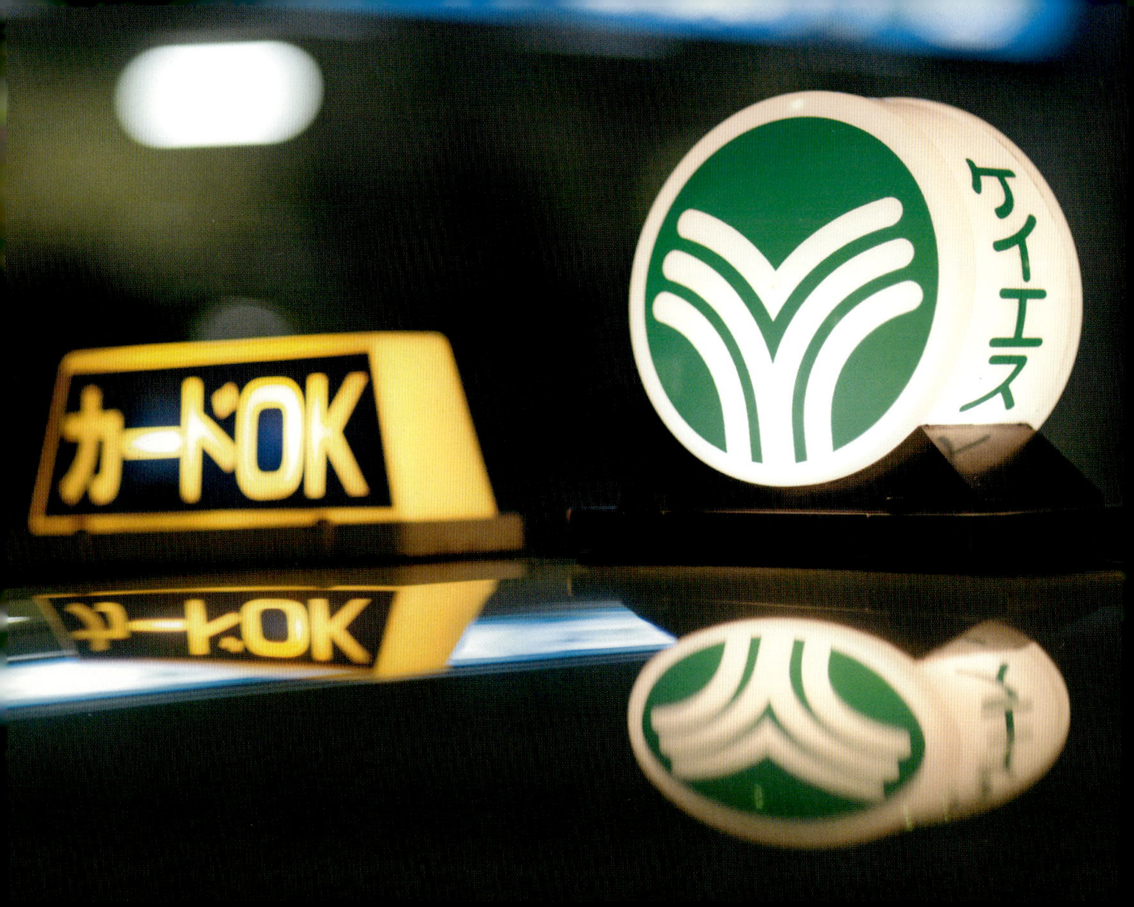
カードOK
ケイエス

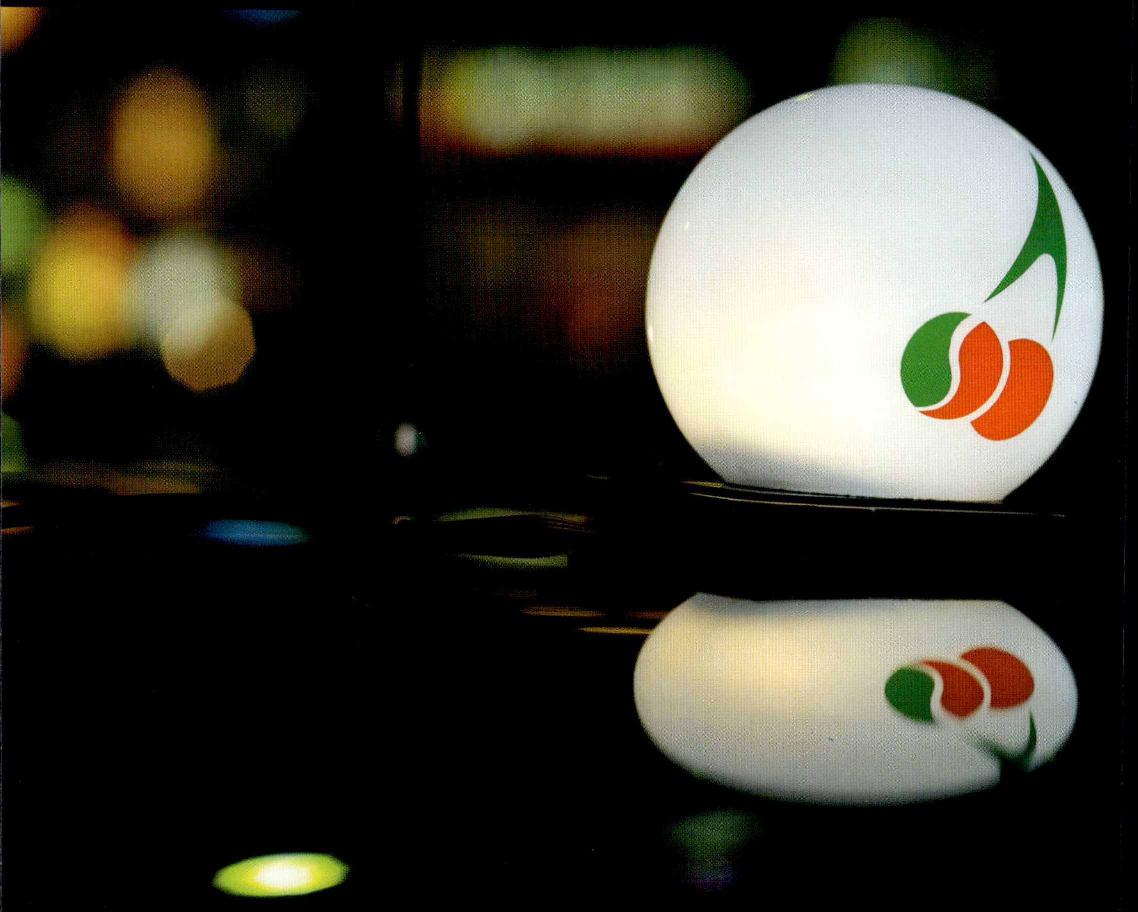

CHERRY TAXI CO.

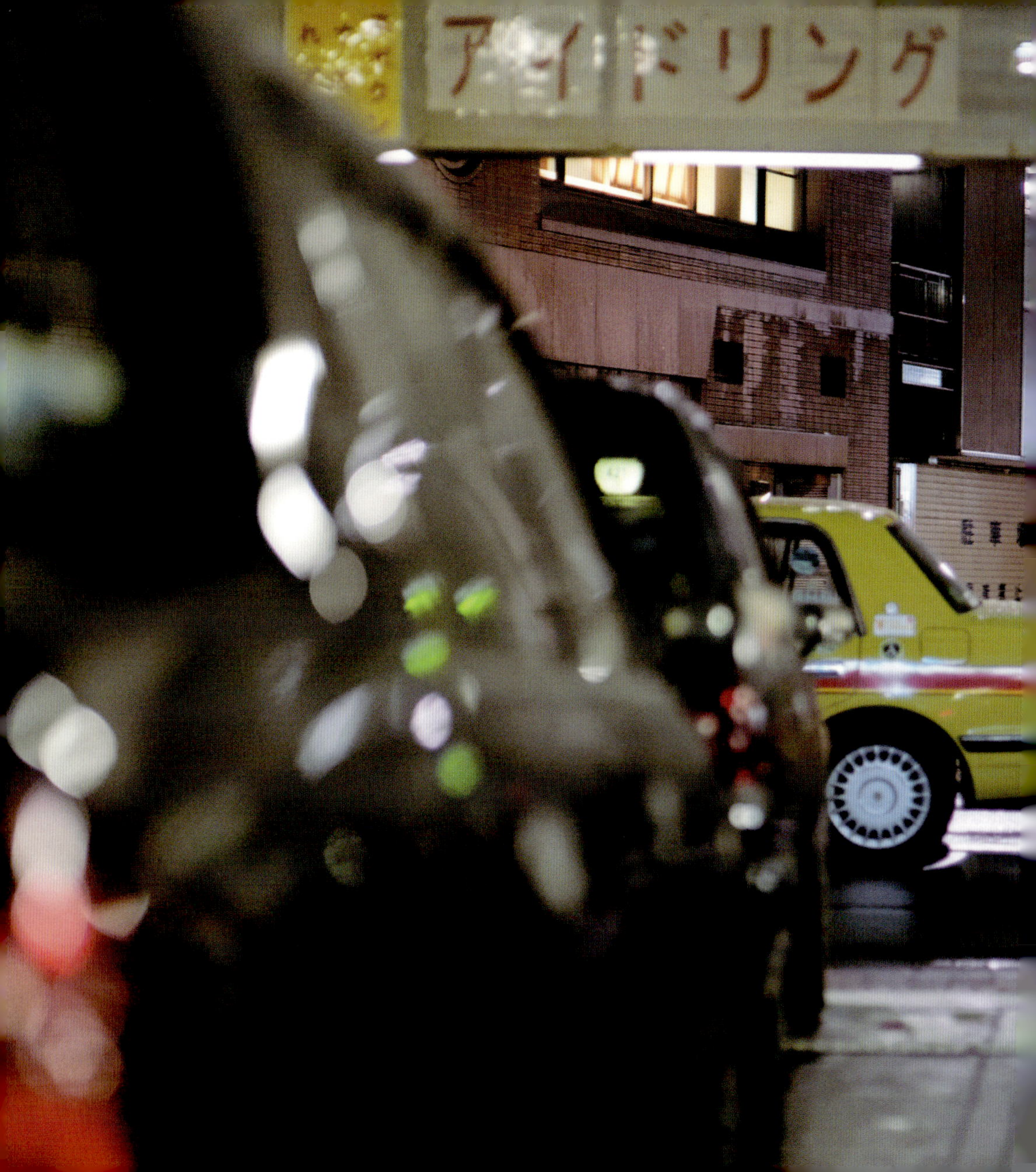
アイドリング

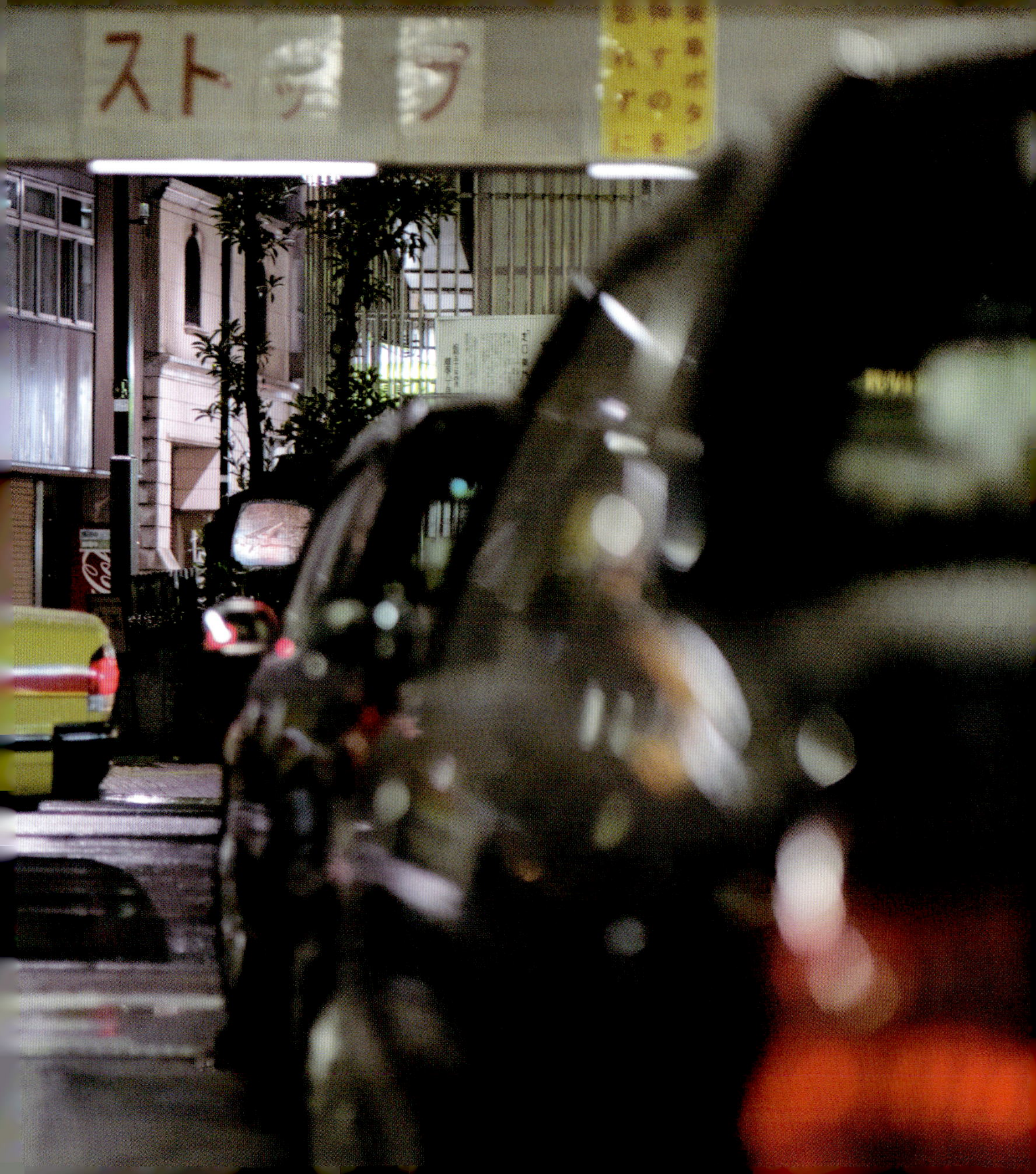

UNNAMED DRIVER

I don't like to get involved when I pick up couples who are arguing. I just drive and say nothing, but they often try to involve me with such questions as, 'What do you think, then? Am I right, or is she right?' I just want to get my job done – get them to their destination, get the fare from them, and move on to the next job.

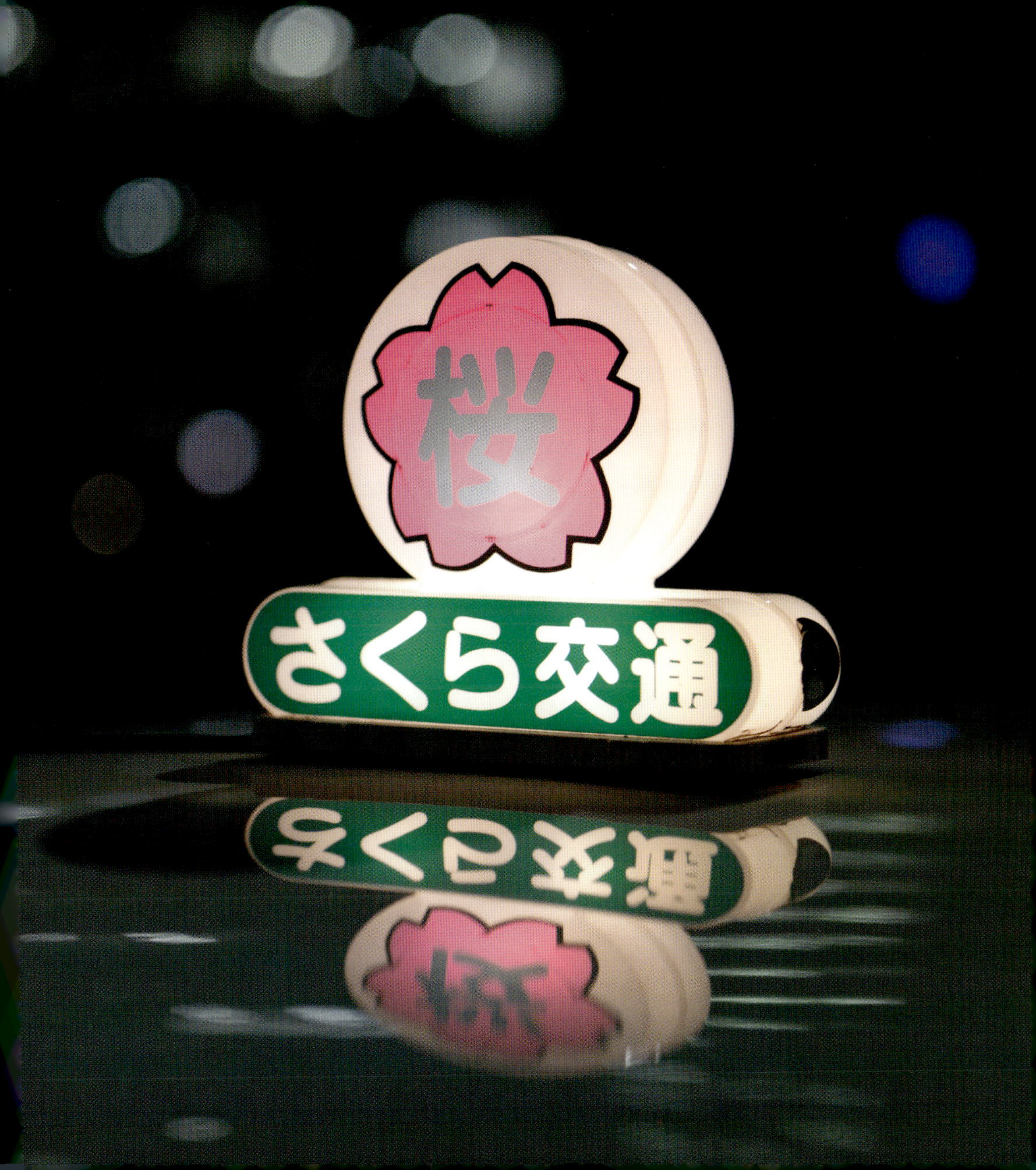
桜
さくら交通

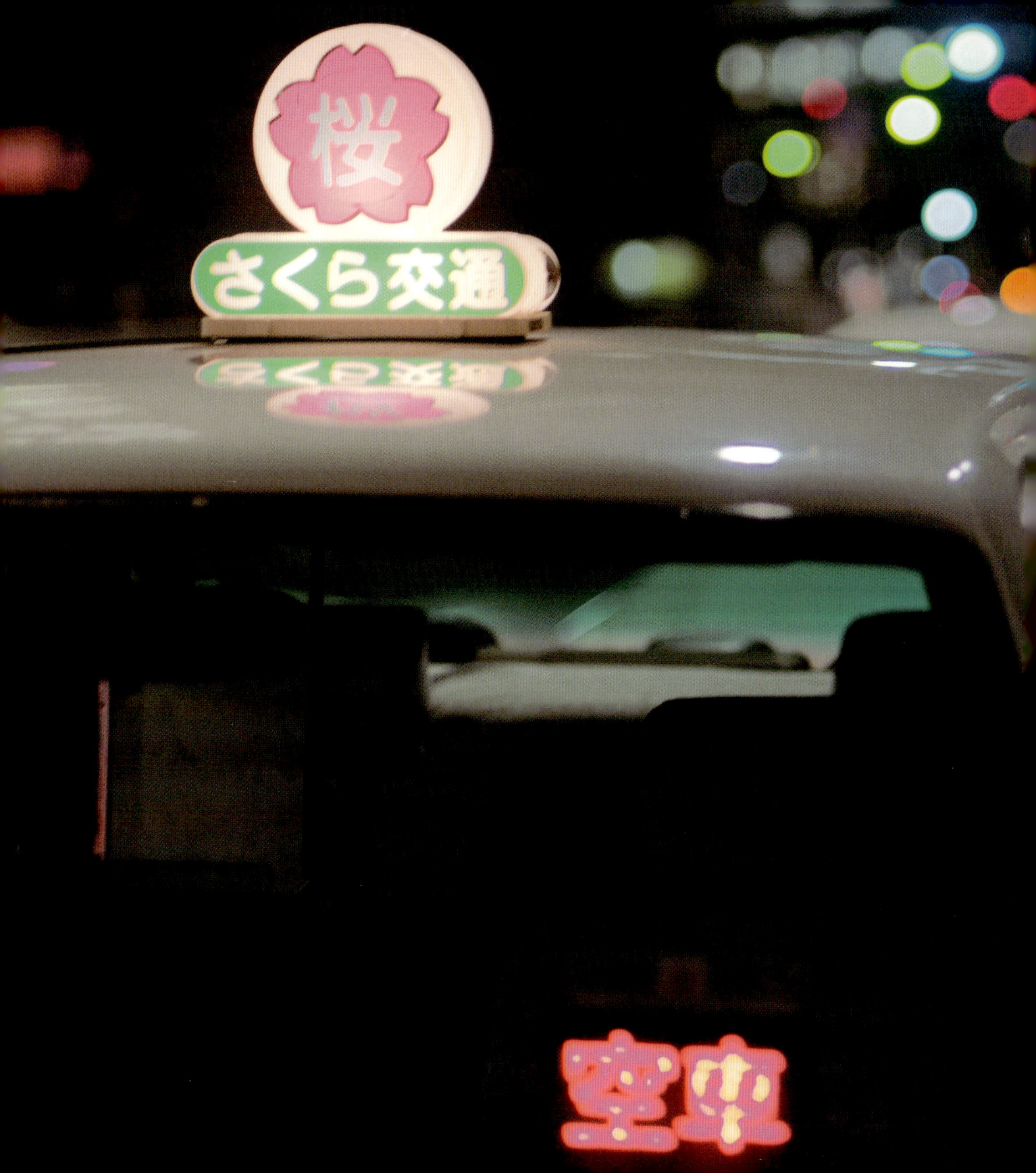
桜
さくら交通
空車

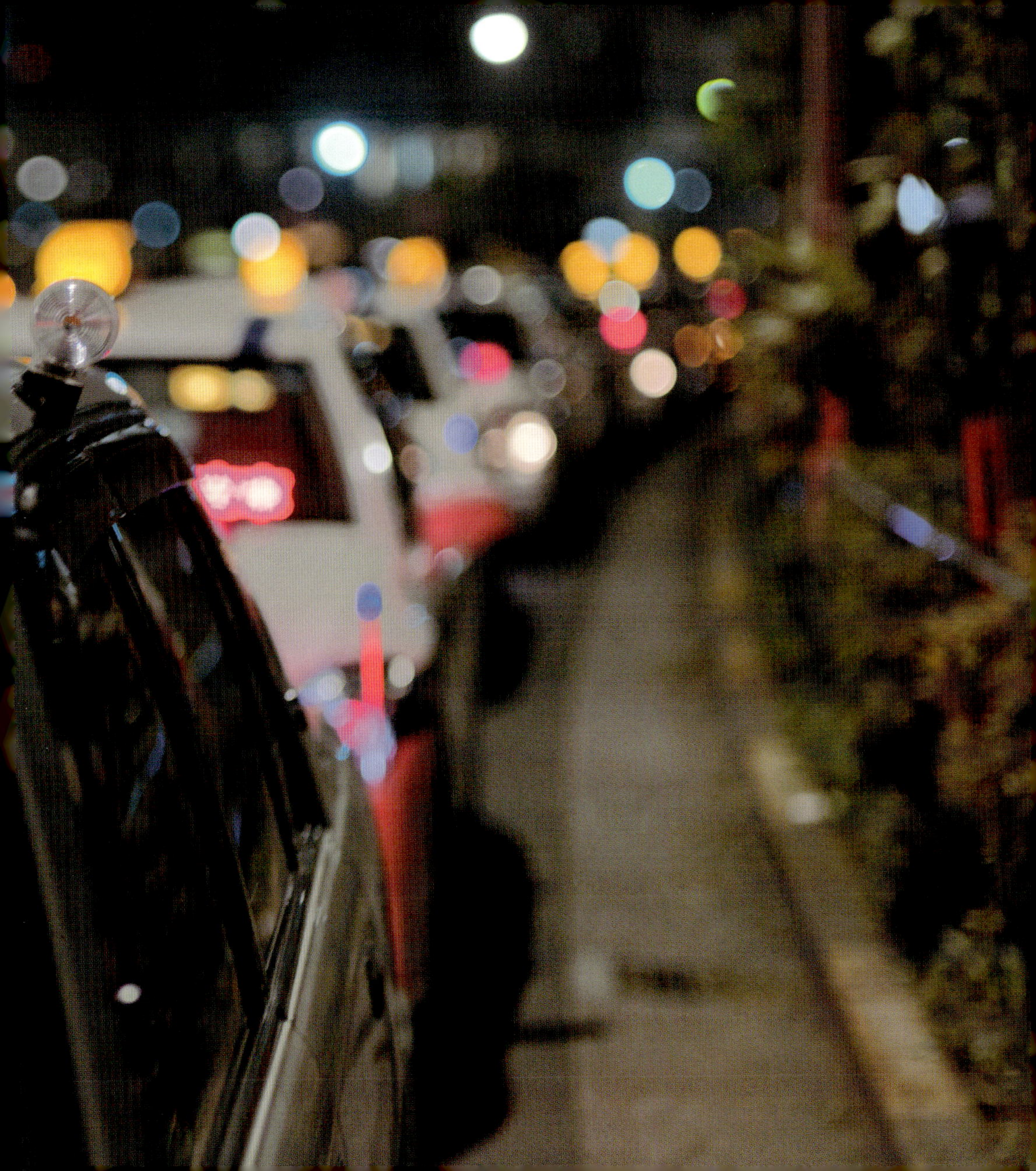

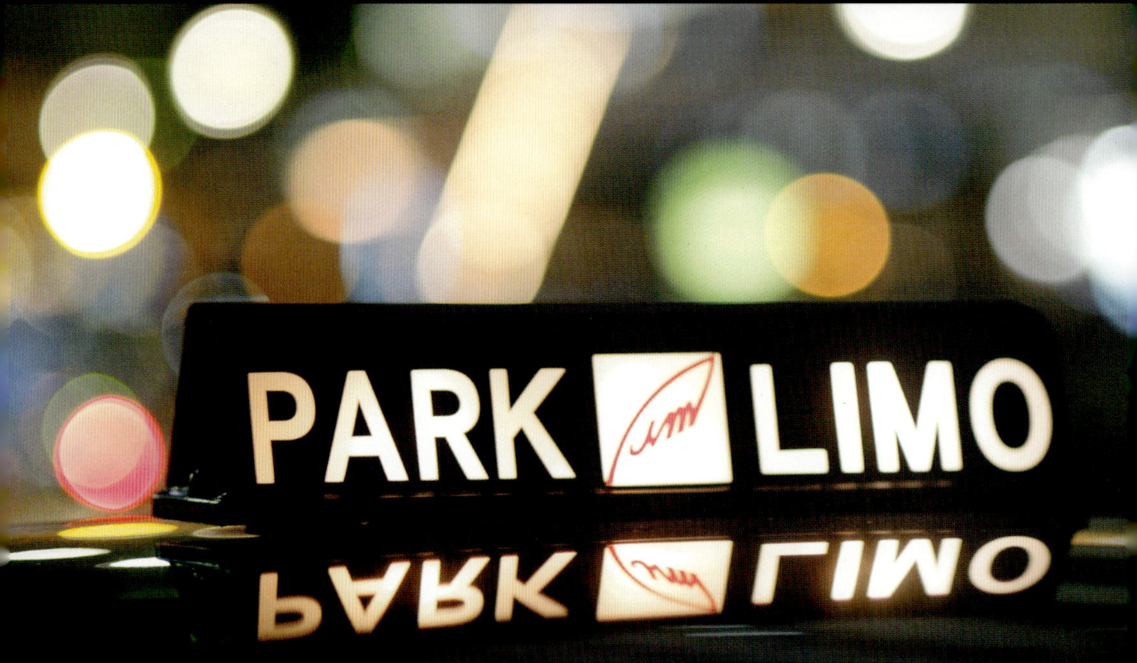

PARK LIMO TAXI

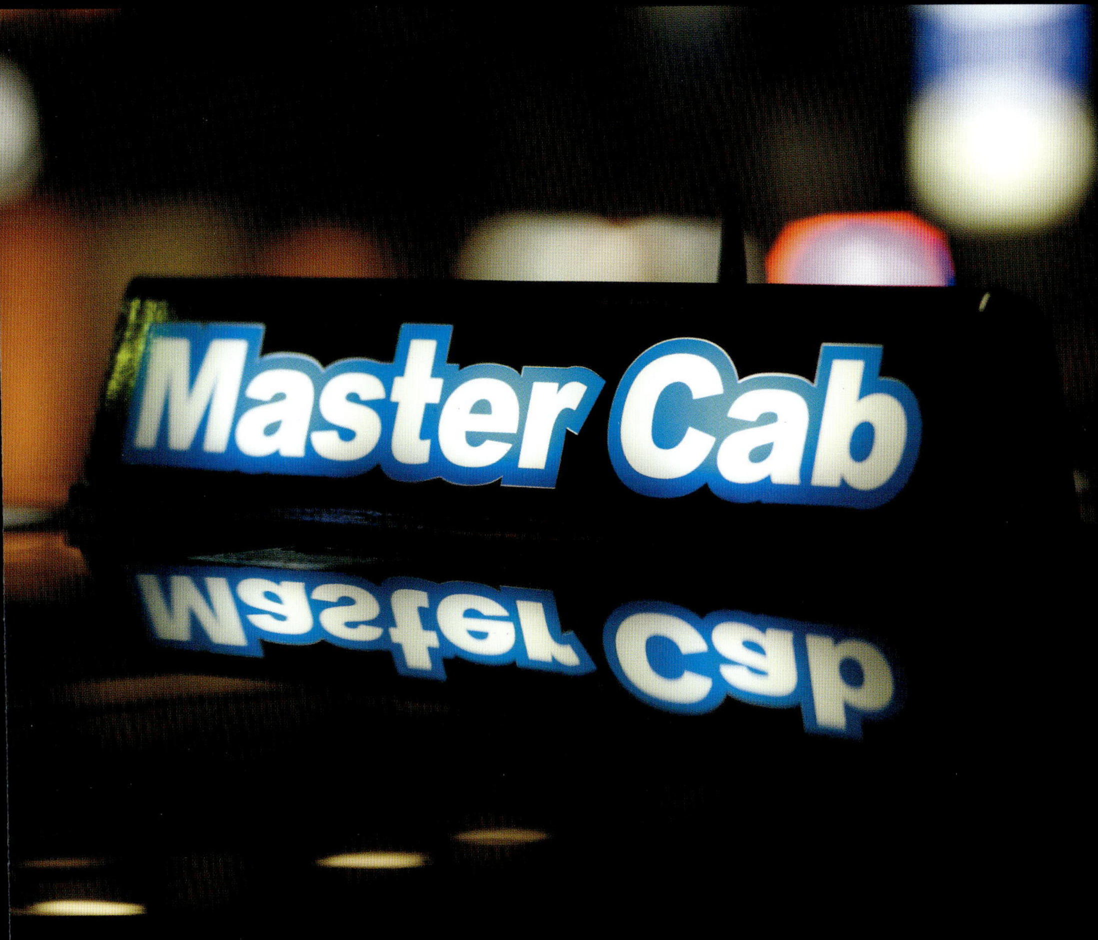

MASTER CAB

DAICHI TAXI CO. 1152

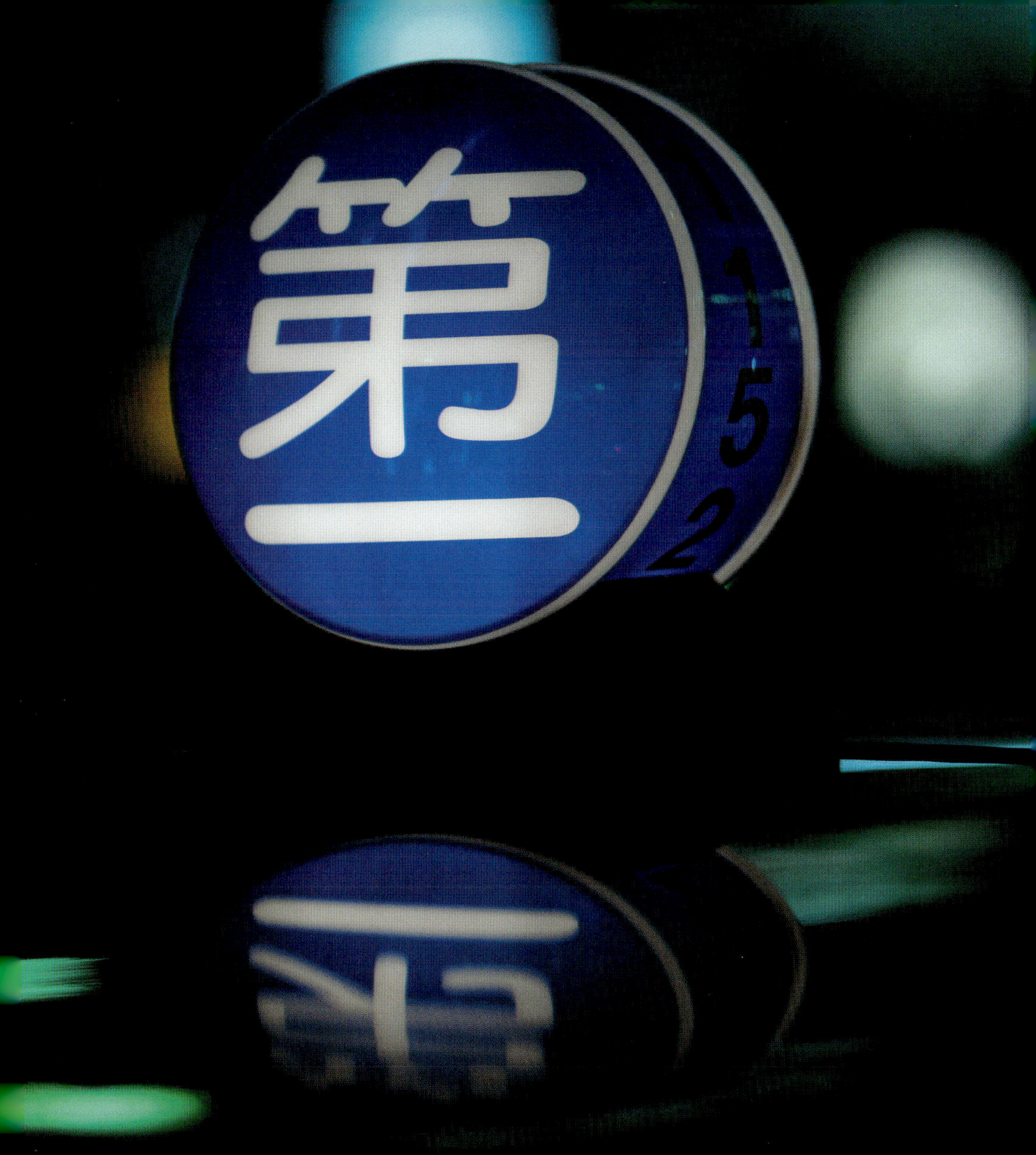
第一

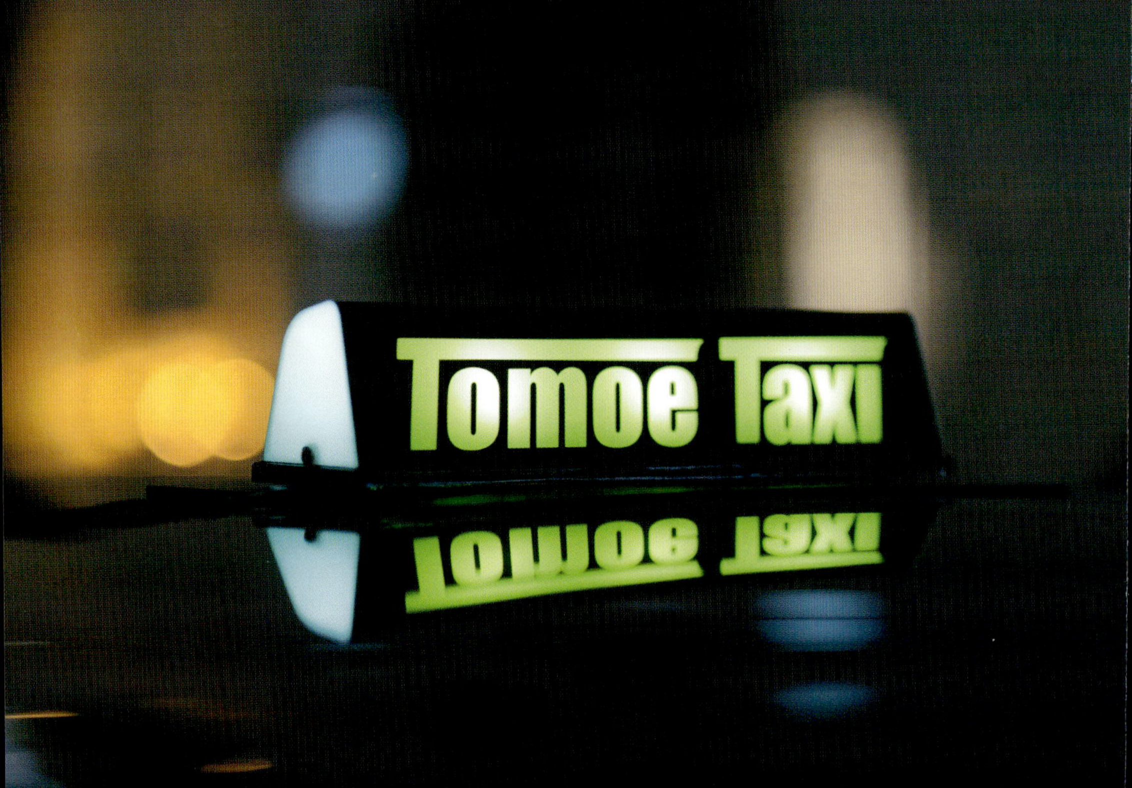
Tomoe Taxi

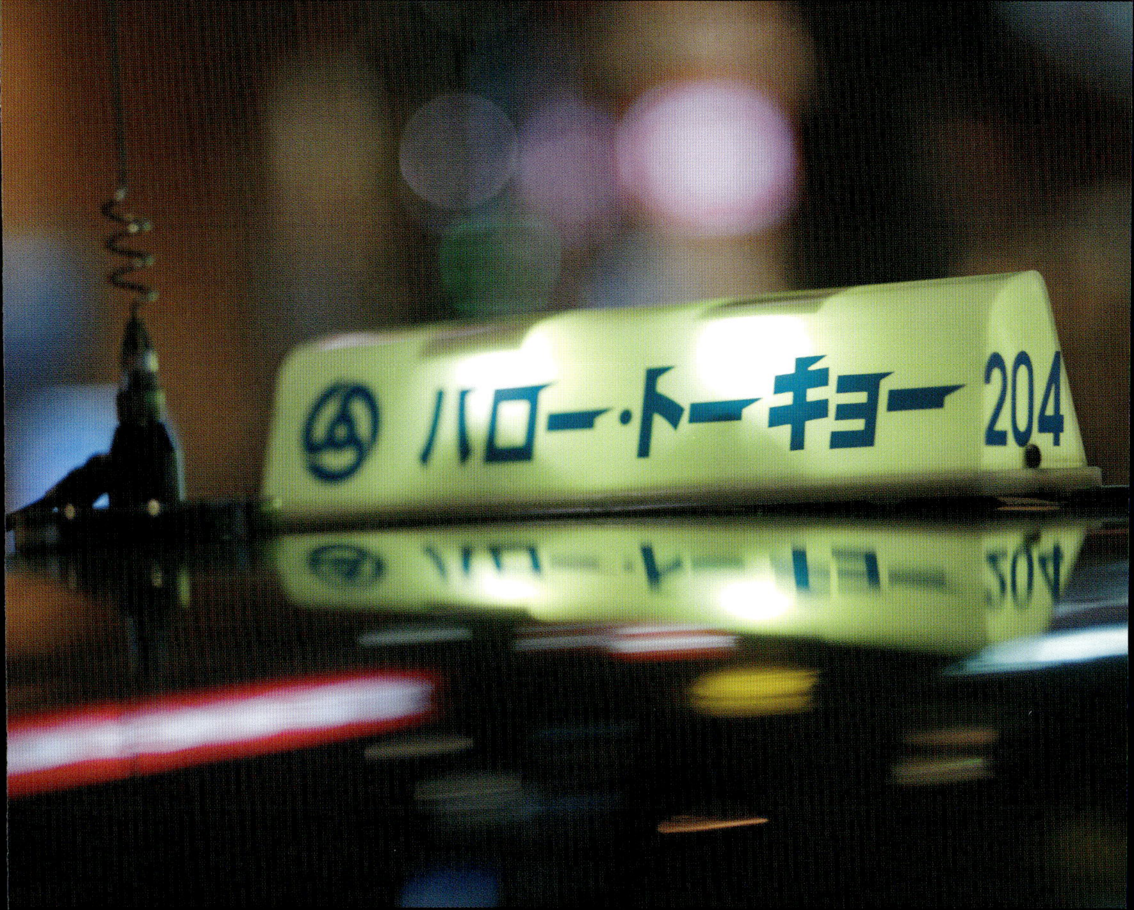

HELLO TOKYO TAXI 204

MR MIZOGUCHI

I found it difficult to adjust to the hours. Mentally I coped just fine, but physically it affected me greatly. My first priority is not to have any kind of accident; my second is never to upset a customer.

Pages 176–77: 'H' TAXI

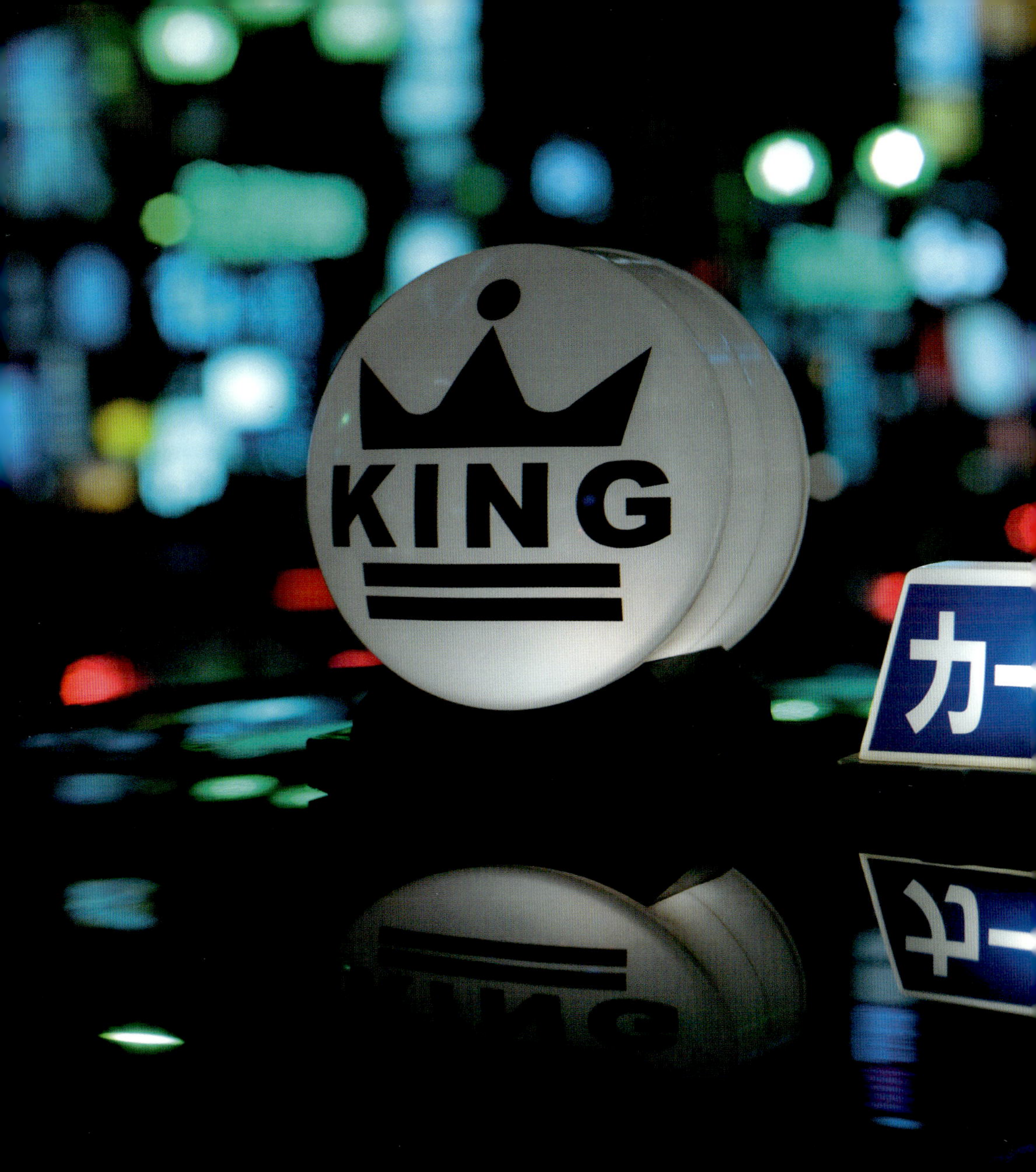
KING
カー

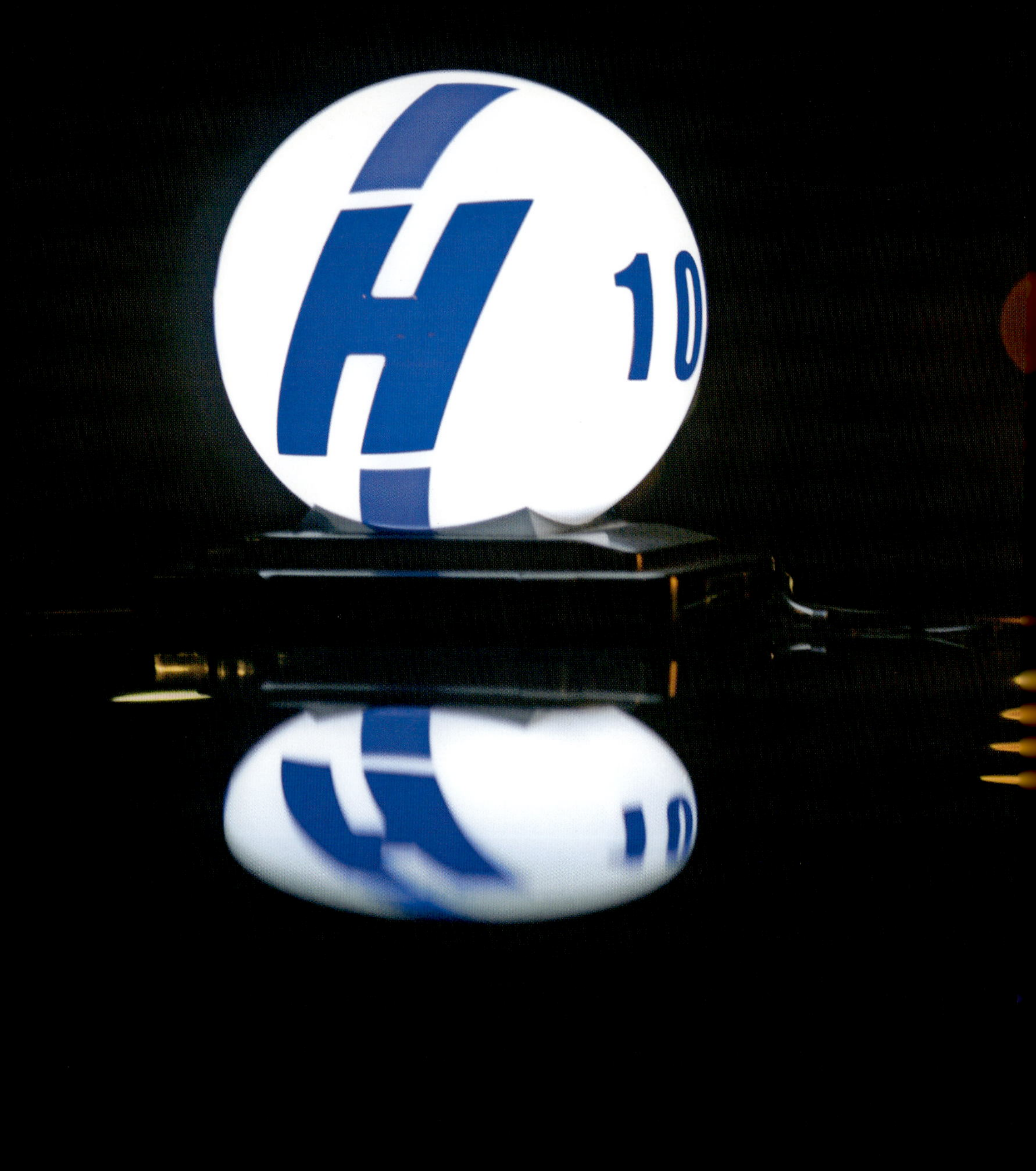
H 10

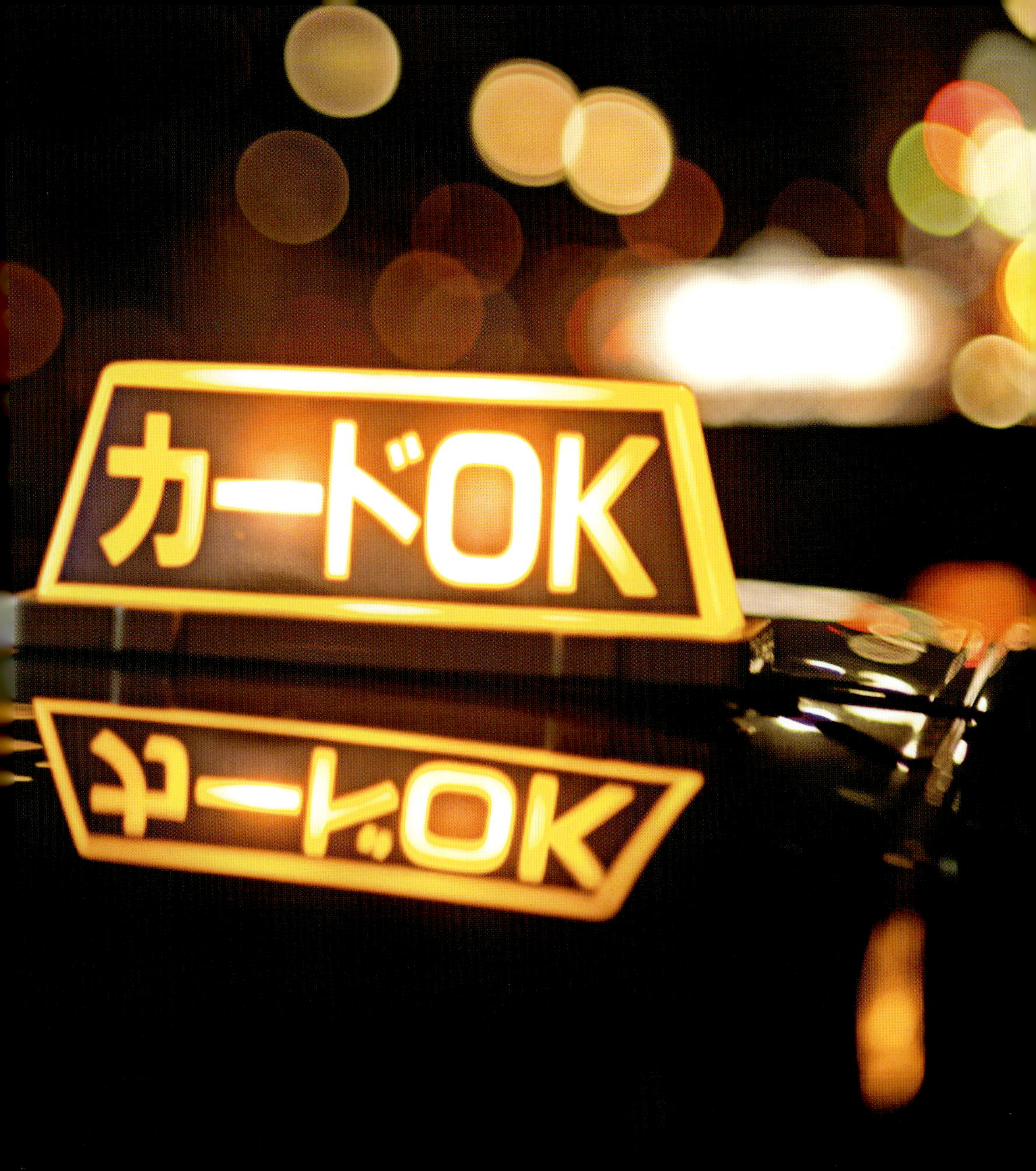
カードOK

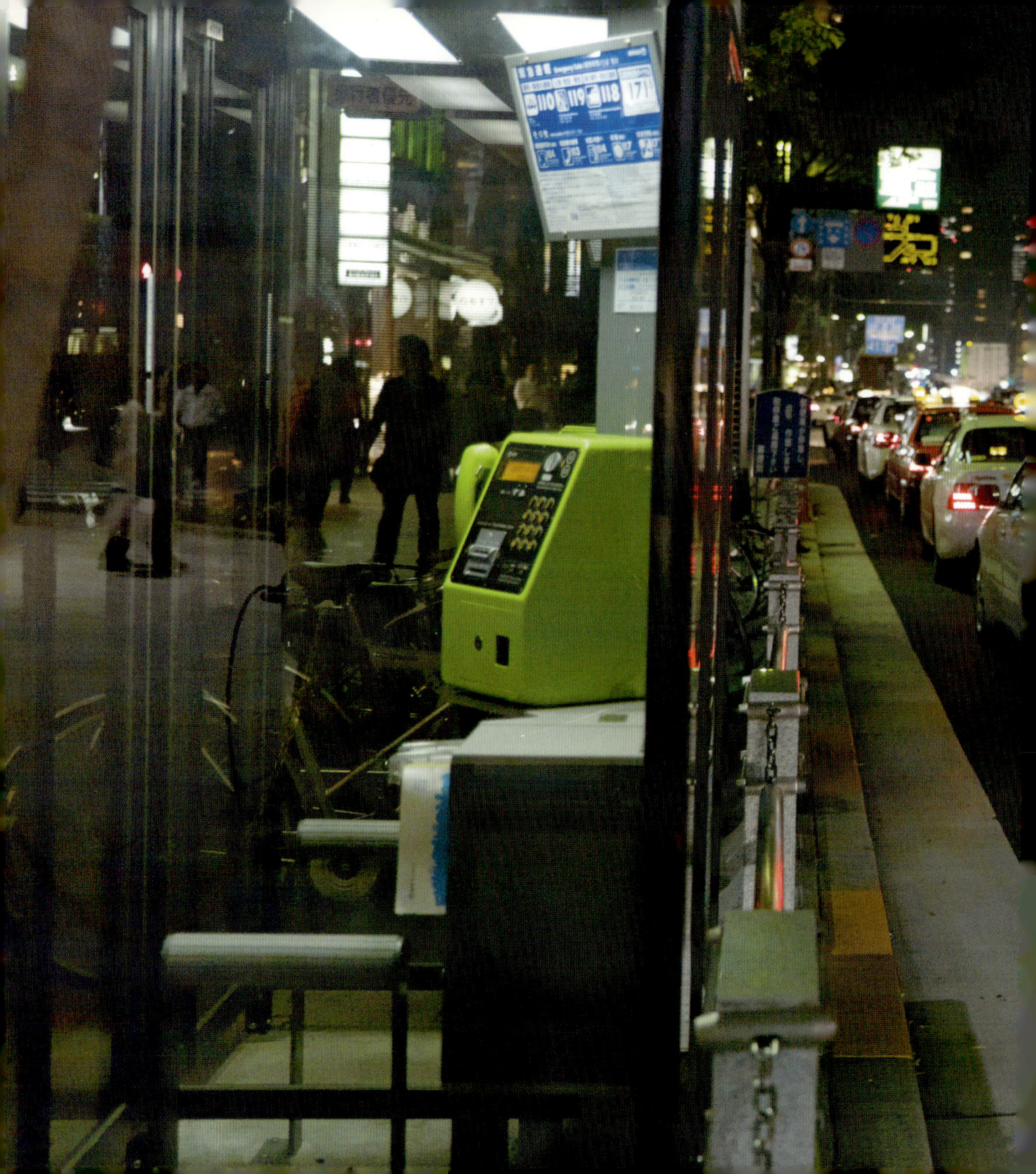
110
119
118
171

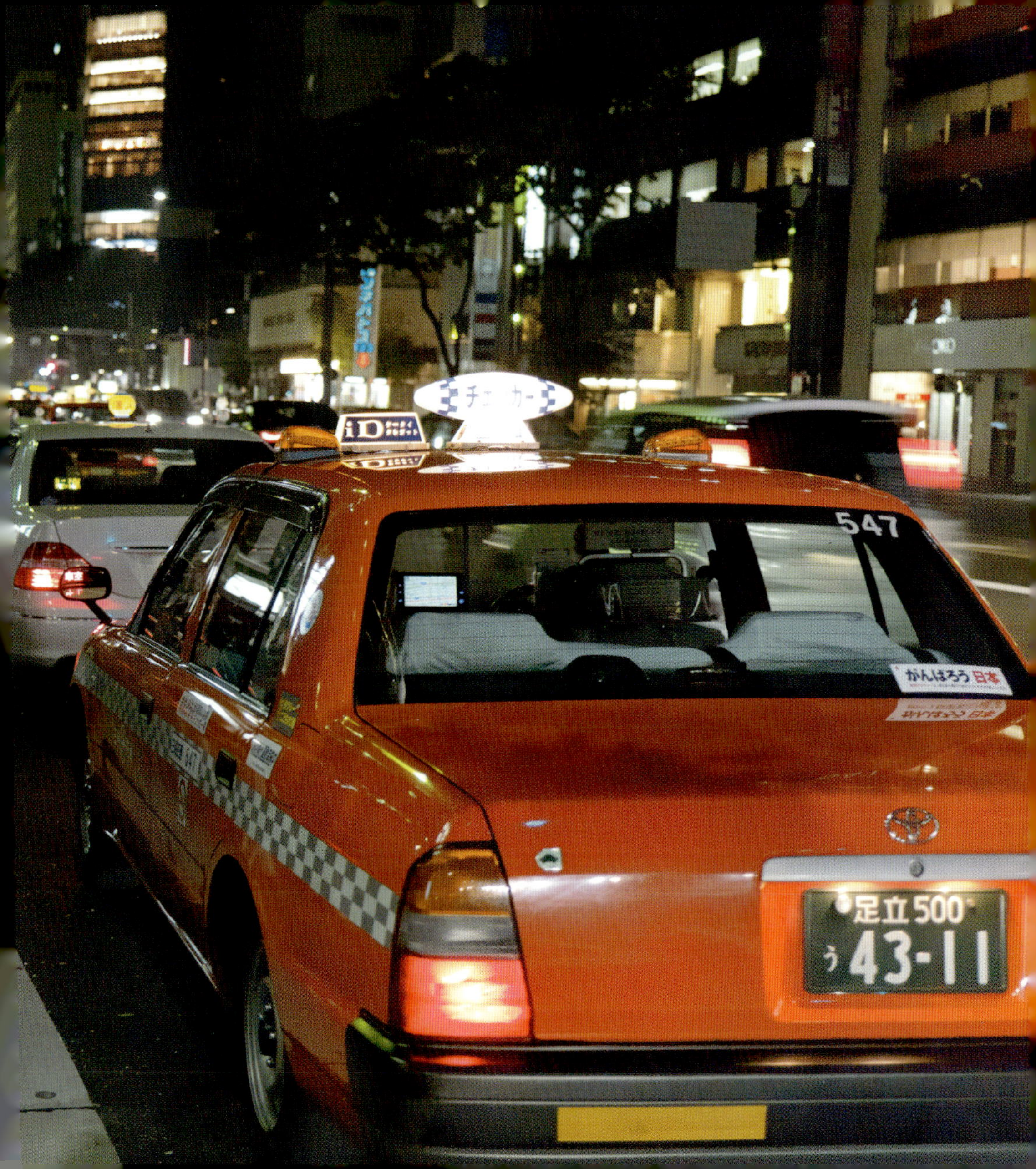
547
がんばろう 日本
足立500
う 43-11

KYOUDOU MUSEN TAXI 6050

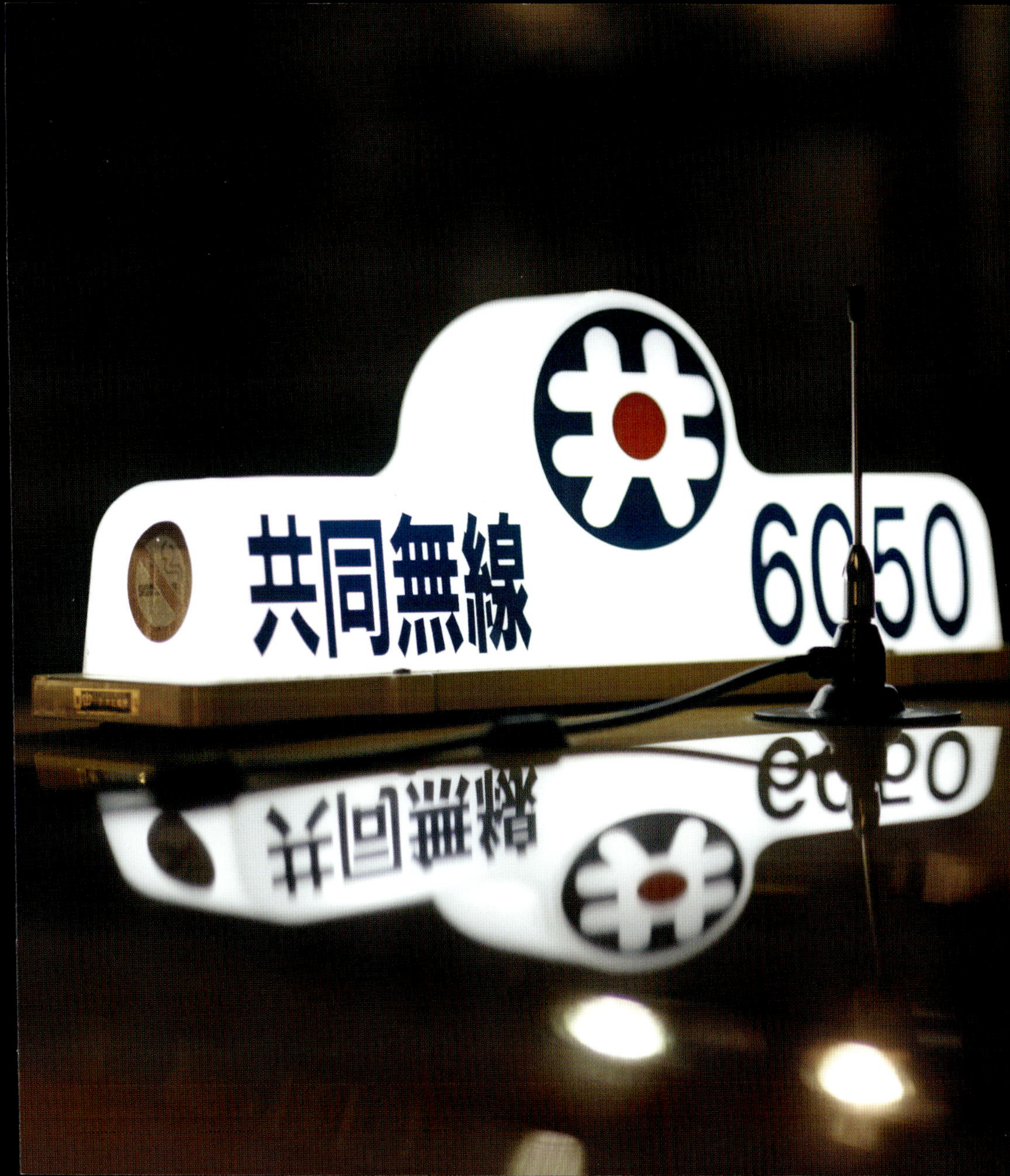
共同無線
6050

EBARA TAXI CO. 662

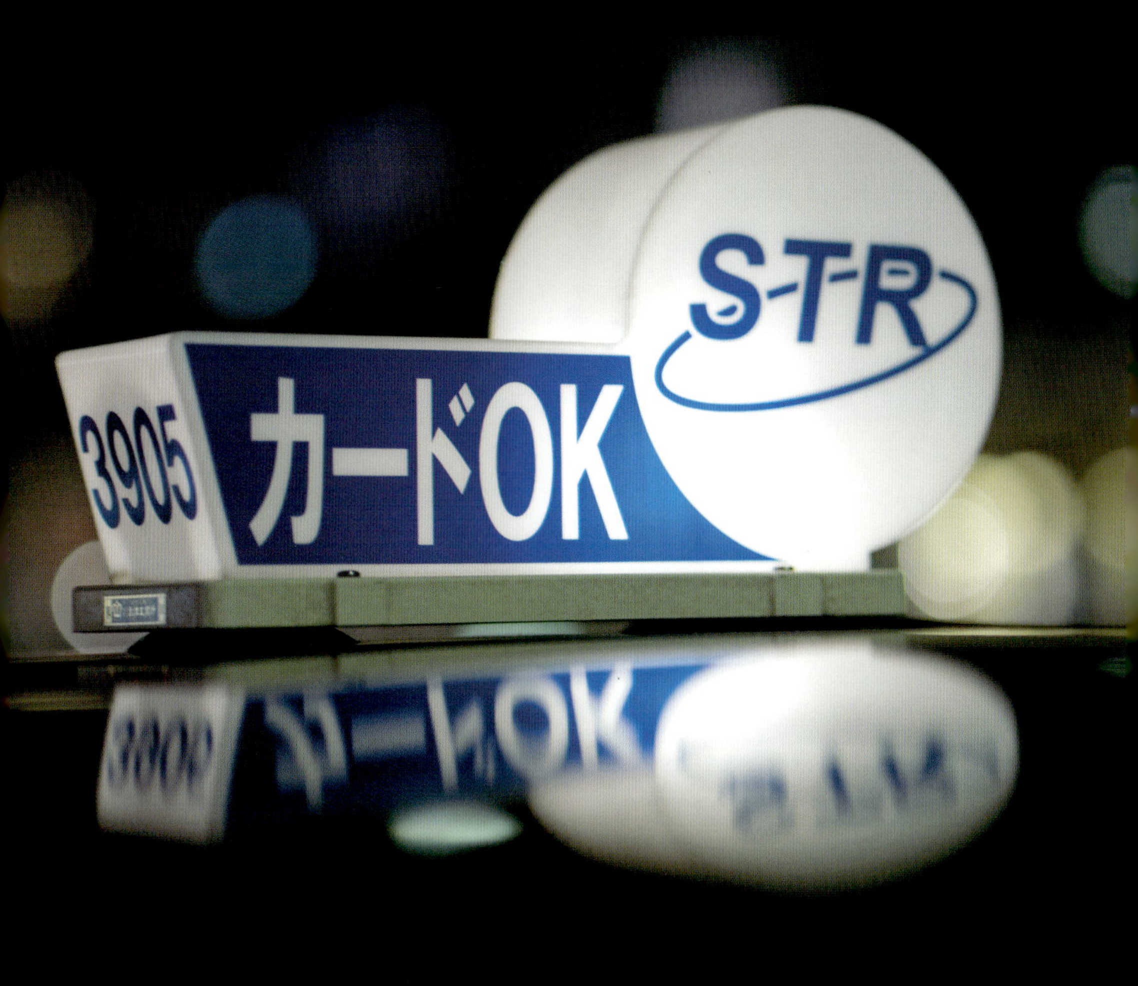

STR TAXI CO. 3905

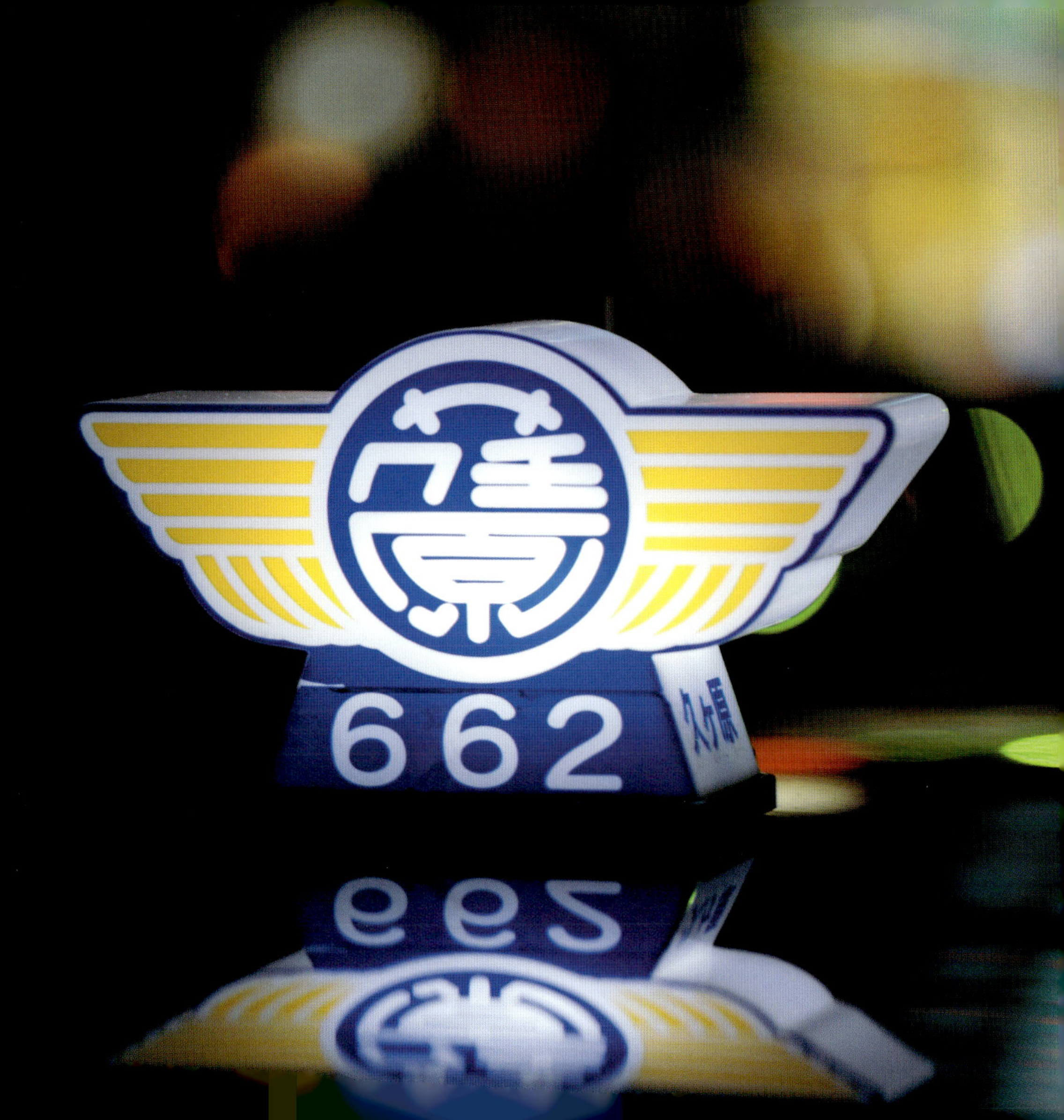
662
久ケ原

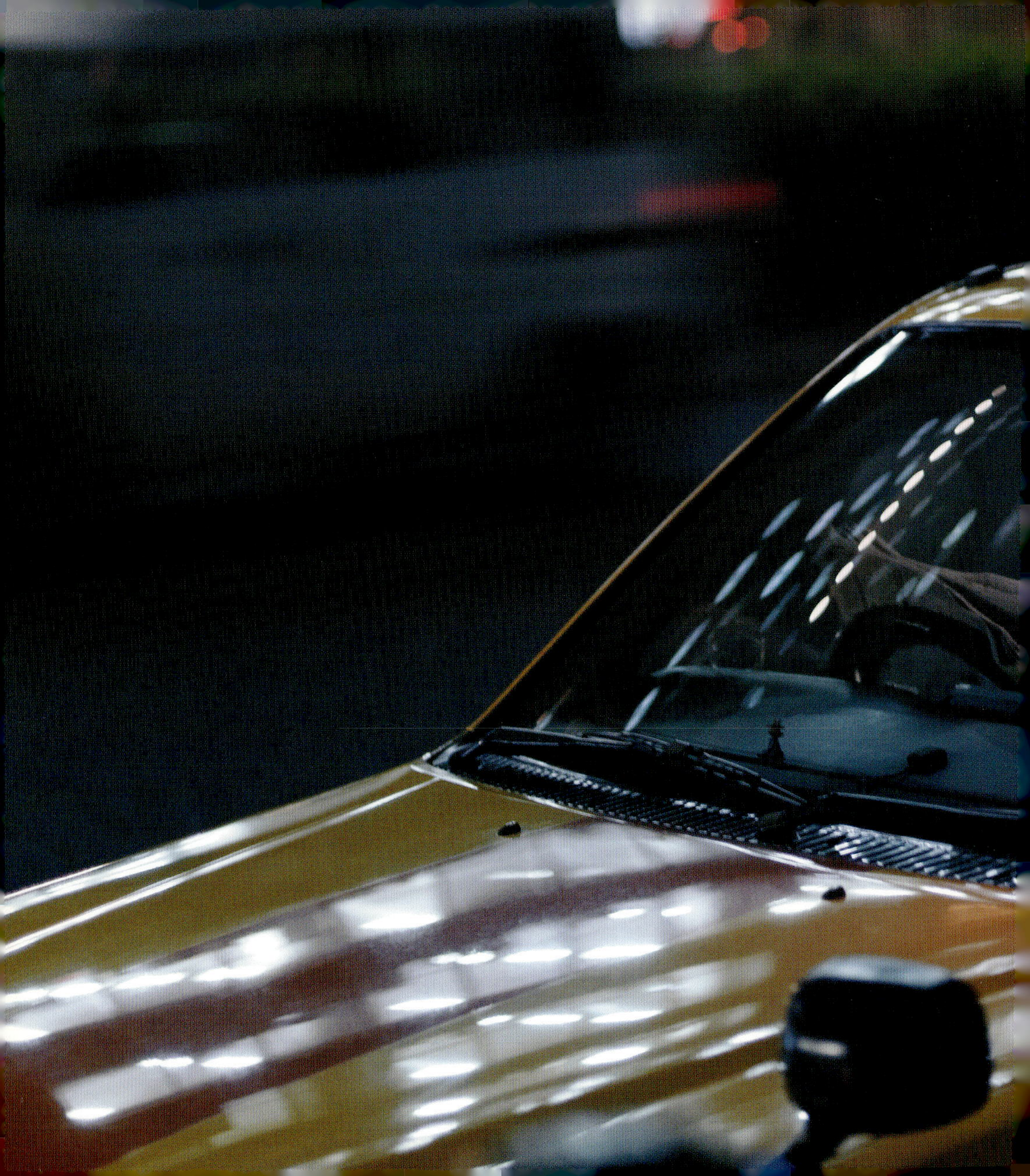

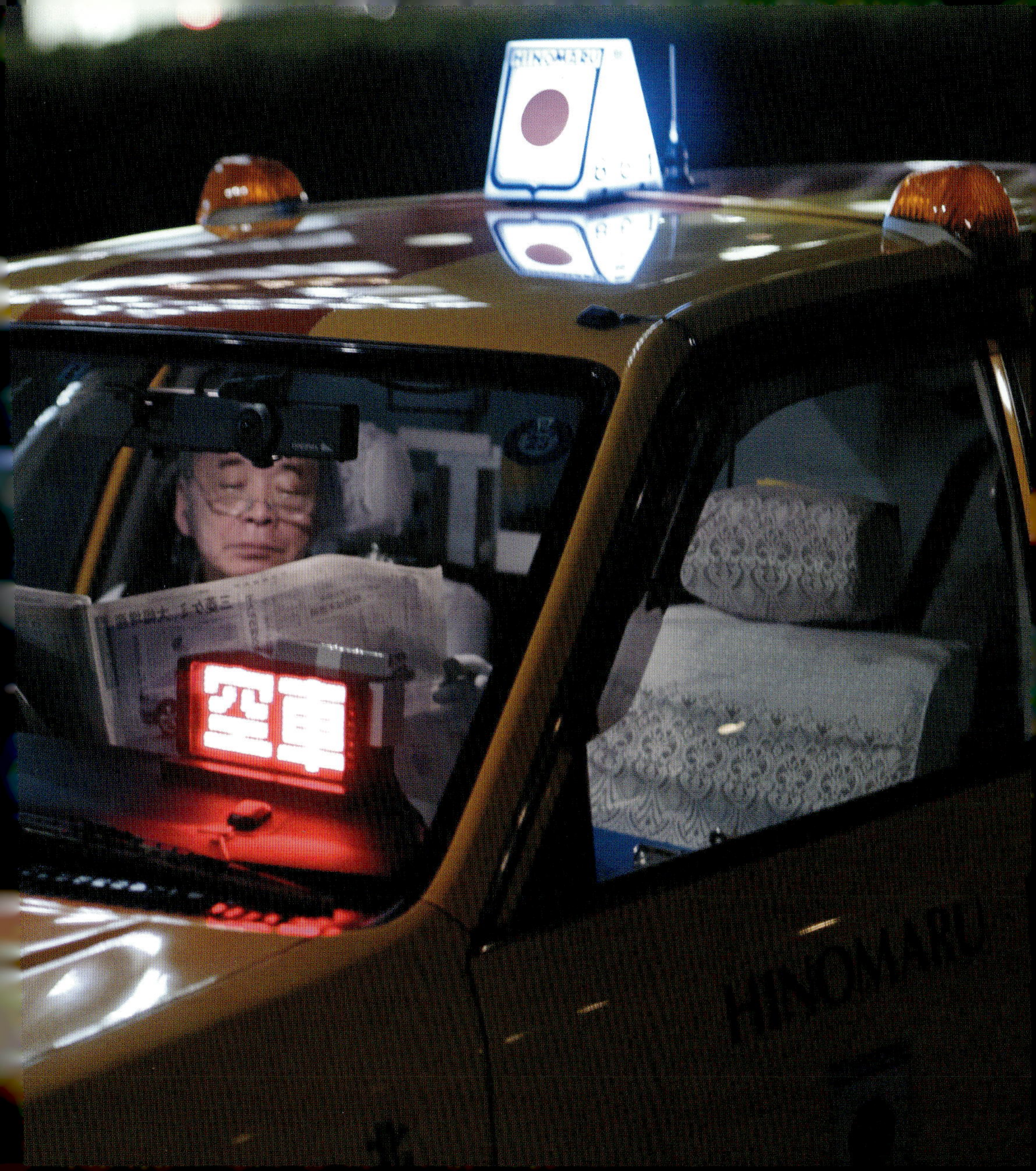
HINOMARU
空車
HINOMARU

HINOMARU TAXI 6739

Pages 188–89: TOKYO MK TAXI

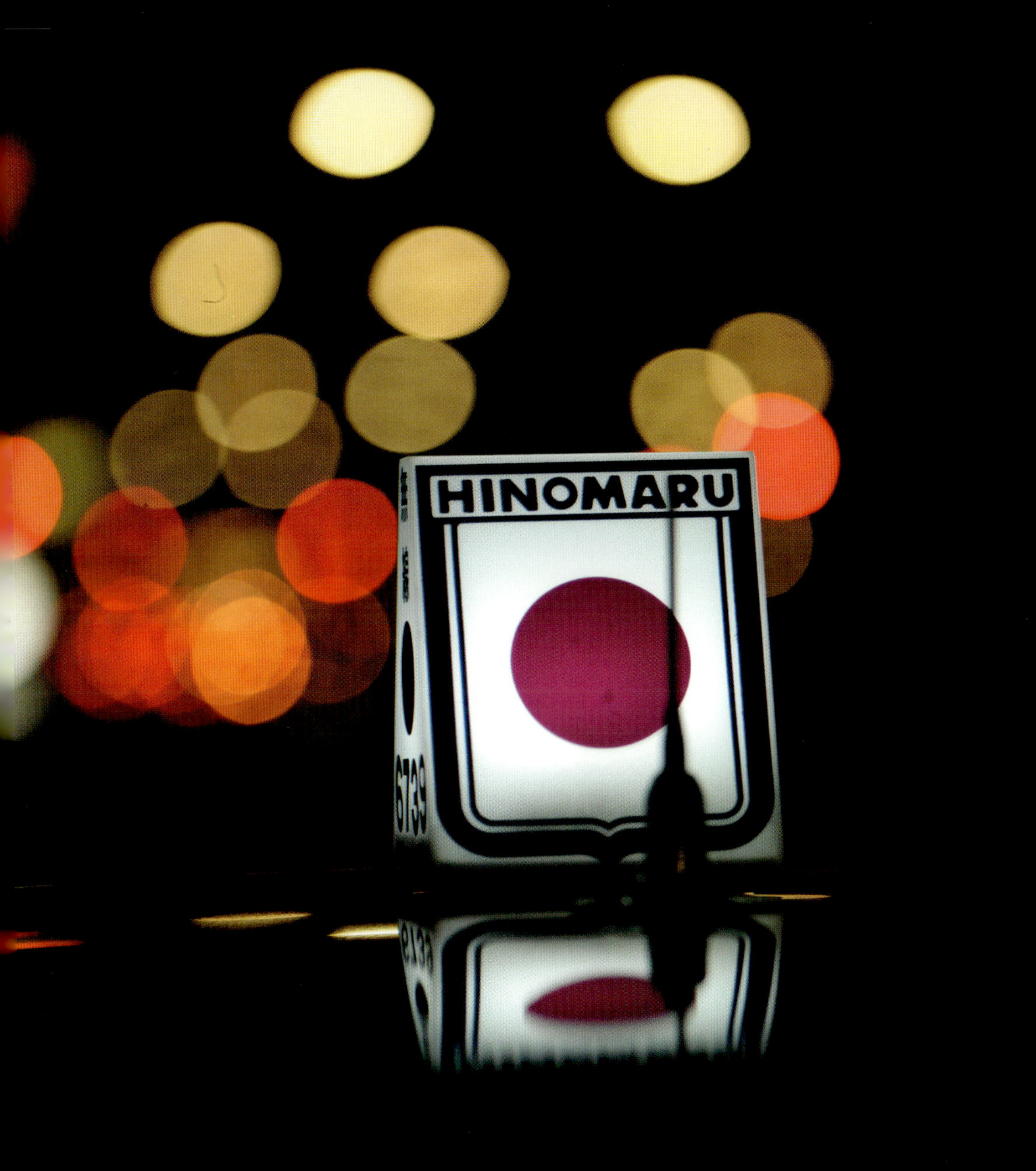
HINOMARU
6739

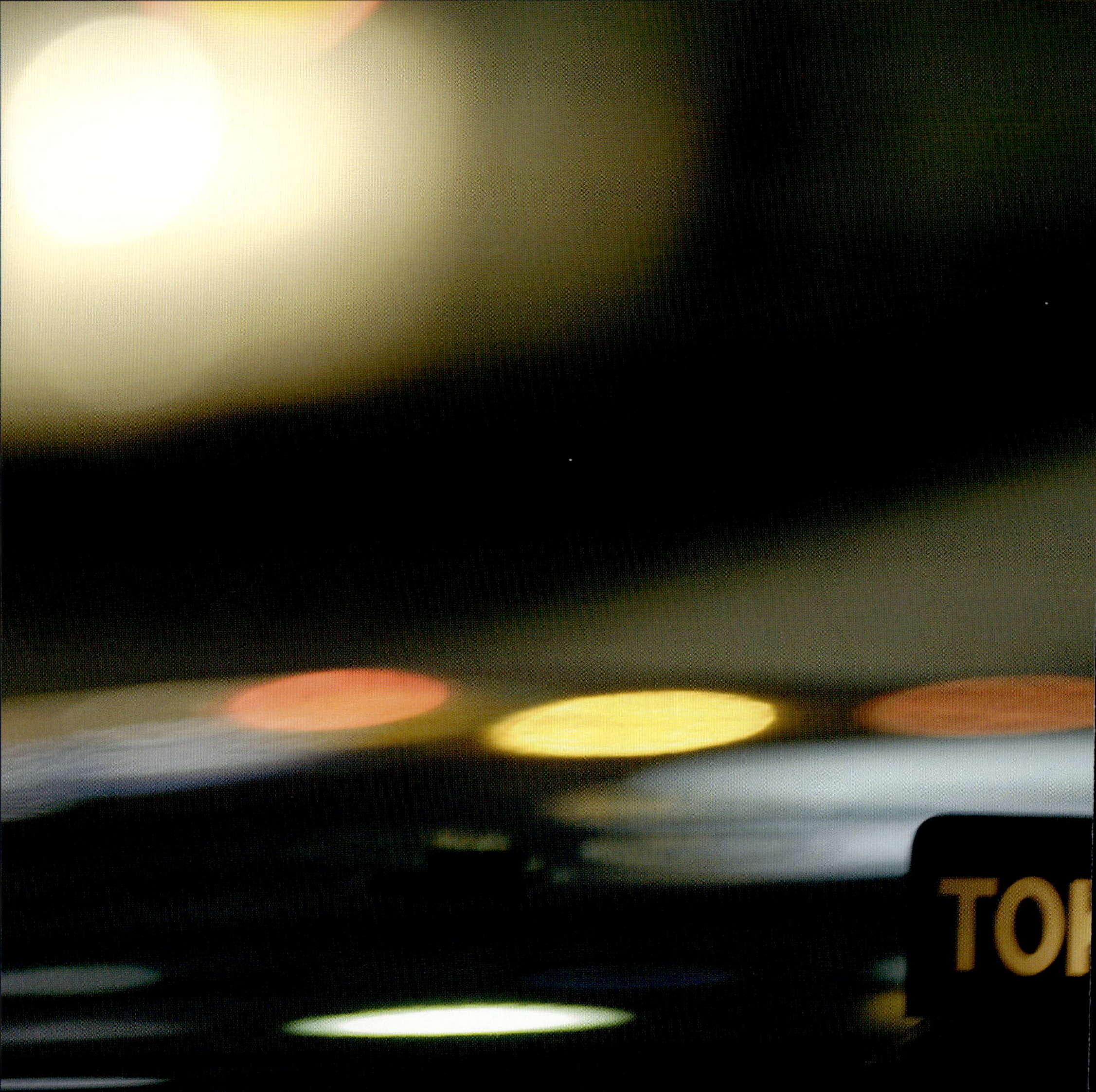

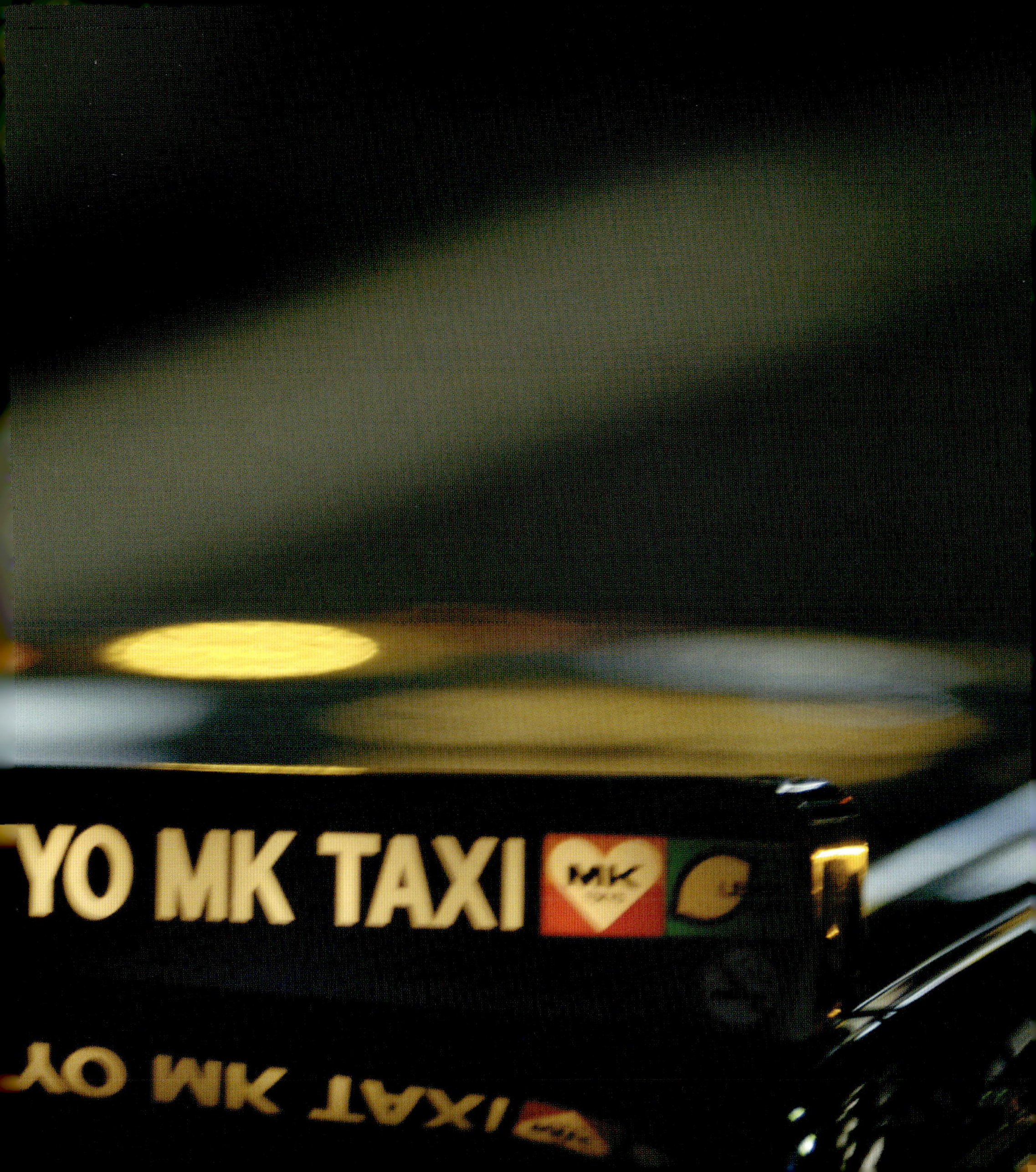

YO MK TAXI
MK

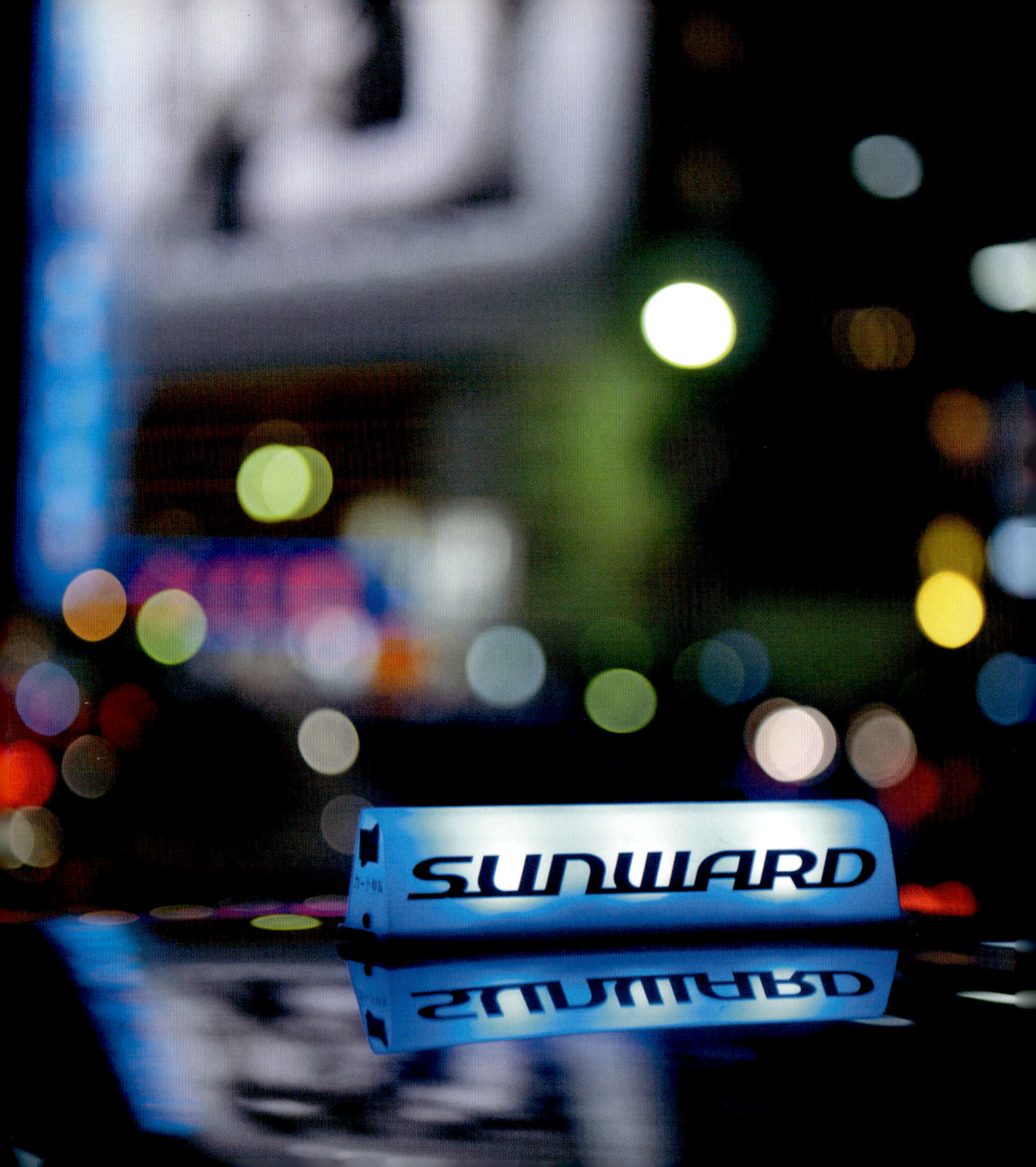
SUNWARD

UNNAMED DRIVER

Things often get left in the cab – bags, mobiles, wallets etc. – and I always make a point of returning them to the office asap, just in case the customer needs their property back urgently. I once picked up a young woman in Akihabara and took her to her hotel. When I dropped her off I didn't notice that she had left a big, expensive-looking bag in the back. Within a few minutes a call came over the radio to say that the lady would wait for me outside her hotel. When I arrived she was looking very anxious, but she was really pleased to see me, so I handed her this bag – I think it was a Prada – and it started to move. That's when I realized it had a small dog in it. She immediately opened the bag, and this hairless little dog jumped up at her

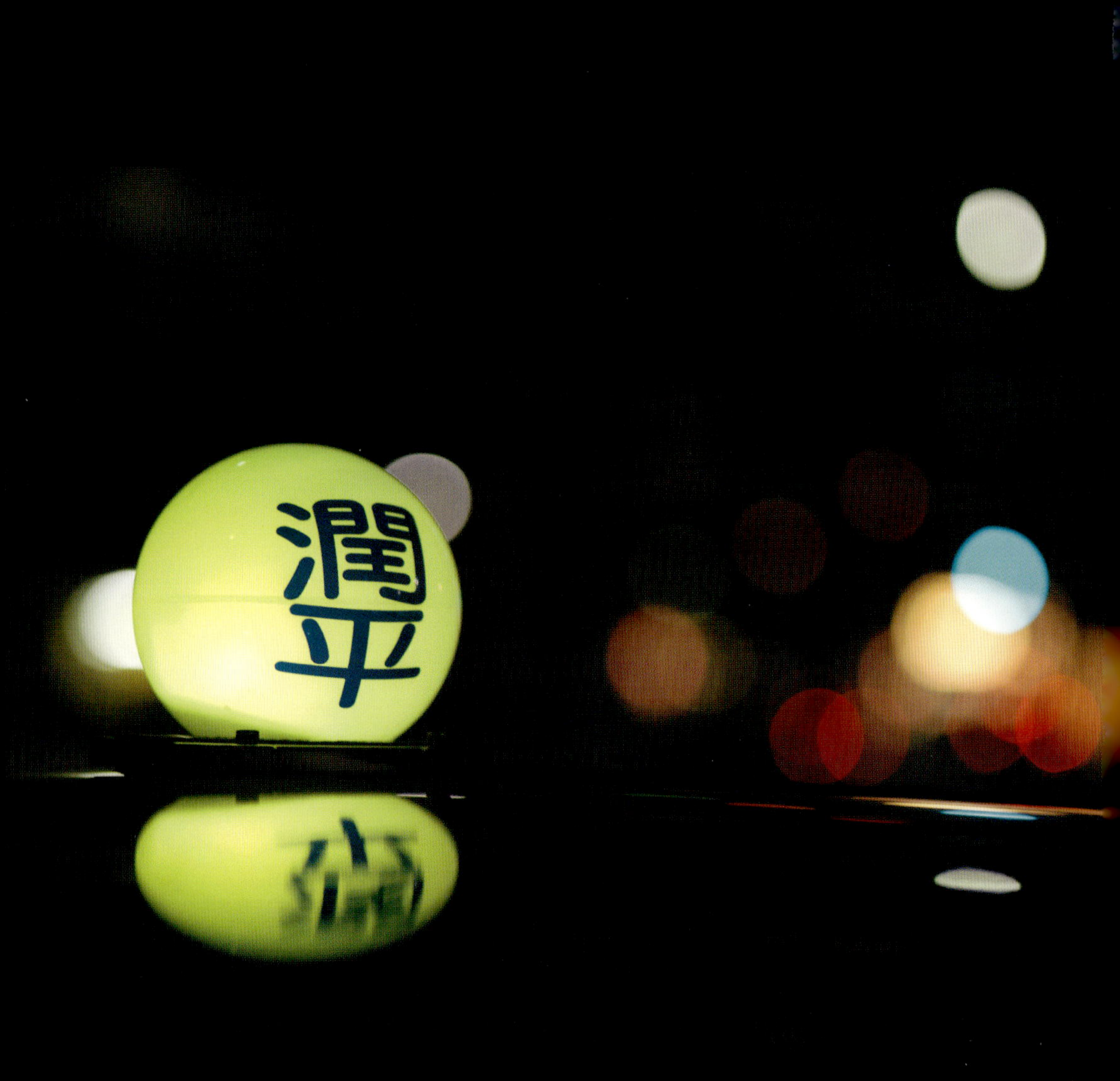

JUNPEI TAXI

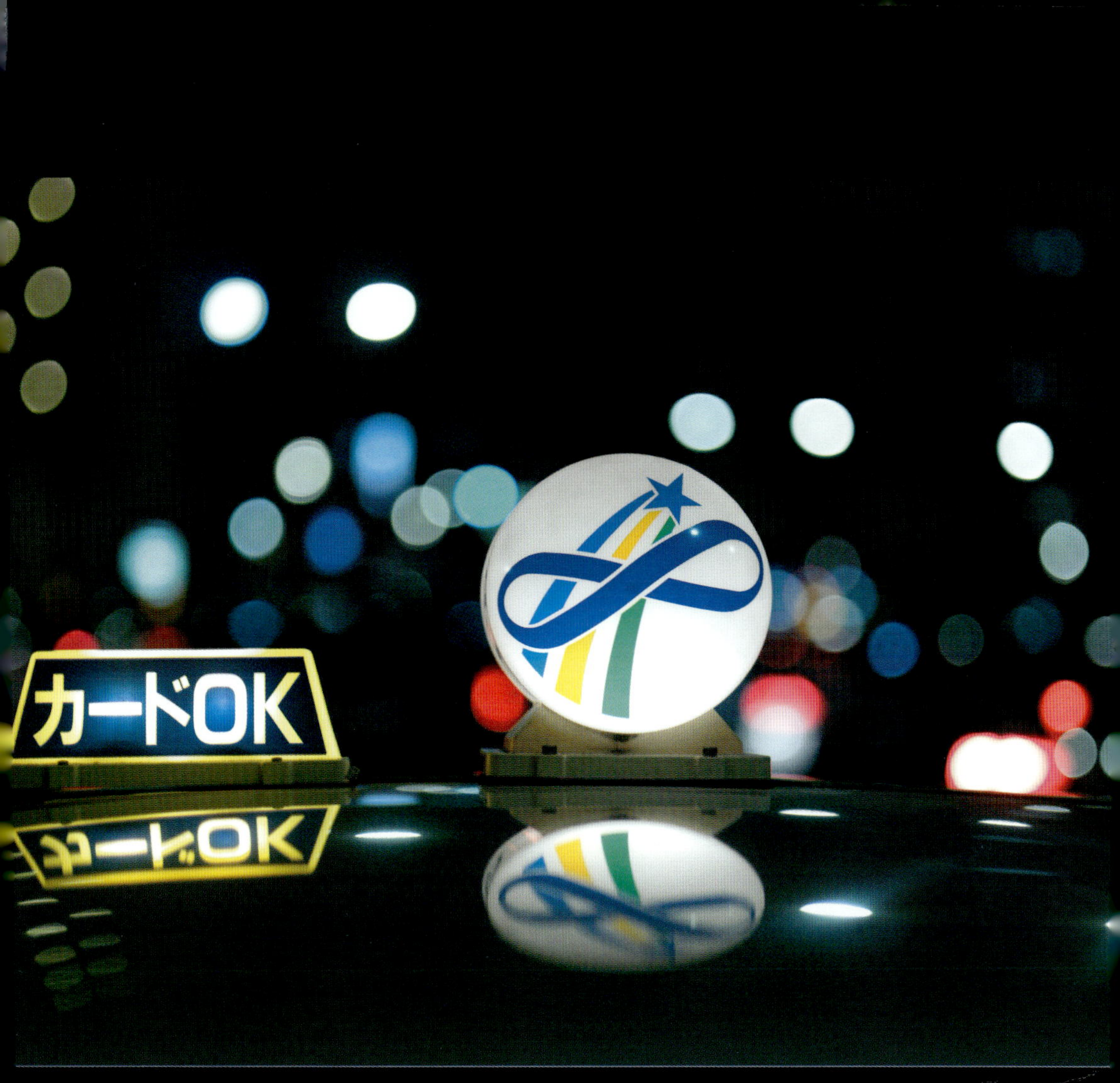

'INFINITY STAR'

YURAKU TAXI

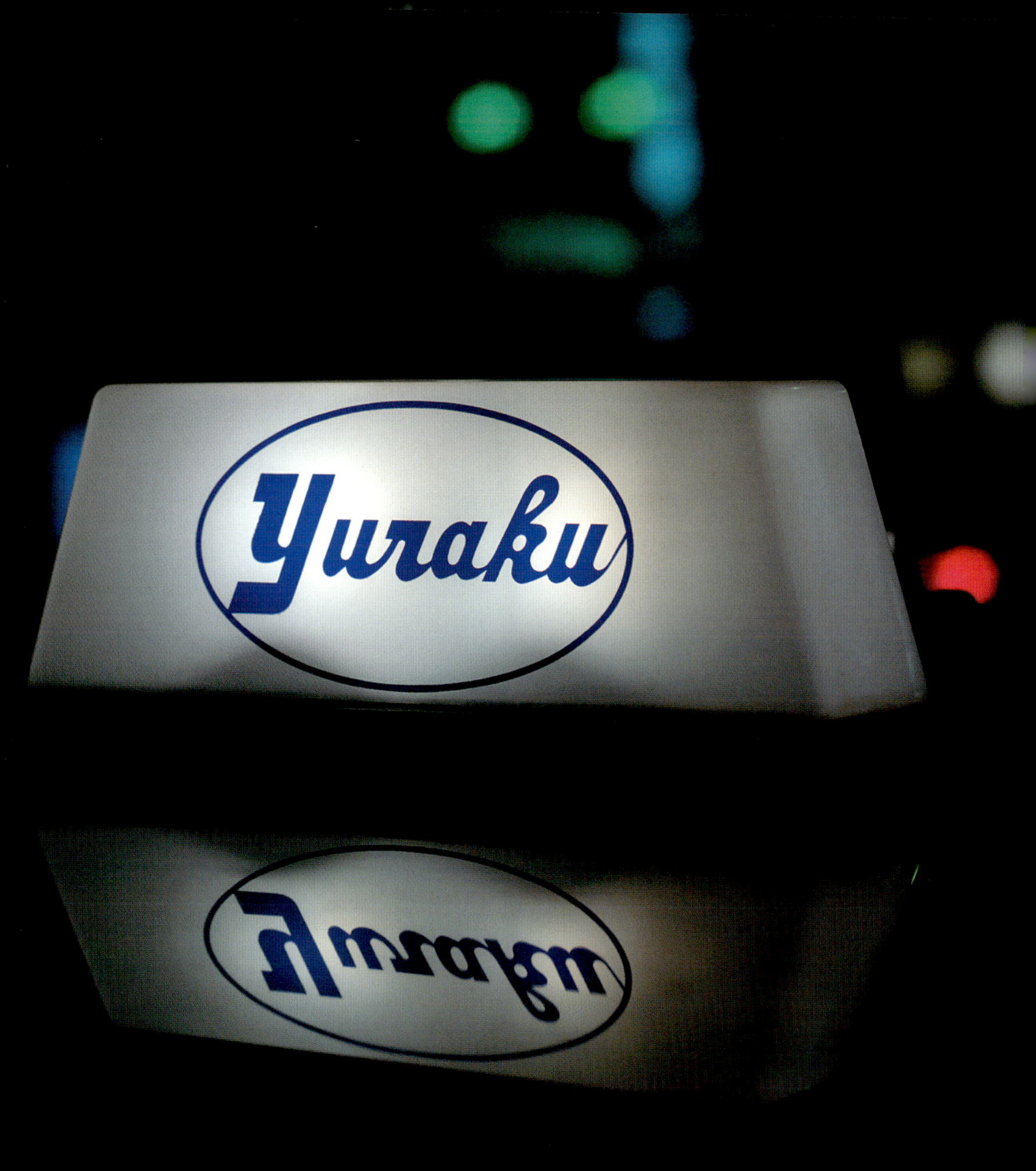
Yuraku

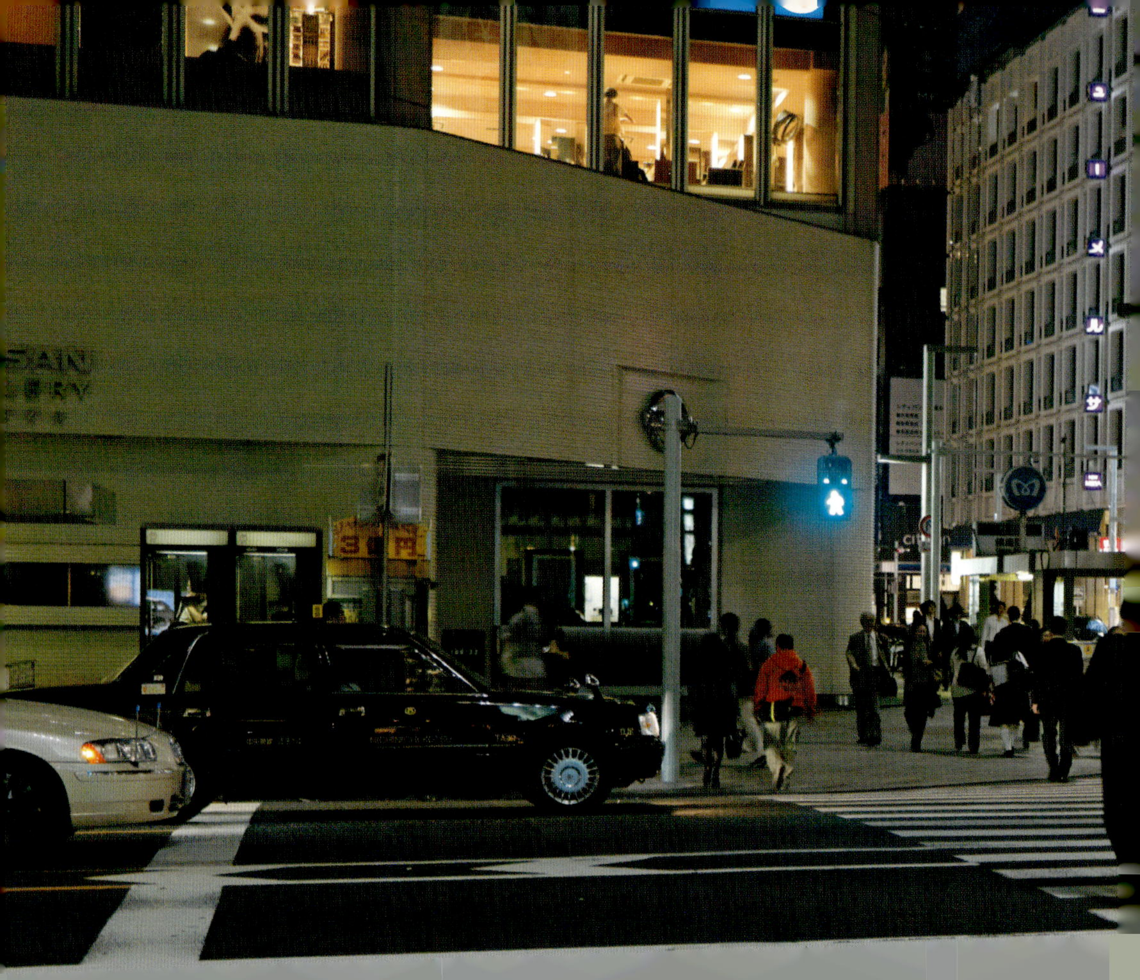

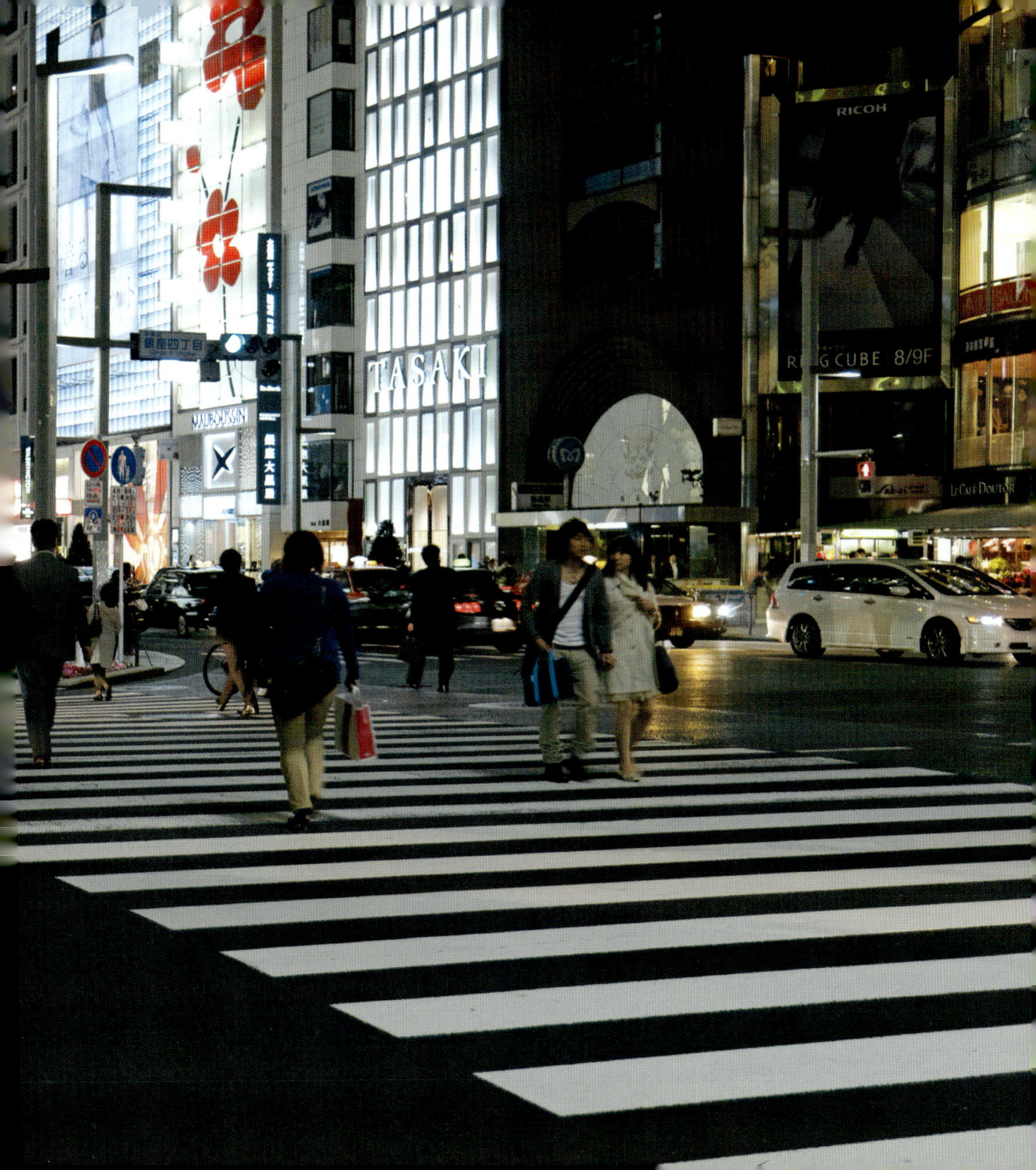

RICOH
TASAKI
MAUBOUSSIN
RING CUBE 8/9F
LE CAFÉ DOUTOR

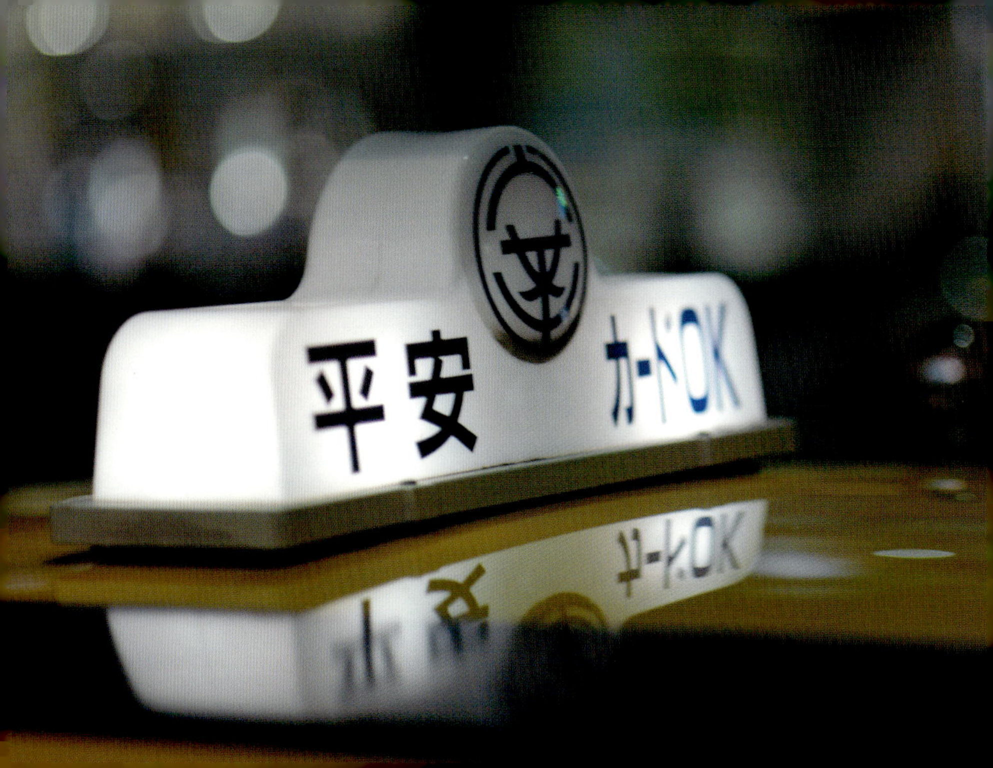
平安
カードOK

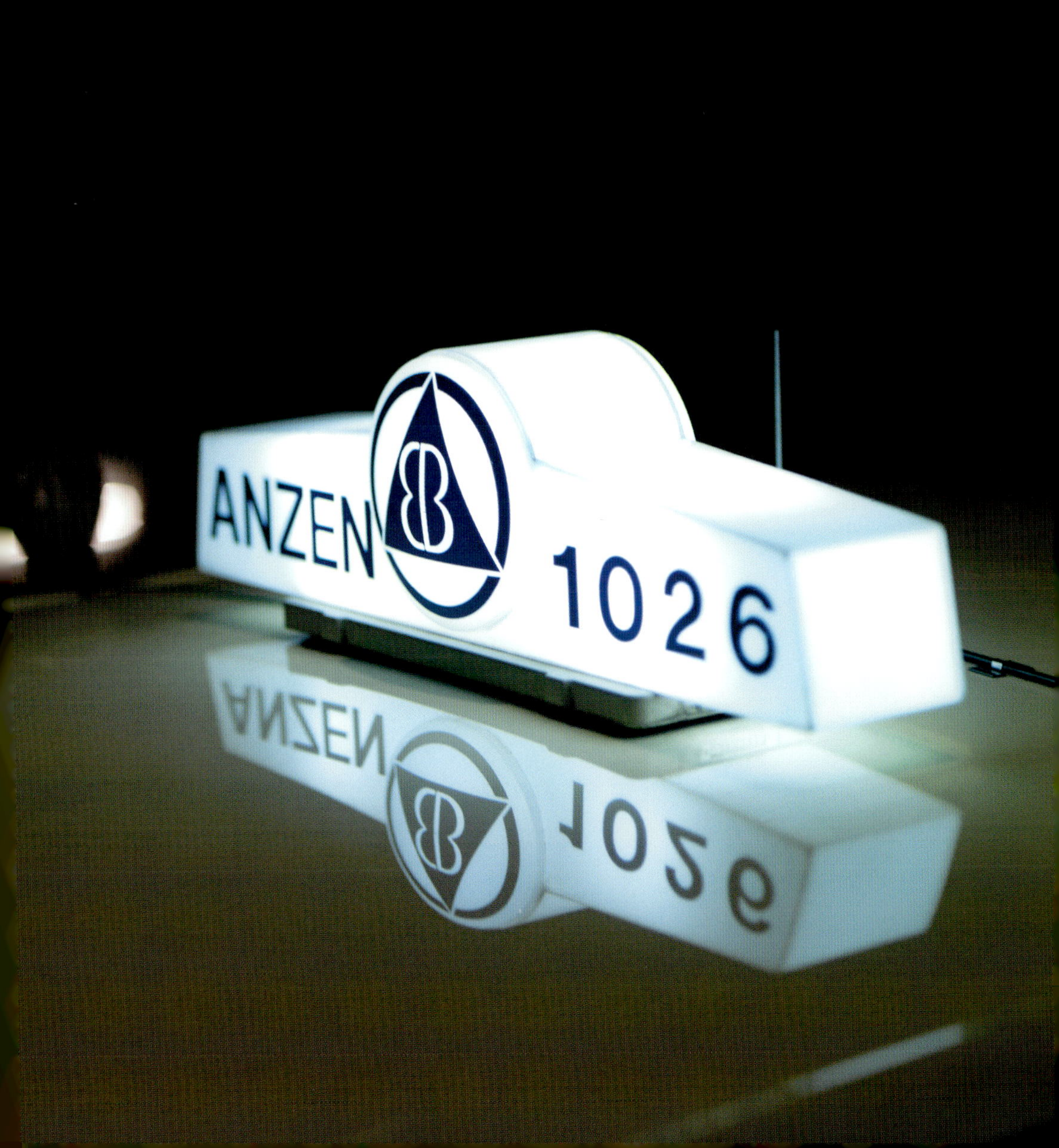
ANZEN
1026

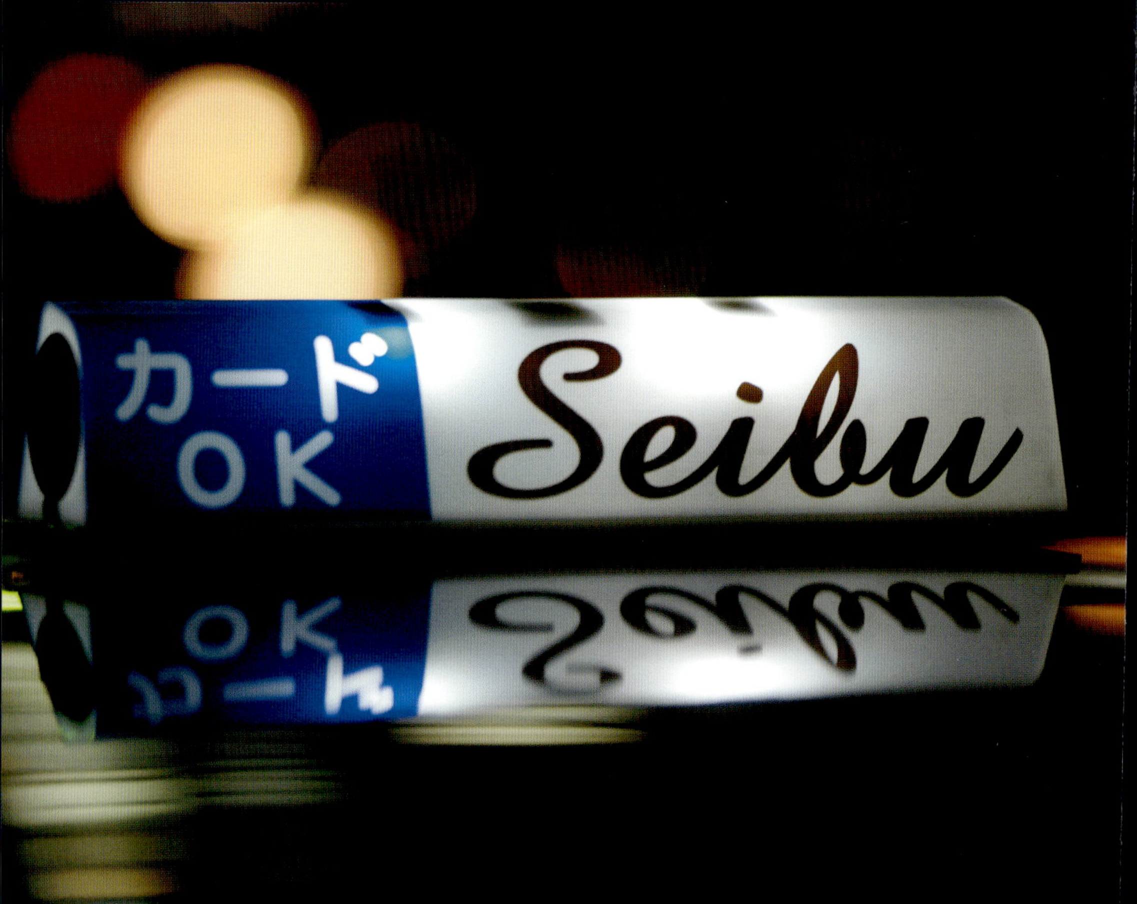
カード
OK
Seibu

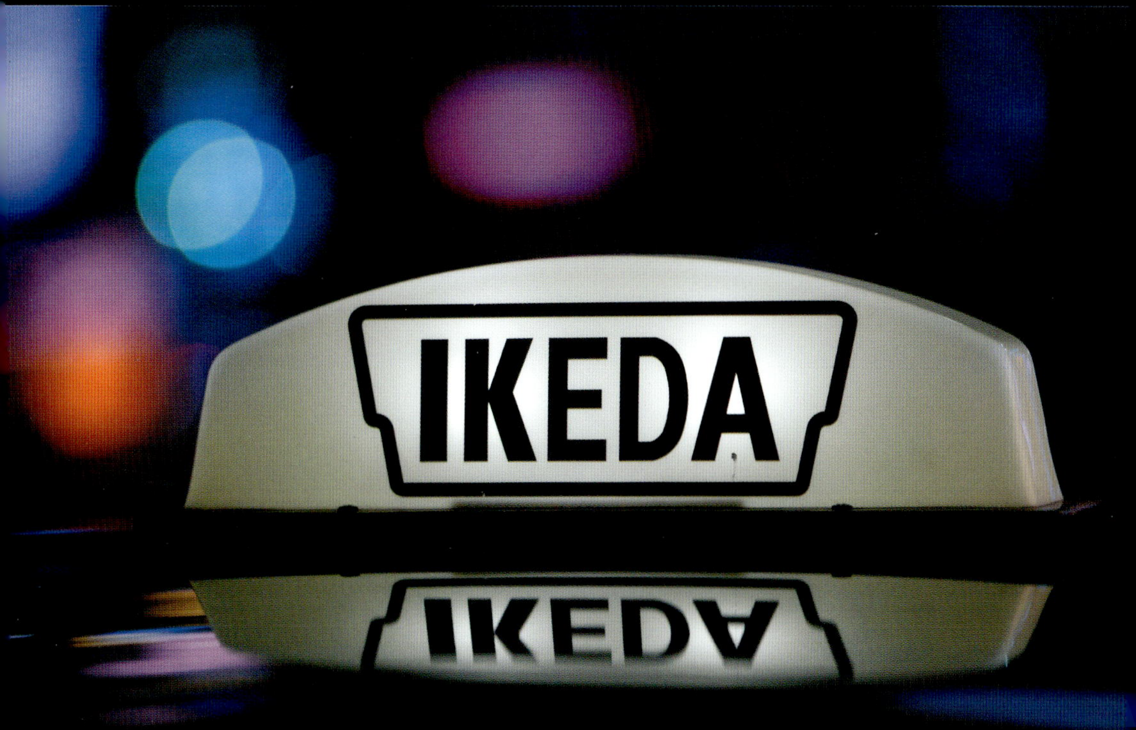

IKEDA TAXI

KOJIN TAXI

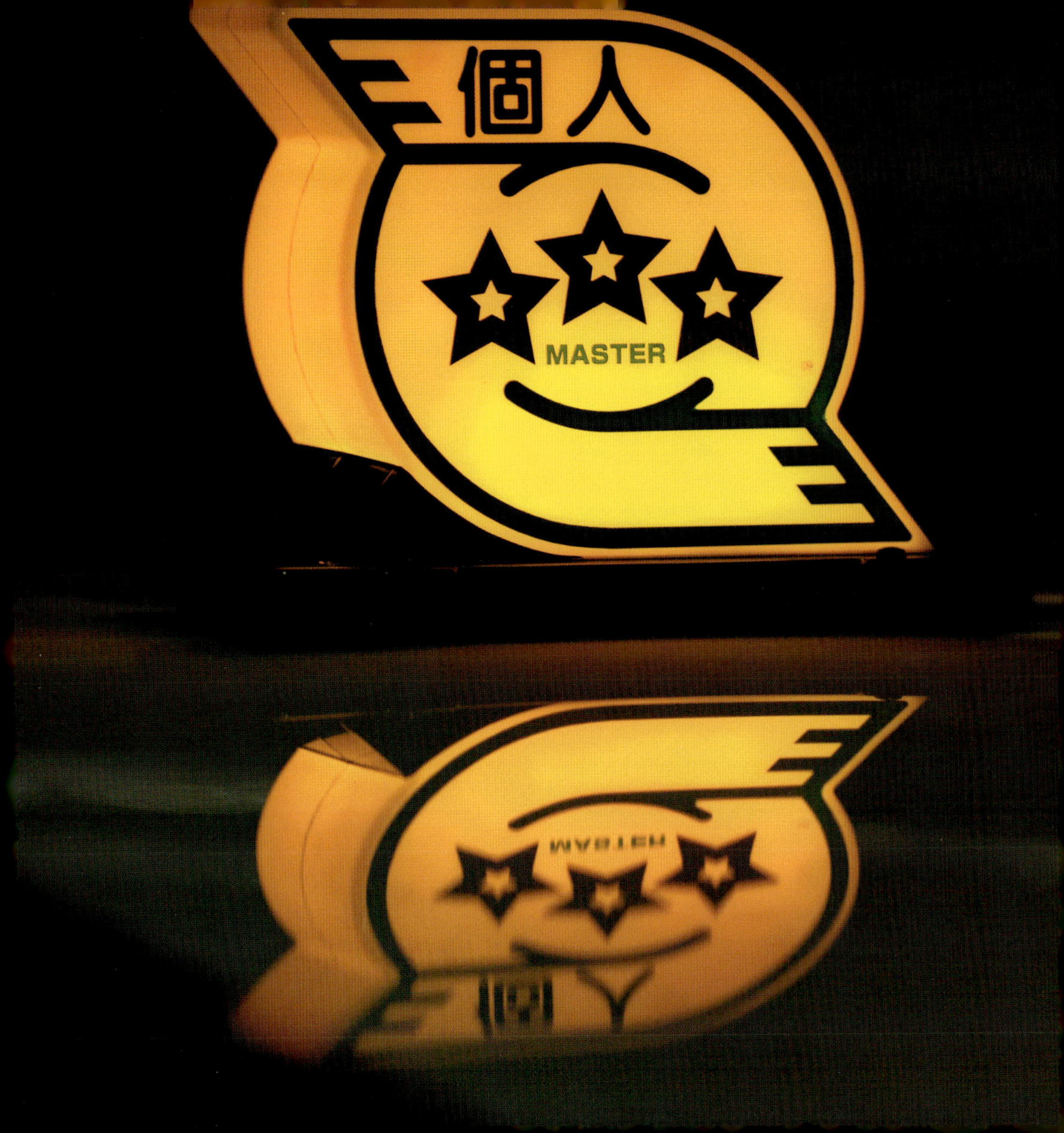
個人
MASTER

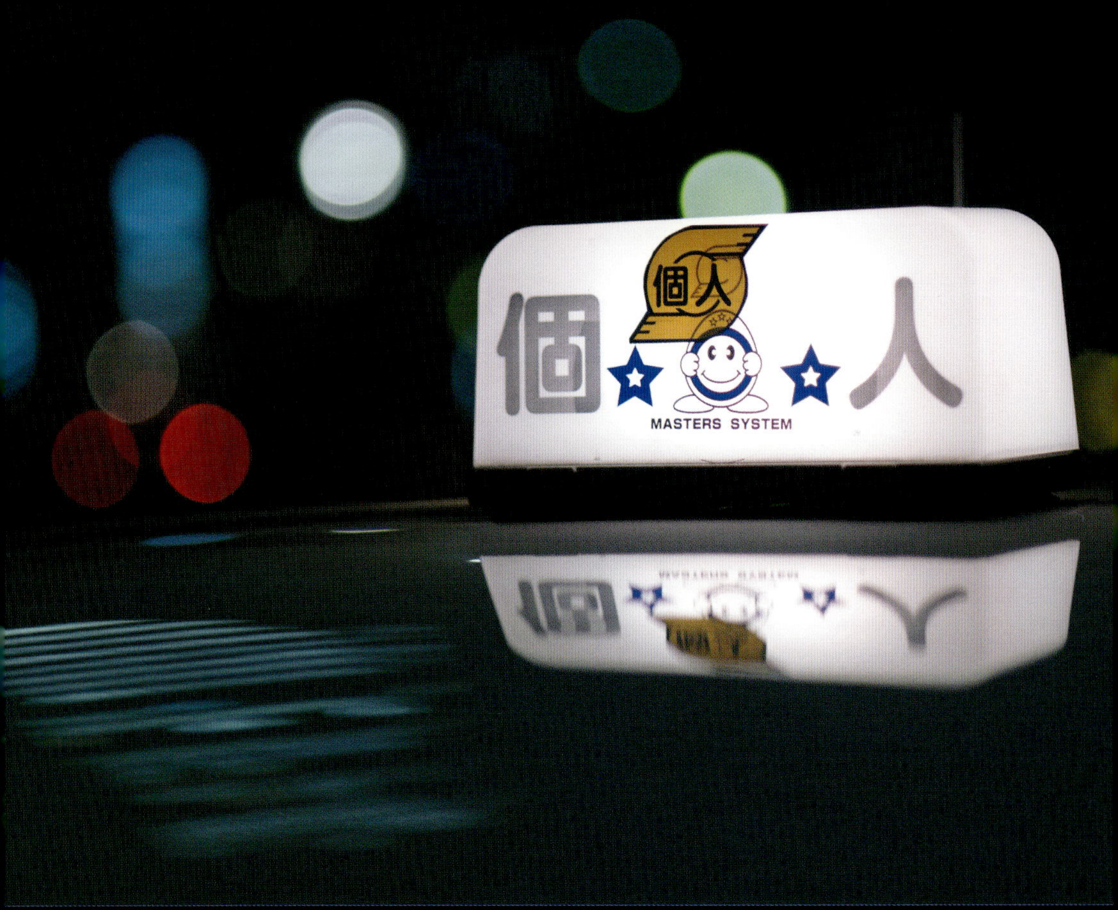

KOJIN TAXI

Pages 206–207: SC TAXI 217

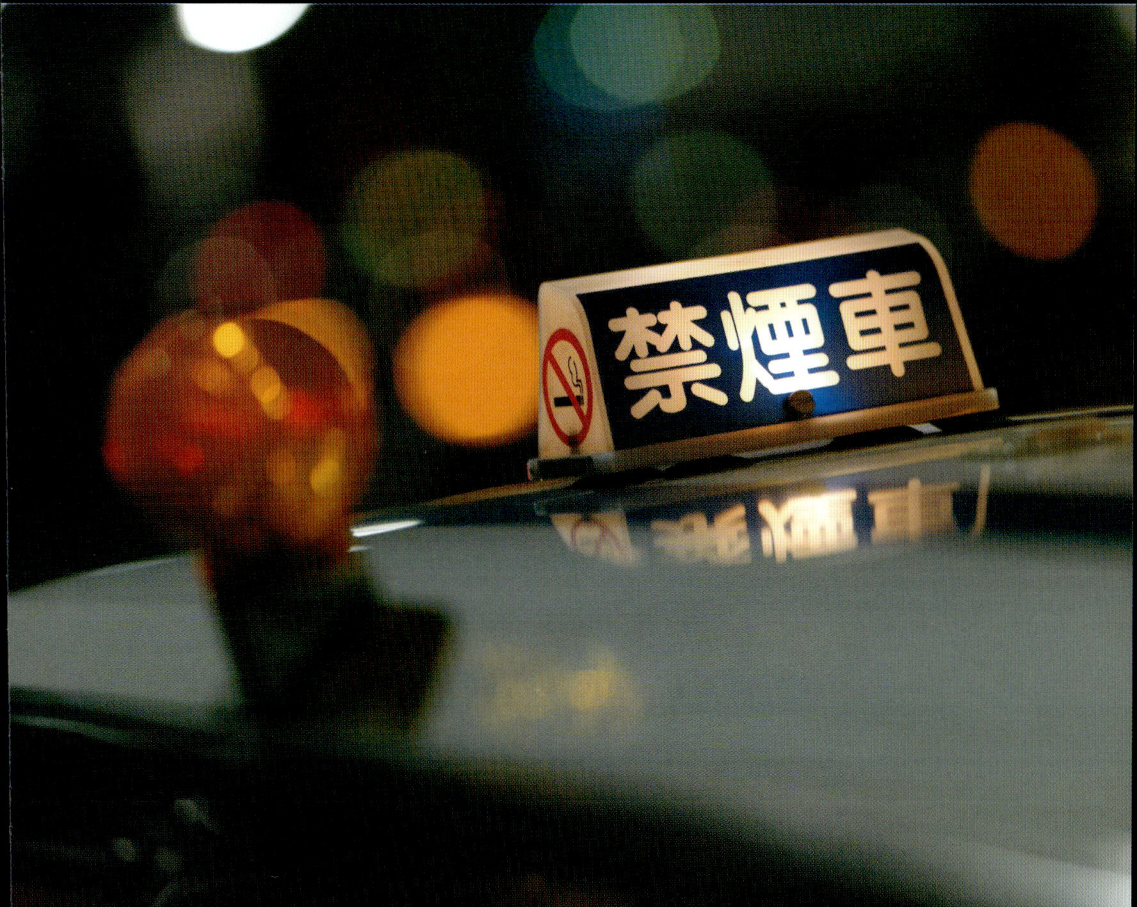

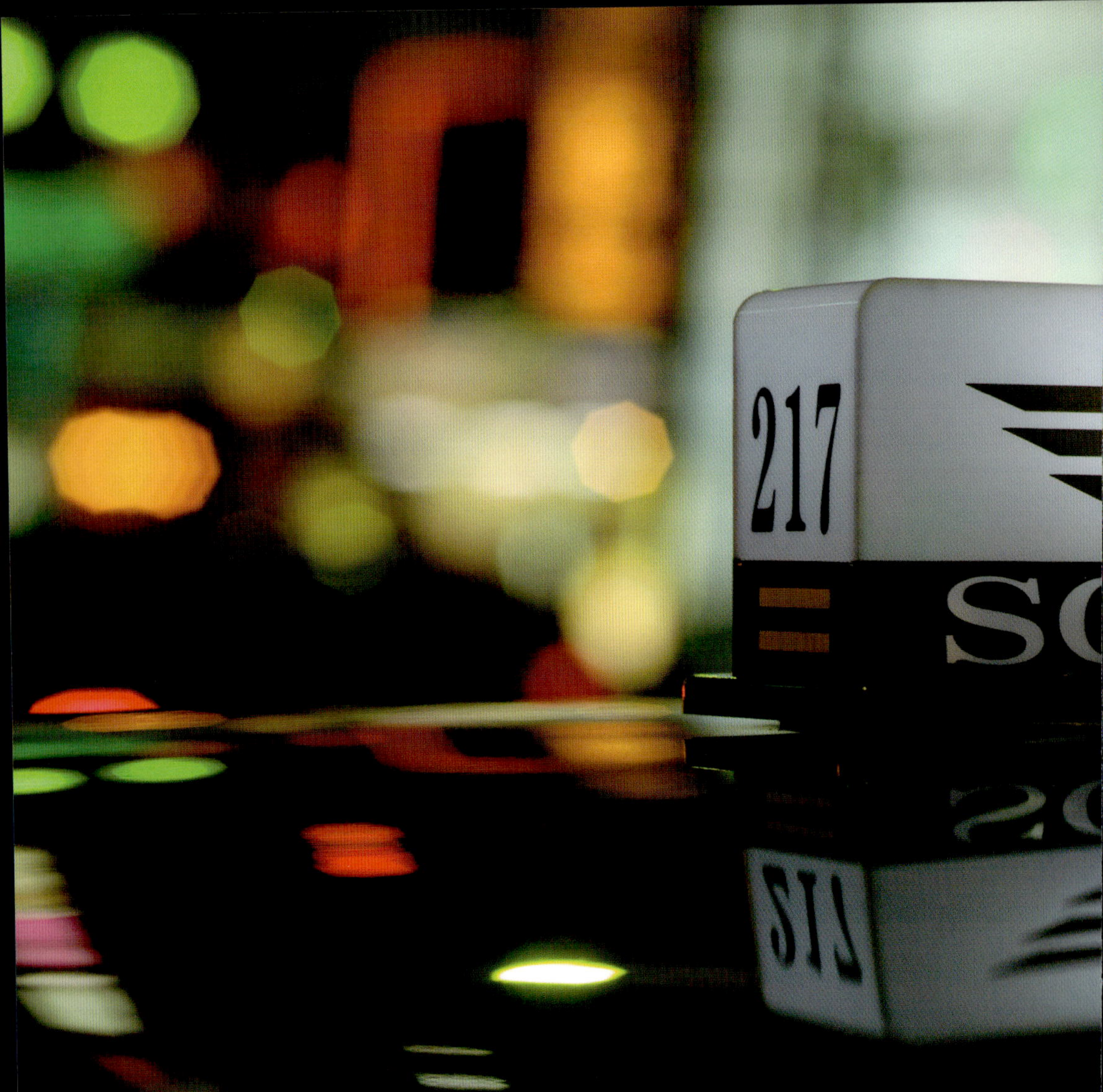
217

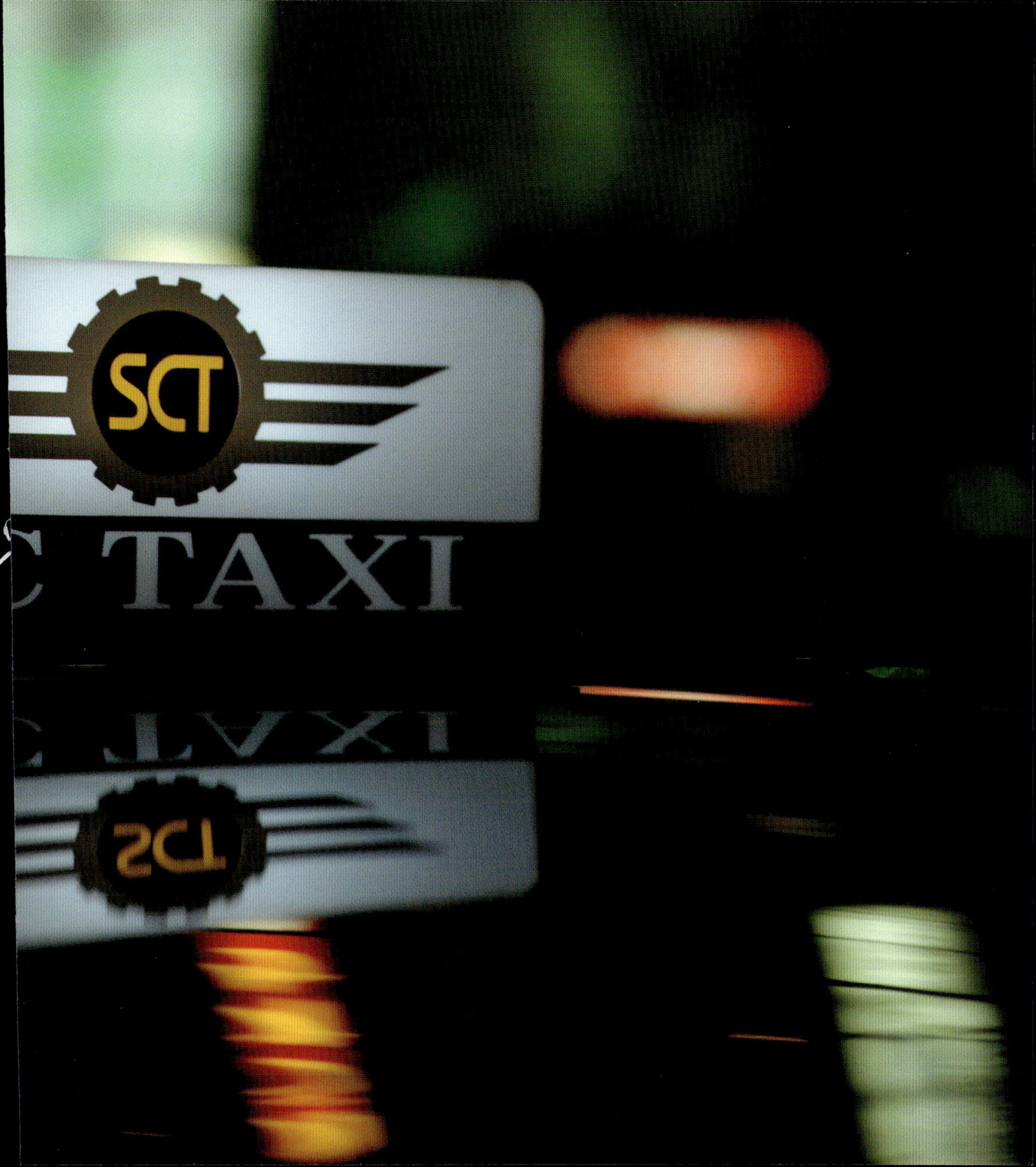
SCT
TAXI

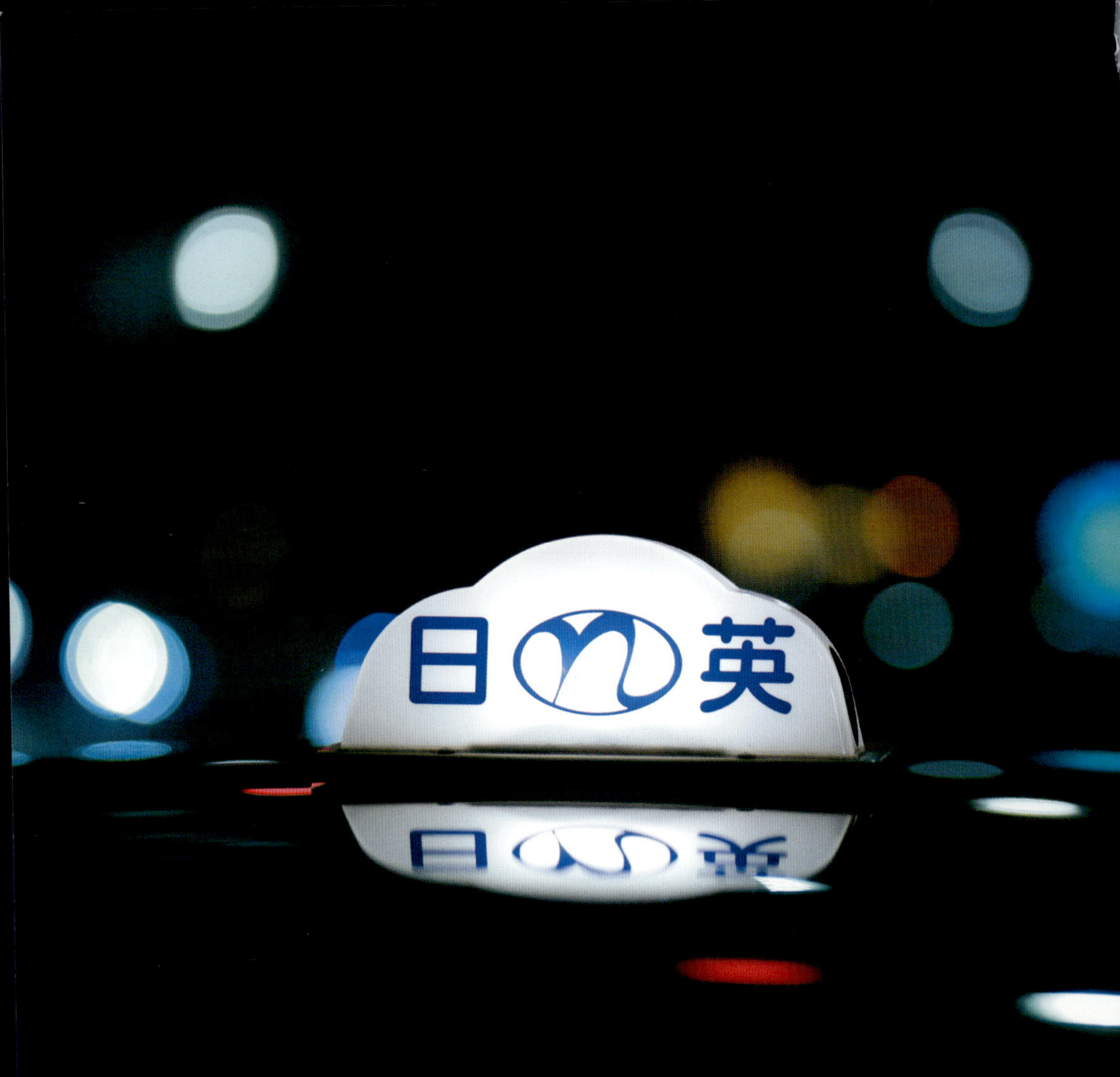

NICHIEI TAXI CO.

Pages 210–11: 'ID PAYMENT ACCEPTED'

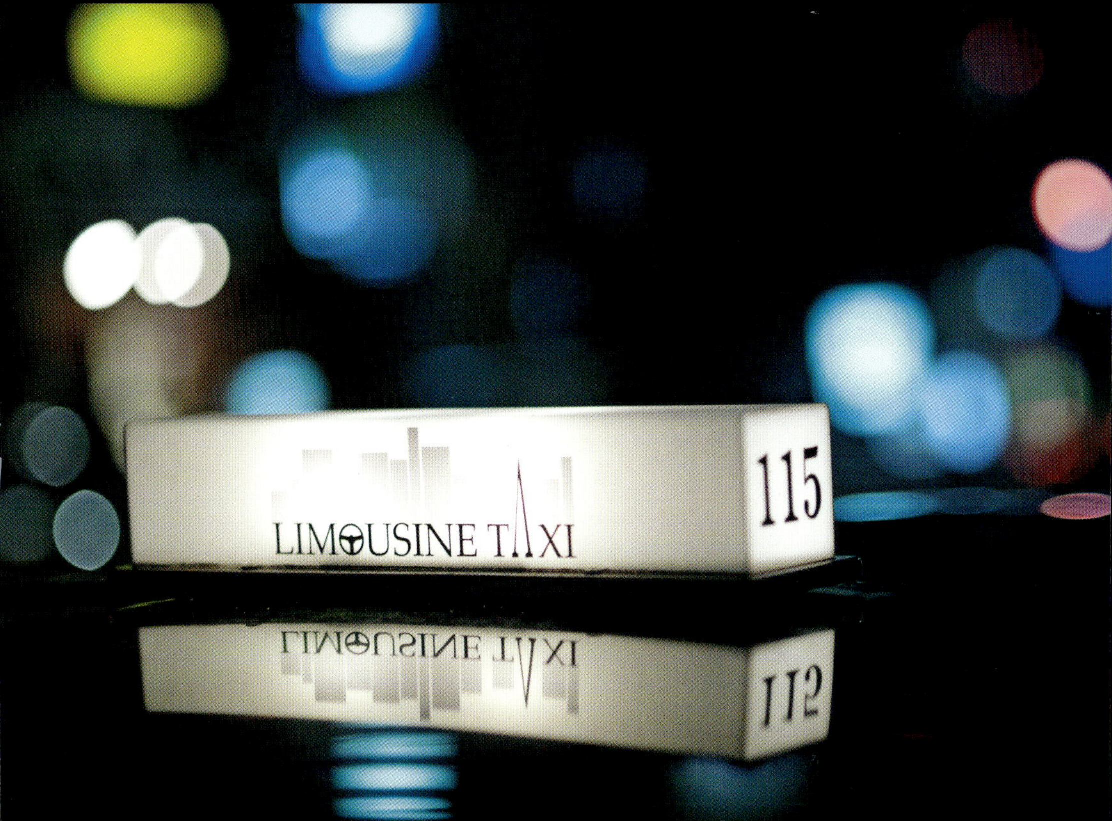

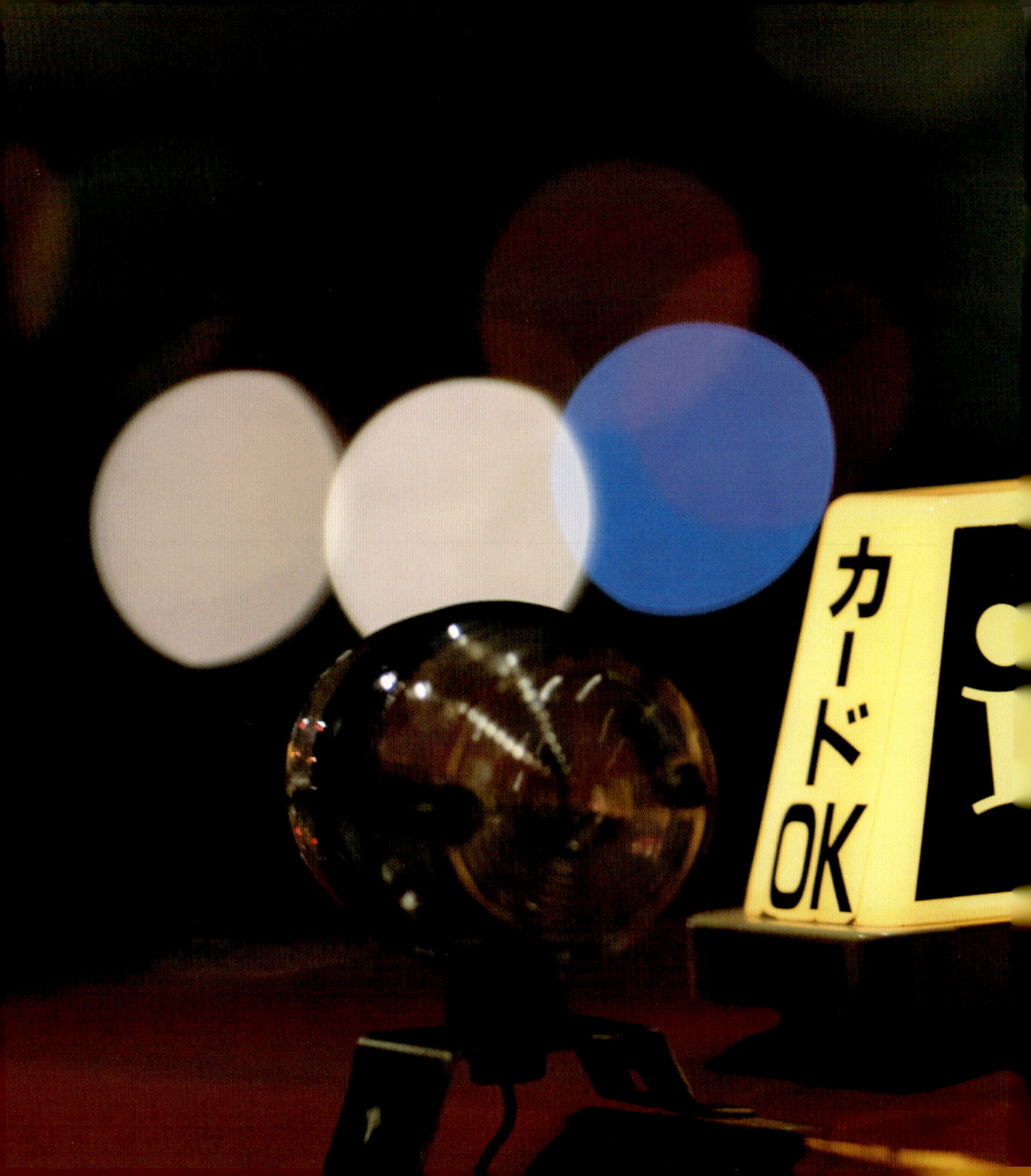
カード
OK

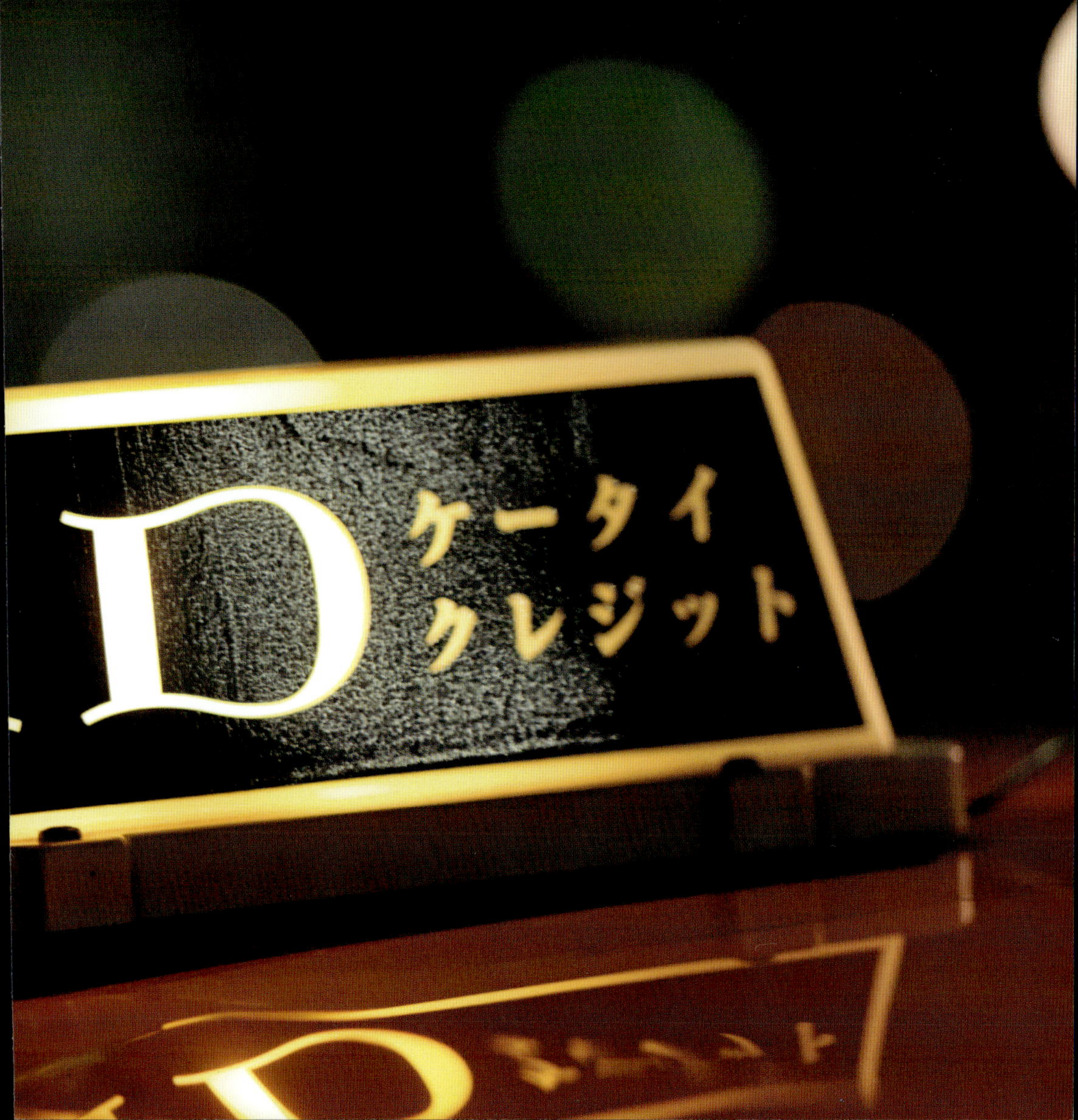
D
ケータイ
クレジット

MR MISAWA

I love my job, and take great pride in my driving skills and the appearance of my taxi. The long and sometimes difficult hours are offset by the interesting people I meet on a daily basis. I have met politicians, celebrities and tourists.

Pages 214–15: CHECKER TAIYO TAXI CO. 450

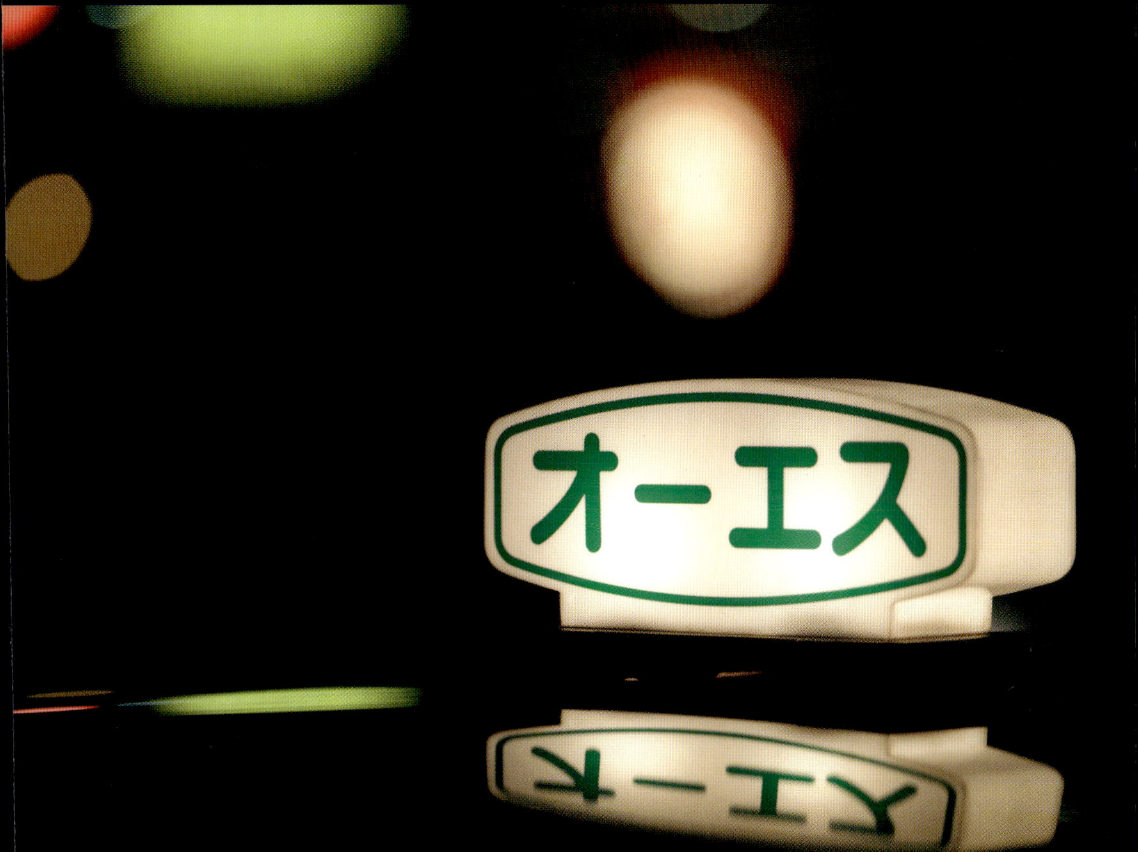

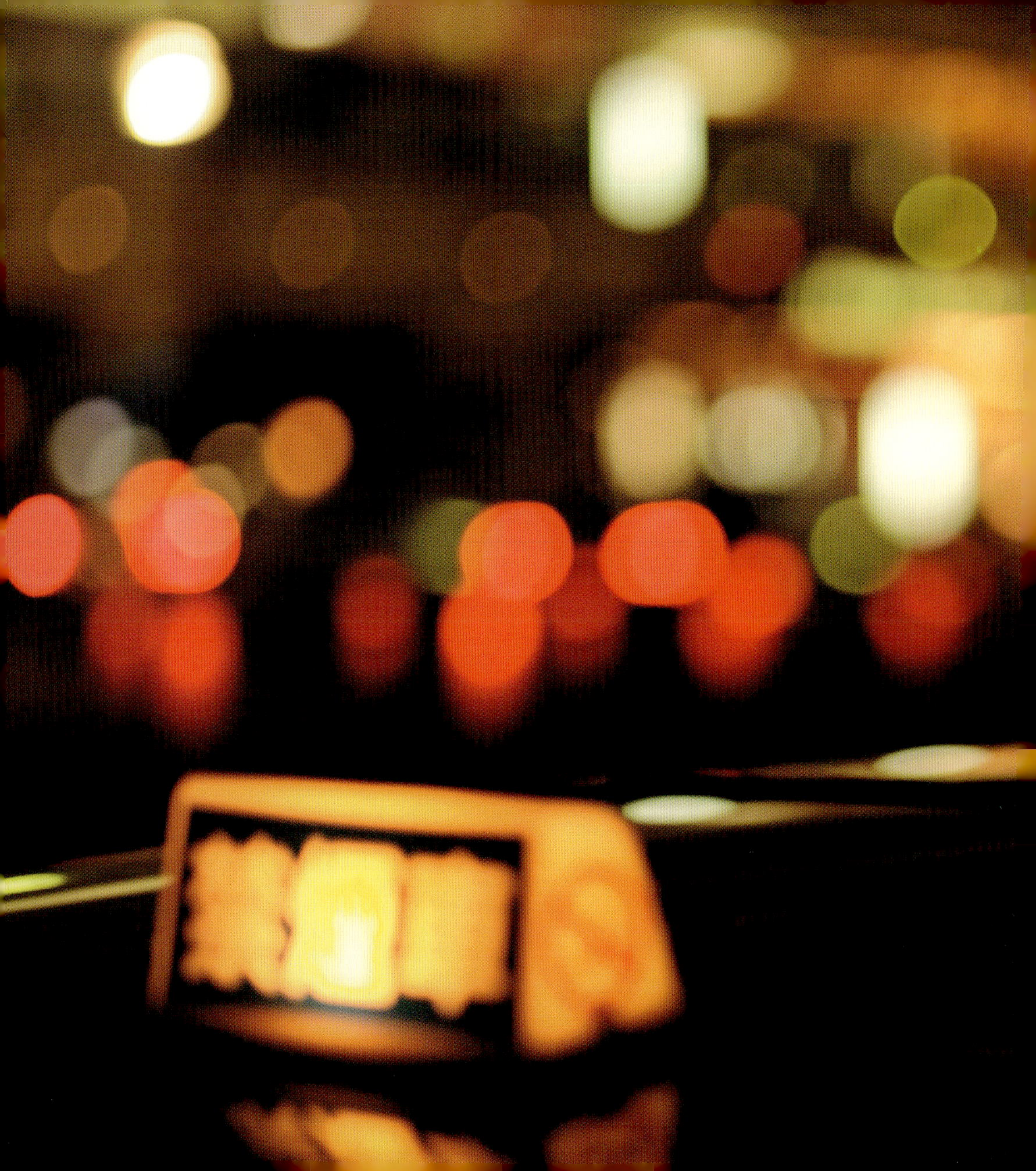

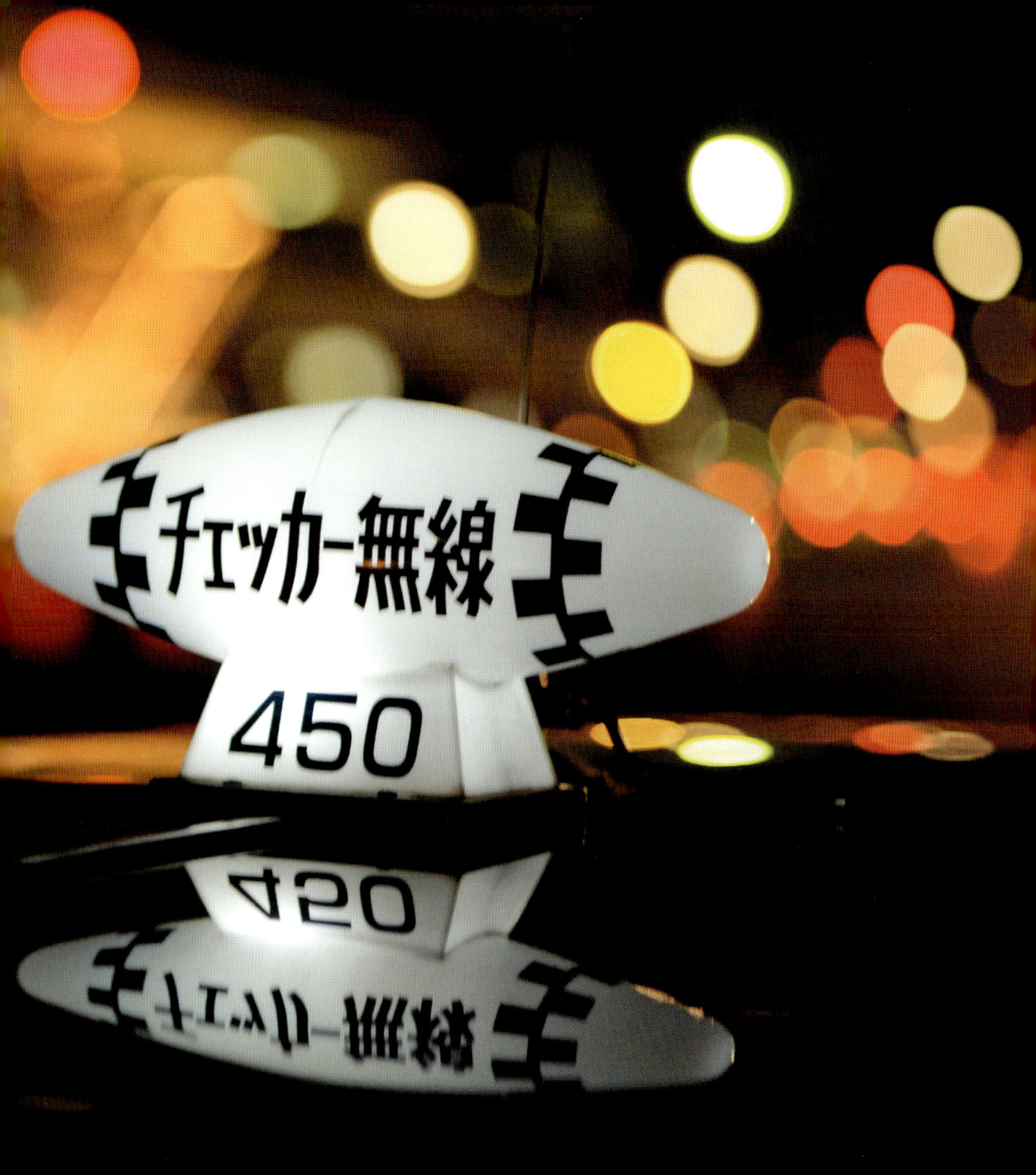
チェッカー無線
450

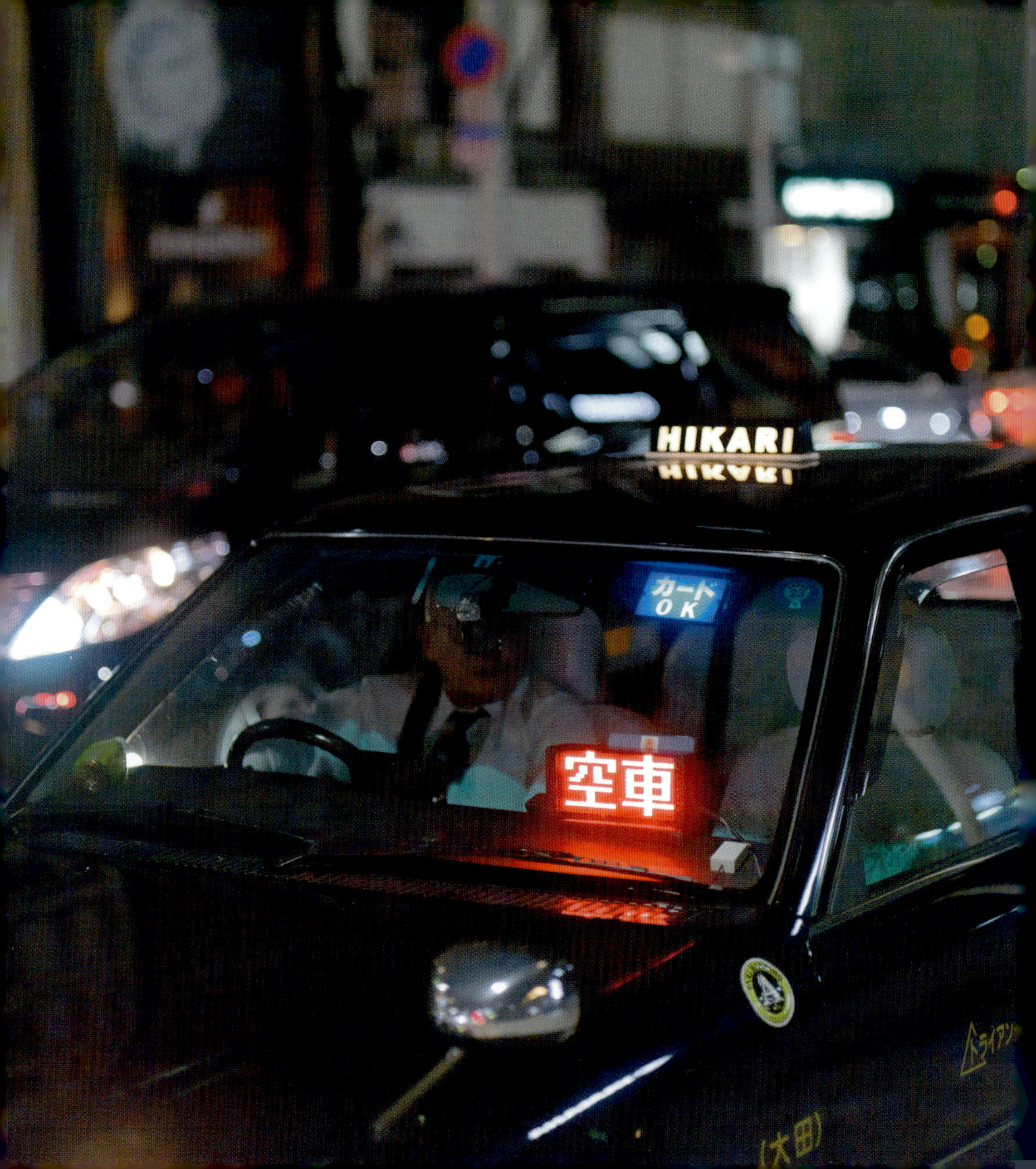
HIKARI
カード
OK
空車

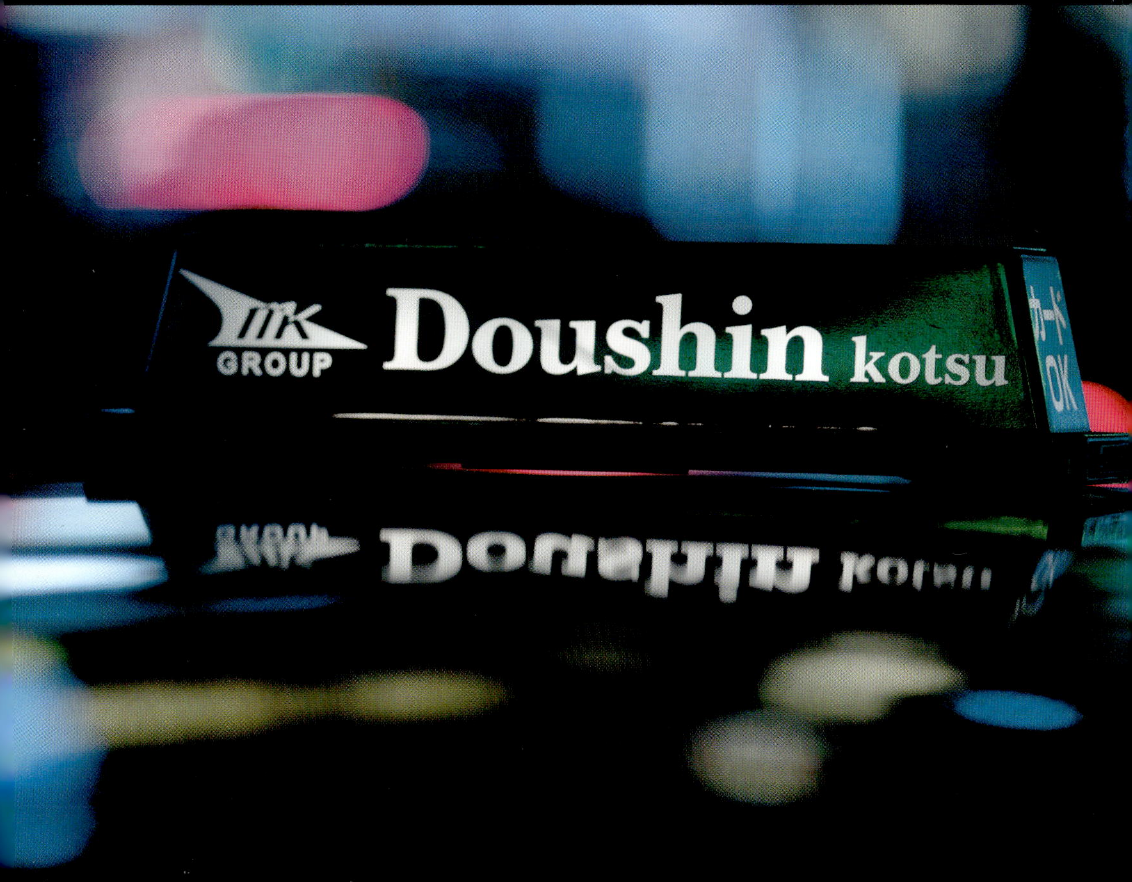

DOUSHIN KOTSU TAXI

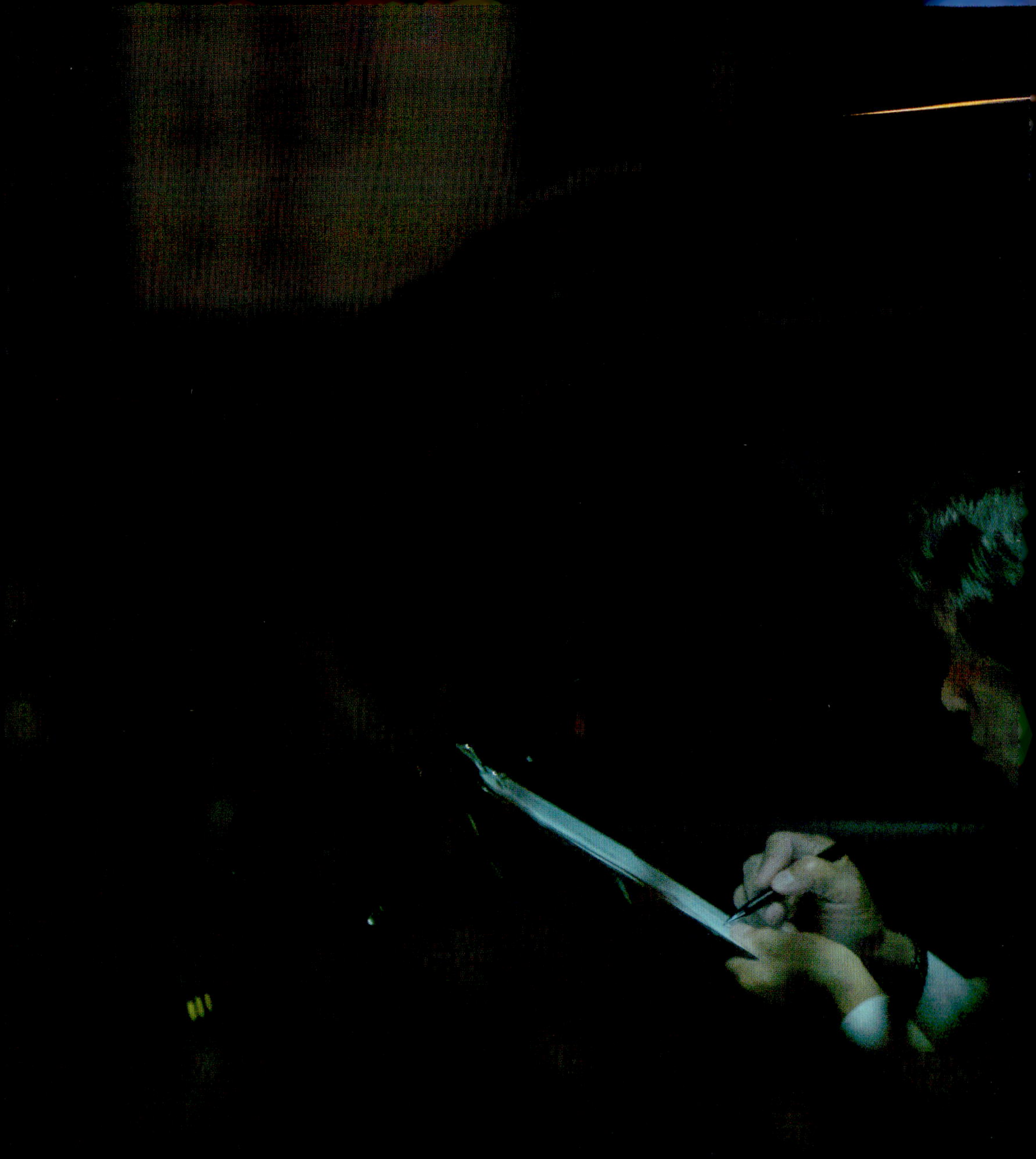

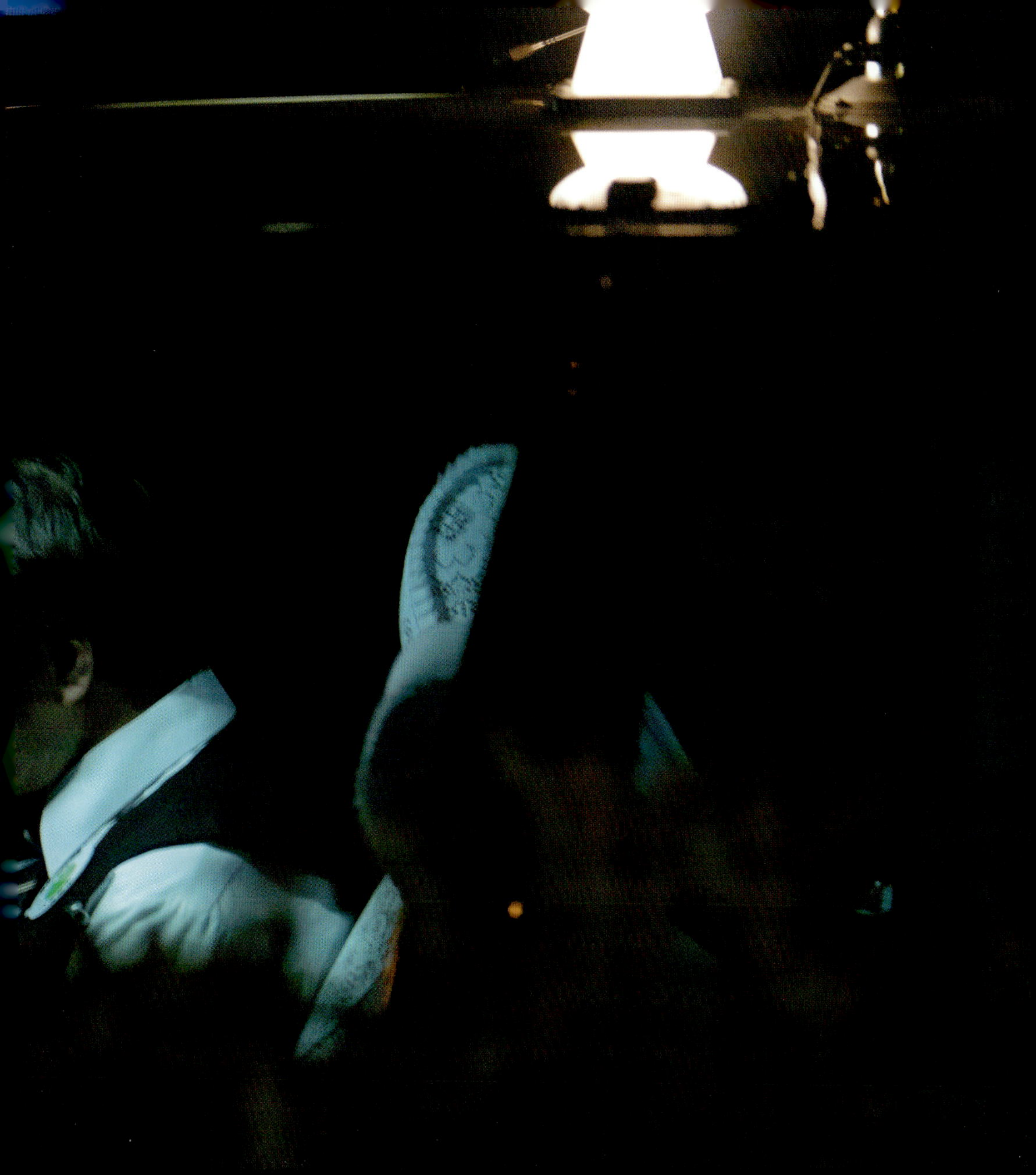

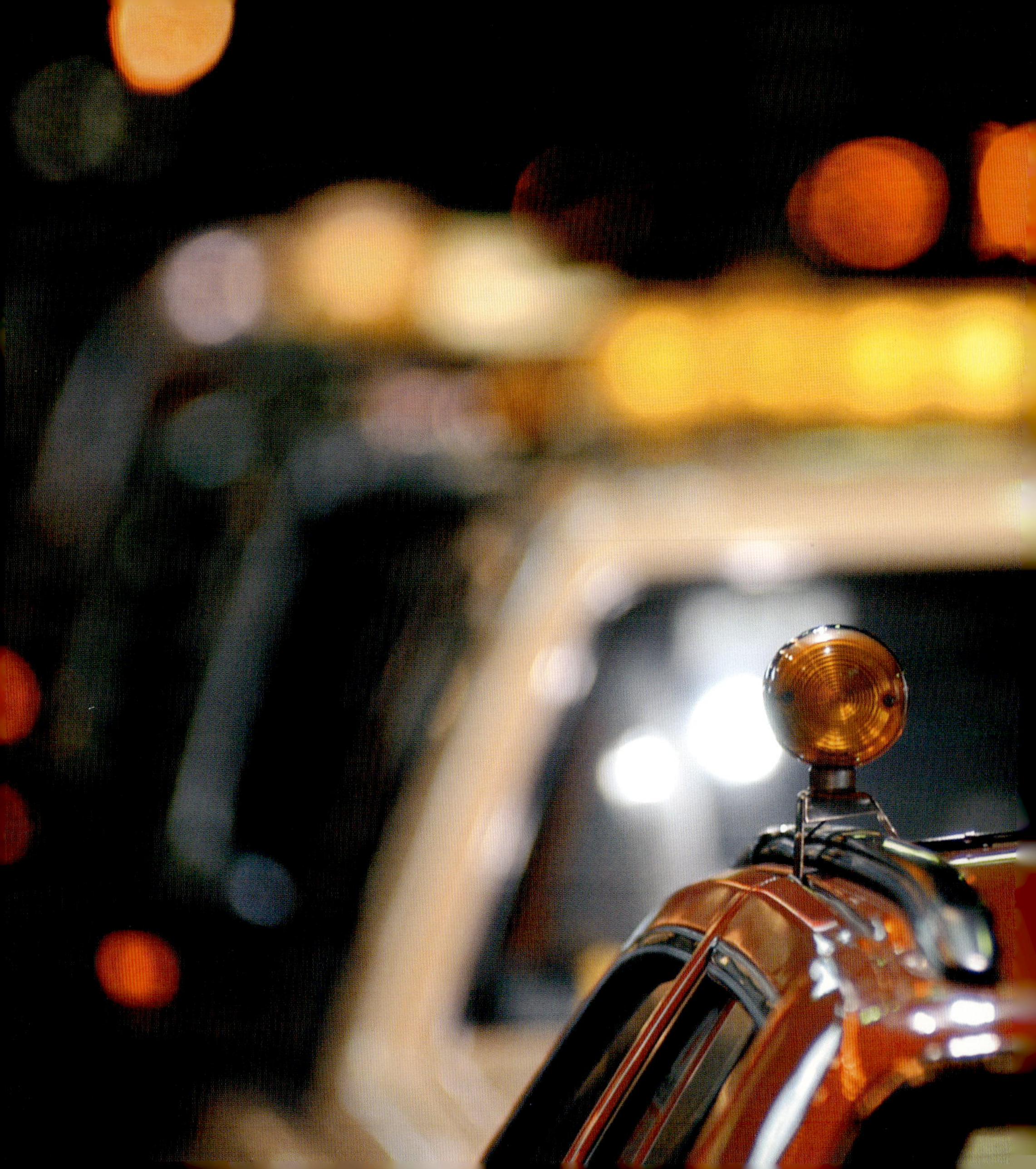

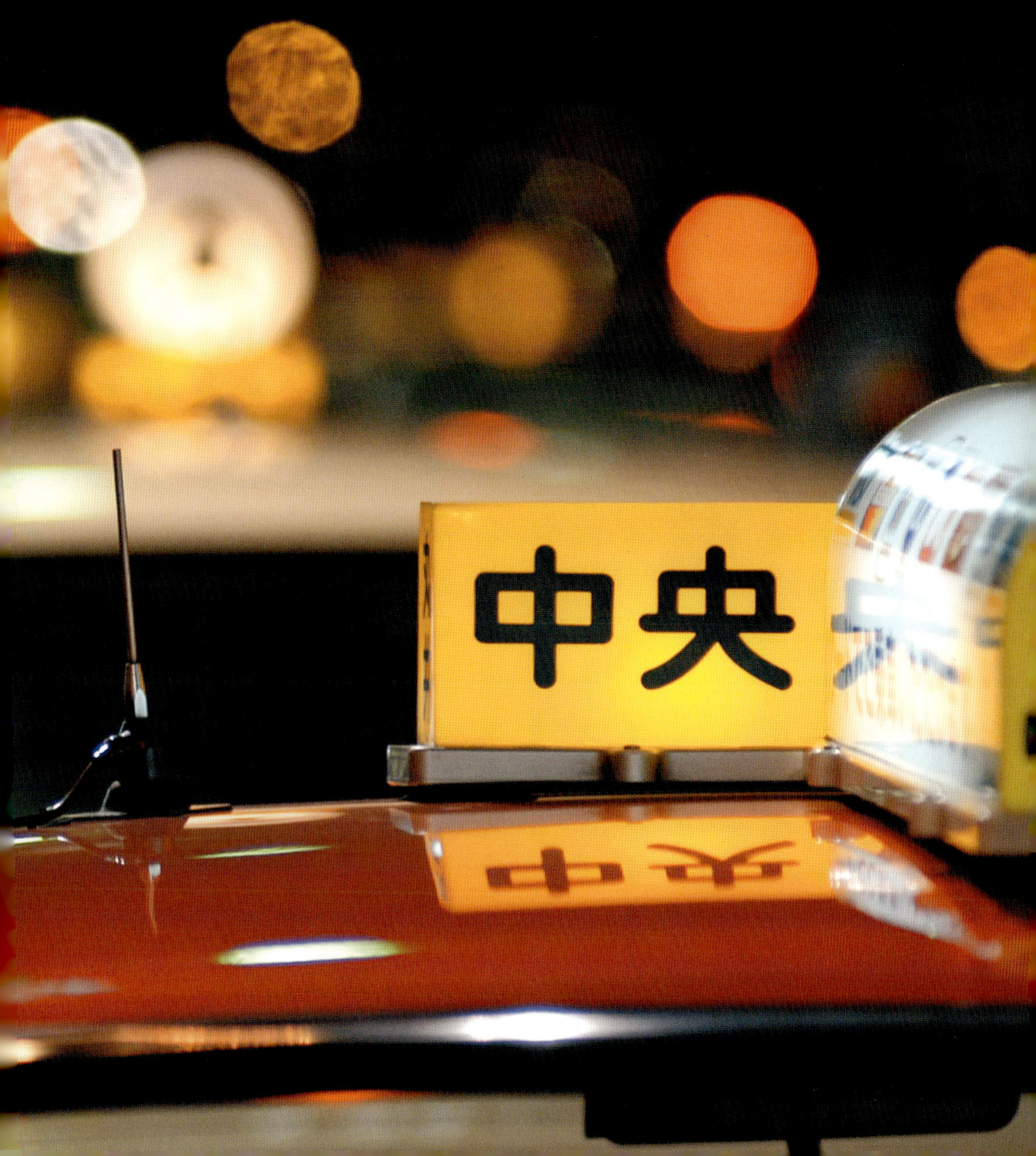
中央

MY THANKS

to the wonderful people of Tokyo for always making me feel so welcome; and to all the taxi drivers who, over the years, have allowed me to document their world, with a special mention to the Teito Taxi Co. office in Shimbashi.

ALEXANDER JAMES

is a critically acclaimed artist whose work has been exhibited around the world. His pieces are always presented 'as shot', without cropping or post-production, and this dedication to in-camera purity forms the focal point of his practice. His recent projects address social, political and environmental issues, and his images have appeared in such publications as *Qvest*, *Design Week*, *Monograph* and the *Los Angeles Times Magazine*. His studio, Distil Ennui (distilennui.com), is based in London.

First published 2012 by

Merrell Publishers Limited
81 Southwark Street
London SE1 0HX

merrellpublishers.com

British Library Cataloguing-in-Publication data:
James, Alexander.
Tokyo taxi.
1. Taxicabs – Japan – Tokyo – Pictorial works.
2. Neon signs – Japan – Tokyo – Pictorial works.
3. Photography, Artistic. 4. James, Alexander.
I. Title
779.9′62922232′0952135-dc23

ISBN 978-1-8589-4569-9

Produced by Merrell Publishers Limited
Designed by Nicola Bailey
Project-managed by Mark Ralph

Printed and bound in China

Front cover: Ebisu Taxi
Back cover: Edosou Group Taxi Co.

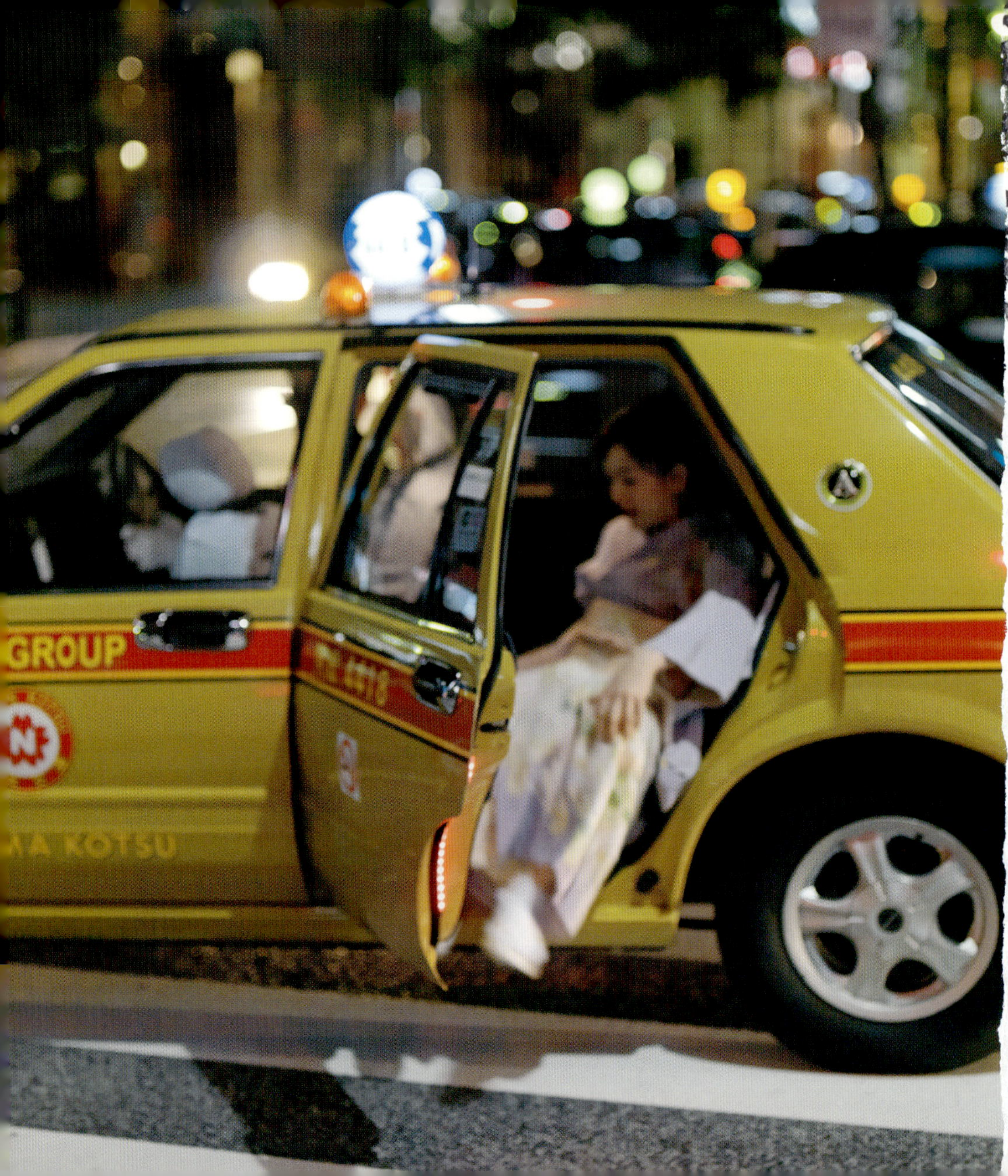
GROUP
MA KOTSU

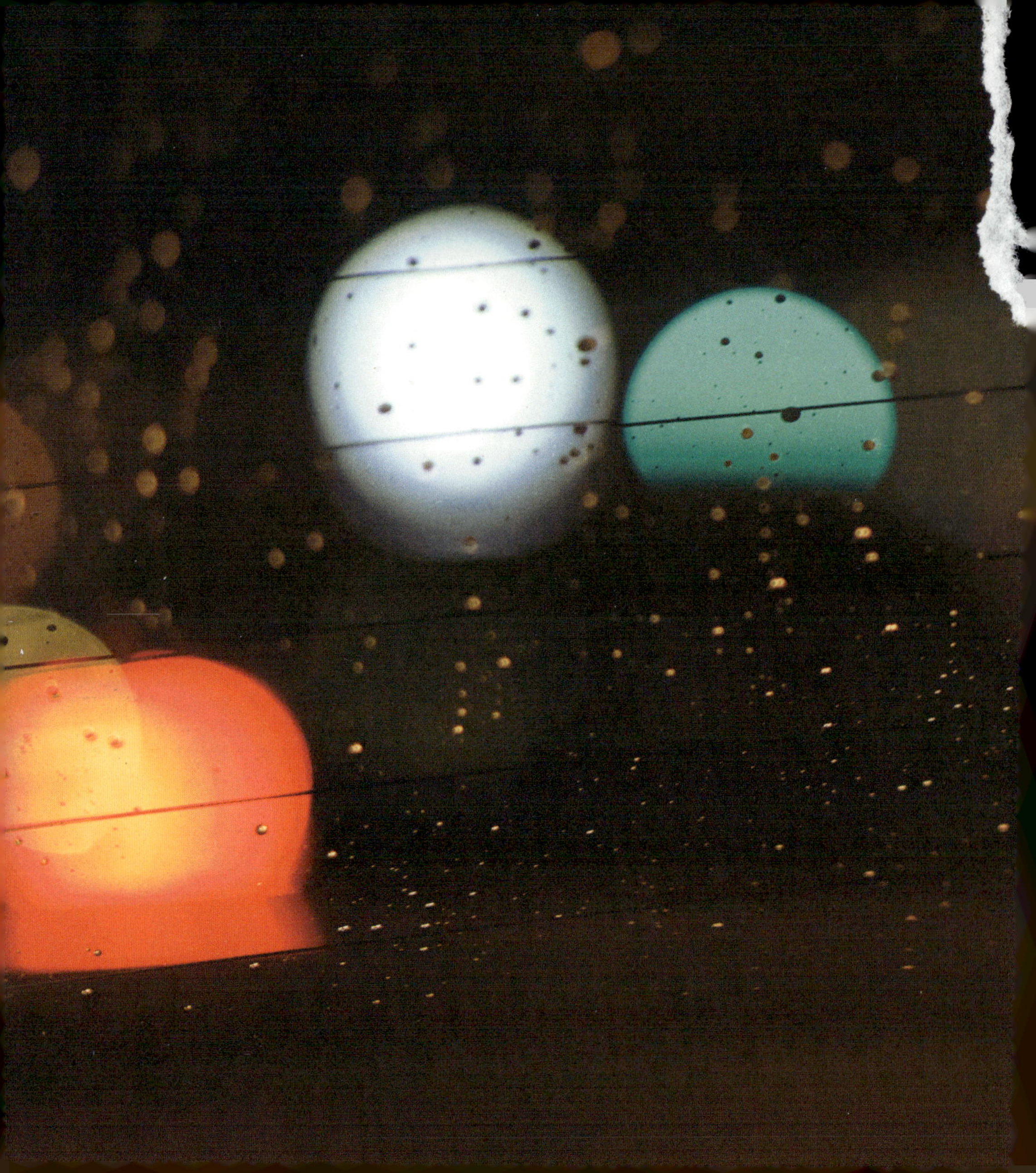